Introduction to Hegel's Philosophy of Religion

SUNY Series in Hegelian Studies
Quentin Lauer, Editor

Introduction to
Hegel's Philosophy of Religion

Raymond Keith Williamson

State University of New York Press
Albany

Published by
State University of New York Press, Albany

© 1984 State University of New York

All rights reserved

Printed in the United States of America

No part of this book may be used or reproduced
in any manner whatsoever without written permission
except in the case of brief quotations embodied in
critical articles and reviews.

For information, address State University of New York
Press, State University Plaza, Albany, N.Y., 12246

Library of Congress Cataloging in Publication Data

Williamson, Raymond Keith, 1941–
    Introduction to Hegel's philosophy of religion.

    Bibliography: p. 305
    1. Hegel, Georg Wilhelm Friedrich, 1770–1831—Religion.
2. Religion—History—19th century. I. Title.
II. Series.
B2949.R3W54 1984   200′.1   83–5081
ISBN 0–87395–827–6
ISBN 0–87395–826–8 (pbk.)

10 9 8 7 6 5 4 3 2 1

Contents

Acknowledgments

This work on Hegel's philosophy of religion commenced in 1976 when I received an Australian government postgraduate research award. For the following three and a half years, I worked with the encouragement and guidance of a number of friends and colleagues in the philosophy department of the University of Newcastle. The two people who served as head of department during that time, Professor Alec Ritchie and Dr. John Lee, gave valuable support and advice, for which I am extremely grateful. The thesis resulting from that research was submitted for the degree of doctor of philosophy in October 1979.

Subsequently, I received a generous offer from Professor Quentin Lauer to consider my work for publication in his Hegelian Studies series. I felt deeply honored by that offer: it was a great compliment, and it has provided renewed stimulation for my work.

During the time of preparing the manuscript for submission to Professor Lauer, Professor Cliff Hooker, the present head of the philosophy department at the University of Newcastle, generously made available the facilities of that department for my use.

To Colleen Ogle and Jan Taylor of the university secretarial staff, who patiently worked through my manuscript in order to produce the typed edition of the thesis, I also owe a special thanks. More recently, I have been deeply grateful to Diane Payne, the secretary of St. John's Theological College, Morpeth, for her willing assistance in preparing the revised manuscript; and to the Reverend George Garnsey, the principal of St. John's College, for his cooperation.

Associate Professor Bill Doniela was the supervisor of my work as a research student, and to him I want to express my deep gratitude. It was he who launched me on this particular project, and the benefit of his wide knowledge and understanding of Hegel, together with his valuable comments on the manuscript, have been of immeasurable assistance. My gratitude to him is even more deeply felt because of his continued assistance in recent times while I have been revising the manuscript: his help has been of the same high value, and has certainly been beyond the requirements of any obligation.

A special thanks must go to Dr. David Dockrill for his friendship and encouragement at all times.

Finally, to my wife, Sue, and daughters Elizabeth and Judy, I want to say that I know something of the burden you have felt throughout the two stages of the progress of this work. Thank you for the patience and understanding that you have shown so often and for your supporting love.

St. James's Rectory,
Morpeth
Australia

18 August 1982

Abbreviations

Hegel's works referred to in this book will be identified as follows:

Aes.   *Aesthetics: Lectures on Fine Art.* Translated by T. M. Knox.
        Oxford: Clarendon Press, 1975.

CR   *Lectures on the Philosophy of Religion.* Part 3. Edited and
        translated by Peter C. Hodgson, under the title *The
        Christian Religion.* Montana: Scholars Press, 1979.

Diff.   *The Difference Between Fichte's and Schelling's System of Phi-
        losophy.* Translated by H. S. Harris and Walter Cerf.
        Albany: State University of New York Press, 1977.

Dok.   *Dokumente zu Hegels Entwicklung.* Edited by Johannes Hoff-
        meister. Stuttgart: Frommann-Holzboog, 1974.

EL   *Logic.* Part 1 of *The Encyclopaedia.* Translated by William
        Wallace in 1873. Oxford: Clarendon Press, 1975.

EM   *Philosophy of Mind.* Part 3 of *The Encyclopaedia.* Translated
        by William Wallace in 1894. Oxford: Clarendon Press,
        1971.

Enz.   *Enzyklopädie der Philosophischen Wissenschaften im Grundrisse.*
        Hamburg: Verlag von Felix Meiner, 1969.

ETW   *Early Theological Writings.* Translated by T. M. Knox. Chicago:
        University of Chicago Press, 1948.

"FHS"   "Fragments of Historical Studies." Translated by Clark Butler.
        *Clio: An Interdisciplinary Journal of Literature, History and
        the Philosophy of History* 7, no. 1 (1977): 113–34.

FK   *Faith and Knowledge.* Translated by H. S. Harris and Walter
        Cerf. Albany: State University of New York Press, 1977.

JR   *Jenaer Realphilosophie.* Edited by Johannes Hoffmeister. Ham-
        burg: Verlag von Felix Meiner, 1969.

LHP   *Lectures on the History of Philosophy.* 3 vols. Translated by
        E. S. Haldane and Frances H. Simpson in 1894. London:
        Routeledge and Kegan Paul, 1955.

LPR   *Lectures on the Philosophy of Religion: Together with a Work on the Proofs of the Existence of God.* 3 vols. Translated by E. B. Speirs and J. Burdon Sanderson in 1892. New York: Humanities Press, 1962.

Phän.   *Phänomenologie des Geistes.* Edited by Johannes Hoffmeister. Hamburg: Verlag Felix Meiner, 1952.

Phen.   *Phenomenology of Spirit.* Translated by A. V. Miller. Oxford: Clarendon Press, 1977.

SL   *Science of Logic.* Translated by A. V. Miller. London: Allen & Unwin, 1969.

"TFL"   "Two Fragments of 1797 on Love." Translated by H. S. Harris and C. Hamlin. *Clio: An Interdisciplinary Journal of Literature, History and the Philosophy of History* 8, no. 2 (1979): 257–65.

VPR   *Vorlesungen über die Philosophie der Religion.* Vols. 16 and 17 of *Werke.* Frankfurt: Suhrkamp Verlag, 1969.

WK   *Werke.* Neu edierte Ausgabe Redaktion Eva Moldenhauer und Karl Markus Michel. Frankfurt am Main: Suhrkamp Verlag, 1970.

Introduction

The hopes and aspirations by which Hegel was motivated, and the questions and problems with which he wrestled, were determined, inevitably, by the age in which he lived. However, his perception of those hopes was more penetrating, and his probing of those questions was deeper than that of any of his contemporaries; and in so doing he formulated a philosophy that dominated his own time and has profoundly influenced the thought of subsequent times. In the shaping of that philosophy, a fundamental role was occupied by Hegel's approach to religion; indeed, it can be said that the whole Hegelian philosophy is sharply savored by—and can really be understood only in the light of—his philosophy of religion, which, in turn, has to be seen as developing within the caldron of upheaval in the social and intellectual environment of late-eighteenth and early-nineteenth-century Europe, and therefore as reflecting Hegel's approach and answer to the aspirations and problems of his era.

Hegel's Program

Hegel's philosophic program was naturally shaped by the contemporary situation, for the Enlightenment and the Christian religion gave rise to three motivating aspirations in the young Hegel. He was impressed by the Enlightenment ambition for the human freedom of self-determination on the basis of autonomous reason, especially in the developed Kantian sense of the individual's courage to fully use reason without looking to the guidance of another person. Secondly, Hegel was filled with the longing for a genuine unity and harmony within human beings and between people and their world, and thus for the overcoming of the feelings of division, separation, and alienation. Thirdly, he aspired to the realization of an expression of religion that was characterized by a reasonableness whereby all claims of religion were assessed by the clear principles of reason.

The place of religion in the development of Hegel's thought is of primary concern and significance. He was a child of a Lutheran

1

family, his boyhood years were spent in the Protestant city of Stuttgart, and his early adult years in the Lutheran seminary *(Stift)* in Tübingen. Thus it is not surprising that, from an early stage, religion provided a fundamental aspect of his thought. Yet, the kind of religion to which Hegel was exposed was not one which he found satisfying or adequate to the needs of man and society. The religion of his home would have been an austere and rigid form of Lutheranism, and in the *Stift* he was subjected to the Tübingen version of rational theology, against both of which he reacted quite adversely. Such a reaction, however, sprang from his own tendency of thought on these matters, but was also naturally affected by the prevailing expectations of the age and the ever-widening criticism of religion. But Hegel never discarded religion, for indeed he accepted religion as providing the fundamental truth by which the contemporary ideals could be realized; yet, this could be so only when the content of religion had been subjected to a major rethinking and reexpression.

This was something Hegel came to only over a period of time, during which he was obviously influenced by the contemporary critique of religion, absorbing carefully the work of Kant, critically assessing that of Fichte and Schelling, and being profoundly affected by the thinking of Hölderlin. But in the end, Hegel went beyond all previous analyses of religion, and he raised far more radical questions in the area of philosophy of religion than anyone before him. To Hegel, all previous analyses had been marked by a one-sidedness. Because they had displayed a sense of an opposition and separation between the divine and the human, and between 'faith', which is supposed to characterize religion, and 'knowledge', which is supposed to be the way of *Wissenschaft*, those analyses had contained a one-sidedness which Hegel desired to remove in his own philosophy of religion. At the end of his *Lectures on the Philosophy of Religion,* in reflecting on the purpose of those lectures, he declared his aim to have been threefold: "to reconcile reason and religion, to show how we know this latter to be in all its manifold forms necessary, and to rediscover in revealed religion the truth and the Idea." [1]

It will be the endeavor of the following inquiry into Hegel's philosophy of religion to examine the manner in which he executed this threefold task.

An adequate understanding of this can be achieved only by tracing the early evolution of his thought in the light of the influences upon him and the ideals which inspired him. Therefore, in Part 1, the development of Hegel's thought, especially its bearing upon the emergence of his philosophy of religion, will be surveyed.

This will be followed, in Part 2, by an exposition of Hegel's understanding of the nature of religion and the place of religion in human thought, drawing the evidence for that exposition primarily from his *Phenomenology of Spirit* and *Lectures on the Philosophy of Religion*. In any discussion of religion it would be natural to expect at least two constantly recurring terms, namely, 'religion' and 'God', and these terms are abundantly present in Hegel's philosophy of religion. But his use of both terms must be heavily qualified, for it will be seen that they certainly cannot be understood in any popular sense. For Hegel, religion and philosophy are one in the sense that they have a common object and share the same content: in this way religion can be said to be philosophy in disguise. However, the nature of the disguise was quite crucial for Hegel: it consisted in religion's mode of apprehension of the content it shares with philosophy, the mode of *Vorstellungen*, which caused religion to occupy, in Hegel's mature thought, an inferior position to philosophy. However, although this meant that Hegel profoundly changed his conception of the Christian religion, and although he reversed his early view about religion's providing the highest form of human knowledge, one can never lose sight of the fact that Hegel came to philosophy to a large extent through Christian theology. He himself never lost the conviction that it was Christianity that supplied the truth philosophy is to comprehend, and that without the Christian religion, philosophy would be without true content and direction.

It will also be observed, in Part 3, that, in its mature form, the Hegelian philosophy of religion has given rise to a continuing debate about the consequence of the profound change that occurred in Hegel's conception of religion, especially of the Christian religion. Does Hegel treat the religious content in such a way that there is nothing left of what could be regarded genuinely as religion, especially as Christianity? The variety of answers that have been given to this question does indicate a certain ambiguity in Hegel's position, particularly in reference to the fundamental issue of the relation between the infinite and finite, where Hegel's use of the term 'God'—though in an other than popular sense—gives rise to much of the ambiguity. It is this matter that will be examined in some detail in Part 3, where it will be suggested that Hegel's philosophy charts a middle course between extremes—neither moving into atheism nor maintaining a traditional theism. It also will be noted just how difficult it is to define that middle. But in the light of an analysis of Hegel's own works and a consideration of relevant literature, an attempt will be made to give some definition of that Hegelian middle—for without it an understanding of Hegel's philosophy of religion is quite impossible.

PART I

Hegel's Early Writings

*The Importance of Religion
in the Life of the People*

Introduction

Hegel's philosophy of religion portrays a definite pattern of evolution, and comes to its maturity during his years at Jena, which culminated in the writing of *Phenomenology of Spirit.* That mature position, however, cannot be adequately comprehended without due regard to the course of its development, and for that reason a study of Hegel's early essays, known as the *Early Theological Writings,*[1] together with those written in the context of his renewed association with Schelling in Jena, is quite crucial.

It is untenable to consider the early essays as unimportant for an understanding of Hegel's philosophy on the grounds that they are nothing more than the theological ponderings of a young man who later discarded all such interests, for these essays reveal the motivating interests of the young Hegel and the development of notions that are vital for his philosophy and that otherwise are easily misunderstood. Rather than seeing Hegel's developed thought as being achieved as a result of a violent overturning of views held in earlier periods, it is important to see it as a process of maturation, consisting in a number of significant stages of growth, which are reflected in his early writings.

But it is equally untenable, or at least totally misleading, while correctly acknowledging the importance of the early essays, to sweepingly designate them as antitheological. Such a description is suggested by Walter Kaufmann,[2] who argues that the only way Hegel's early writings could be described as 'theological' is by giving that term such a wide definition that it ceases to have a clear meaning. He says these essays "consistently deprecate theology in any customary sense of the term." [3] Georg Lukács is another, though from a Marxist stance, who dismisses the 'theological' description of Hegel's early essays as "a legend created and fostered by the reactionary apologists of imperialism." [4] He argues that the truth is that these works contain a "tone of sustained hostility" toward theology.[5] However, the difficulty with the word 'theological' as a description of Hegel's early writings lies in a distinction between theology and religion, for while there is some argument about the use of the term 'theological', there can be no serious quarrel about Hegel's clearly being concerned with religion.[6] Admittedly, he was not concerned

7

with theology in the sense in which it was practiced at that time; but was he concerned with theology in any sense? That is a question requiring further consideration.

It would be incorrect to suggest that these writings comprise a theological work in the sense that they are definitive of Hegel's theological position. Far from being definitive, they are a collection of writings that reflect a keen young mind's wrestling with contemporary issues and endeavoring to work out a position in regard to those issues, and in the course of which, themes and concepts emerge that become important in his later works. Only in regard to those later works can one speak of a definitive theological position. Even though it then was the work of Hegel, the philosopher, for whom theological, and all religious, thought is sublated in philosophical thought, it is clear that his system of philosophy is a theological system—he may then be described as a *speculative theologian*—since the ultimate concern of theology is God and, for Hegel, God is the object of philosophy. But that definitive system grew out of Hegel's concerns in the *ETW*, and these early writings therefore can be seen to have a basic theological theme.

It would be equally incorrect to suggest that these writings comprise a theological work in the sense that they are akin to the typical theology of his time. Indeed, in that sense they may be described as 'antitheological', for they were written in the context of his own markedly adverse reaction to the theological tradition of his home city and of the Tübingen *Stift*.[7] However, theology per se is not to be equated with one way of doing, or one kind of, theology; and so Hegel's opposition to the contemporary theology does not indicate a general antitheological position on his part. That the contrary is true can be discerned from his most fundamental interest and endeavor. From an early stage Hegel was strongly opposed to Christianity in its contemporary ecclesiastical expression, which either sought to accommodate the spirit of the Enlightenment while retaining the tradition intact, or kept itself completely divorced from the life of the world. But Hegel's opposition to this can be adequately understood only in light of his abiding interest in the life of the people and the achievement of a truly integrated society, for it was his conviction that such a society could be realized only on the basis of a genuinely living—'subjective'—religion, a *Volksreligion*. Yet, his experience of contemporary religion convinced him that it was a dead—'objective'—religion.[8] Therefore, the question of how religion is to be transformed was one of fundamental importance for Hegel: it is only on the foundation of a genuine religious transformation that adequate reform of society can be achieved, and this is why it can accurately be said that "the core of his work here is religious."

But at the heart of the desired transformation of religion is the restoration of a true understanding of the relation between the world and God, the finite and infinite, and, as this question is at the center of all theology, Hegel's work here can also be said to be theological.

Therefore, it can be concluded that while not being a definitive theological work, the *ETW* is neither antitheological, in the sense of being opposed to theology per se, nor nontheological, in the sense of not touching upon issues pertaining to theology. In fact, it is the case that these writings touch very heavily upon such issues: they contain the young Hegel's discussion of folk religion and Christianity, his writing of a life of Jesus, and his examination of the positivity of the Christian religion and of the spirit of Judaism and of Christianity. These themes all fall within the subject matter of theology, the ultimate concern of which is with God, but whose task embraces a critical examination of theological claims: an exploration of their foundation and history; a questioning of particular expressions of those claims at a given time to determine whether such expressions maintain the truth, or stray into a falsity, of the foundational claims; a consideration of the appropriateness or inappropriateness for the time of religious practices to which a particular theology gives rise; and then a consolidation, by clarifying, or a renewal, by purifying, of the theological claims. Given this understanding of the task and subject matter of theology, it seems quite clear that Hegel can be said to have been doing theology in these early writings—and in that sense they are theological.

Chapter 1
The Tübingen Period
The Concept of Volksreligion.

By the time Hegel began his study in Tübingen in 1788, there were already strong indications of his historical and social concern. Although he cannot be associated with the antireligious strand of the Enlightenment,[1] Hegel was nevertheless a child of the Enlightenment. Two Enlightenment ideals—the theoretical ideal of understanding and the practical ideal of reform[2]—showed themselves in Hegel's great interest in human history, from which he sought to gain an understanding of the origins of his own society, and in his deep sense of social responsibility and concern for the reform of his society. Any tension that possibly may be seen between these two ideals did not exist for Hegel: to reform the ills of society one must know how such ills occurred, so that reform necessitates understanding, and understanding can be gained only through historical inquiry. However, Hegel realized very clearly that it is not the case that theoretical understanding will always be converted into personal knowledge and issue in existential action, and he felt that this was distressingly true of his own society: understanding was without life, it was purely theoretical and not applied existentially. But if this was true of society in general, his experience of religion, and particularly the more intensive experience in the Tübingen *Stift*, convinced him that religion, too, was without life.

This opinion of the contemporary situation developed from, and was consolidated by, his historical inquiry, from which he derived

an unrivalled admiration for the culture of ancient Greece. The
contrast he drew between this and his own society was very sharp,
seeing the former as being characterized by a natural spontaneity
and the latter by an unnatural artificiality. It is in this contrast that
is to be found the origin of some key Hegelian concepts: alienation,
positivity, and objectivity as opposed to autonomy, freedom, and
subjectivity. His study of history led Hegel to the opinion that the
Greek city-state provided an ideal model of society, for it was a
harmonious and integrated society, enjoying a genuine freedom
whereby external authority gave way to internal self-determination.
In sharp contrast, he regarded his contemporary society as one marked
by disharmony and disintegration, one in which life was lived in
subservience to external authority: that is, in Hegel's terminology, it
was an alienated or 'positive' society.

This general comparison between the two societies dominated his
thinking during his Tübingen years, but it seems first to have suggested itself to Hegel in the form of a contrast between ancient
writers and modern ones,[3] in which Hegel detected two quite different
attitudes toward experience. On the one hand, there is that attitude
and reaction to experience that results in an understanding that is
merely theoretical, the product of booklearning, which is objective
and 'dead' for it is not related to life; on the other hand, there is
that which results in knowledge that is personal and practically
effective, and is 'living' because it has an existential application.
These two attitudes were explained by Hegel by means of two very
distinct kinds of mental activity, understanding and reason, for which
he used the terms *Verstand* and *Vernunft*.[4] This is an important
distinction for Hegel, for in it he found the key to comprehending
the nature of the problems of his own society—simply, he saw it
as characterized by *Verstand*, whereas Greek society had been characterized by *Vernunft*—and in it he found the clue to the means
whereby contemporary society might be reformed and renewed.

In Hegel's view, the problems of contemporary society—its disharmony, disintegration, alienation—permeate all spheres of life, not
least the religious life of the society. Indeed, this is of particular
importance in Hegel's view of society because he saw religion playing
a decisive and formative role in the life of a society. Therefore, the
cause of the problems of his society was more clearly apparent to
the young Hegel as a result of his consideration of religion, and
again it was his study of history that brought him to his conclusion.
It is with regard to religion that the stark contrast between the Greek
culture and that of his own society was most strongly noted.

Here, too, the comparison corresponds to the distinction between
Verstand and *Vernunft*: religion that is the work of *Verstand* is objective

religion, imposed from without by an authority and therefore alien to the society and individuals, being divorced from their spirit and needs; on the other hand, religion that is the work of *Vernunft* is subjective religion, arising out of and reflecting the experience of people and so having a capacity for meeting their needs. For Hegel, Christianity, as expressed in his own society, was nothing more than objective religion, a religion of *Verstand;* it had its origin in another land and amongst other people and so was alien to Germany; and barren, it was divorced from the spirit and needs of his generation, being imposed on individual Germans by an external authority: It was concerned only with the content of faith, with creeds, dogmas, and ceremonies—merely the work of *Verstand* and *Gedächtnis* (memory)—and so was a religion of subservience and death, not of freedom and life. Greek religion, on the other hand, he regarded as having been deeply rooted in the spirit of the Greek people, arising out of and reflecting the experience of those people in their situation, and so forming an integral part of their culture. For Hegel, Greek religion was therefore a subjective religion: it was a matter of direct experience, it was essentially personal, the work of *Vernunft,* and consequently the source of the self-liberation of the people.

Thus, Hegel's view of Christianity and his contrasting ideal of religion at this stage were molded by two mutually supporting factors: his study and love of classical Greece and his experience of, and disdain for, contemporary Christianity. His experience of theology at Tübingen convinced Hegel that Christianity was being treated in a way that reduced it to nothing more than a matter of book learning, and convinced him as well that rather than use new Enlightenment insights to rethink Christian theology in the contemporary situation, those insights were being used, even being distorted, in order to defend and maintain the traditional theological position—a biblical supernaturalism—of the *Stift.*

The comparison that Hegel drew between the religion of the ancient Greeks and the Christianity of contemporary Germany occupied much of his thinking during the Tübingen years, and not only issued in his understanding of objective and subjective religion, but also in the consolidation of his related concept of *Volksreligion* (national religion). This is the concept of a religion that is intimately related to the spirit of a people and forms a significant element in the culture of that people. This was not something Hegel came to only in Tübingen, for again the first indication of this concept of *Volksreligion* is to be found in an important school essay, written in August 1787;[5] and again it is clear that his ideal of *Volksreligion* is afforded by that of classical Greece, whose philosophers, he said, offer us far more enlightened and sublime concepts of the Godhead, especially in respect of the fate of man. They taught that God gives to every man sufficient means and power to achieve happiness, and has so ordered the nature of things that true happiness is achieved through wisdom and moral goodness. (Hoffmeister, 47; trans. by Harris, 33)

It was a concept that certainly dominated his thought at Tübingen, as did his important distinction between objective and subjective religion. There these concepts were developed and consolidated and committed to writing in an essay, *Religion ist eine,*[6] which Hegel wrote during a short visit to Stuttgart (July-August 1793), at the end of his time at the *Stift*[7] and prior to taking up a private tutorship in Bern.

In this fragment, Hegel's primary concern was to show that abstract intellectualism in the study of religion—the kind he had just experienced at Tübingen—was simply not good enough if religion was to have a practical purpose and become an active social force in the necessary reshaping of society. That religion does have such a purpose and role is quite apparent in Hegel's view: he likened religion to the hub of a wheel and asserted that "religion is one of the most important concerns of our life."[8] And it is assertions of this kind that distinguish Hegel from the antireligious French *Aufklärer*, for Hegel's desired renewal of society was based on a fundamental enlivening of religion.[9] But this Hegelian essay is clearly the product of *Aufklärung* aspirations: Kant was obviously a dominating influence, for Hegel's abiding concern was with practical reason;[10] but it was an influence modified by the works of Rousseau, Mendelssohn, and Lessing, the last of whom is frequently quoted.

If religion is therefore such a crucial concern of our life, it is important to clarify what is the adequate kind of religion for such a purpose; and it was here that his distinction between objective and subjective religion, with which he began the fragment, was relevant.

Objective religion, in which only *Verstand* and *Gedächtnis* are operative, is concerned merely with the content of faith—with doctrines and ceremonies. Religion becomes objective when it is systematized, set down in writing, and so reduced to something that can be verbally taught. Thus, it is something imposed by an external authority, living experience being quite absent. On the other hand, religion is subjective when it originates in the direct experience of feelings and actions; "subjective religion is alive, it is effective in the inwardness of our being, and active in our outward behaviour." Subjective religion was likened to the living things of nature, whereas objective religion was said to be akin to natural species preserved in the naturalist's cabinet, where they are all arranged for a specific purpose of study in contrast to their natural infinite and interlocking variety of purposes.[11]

When Hegel stated that "a few fundamental propositions lie at the base of every religion; they are merely modified or deformed to a greater or lesser degree in the different religions," and when he spoke of these propositions being "of God and immortality," [12] the influence of Kant,[13] Mendelssohn,[14] and Lessing[15] is apparent. It is this common element that is fundamental to subjective religion. It was not the differing manifestations of that common element that Hegel regarded as important, for such matters as dogmas, ceremonies, and codes of behavior—the content of objective religion—are the concern of the theologians who argue about them; they are the subjects of mere book learning, of cold and critical evaluation by the understanding, and consequently are matters concerning which there is a complete absence of any comprehension of meaning.[16] The understanding, which "serves only objective religion," might be useful, through abstract argument, in clarifying principles and in making us cleverer, but really the understanding contributes little to religion, for it does not render the principles into practical action or make us better.[17] First, because the understanding does not make the principles part of ourselves—its activity is abstract and the principles remain objective, whereas religion must be truly subjective.[18] Secondly, because something other than rational argument is needed, namely, wisdom, which—again reflecting *Nathan*—is not convictions purchased in the market where knowledge is given out for a price, but is that which "speaks rather from the fullness of the heart." [19] What is important about subjective religion is that it is a matter of the heart:

It is inherent in the concept of religion that it is not mere science of God, of his attributes, of our relation and the relation of the world to him and of the enduring survival of our souls—all of this might be admitted by mere Reason, or known to us in some other way—but religion is not a merely historical or rational knowledge, it is a concern of the heart, it has an influence on our feelings and on the determination of our will—partly because our duties and the laws make a stronger impression on us when they are presented to us as the laws of God; and partly because the image *(Vorstellung)* of the sublimity and the goodness of God towards us fills our hearts with wonder and with a sense of humility and gratitude. (Harris's trans., 482)

In subjective religion it is the heart that must speak louder than the understanding, as in the case of the friar in Lessing's *Nathan* and in Jesus' accepting "with love and goodwill the anointing of his body by a woman who had formerly lived a life of ill-fame." [20] It is from the heart that there comes the rendering of principles into action and the living of better lives; and the underlying principles known by the heart are those common to all religions. And it is these common elements and practical action that, for Hegel, were the essence of subjective religion.

But because these universal truths have been "grasped with whole heart and cloven to with love" only by "outstanding men in every age," they cannot "constitute a religion for the general populace"; additional elements have to be added for such a popular religion (*Volksreligion*), and the pure principles have to be "embedded in a sensible shell." [21] But it cannot be just *any* additional elements or *any* sensible shell! What, then, are the criteria for a *healthy Volksreligion*? Hegel answered this question in the following way:

I.   Its doctrines must be grounded on universal Reason.
II.   Fancy, heart, and sensibility must not thereby go empty away.
III. It must be so constituted that all the needs of life—the public affairs of the State are tied in with it.

(Harris trans., 499)

Early in this essay Hegel had stated that his object was to make the necessary inquiries into that which is requisite "in order that religion should become wholly subjective." [22] In turning to discuss the characteristics of *Volksreligion*, he did not cease to be concerned with subjective religion. Indeed, a *Volksreligion* has the same qualities as subjective religion, but whereas the latter primarily suggests personal and individual religion, the former is subjective religion of the community: the former, Harris says, "is like the order of living nature, where every creature lives its own life and has its own purposes, but they all nevertheless depend on one another." [23] Thus, in turning to *Volksreligion*, Hegel was discussing the meaning of subjective religion for the community, and in doing so he was displaying his involvement in the question of popular education for the pursuit of the desired transformation of society.[24]

A healthy *Volksreligion*, in Hegel's view, is the primary instrument in popular education and social reform, and therefore it is crucial to determine the nature of a genuine *Volksreligion*. First, religion should not remain on the level of *Verstand*, since as such it is merely a theoretical discussion about doctrines and does not meet the requirements of *Vernunft*. In order to meet those requirements, doctrines—

even if it is claimed that they rest on divine revelation—must be "authorized really by the universal Reason of mankind"; they "must also be simple," not based on obscure and complex arguments; and they must be "humane" in the sense that they must reflect a realization of the fact that people are not abstract beings, but real persons, and must be met where they are in their existential situations. Thus, doctrines must be "appropriate to the spiritual culture and stage of morality that a people has reached." [25] A religion becomes burdensome if its doctrines are imprisoned in formulations of the past, and it becomes unrealistic if they are adopted as universal maxims: while being grounded on universal Reason, they must be expressed in a way that is meaningful to each contemporary situation.

The implied criticism of Kant here becomes more obvious in Hegel's assertion that Reason alone, however, is insufficient,[26] for, secondly, religion that is to serve as a *Volksreligion* should not neglect the senses and emotions of people. The three elements of religion—concepts, essential practices (such as Baptism and Eucharist in Christianity), and ceremonies—should accommodate heart and fancy. Concepts should be expressed in beautiful images and myths; essential practices should be structured in a way that springs from "the spirit of the people," for "otherwise they are gone through without life, coldly, without force"; and in ceremonies use should be made of color, drama, national festivals, etc., though care should always be taken to ensure, as far as possible, that ceremonies are not constituted in such a way that the mere performance of them will be "taken as the essence of religion." [27]

Thirdly, there should be no discrepancy between the doctrine that is accepted and the way of life that is practiced; and, of course, Hegel did not mean only the life-style of an individual, but also that of the society. Indeed, as Harris says, "folk-religion goes hand in hand with political freedom because it arouses and nourishes the noble emotions (*große Gesinnungen*) that sustain a free constitution. The religion, the historical tradition, and the political constitution of a people together constitute the *Volksgeist*." [28] Thus, one can conclude with Lukács that "even the Tübingen student already conceives of subjective, public religion as the religion of a self-liberation of the people." [29]

In the Introduction it was noted that three aspirations motivated the young Hegel,[30] namely, the freedom of self-determination, unity and wholeness, and the Christian religion. It can now be said that the "Tübingen Fragment" shows how Hegel perceived the notion of the freedom of self-determination in regard to religion: religion should not remain external and objective, but must spring from experience and be an integrated part of life; and this is so not just for private religion but also for public religion, which must spring from the spirit of the community and be geared to the level attained by the people rather than being imposed from an alien culture. Further, the Fragment displays Hegel's application of the notion of wholeness and the desire for the healing of divisions: this is to be realized within each individual, for religion is not just a matter of reason, but of the whole person whose various aspects are not at odds with each other.[31] But this wholeness is also to be realized within the relationships between individuals and realized for a people—a community or nation—so that Hegel's aspirations have a social and political import.[32]

Chapter 2
The Bern Period

A Rational Foundation in Kantian Terms for a Christian Volksreligion, *and the Concept of* Positivity.

The date of the "Tübingen Fragment" indicates that it embodies the ideals and aspirations Hegel carried with him when he took up his new position in Bern in October 1793. They were aspirations that amounted to the regeneration of society, the achievement of which he saw in terms of the establishment of a genuine *Volksreligion*. But they were aspirations that presented certain questions, such as: How does one reform a corrupt society? How does a reformer successfully work within an educational process that has become degenerate? In particular, how does the third basic element in Hegel's thought— the Christian religion—fit in with the aspirations spelled out in the "Tübingen Fragment"? The question had not really been considered there, but it can be said that the Christian religion appears to fit "very uneasily" with his ideal of a *Volksreligion*.[1] This was something Hegel seems to have realized increasingly in Bern, where most of his initial fragments are concerned with this question. At first, this tension in his thought showed itself in strong criticism of Christianity, and it was Kant who provided the clue for the way Hegel sought to resolve the tension—though that solution proved to be only temporary.

In an early Bern fragment, *Außer dem mündlichen Unterricht,* [2] Hegel highlighted the problem of the intended reformer of a corrupt society. In it he turned his attention to notable individual teachers of their respective societies, and in particular he drew a sharp contrast between Socrates and Jesus[3]—thus indicating the extent of his critical attitude toward Christianity at this stage. Hegel suggested that the very different ways in which Socrates and Jesus went about their teaching was made necessary by the differences between their respective societies. Jesus deliberately chose to become a private teacher, seeking to separate both himself and his followers from his society because he recognized its corruption. But that corruption and the authoritarian nature of that society made it impossible for Jesus to completely separate himself and to achieve a personal freedom for his followers: the use of such titles as the "Twelve" and the "Chosen" was an indication of a conformity to the spirit of the society.

Socrates, according to Hegel's comparison, made no such attempt to escape from his society, and he remained a public teacher. He was fully involved in the life of his society, but at the same time enjoyed a personal freedom that he sought to impart to his circle of friends. Furthermore, this group of friends was deemed to be completely open, rather than being restricted in number; and Socrates was said to have given every encouragement and assistance to enable them to develop their own gifts and follow their own purposes as distinct individuals. For Hegel, as a result of this kind of examination of notable individual teachers, "the proposition is proved, 'the mode of instruction must always be directed in accordance with the spirit *(Genie)* and tone that is established among the people.' " [4]

In another Bern fragment, *Die Staatsverfassungen,* [5] Hegel argued that Christianity was not in accordance with the spirit of the people of his society and cannot bring about the regeneration and maturity of society. Societies, he said, like individuals, pass through a cycle of development, and the state of maturity, for both the individual and society, is the state of being ruled by *Vernunft*—a condition for which religion is the primary instrument. However, where responsibility for religion is in the hands of a privileged group—which is very probable in a situation where the religion is of an alien origin (and he regarded Christianity as such)—there exists a barrier to the full realization of the cycle of development. This barrier becomes even more imposing if the religion is closely connected with the prevailing political system of the society, for then it can become a tool of the forces of reaction. The barrier is caused by such privileged groups being concerned with serving their own interests, which involves keeping the people in a state of 'childhood'. Childhood is characterized by dependence, and people are forced to depend on the *Verstand* of religious experts rather than being enabled to depend on their own *Vernunft*. To understand the true essence of religion is a work of *Vernunft*, and of course, is opposed by the privileged "defenders" of religion. Therefore, theological concepts are the last to feel the effect of any advance of reason; and this was why the Reformation failed. Hegel tended to regard the Reformation as an attempt to restore the spirit of religion and as coinciding with the German people passing from childhood to maturity; but he believed it failed because it resorted to the principle of authority, a product of *Verstand*,[6] and so prevented the flowering of *Vernunft*. Indeed, in Hegel's view, wherever religion has the role of an authority it is impossible for the ideals of self-determination and wholeness, expressed in ethical life *(Sittlichkeit)*, to be realized.[7]

In *Unter objektiver Religion*—"The Bern Plan of 1794"[8]—Hegel set down a plan for his analysis of the problem of how a renewed society is to be achieved through a genuine *Volksreligion*.[9] He made it clear that he regarded the structure of society as one in which there is no sharp distinction between church and state; the political community is also a religious and moral community. Therefore, it should be a concern of the state to facilitate the development of moral character and a sense of purpose in the society, and in Hegel's terms, this can be achieved only by making "objective religion subjective," a task that is therefore "the great concern of the state."[10] Yet, in spite of his deprecating comments, the third motivating aspect of Hegel's thought has not been discarded, for he asked, "How far is the Christian religion qualified for this purpose?" The pursuit of this question involved Hegel in a critical examination of fundamental doctrines of Christianity to determine the extent to which it meets the requirements of a healthy *Volksreligion*.

In two essays of 1794, *Es sollte eine schwere Aufgabe*[11] and *Wenn man von der christlichen Religion*,[12] Hegel embarked on such an examination. A main thrust of his argument is the assertion of "the proper rational purpose of religion" as "the strengthening of *Sittlichkeit* by establishing the *Idee* of God as giver of the moral law and guarantor of the highest good (i.e., the harmony of virtue and happiness postulated by Kant)."[13]

If religion has such a purpose, however, it cannot admit incomprehensible doctrines and religious mysteries: "reason must reject [such things]—in its demand for moral goodness it can permit no giving-in."[14] Similarly, it follows that any claim that "those (religious) doctrines are above reason, but not against reason" must equally be repudiated, for perhaps "the doctrines as such are not against reason, but it is against reason to believe them."[15] Another thrust conerns the foreign origin of Christianity and what Hegel took to be its consequent authoritarian character, which means that "the ordinary man is inevitably obliged to depend on the *Verstand* of experts instead of being spurred to use and rely on his own *Vernunft*. This dependence destroys the proper character of religious faith itself, the very thing that gives religion its practical value and importance. For it ought to be a 'stretching of the soul' *[Spannung der Seele]*, not a 'function of the memory' *[Sache des Gedachtnisses]*." [16]

In contrast to this product of *Verstand*—these requirements of orthodox religion—*Vernunft* tells us that what is pleasing to God is the fostering of a disposition that is inclined to the moral law, and Hegel was of the opinion that, if properly understood, the teaching of Jesus would be seen as being of the kind that cultivates such a disposition. However, Hegel was also of the opinion that, due to historical circumstances and other factors, the teaching of Jesus had been distorted from a creative force of this kind to an objective authority that restricts the growth of moral character because it maintains a condition of dependence. Therefore, given this conviction about the strength of Jesus' message, at this stage Hegel seems to have been convinced of the necessity to rediscover that message; that he believed it possible to do so was based on a firm confidence in *Vernunft* to achieve its requirements for an adequate *Volksreligion*. Those requirements amounted to the establishment of religion on a rational foundation that would cultivate a disposition toward the moral law; and that Christianity had such a rational foundation was the view Hegel expressed in his work "The Life of Jesus," [17] which he commenced on 8 May and completed on 24 July 1795. The problem of Christianity for Hegel now was that Jesus had been divinized by his followers, and thus his true nature and the character of his message had been distorted; but once the veil of divinity was removed by *Vernunft*, the picture of Jesus that emerged for Hegel in 1795 was that of Kant's ideal moral teacher.[18]

Another important aspect of the background in which "Life of Jesus" was written was the recollection of the situation in the seminary, where Kant was used by the teachers to demonstrate their own theological position, particularly with regard to revelation.[19] This recollection was prompted by correspondence with Schelling, who, in a letter to Hegel early in 1795, complained that in Tübingen the *Critique of Practical Reason* had infused new life into reactionary orthodox theology.[20] Therefore, partly to defend Kant against the treatment he was receiving at the hands of the Tübingen teachers, but more importantly to pursue his own creative purpose, Hegel wrote "Life of Jesus." This result of his independent mind was an essay in which he claimed to have shown precisely what could be done with Kantian terms when properly used: they could provide the means for a reinterpretation of Christianity that would serve as the rational foundation of a genuine *Volksreligion.*

"The Life of Jesus."

In writing "The Life of Jesus," [21] Hegel's purpose was to give an account of Jesus' life in such a way as to show that his own concept of *Volksreligion* had a scriptual basis. He did not take this to involve any deliberate alteration of the life of Jesus,[22] but merely a purging of the halo of divinity that had later been bestowed on Jesus, and a clarification of the teachings of Jesus, which then would be seen to be the basis of a genuine *Volksreligion.* Furthermore, in this work Hegel was not intentionally setting out to undermine the faith of the devout religious people of his day, but rather to properly direct their devotion by breaking through the accretions contained in the historical record, and thereby presenting a right understanding of what Jesus did and said. Hegel sought "with quite dedicated intentness to give *the most literal account possible of what Jesus meant.*" [23] The implication, naturally, is that Hegel believed his account to be compatible with Jesus' own intentions; but inevitably, some Hegelian critics see Hegel's work as being beyond the limits of what can be justified by the original texts.[24] However, while it is fairly obvious that much of Hegel's interpretation is forced, there is no warrant for a dismissal of it as antitheological, for his intention to present a "proper grasp of what Jesus *meant*" is no different from the intentions of any biblical commentator or theologian.

The result, in Hegel's "Life of Jesus," is a presentation of Jesus as the supreme moral teacher, with all aspects of the Gospel records that do not provide a moral lesson being omitted—this is the employment of *Vernunft* for the formation of an adequate foundation for a *Volksreligion,* casting off whatever conflicts with its own requirements. Therefore, the miraculous element that, on a literal interpretation, the Gospels seem to possess, is eliminated, with reference being made only to those 'miracle' stories that are capable of a naturalistic interpretation and from which a moral lesson can be drawn. Consequently, there is no mention of a miraculous virgin birth, Jesus being simply described as the son of Joseph and Mary;[25] and the work is brought to an end with the death and burial of Jesus, [26] so that Hegel does not even mention the Resurrection. On the other hand, there are miracle stories of healing, but these are taken to refer to experiences of spiritual conversion and rational illumination: Jesus' statement to Nicodemus that a man must be "born again" is interpreted as meaning that a man must recognize his essential freedom; and the assurance of forgiveness of sins that Jesus is reported to have given to many individuals is said to be a statement of recognition by Jesus that the particular individual had found for himself the courage to begin a new life.

Hegel's "Life of Jesus" is an attempt to express the Gospels in terms of Kantian philosophy:[27] Jesus is depicted as being exclusively a moral teacher who expounds Kantian ethics. Thus, Hegel has Jesus say: "What you can will to be a universal law among men, valid also against yourselves, according to such maxim act—this is the basic law of ethics, the content of all legislation, and of the sacred books of all peoples." [28] At the time of writing "Life of Jesus," Hegel held the opinion that the clearest articulation of the practical implications for a life lived in accordance with *Vernunft* was to be found in Kantian philosophy—and therefore in this particular essay the contrast between, for example, Kant's Categorical Imperative and the Golden Rule of the Gospels is a clear suggestion that Hegel saw the Kantian formulation as the ethical law that Jesus preached.

Hegel was expressing an unqualified belief in *Vernunft* and openly appealing to rationality as the principle of genuine *Volksreligion;* indeed, in his opening statement he identified this principle with the Godhead itself:

> Reason *[Vernunft]* pure and exceeding all limits is the Godhead itself—According to Reason therefore is the plan of the world in general ordered (John 1); Reason it is which teaches man to recognize his vocation *[Bestimmung]*, an unconditional purpose of his life; often indeed it is obscured but never wholly quenched, even in the darkness he has always retained a faint glimmer of it—. (Nohl, 75; trans. by Harris, 198)

But it was in Jesus that this principle was supremely represented, and this central theme of this essay is marked by an important contrast: on the one hand, the virtuous Jesus acts dutifully for the sake of the moral law that is the requirement of *Vernunft;* while on the other hand, the Jewish priesthood calls for the meticulous observance of a set of irrational rules said to be commanded by God, but which are only burdensome additions to the requirements of *Vernunft.* The contrast is between those who follow the letter of the law and one who taught and acted in its spirit.

Action in the spirit of the law is not action based on authority, and in Hegel's interpretation, Jesus never intentionally acted or spoke in a way that would create a special faith in him or a belief founded on the authority of his name. It is the unhindered operation of enlightened *Vernunft* in every individual that is the true vocation of each person, and this cannot be achieved through obedience to authority, but only as the free response of each individual. Thus, one cannot fail to notice Hegel's stress on that motivating aspiration of human freedom and autonomy. It is this that Hegel saw Jesus encouraging through his words and deeds, and he therefore presented Jesus as the one who supremely represents the principle of *Vernunft* that Hegel had stated at the outset of this essay.

The Concept of *Positivity*

Thus, in this essay, "Life of Jesus," Hegel provided an answer to his own question that he had posed in his "Plan of 1794," namely, to what extent is Christianity equipped to be a *Volksreligion*, performing the function of developing morality in society? While he had already determined three criteria for a *Volksreligion*, his answer, as contained in "Life of Jesus," was directed at demonstrating that Christianity has the capacity to fulfill the first criterion, namely, of being grounded on universal Reason. With his thinking dominated, at this period, by the Kantian notion of a practical *Vernunftreligion*, Hegel, seeking to restore a 'true' understanding of Jesus as the teacher of rational morality, claimed to have shown that Christianity possessed a rational foundation and thereby also possessed the capacity to be the desired *Volksreligion*. However, this claim about Christianity posed a further difficulty: since the contemporary expression of Christianity did not show signs of having such a rational basis, the obvious task was to analyze the cause of the deterioration.

This analysis issued in the writing of the "Positivity" essay,[29] which was completed in November 1795. Within the next seven months, however, Hegel had written two postscripts to this essay, *Ein positiver Glauben*[30] and *Jedes Volk hat ihm eigene Gegenstände*,[31] and these three writings together are of utmost importance for their presentation of the Hegelian notion of 'positivity'. But the two postscripts must, in an equally significant way, be separated from the essay because they reflect the development of a new dimension in Hegel's thought that marks the end of the period in which Kant exerted a dominant, though never exclusive, influence on his thought.

The "Positivity" essay itself, however, like "Life of Jesus," reflects the Hegelian thought that is still geared to the Kantian notion of the practical purpose and rational basis of religion, and because these two writings also complement each other in their analysis of Christianity, it is apparent that they form a unity. It is probable that Hegel conceived of both at the same time.

In the preface of the "Positivity" essay, Hegel reiterated the view
that religion is concerned with morality:

". . . the general principle to be laid down as a foundation for
all judgments on the varying modifications, forms, and spirit of
the Christian religion is this—that the aim and essence of all
true religion, our religion included, is human morality, and that
all the more detailed doctrines of Christianity, all means of
propagating them, and all its obligations (whether obligations to
believe or obligations to perform actions in themselves otherwise
arbitrary) have their worth and their sanctity appraised according
to their close or distant connection with that aim. (*ETW*, 68)

An understanding of the true nature of that aim clarifies what Hegel
meant by 'positivity': the positivity of the Christian religion is its
authoritarian character. Yet, true morality is the free, spontaneous
cultivation of virtue for its own sake, not out of obedience to authority
or for fear of punishment.[32]

Thus, the explanation, given in this essay, for the corruption of
the original and true character of Christianity is that it has been
made a positive faith. The reasons why this has occurred, according
to Hegel, are to be found in Jesus himself, in the disciples, and in
the nature of the later expansion of Christianity. The environment
in which it was being expressed at any particular time always had
an important bearing on its development, and this was particularly
true regarding the origin and early life of Christianity: the reason
why elements of positivity are to be found in Jesus and his disciples
is in the nature of Judaism, a highly authoritarian religion.

Of course, this does not mean that Hegel had moved away from
his interpretation of Jesus as the teacher of rational morality, and he
certainly made every effort to avoid any suggestion that Jesus had
intended to establish a positive faith. Jesus is presented as being free
from the ailments of his own society and as taking upon himself
the task of bursting the strict legality of Jewish law: "he undertook
to raise religion and virtue to morality and to restore to morality the
freedom which is its essence."[33] Jesus did not endeavor to achieve
this by introducing novel doctrines or new moral principles, but he
sought to restore and develop the implications of the true meaning
of the existing tradition as contained in the sacred writings of his
people. When Jesus said "be perfect," he was advocating living *in*
the law as the way to realizing fullness of life and contrasting it
with living in subjection *under* the law, which is the way to death.
Similarly, Jesus advocated the value of virtue as opposed to the
worthlessness of outward religious exercises that merely give rise to

hypocrisy; and the virtue that is to be valued is that which springs from one's own being, as opposed to that which is grounded on authority.

So Hegel presented Jesus as the teacher of moral religion and denied that he was a teacher of a positive faith; but Hegel recognized that there are those who do not agree and who assert that while the religion Jesus taught "contains principles of virtue, it also contains positive prescriptions for acquiring God's favour by exercises, feelings and actions rather than by morality." [34] However, amongst those who do not agree with him, Hegel distinguished two opinions: those who feel that such positive prescriptions are "inessential and even reprehensible" (it would seem that here he is referring to Kant); and those who put "the pre-eminence of Jesus' religion precisely in this positive element" (it would seem that here it is the Tübingen professors whom he had in mind). But neither view was that of Hegel, and his interpretation of Jesus inevitably raised the question: Why did the teaching of Jesus lead to the creation of a positive religion?

The general answer that Hegel gave to this question is that it was due to the external circumstances and the spirit of the times. Such factors meant that even in Jesus himself elements of positivity were present in spite of the fact that it was his prime aim to teach rational morality. The spirit of the Jews was "overwhelmed by a burden of statutory commands," [35] and the people therefore had lost sight of the essential freedom in morality; instead, they regarded virtue as consisting in the slavish obedience to dead formulas that were seen to derive their authority from the divine will. In such circumstances reason had been deadened, and therefore it would have been futile for Jesus to base his appeal on reason. Instead, he "was compelled . . . to speak a great deal about himself" in order for his message to be accessible to the people.

The Jews believed they were God's chosen people, and that their entire law was of divine origin, so that no aspect of their faith was open to the scrutiny of speculative reason, but all was a matter of "blind obedience to these authoritarian commands." Therefore, any teacher who sought to reinterpret these commands and to challenge people on the adequacy of their faith "must of necessity have based his assertions on a like authority"; to have appealed to reason would have been like "preaching to fish," because the Jews had lost the awareness of possessing an autonomous reason, and so "had no means of apprehending a challenge of that kind." [36] Jesus' only alternative was to speak of himself as being sent by God and thus as the one in whom people were to have faith, for he could not have obtained even a hearing from the Jews of his day if he had not claimed God's authority for his teaching: "Jesus therefore demands attention for his teachings, not because they are adapted to the moral needs of our spirit, but because they are God's will. This . . . gave him his authority." [37] In speaking of himself as the Messiah, Jesus was using the language that his listeners would understand, since the expectation of a Messiah was part of their religious faith, and it would have been indicative of a claim to divine authority.

Thus, Hegel identified elements of positivity in Jesus' teaching, but he was adamant that it was not Jesus' intention to exercise authority over others; his appeal to authority was merely in order to attract people to his message, which was one of rational morality. But although this was Jesus' intention, he failed in the attempt; and the most serious cause of his failure occurred when, because of hostility toward him, he turned away from the public life of his people and concentrated his attention on a group of selected followers. The choice of the Twelve provided the greatest opportunity for the emergence of a positive religion, since "the result of restricting the highest standing to a specific number of men was the ascription of high standing to certain individuals, and this became something continually more essential in the later constitution of the Christian Church." [38] These men were people of their own time, and while they themselves did not possess any great spiritual energy, they shared the authoritarian character of their society, and therefore it was they who developed the positive elements into a sectarian religion. Unlike Socrates' pupils, the disciples of Jesus lacked great gifts of insight, and so their sole interest was in an absolute adherence to Jesus' teaching rather than in working on it to draw out its implications for themselves.

Hegel's treatment of the relations between Jesus and the disciples and this sharp contrast between Jesus' disciples and those of Socrates are a strong indication that he did not want to present Jesus as the teacher of a positive religion. An equally strong indication is given by Hegel's treatment of miracles. The way in which miracle stories have been retold by the disciples and handed down to succeeding generations has been the largest factor in making Christianity positive. Hegel's discussion of miracles certainly casts doubt upon their literal interpretation, for he said that they were miracles in the eyes of Jesus' friends, while "more learned contemporaries" were simply not impressed. But being viewed in this way by his followers, the miracles became the basis of authority. This, however, was not Jesus' intention.

> Although Jesus wanted faith, not on the strength of his miracles, but on the strength of his teaching, although eternal truths are of such a nature that, if they are to be necessary and universally valid, they can be based on the essence of reason alone and

not on phenomena in the external world which for reason are mere accidents, still the conviction of man's obligation to be virtuous took the following road: Miracles, loyally and faithfully accepted, became the basis of a faith in the man who worked them and the ground of his authority. This authority of his became the underlying principle of the obligation to act morally. (*ETW*, 78–79)

So the essentiality of virtue in itself is lost, and becomes essential only because obedience to the authority of Jesus requires it, not because reason—the proper basis of virtue—requires it.

The result of this was to make reason a purely receptive faculty, instead of a legislative one, to make whatever could be proved to be the teaching of Jesus or, later, of his vicars, an object of reverence purely and simply because it was the teaching of Jesus or God's will, and something bound up with salvation or damnation. Even moral doctrines, now made obligatory in a positive sense, i.e., not on their own account, but as commanded by Jesus, lost the inner criterion whereby their necessity is established, and were placed on the same level with every other positive, specific command, with every external ordinance grounded in circumstances or on mere prudence. And although this is otherwise a contradictory conception, the religion of Jesus became a *positive* doctrine about *virtue*. (*ETW*, 85–86)

Thus, the positive character became the root of evil, and as expansion occurred, the religion of Jesus became increasingly diverted from the essence of true religion. On the one hand, expansion resulted in the loss of certain characteristics that had been possible in a small group, such as the community of goods, the principle of equality, and the spontaneous nature of the Lord's Supper. On the other hand, expansion resulted in the acquisition of other characteristics, such as zeal for further expansion and an exclusive attitude that viewed salvation as being dependent on its own distinctive doctrines. The final step in the degeneration of the religion of Jesus into a positive religion occurred when it became identified with the state, for then it was based on an even more pressing authority, namely, that of the state.

From this point the essay ceases to be primarily concerned with a diagnosis of the process of the deterioration of Christianity, for Hegel's fundamental concern turned to the proper relation between church and state. His major points were that rational morality, which is the proper concern of religion, cannot be enacted by the state or any other authority; that religion must be a matter of free choice, with any coercion being an infringement of a basic human right; and further, such coercion involves the subjugation of human reason, and therefore it is the responsibility of the enlightened state to prevent such a possibility. However, unless coercive authorities manage to blot out the rational part of human nature, reason will assert itself and break through the restraints of such coercion: the tragedy is, of course, that such breakthroughs usually result in becoming a new form of rigidity and coercion.

The overriding point of this "Positivity" essay—the lesson Hegel believed it important for his contemporary society to understand as the way to achieve renewal of that society—is that the true message of Jesus must become effectual. Moral autonomy, the freedom for self-determination, must be realized, and to enable this realization, all positive aspects of religion—every appeal to absolute authority—must be eradicated.

Preparation for a Significant Development.

Hegel's endeavor to demonstrate that Christianity meets the requirements of a genuine *Volksreligion* in having a rational foundation in Jesus' teaching, and his task of rationally examining the course of Christianity's subsequent degeneration, can be seen to have come to an end at this stage in his early writings. He had concluded that the result of this degeneration of Christianity is that *Vernunft* is no longer employed in the expression of the Christian religion: man has lost his liberty of thought, his moral liberty has been eroded, and thus man has been alienated from his true self and can be said to be also alienated from God.

The way forward must be a way that will heal this alienation, and it was the search for such an advance that brought about a significant development in Hegel's early thought, eventually (but not yet) resulting in a move away from his conception of Kant's rational religion, with its morality of law, as the goal of human progress, toward his own formulation of a morality of love.

Positivity, the characteristic that, according to Hegel, must be eradicated from religion, is marked by separation and alienation, and by the suspension of moral autonomy; it is a characteristic that, being essentially authoritarian, involves a denial of the use of *Vernunft*. However, the true vocation of each person is the unhindered operation of *Vernunft*, although this in itself, while it can recognize this separation and alienation, cannot heal alienation or overcome opposition. This inability of *Vernunft* is so because the freedom of the individual may lead one person to oppose another, or moreover, within each individual reason may become an authority as great as any external authority, so that he becomes a slave to himself, and alienation persists. This inability of reason to overcome alienation means that all forms of reflective religion—and, as Hegel will eventually conclude, this embraces even the highest form, the Kantian *Vernunftreligion*—are forms of positive religion. As Hegel had already suggested the inadequacy of traditional positive religion, so he soon will suggest that religious faith of the Kantian rational kind is just as inadequate in annulling all the division and alienation that exists in a sundered world.

The year 1795 saw Hegel pass through a 'Kantian interlude' during which he regarded Kant as offering the most adequate formulation of moral freedom and rational autonomy. However, Harris refers to this interlude as being "only like the exposed tip of an iceberg" [39] in the sense that it simply revealed an underlying immovable Hegelian conviction regarding the essentiality of moral freedom and rational autonomy. While that conviction was to remain, its Kantian manifestation would soon begin to disappear in 1797, when earlier differences with Kant would be reaffirmed and additional ones would emerge.

That movement in Hegel's thinking, at this stage, was still in the future, and would occur only after his renewed contact with Hölderlin in Frankfurt. However, what can be detected in his writings during his final year in Bern is a preparation—though unintentional at that time—for the subsequent rejection of Kant. Part of that unintentional preparation was in the writing of two essays between December 1795 and June 1796, which may be regarded as postscripts to the "Positivity" essay.

In the first of these writings, *Ein positiver Glauben*,[40] Hegel temporarily turned away from his historical consideration of religion to look at the contemporary situation regarding the nature of positive faith. His concept of such a faith, and its relation to his concepts of objectivity and subjectivity, are reiterated at the outset:

A positive faith is a system of religious propositions which are true for us because they have been presented to us by an authority which we cannot flout. In the first instance the concept implies a system of religious propositions or truths which must be held to be truths independently of our own opinions, and which even if no man has ever perceived them and even if no man has ever considered them to be truths, nevertheless remain truths. These truths are often said to be objective truths and what is required of them is that they should now become subjective truths, truths for us. (Nohl, 233; quoted in trans. by Lukács, 18)

Again it is the theology of the Tübingen Seminary that he particularly seems to have had in mind, and it is the arguments of that school in defense of such a faith that Hegel began to examine. While he realized that the Tübingen theology gave a place to reason and represented an attempt to absorb the achievements of human reason into the system of revealed truth, for Hegel, the problem with this kind of defense of positive faith was that it still regarded truth as objective.

Therefore, his examination of positivity in this postscript amounted to a strong criticism of all 'orthodox' theology. The older and most common theological outlook was heavily positive in character, for it so stressed the otherness and transcendence of God that human reason was regarded as completely incapable of comprehending anything of God.[41] However, though some theologians, like those Hegel had experienced at Tübingen, recognized a place for reason in theology, this place was only one of justifying the miraculous and articulating the 'truths' known through divine revelation. This was still a positive faith in Hegel's view, for it continued to present God as

an alien being, in whom the control over nature resides, a control which nature misses and which it can no longer afford to despise.

   In this philosophy faith means a lack of awareness that reason is absolute, complete unto itself—that its infinite idea must be created from itself alone, free from the admixture of anything alien to it, and that this can be achieved only through the removal of that intruder and not through his presence. (Nohl, 238; quoted in trans. by Lukács, 53)[42]

While it is true that Hegel's turn against Kant had not yet occurred, one can, with some justification, speak of a preparation being made—though unintentionally—for that turn. As elaborated in this first postscript, Hegel's concept of positivity in religion consists in an idea of God as an objective, alien being who is an object of faith beyond the bounds of human reason; and positivity also exists wherever reason is not truly autonomous. These criticisms were to be directed against Kant at a later time, but, with hindsight, one can identify the groundwork being made at this time.

   Georg Lukács is surely correct when he says that "the philosophically and historically crucial concept of Hegel's thought in this period is that of positivity." Philosophically, "positivity contains the seeds of a problem that will prove central to the later development of the dialectic";[43] but Hegel came to the concept through his historical inquiries, and it is central to his understanding of the historical process. Therefore, it was consistent with his chief interest in Bern that he returned to his historical considerations in the second postscript, *Jedes Volk hat ihm eigene Gegenstände*,[44] which, however, like the first, shows signs of the groundwork for his as-yet-unanticipated move away from Kant.

In his Bern period, Lukács says, "Hegel saw the historical process as possessing a single great triadic structure: 1) the original freedom and self-activation of human society—2) the loss of this freedom under the hegemony of positivity—3) the recovery of the lost freedom." [45] A question that occupied much of Hegel's attention in this second postscript was that of the reason why the original freedom of the classical period had been lost and Christianity had triumphed. His answer was that the cause of the loss was to be found in the spirit of the age, which, in turn, made possible the expansion of Christianity:

> Great revolutions which strike the eye at a glance must have been preceded by a still and secret revolution in the spirit of the age, a revolution not visible to every eye, especially imperceptible to contemporaries, and as hard to discern as to describe in words. . . . The supersession of a native and immemorial religion by a foreign one is a revolution which occurs in the spiritual realm itself, and it is thus of a kind whose causes must be found all the more directly in the spirit of the times. (*ETW*, 152)

Thus, one is forced to ask what must have been the character of that age. And, in response, Hegel said that the Greek and Roman gods were natural gods, and as such ruled man's passions and emotions; but, over against this, man set his own self and the freedom of his will: everyone had the right to have a will of his own, and no one imposed a moral system on others. Man's duty was found in himself, not in others, and not even in divine commands, for there was an individual responsibility to seek his own good that was regarded as inseparable from the good of the community. Gradually this freedom was lost, however, as a ruling class emerged through the acquisition of wealth and power; then government and authority were imposed from without, bearing down upon the individual, who came to regard his life as an individual possession that had to be preserved irrespective of the community that had previously given him fulfillment.

> Thus the despotism of the Roman emperors had chased the human spirit from the earth and spread a misery which compelled men to seek and expect happiness in heaven; robbed of freedom, their spirit, their eternal and absolute element, was forced to take flight to the deity. (*ETW*, 162–63)

In Hegel's opinion, the individual had previously enjoyed a freedom to satisfy the demands of reason in religious and moral matters, and Hegel saw such an individual as an expression of the Kantian ideal of the autonomy of individual reason. But the loss of such freedom did not mean that the demands of reason were surrendered. Now they "were no longer to be met with in man's will"; they "showed themselves in the deity proffered by the Christian religion, a deity beyond the reach of our powers and of our wills but not of our supplications and prayers." [46] There could be no active human contribution toward "the realization of a moral ideal," [47] for this would be brought about only by the activity of God while human beings passively observed. This meant that the human concepts of such ideals became more grandiose, because God was perceived as capable of achieving anything of which the imagination could conceive. These ideals became so remote from the human situation that they were thought of as being of divine origin; and indeed, all matters of religious faith and morals came to be seen as imposed by God, and in practice, came to be imposed from without by an ecclesiastical hierarchy. Then, with the acceptance of Christianity by the Roman Empire, Christianity became enslaved to this corrupting path, in which freedom and autonomy were lost.

Hegel understood this to be a product of the spirit of that age. The conception of God as something objective and dwelling in another world in which humanity has no part was a conception that arose out of the corruption and slavery of that human situation. God, therefore, was perceived as an objective thing to be studied, and an external moral authority to be obeyed, rather than as the divine spark of life and source of moral ideals dwelling in everyone.[48]

Again, one can identify aspects of a preparation for that impending, though still unforeseen, turn against Kant. Hegel's examination of positivity was such that he regarded faith as positive wherever there is an authoritative agent present. In this postscript, that authority was still seen as being imposed by an external agent, but it was Hegel's thinking along these lines that was important for that subsequent quarrel with Kant, the basic element in which was Hegel's realization that reason itself could be reduced to an authoritative agent, albeit an internal authority. He had never been a totally convinced Kantian, for there had been early signs of disagreement, but the move toward his final rejection of Kant came with the awareness that reason could become an authority, an agent of positivity.

Other aspects of his thought needed to develop, however, before that awareness emerged, and the crucial development was his conviction that something more than reason was required, namely an involvement of the whole person. Of course, this was not a new feature in Hegel's thought, for in 1793 he had written regarding *Volksreligion:* "imagination, heart and the senses must not go out empty." While it seems true that it would be the renewed contact with Hölderlin in Frankfurt that encouraged Hegel to develop the implications of this position, it had begun to resurface even in the "Positivity" essay where he had spoken of Jesus' teaching being founded on the heart as well as reason.[49] But it is in the second postscript—when, in examining the cause of the loss of the freedom of antiquity and the triumph of Christianity, his thoughts returned to the Greek ideal—that he came to consider seriously the needs of human sensibility, for he believed those needs to have been truly and adequately catered for in the classical period.

However, Hegel believed equally strongly that in the contemporary situation 'positive' Christianity was not meeting those needs. Such needs are an important element in the spirit of a nation that is largely built up by its traditions of religious mythology and political legends of national leaders. Therefore, a genuine *Volksreligion* will satisfy these needs on the religious side; but, rather than achieving that,

> Christianity has emptied Valhalla [i.e., the home of ancient German gods], felled the sacred groves, extirpated the national imagery as a shameful superstition, as a devilish poison, and given us instead the imagery of a nation whose climate, laws, culture and interests are strange to us and whose history has no connection whatever with our own. . . . Thus we are without any religious imagery which is homegrown or linked with our history. (*ETW*, 146–47)

Furthermore,

> In proportion as the imagination loves freedom, it requires that the religious imagery of a people shall be permanent, i.e., shall be less linked with specific dates than with certain familiar places. For the vulgar, familiarity with the place is generally one proof more, or the most certain proof, that the story told of it is true. (*ETW*, 149)

In this connection Hegel thought that Catholics had done better than Protestants, for they placed great stress on local saints and miracle stories; but even so, they failed to adequately satisfy the needs of imagination, since the legends of such people or events were made to appear as historical realities rather than being left as myths. Whenever this happens one can only either accept the objective aspect of such religious legends as being historically real and therefore of total significance (but this violates Hegel's first condition of a _Volksreligion_), or completely reject it, dismissing the supposed objective aspects by means of some rational explanation (and this violates his second condition of a _Volksreligion_, since imagination is thereby sent away empty). In Hegel's view a religious experience must have an objective aspect, even though it is of no value in itself, for it somehow satisfies the imagination; but Christianity, as Hegel saw it being expressed, did not permit such satisfaction.

A significant move in Hegel's thought toward the recognition of the inability of reason to rise above the sundered world and to meet the needs of human sensibility in religion is reflected in the fragment _eine Ethik_, which may have been written during the summer of 1796 prior to Hegel's leaving Bern.[50] In this fragment Hegel began to stress the importance of an aesthetic sense and proceeded to what he described as a novel idea, namely, that we must have a new mythology—"a mythology of reason".

In spite of this novel idea, however, the fragment _eine Ethik_[51] reveals a presence of focal concerns of Hegel during the Bern period. The essay focuses on moral theory, and it is clear that he still conceived of such a purpose in Kantian terms when he said that "this Ethics will be nothing less than a complete system of . . . all practical postulates," though this was to be a more exhaustive treatment than Kant's, who had "given only an example" and thus had left the task incomplete.[52] Further, Hegel's Bern reflections convinced him that some contemporary theologians misused Kant's philosophy in their attempts to provide a rational basis for their dogmas, and reference to this is also to be found in this fragment, where the author referred to superstition in theology as "the prosecution of the priesthood which of late poses as rational," and where the author also spoke of the necessity for all such superstition to be uprooted "at the bar of Reason itself." [53]

Being concerned with moral theory, in this fragment "the first Idea is, of course, the presentation [_Vorst(ellung)_] of my self as an absolutely free entity [_Wesen_] ";[54] but it is recognized that the self does not stand alone, for along with the free, self-conscious being there stands 'an entire world', the context in which moral theory is to be applied. Then, in its elaboration of the content of moral theory, one finds that the fragment passes from 'nature' to the 'work of man' and the State; but "in this sphere all the Ideas, of perpetual peace, etc., are only *subordinate* Ideas under a higher one," [55] and so the ethical program must move on to such a higher idea. It was the search for that overarching idea, under which other ethical ideas can be united, that led to an emergence of a stress on the aesthetic sense:

> The Idea that unites all the rest, the Idea of beauty [*Schönheit*] taking the word in the higher platonic sense. I am now convinced that the highest act of Reason, that one through which it encompasses all Ideas, is an aesthetic act, and that truth and goodness only become sisters in beauty—the philosopher must possess just as much aesthetic power as the poet . . . The philosophy of the spirit as an aesthetic philosophy. (Hoffmeister, 220; trans. by Harris, 511)

This was a major development in Hegel's understanding of human nature, since it involved a considerable change in his thinking regarding the relation between *Vernunft* and *Phantasie*, and this change contributed significantly to his final rejection of Kant. Hegel had already expressed the necessity of a religion of the senses for the majority of ordinary people, but now he was saying that a religion that appeals to the senses is necessary also for the philosopher. Clearly this was a radical departure from his conception of Kant's *Vernunftreligion* as the goal of human progress, but it was a natural outgrowth of his concern in *Jedes Volk hat ihm eigene Gegenstände*, and it led him to present an idea that, to his knowledge, had not occurred to anyone else:

> We must have a new mythology, but this mythology must be in the service of the Ideas, it must be a mythology of Reason.
>   Until we express the Ideas aesthetically, i.e., mythologically, they have no interest for the people, and conversely until mythology is rational the philosopher must be ashamed of it. Thus in the end enlightened and unenlightened must clasp hands, mythology must become philosophical in order to make the people rational, and philosophy must become mythological in order to make philosophers sensible [*sinnl(ich)*]. Then reigns eternal unity among us" (*Dok.*, 221; trans. by Harris (1972), 511–12).

Hegel's point was that it is necessary for ideas to be expressed mythologically rather than merely expressed as objective statements of fact: he has moved away from his recognition of rational religion as the ideal to a new recognition of the need for religious truth to be expressed mythologically in order for there to be a truly subjective religion[56]—for only then will the truth have an appeal to the whole person, since then "imagination, heart and sensibility" will not be ignored. Having turned his attention to the principle of *Herz* and become aware of the importance of the aesthetic sense, it would be natural that just as he had obviously reflected on the Fourth Gospel's statement that God is Logos (Reason), so, too, he would now reflect upon the fact that the same author also says "God is *Love.*" This turn to a consideration of aesthetic needs in religion led Hegel to become aware of the importance of *love* in genuine religion, which he came to regard as a new spirit of equality and freedom, and about which the fundamental thesis was "*Religion ist eins mit der Liebe.*"

One can conclude at this point by saying that, with the advantage of hindsight, it is clear that Hegel was on the brink of a significant development. His Bern period had been strongly, though never totally, Kantian in the problems raised and the solution sought, but in his work during his last year in that city fruitful ground for the final break with Kant is detectable. The two postscripts to the "Positivity" essay, which he wrote between late 1795 and mid-1796, contain critical ideas that he was soon to recognize as applying to Kant's philosophy. But above all, it was his turning to a consideration of aesthetic needs in religion—the reemergence of his stress on the needs of the whole person rather than on those of reason alone, his discovery of "a mythology of Reason", and his coming to an awareness of the importance of love—that was the seed that, when enabled to draw sustenance from the sharing of ideas with the "*Bund der Geister*" in Frankfurt, grew and bore fruit in the form of important Hegelian concepts.

Chapter 3

The Frankfurt Period

The Concepts of Love, Life, *and* Spirit.

The subsequent development of Hegel's thought gave sequential prominence to three closely similar concepts: *Love, Life,* and *Spirit.* In these concepts Hegel proposed the means by which the sundered world of the reflective intellect may be transcended, the divisions and oppositions of that world resolved, and all alienation healed.

The concept of alienation was an underlying concept, running through the whole of Hegel's thought, and it was present in his thought because of his own observation of society. He regarded his society as marked by a feeling of isolation and separation, an absence of autonomy, a sense of dependence on something 'other' with which one does not feel identified; and in social terms, it was the experience of a society as 'other', in which one does not feel 'at home'. Such divisions and alienation arise out of the reflective intellect that regards everything in the finite universe as limited and as being in a subject-object relation with every other finite thing. Furthermore, on this level of reflection, the finite universe as a whole is seen as a multiplicity of finite particulars, and the relationship between the world and God is also understood in terms of a subject-object relation.

This, according to Hegel, is the view of things on the level of reflective thought—a level on which he was soon firmly to place Kant's philosophy—and it was by means of these concepts of love, life, and spirit that he sought to transcend this level of reflection. That it is an inadequate level, and therefore needs to be transcended, was apparent to Hegel not least because of its concept of God: although God is spoken of as infinite, the idea of God as separated from the world of particulars really reduces God to just another finite object standing in an external relationship with a world that is a mere multiplicity of finite particulars.

In the light of these concepts of love, life, and spirit, and because of their prominence in Hegel's thought, it is often said that his Frankfurt period marked a dramatic change. However, while there is a certain truth in this, for clearly it was a period that witnessed a considerable development of his thought, it does seem true to say that to interpret it as an abrupt change requires overlooking certain aspects that had been present—though undeveloped—in his thought from an early stage. It is for this reason that Harris speaks of "a continuity of development in Hegel's reflections." [1]

On the other hand, Lukács describes the Frankfurt period as having been a time of crisis for Hegel,[2] and Henrich refers to "the abrupt change in Hegel's position that occurred so soon in Frankfurt." [3] Briefly, Lukács argues that Hegel's concern about social problems now turned into one about individual morality; the category that provided the focus for this concern was *love*, and it was this category that made it inevitable that Hegel be led into the arms of religion and seek a reconciliation with Christianity. Of course, it is correct to identify the central role of the category of love in Hegel's thought, but it does not seem to be accurate to speak of a change from social problems to those of individual morality, for Hegel consistently regarded the two as ineluctably interrelated. Nor does it seem accurate to speak of Hegel's being led into the arms of religion and seeking a reconciliation with Christianity, for Hegel always gave a central place to religion—which Lukács does recognize, making it difficult to understand why he speaks in this way—though Hegel had been, and remained, critical of institutional Christianity while, at the same time, finding Jesus' teaching to be an expression of truth.

In Henrich's case, his view about "the abrupt change in Hegel's position" is really dependent upon his preceding assertion that "Hegel arrived in Frankfurt as a dedicated follower of Kant." [4] Again, there is a genuine truth in such an assertion, but it does require some modification along the lines suggested above. It is true that Hegel was dedicated to the aspiration for freedom and autonomy in its Kantian form, but it is also true that, from an early stage, he was equally dedicated to the aspiration for expressive unity and wholeness and the healing of all alienation. Hegel's grappling with this problem of the overcoming of alienation and the role of religion in relation to it had led him first to Kant's conception of rational religion, with its morality of law, as the goal of human progress. But already, prior to his arrival in Frankfurt, he had discussed ideas in a manner that can now be seen to have been groundwork for his imminent awareness of the Kantian position as being at odds with expressive unity, and he had begun to formulate his own ethical program, which would be based on a morality of love and spontaneity rather than the Kantian morality of law and obligation.

What Henrich makes clear is that it was Hegel's renewed association with Hölderlin and his participation in intense discussions with Hölderlin's circle of friends that enabled Hegel to discover the way to develop his thought. Hölderlin had already worked out his philosophy, having derived important elements from Schiller and Fichte. From Schiller he had resolved how love and selfhood could be extricated from their opposition, for Schiller had perceived love not as "willingness to surrender the self," but as "an act of self-expansion," "the acquisition of what is already its own, not an overpowering of what is alien to it." [5]

With these insights molded into his philosophy, Hölderlin was able to show Hegel how to resolve the apparent conflict between the principle of freedom and autonomy and the principle of unification by means of a philosophy based on the category of love. It might be true to say that Hölderlin provided inspiration and insight that enabled Hegel to develop such a philosophy, but it is not correct to suggest his rejection of Kantianism and his Frankfurt development were totally due to Hölderlin, for Hegel himself had already planted the seed through the evolution of his own ideas. For this reason it is preferable to acknowledge an important change in Hegel's thought during his Frankfurt period, while, at the same time, recognizing it as continuous with, rather than sharply breaking from, his earlier philosophical thought and ambition.[6]

Furthermore, just as Hegel's position, as it evolved at Frankfurt, was not totally dependent on Hölderlin for its origin, so it was not fully reliant on Hölderlin for the direction of its growth. Henrich makes this clear when he says that "Hegel soon recognized that he had to explicate Hölderlin's insight quite differently than Hölderlin ever could." [7] From Fichte, Hölderlin had adopted a notion of a ground of unity, for Fichte had proposed a pure or absolute Ego as an activity that is immanent in consciousness and in which all consciousness is grounded. Hölderlin had to modify the meaning of Fichte's arguments: "Hölderlin came to presuppose a unity previous to consciousness and the self, which he conceived, like Spinoza, as a state of being *[Sein]* for all existence *[Dasein]* and, like Fichte, as the basis for all opposition;" [8] and here was the stimulus for a novel development in Hegel's thought. In this regard, his renewed contact with Hölderlin must have served as a reminder of the puzzlement caused by a letter from Schelling, who had lightly dismissed the existence of "the personal individual being who reigns above in Heaven"; and in a subsequent letter, he had explained to Hegel "why it is a mistake to conceive of Fichte's transcendental Ego as a conscious individual or person." [9]

Hegel was not attracted at that stage by an idea that seemed to involve the surrendering of personal identity of either finite individuals or God; however, with the concept of love, which did not mean the surrendering of selfhood but an act of self-expression, Hegel was able to adopt as his own the notion of God as the principle of unity. But in doing so, Hegel immediately became aware of the difficult question of how the original state of unity "can produce opposites through divisions." [10] Hölderlin seems to have avoided such a question, and in pursuing it Hegel went beyond Hölderlin's philosophy and adopted a position of his own that was reflected in his replacing the concept of Love, first by 'Life' and then by 'Spirit'.

On *Love*

Enabled by the insights gained through his new experiences in Frankfurt, Hegel's accelerated progress in assimilating the doctrine of love was revealed in "Two Fragments of 1797 on Love," [11] written during the first half of 1797: *Moralität, Liebe, Religion*[12] and *Liebe und Religion*.[13]

In the first of these two fragments Hegel began by immediately taking up again the notion of positivity, in both religion and morality, and doing so in terms that are reminiscent of his earlier discussion:[14] "We call that faith positive in which the practical is theoretically present— . . . a religion which establishes representations of something objective, which cannot become subjective, as a principle of life and action";[15] and a moral concept is called positive when it "is so constituted that it is not a reflected activity of ourselves." [16]

A moral concept is a positive one when it is something given and objective, imposed by some authority "which awakens respect or fear" and from which the concept receives its force and effectiveness. This is how Hegel understood a positive moral concept as being "not a reflected activity of ourselves"; but not only would a concept be not a true reflection of ourselves when imposed by some external source, it would also fail to be a true reflection of ourselves if the self is internally divided—as Kant understood reason to be at variance with inclinations—and a moral law is imposed by the internal authority of reason. "All moral laws are commands to assert this unity against impulses," [17] and in this way Kant's position can also be positive. However, a positive moral concept can be transformed into one of freedom: "The positive moral concept is capable of losing the character of positivity, if the activity which it expresses is developed itself and receives power";[18] though this is normally unachievable.

Similarly, a positive faith is one that is naively adopted by a believer on the basis of "a powerful and commanding objective (authority)." [19] This kind of faith can be described as naive because it admits no capability of comprehension: the object of faith is totally other than the subject, and "its modes of operation must be a miracle for us." This, for Hegel, is the kind of faith that is quite unacceptable, for it has no sense of the autonomy of the subject, who is totally in the command of another. However, Hegel regarded the opposite extreme as equally unacceptable, namely, complete subjective religion in which the subject claims to be in command, for everything is a matter of inner determination.

His brief analysis of subjective religion, to which he turned in the second part of this fragment, and his contrast of this with objective positive religion, led Hegel at this point to an answer he had been seeking since his earliest concerns with *Volksreligion*, namely, an answer to the question: "What is the basis on which a religion can be truly founded?" Here his answer was that it must be founded on love: "only in love alone is one at one with the object, it does not command and is not commanded." [20]

Love achieves unification: the subject loses its form of subject and the object loses its form of object—subject and object, freedom and nature, are united. Once the gods were understood to walk among men, but distance and separation have been set up, and "sacrifices, incense and service" have been offered to these detached gods to appease that which otherwise can only be feared. It is love that makes the fundamental difference, for "love can only take place against its equal, against the mirror, against the echo of our existence." [21]

This theme was continued by Hegel in the second of these two 1797 fragments. Positivity exists, where in the face of misfortune one does not have the strength to endure and accept it, but establishes an idea of a future state (a heaven) where the unity of one's longings and the actuality will be realized through the initiative of one's God. In contrast to this state of positivity, the experience of being at one with reality is the ideal of religion, and this is achieved by love. Therefore, "religion is one with love. The beloved is not opposed to us, he is one with our essential being; we see only ourselves in him." [22]

In another fragment, *die Liebe*,[23] written in Frankfurt late in 1797,

Hegel took up a more specific examination of the nature of separation *(Trennung)* or alienation, and of love as the principle of union *(Ver-einigung)*. Separation is a mark of positivity: the self is perceived by itself to stand over against the world; a disjunction between subject (the self) and object (the world) is presupposed, and is manifested, for example, in feelings of dominion over other people and things. In a situation of this kind "there is no living union between the individual and his world," and there can be no genuine love.

The consciousness of separation understands relationships in terms of distinctions, restrictions and oppositions, and gives rise to a feeling of fear, since fear is the product of being limited and opposed by something seen as an object standing against oneself as subject. Hegel's response to this situation was that in order to correct it man must rise above this consciousness of separation and realize that neither subject nor object are absolutes themselves, that "nothing is unconditioned; nothing carries the root of its own being in itself." This realization is achieved through genuine love, which "neither restricts nor is restricted; it is not finite at all." [24] Love is the principle of union that enables one to rise above the consciousness of distinctions and separations and to realize that the relation between God and the world is not one between subject and object, but that it is a relationship that can only be truly conceived of as a union of love; and further, that in this relationship all distinctions between subjects and objects in the finite world—between man and nature, man and man—are dissolved.

Genuine love transcends divisions: it creates a true union "between living beings who are alike in power and thus in one another's eyes living beings from every point of view." [25] Such love is not a matter of *Verstand*, "whose unity is always a unity of opposites," [26] and which thereby reduces the integral unity of the world to a complex balance of opposing forces. Nor is genuine love a matter of *Vernunft*, "because reason sharply opposes its determining power to what is determined"; [27] that is, in the Kantian view there is a clear opposition between reason and the phenomena it is considering. Love is a feeling *(Gefühl)*, although not a single feeling, for then it would be distinct from other feelings and would be only a part of life *(Teilleben)* and not the whole of life *(das ganze Leben)*; yet genuine love is the whole of life—the feeling of love is the feeling of being "entirely alive", the sense of life itself.

However, this sense of love and the complete unity that it produces is the result of a process of development from a state of immaturity to one of maturity. The immature state is obviously one of oppositions and cleavages between oneself and the world, and Hegel said that the process of development proceeds by means of reflection whereby the overcoming of one instance of separation gives rise to an awareness of others and so on until a union of love has been realized.[28] Thus,

> finally, a love completely destroys objectivity and thereby annuls and transcends reflection (Reflexion), deprives man's opposite of all foreign character, and discovers life itself without any further defect. In love the separate does still remain, but as something united and no longer as something separate; life [in the subject] senses life [in the object]. (ETW, 305)

In the fragment die Liebe, Hegel expounded love as the principle of union that annuls division and opposition, and thus he implied the inadequacy of both kinds of religious faith—the traditional positive kind and also the Kantian rationalist kind—which he regarded as failing to overcome such separation. But what is implicit in die Liebe becomes explicit in another fragment, written shortly afterward, Glauben ist die Art,[29] in which Hegel offered an analysis of the concept of faith. His opening statment gives his understanding of the concept of faith: "Faith [Belief] is the mode, in which the unity, whereby an antinomy has been united, is present in our Vorstellung. The union is the activity; this activity reflected as object is what is believed." The antinomy involved here is that between knowledge of what is the case and opinion about what is true; and belief is the activity whereby this antinomy is united. But Hegel said this union is on the level of Vorstellungen, and his concern in this fragment was to demonstrate the inadequacy of such a union.

The most significant words in this fragment are that "Union and Being are synonymous," [30] for Hegel was beginning to develop his criticism of the traditional concept of God together with his assertion that any statement, on the level of Vorstellungen, of the union of God and the believer is an inadequate view of union. The traditional concept of God emphasizes the notion of otherness of God as an object over against the believer, and any union between the believer and the object of religious faith would be seen only in terms of the believer doing the will of God, and this would be a very incomplete union that is far short of that union of love between the lover and beloved. In every genuine union, Hegel said, "there is a determining and a being determined, which are one, but in positive religion the determining factor is supposed, even so far as it determines, to be determined." [31] The 'determining' and the 'being determined' in the incomplete union of doing God's will is the believer's resolve to obey God's will and the actual fulfilling of that resolve, but Hegel said that in positive religion this resolve on the part of the believer is seen as itself being determined, since the believer can have such a resolve, according to positive faith, only if given it by the grace of God. Thus, even here, in positive faith, the 'sundering' is maintained:

> in the deed, which is done out of positive faith, that which has been united is itself once more an opposite, which determines its opposite, and [so] there is here only imperfect [incomplete] union, since both terms remain opposed, the one is the determining factor and the other the determined; and the determining factor itself is [what it is] *qua* active, but the form of the activity is determined by another; i.e., what has been given, the active factor, so far as it is active, is supposed to be a determined factor; that which determines the activity must *(muß)* as an existent being have previously been united, and if in this union too the determining factor is supposed to have determined, then it was determined by another and so on, [and] the positive believer would have to be an exclusively passive thing, an absolutely determined factor, which is contradictory.—Hence all positive religions set up a more or less narrow boundary within which they confine [human] activity. (Nohl, 384; trans. by Harris, 514)

Thus, the positive believer remains separated from and opposed to the object of his belief, and the union that the act of belief achieves is only at the level of *Vorstellungen*, and is a very incomplete union because even in the union the believer is dominated by the object of belief so that the separation and opposition remain. However, now Hegel also definitely has moved to the position where he said that even Kant's rational moral agent is in an analogous situation to that of the positive believer. The rational moralist may be freed from the imposition of external laws, but he is not freed from internal laws, for he is a slave to himself in that he is mastered by his own rational moral law. The moral imperative, though a product of one's own reason, becomes an imposition equal to that of the external law, if reached at one particular moment and applied to a later situation without further reflection. But while this criticism of Kant—although anticipated earlier—only begins to blossom in this fragment, it is not until the essay "The Spirit of Christianity and its Fate" that it emerges in full bloom.

However, before proceeding to that important essay, one ought to ask, in more specific terms, what these fragments tell us about Hegel's position at this stage concerning the notion of God and the union of God and man, as this is directly relevant to the main objective of this discussion.

In the last considered fragment Hegel had spoken of One Being—"The sundered thing finds only in One Being *[Einem Sein]* its union"[32]—and in this connection he referred to a "one and only possible union" and a "one and only possible being". One can then proceed to say that—by recalling Hegel's words that "Union and Being are synonymous," and by referring back to *"die Liebe,"* where he had spoken of love as the principle of union—it seems that for Hegel, by the beginning of 1798, *Love* is the "one and only possible union" and the "one and only possible being" in which sundered beings can be properly united.

The introduction of the term 'One Being' in this fragment is of considerable importance not least because of its overtones of Spinozism. As early as 1791 Hegel and Hölderlin had become interested in the controversy over Lessing's Spinozism and in the subsequent rejuvenation of Spinoza's philosophy;[33] and the two young Tübingen students had taken up the phrase εν και παν as an expression of their perception of the living unity of all life.[34] But it is fairly clear that at that stage neither Hegel nor Hölderlin took the εν και παν to involve the surrender of the idea of God as 'the personal individual Being'.[35]

Now in Frankfurt, together with Hölderlin again, Hegel had come to share the modification of this concept of God that Hölderlin had already made in his own thought: the concept of Divinity, of One Being, was now seen in terms of a principle of unity or a unifying force from which the unification of all things is derived. For this principle of unity Hegel, following Hölderlin, used the term "Being",[36] thereby suggesting that it is a unity that is prior to all particular objects that are seen to be separated and in opposition to unity, but from which those separated and opposing things are produced.[37] But Hegel was never content with such a view, and he continued to grapple with it, eventually coming to the conviction that the correct view is conveyed by the word 'spirit' rather than 'being'.[38] The concept of Spirit was to become important for Hegel also as a distinction from Spinoza's Substance, for Hegel was convinced that, although Spinoza had fully grasped the notion of unity, he had done so only by putting at risk all individuality—and, having learned from Kant the stress on individual freedom, Hegel would never consent to a loss of individuality.

The search for a synthesis that would provide the underlying unity while not losing individuality, and the search for a solution to the question of the derivation of opposites from an original unity, were therefore important ones for Hegel. Together they constituted an inquiry that issued in the development of his concept of Spirit, made possible for him by his renewed and catalytic association with Hölderlin, which brought to the forefront of Hegel's thinking the notion of *love* as the principle of union. This was the notion that stirred his thinking in 1798, and it therefore dominated the writings of that time, which are the most important of all the early writings.

"The Spirit of Christianity and Its Fate"

From the beginning of his acquaintance with Kant's philosophy Hegel had agreed that the really free man is the completely rational man, and it had been from this conviction that he had stipulated the satisfaction of the requirements of reason as the first condition of a genuine *Volksreligion*. Hegel felt that this was the link between the Greeks and Kant: the Greeks had achieved it in practice and Kant had recently provided an account of it in theory, that is, on the level of reflection. But Hegel was convinced that it was no longer being achieved in practice, in the experience of life; and the early dissatisfaction with the dualism inherent in Kant's philosophy now became fully explicit in Hegel's writings[39]—revealing Kant's thought to be inadequate for the annulling of division and alienation, since it presupposed a cleavage between reason and inclination, leaving the individual in a state of bondage, as a slave to his own reason. Such philosophy, confined to the level of reflection, therefore needs to be transcended in order to achieve the level of 'life' that is characterized by unity and harmony as well as rationality.

Hegel's understanding of this new level of life—his morality of love—was spelled out in "The Spirit of Christianity and Its Fate," [40] where he undertook an analysis of the life of Jesus in whom alone life (love) achieved a complete self-consciousness, for the spirit of Jesus was totally contrary to all bondage and alienation. But what was seen in Jesus is indicative of humanity and of the whole living order of things, namely, the presence of the divine infinite in the finite. All processes of life, and supremely human life, are manifestations of divine life, and it is in the grasping of this notion and in the consequent living of it that division and opposition are transcended and the meaning of life is recognized as being found not in abstract speculation but in the concrete history of human life.

Hegel's involvement in the study and understanding of history is keenly revealed in these manuscripts, for not only did he present his analysis of the life of Jesus in the context of a very explicit criticism of Kant's rational morality (thereby sharply distinguishing this from his Bern presentation of Jesus), but he also proceeded largely by means of contrast with the "spirit" of the Jews and their history in which their "fate" was worked out.[41]

The Spirit of Judaism

The Jewish spirit,[42] which had its origin in Abraham,[43] is characterized by an exclusive consciousness, and the Jews' consequent fate, expressed in the Mosaic religion, was to be alienated from all other life and to be totally subjected to their God, to whom they owed a slavish obedience in the form of adherence to 'divine' law.

In this essay Hegel presented Abraham as having been characterized by a voluntary spurning of relationships with other people and with nature:

> he tore himself free altogether from his family as well, in order to be a wholly self-subsistent, independent man, to be an overlord himself. He did this without having been injured or disowned, without the grief which after a wrong or an outrage signifies love's enduring need, when love, injured indeed but not lost, goes in quest of a new fatherland in order to flourish and enjoy itself there. The first act which made Abraham the progenitor of a nation is a disseverance which snaps the bonds of communal life and love. (*ETW*, 185)

He wanted to be free from all such relationships—his ultimate concern was his own existence—and so "he wanted *not* to love, wanted to be free by not loving." [44] This attitude to life was the *spirit* of Abraham; it was what marked his encounters with other peoples and other lands throughout his life—"this was the spirit of self-maintenance in strict opposition to everything." [45] For example, he was never prepared to settle, to become attached to a place by cultivating and improving the land and so to make it part of his world; he used the land only when it suited his own purposes, and similarly he used other people—"he was a stranger on earth, a stranger to the soil and to men alike." [46] The spirit of Abraham was such that he saw the whole world as in opposition—in separation (*Trennung*)—to himself, and thus as hostile; and it followed that the only possible relationship was a relation of domination (*Herrschaft*) in which one became the master and the other the mastered.

Thus, at the very foundation of Jewish life, in Hegel's view, was a sense of alienation whereby all nature, other people, and even their God were regarded as alien and therefore as threatening. But the basis of this sense of alienation was the Jews' understanding of their relationship with God: God was conceived of as the Almighty

Sovereign, separated from them and dominating their lives through the law they were to obey. The fate of the Jews was a lifeless subservience.

However, Hegel saw this fate emerging only when the force of circumstances compelled Jacob to become attached to a permanent abode. This was an act contrary to the spirit of Abraham, though not entirely so, for it was an involuntary action and not motivated by a desire to unite with the environment. But whereas Abraham had voluntarily separated from his environment and, as a result, built up a consciousness of a union with his God, the Jewish people now felt themselves to be in a state of separation from their environment not because of their own choice but because a condition of slavery had been foisted upon them. Consequently, they no longer felt a consciousness of a union with their God, but became conscious of a relationship of servitude that they fulfilled through obedience to the laws of their God—and this was an obedience that was regarded as necessary for their survival rather than as a free expression of life. "For the first time they became subject to fate." [47]

The spirit of Abraham found a renewed but solitary expression in Moses—"an isolated enthusiast for the liberation of his people" [48]—but he was not able to arouse this spirit in the people whom he led. Indeed, they could be forced to follow Moses only by the performing of tricks and wonders that to them were signs of their God. The Jews did not see their liberation as something they "inaugurate with heroic deeds of their own," but as something that was being done for them by their God. So this concept of his mastery over them as well as over all nature and people was deepened—the Jewish nation "in its emancipation bore the most slavelike demeanour" [49]—and thus the *Trennung* between themselves and their God was confirmed in their own consciousness. Their relationship of servitude was consolidated in a covenant formed at Sinai in which God was believed to have promised to be their God, while their part of the covenant was taken to be a promise to obey the divinely given laws. This also confirmed the *Trennung* between the Jewish people and their fellow human beings in other nations, for God was not only the God of the Jews, he was master of all—but their own relationship with God was of a special kind.

> The subsequent circumstances of the Jewish people . . . have all of them been simply consequences and elaborations of their original fate. By this fate—an infinite power which they set over against themselves and could never conquer—they have been maltreated and will continually be maltreated until they appease

it by the spirit of beauty and so annul it by reconciliation. (*ETW*, 199–200) [50]

The Moral Teaching of Jesus: As Contrasted with the Mosaic Law and the Ethics of Kant

In turning to a new account of Jesus' life, Hegel said that Jesus set himself against the whole of the Jewish fate although it was inevitable that he become a victim of that fate. Jesus rose above the Jewish fate and he also sought to raise the Jewish people above it, but all except a few were far too preoccupied with it to heed the message of Jesus, and so Jesus felt compelled to separate himself and his disciples. But from that separation there came the inevitability that he become a victim of fate,[51] even though he had set himself against it.

In saying that Jesus set himself against the Jewish fate, Hegel was asserting the marked contrast between Jesus' message and the Mosaic Law; and in so doing Hegel was also intent on very explicitly contrasting the teaching of Jesus with the ethics of Kant. At the very foundation of the Jewish fate was a sense of alienation whereby all nature, other people, and God were regarded as alien and therefore as threatening. That is why the life of the Jews was regulated by law that expressed the *ought* of divine commands. Similarly, Kantian ethics also contained an *ought*, which is expressed in the moral law, the categorical imperative. The difference here is that the moral law is a product of man's own reason and not imposed by some external or alien authority; and therefore, to follow it, in Kant's view, is to be free, since true freedom is found in the autonomy of the rational man. But Hegel was now clearly of the opinion that Kant's universal moral law, because there are only particular situations to which it can have application, also is to be seen as a "master",[52] and that the individual is in bondage to his own reason, a slave to himself. Further, this moral law, expressing an *ought*, the product of man's reason, presupposes a cleavage between reason and inclination. Therefore, here also the consequence of law is the same, namely, the individual is in a state of bondage to his own reason—he becomes a slave to himself.[53]

However, the spirit of Jesus transcended all alienation and provided liberation from all such bondage to law, whether it be law imposed by some internal sovereign (viz., reason) or an external Lord.

The spirit of Jesus, a spirit raised above morality, is visible, directly attacking laws, in the Sermon on the Mount, which is an attempt elaborated in numerous examples, to strip the laws of legality, of their legal form. The Sermon does not teach reverence for the law; on the contrary, it exhibits that which fulfils the law but annuls it as law and so is something higher than obedience to law and makes law superfluous. (*ETW*, 212)

This superfluity of law is due to the spirit of Jesus, which is the spirit of love, and love transcends all cleavage and alienation, thus abolishing all thought of duty. The *ought* expressed in law becomes transformed into an *is (Sein)*, a "modification of life":[54] there is no longer a cleavage between the demands of law or of reason and inclination, for love overcomes such a cleavage and achieves a correspondence, or identity, between them. Therefore, the requirements of law are not abolished; they simply lose their appearance as law.

This correspondence with inclination is the πλήρωμα [fulfillment] of the law; i.e., it is an 'is', which, to use an old expression, is the 'complement of possibility', since possibility is the object of something thought, as a universal, while 'is' is the synthesis of subject and object, in which subject and object have lost their opposition. (*ETW*, 214)

This, of course, is in sharp contrast to the Kantian conception in which the opposition between law and inclination remain.

The correspondence of inclination with law is such that law and inclination are no longer different; and the expression 'correspondence of inclination with the law' is therefore wholly unsatisfactory because it implies that law and inclination are still particulars, still opposites. . . . In the 'fulfilment' of both the law and duty, their concomitant, however, the moral disposition, etc., ceases to be the universal, opposed to inclination, and inclination ceases to be particular, opposed to the law, and therefore this correspondence of law and inclination is life and, as the relation of differents to one another, love" (*ETW*, 214–15)

So love is seen as congruent with both law and inclination because it is a synthesis of them, making any suggestion of a distinction between law and inclination superfluous.

That the spirit of Jesus rises above both Judaic and Kantian morality Hegel found illustrated by a number of examples from the Sermon on the Mount. One illustration of how Hegel saw the spirit of Jesus transcending the demands of law is to be found in his treatment of the commandment "You shall not kill." This, Hegel said, "is a maxim which is recognized as valid for the will of every rational being and which can be valid as a principle of a universal legislation. Against such a command Jesus sets the higher genius of reconcilability (a modification of love) which not only does not act counter to this law but makes it wholly superfluous; it has in itself a so much richer, more living, fulness that so poor a thing as a law is nothing for it at all." [55]

Thus, the point of this essay is the comparison between the spirit of Jesus (the spirit of love) and a morality that is built on a consciousness of separation—such as the morality of Judaism, which was based on the separation of man from God, and Kantian morality, with its rift between reason and inclination—and that leads to relations of domination and servitude. But Hegel regarded love as enabling the resolution of all separation and opposition, and thus the healing of all alienation: in other words, as enabling the recognition of unity. In the spirit of love one spontaneously fulfills the requirements of law, not because they are law and there is a duty to obey, but because one spontaneously acts in that way through love. Therefore, love, which is in contrast with law, transforms law "not in content but in its form": the requirements of law may still be fulfilled, but they no longer have the appearance of law. Thus, Hegel's formulation of the morality of love transformed the morality of law.

The Moral Teaching of Jesus: Regarding Punishment and Fate

From this contrast between the morality of love and the morality of law, Hegel now turns to consider "love as the transcending of penal justice and the reconciliation of fate." [56]

A person who violates a law negates the content of the law, and according to the law such a trespass deserves punishment, and, so long as the form of law remains, there exists a division between those who judge and those who are judged. An individual's action is a particular action; but, in contrast, the law is regarded as having universality, and the particular action is seen as either conforming to or contravening the universal law. If the action contravenes it, then the content of the law is broken though the universal form of the law remains, and thereby the sense of alienation is inevitable and "no reconciliation is possible, not even through suffering punishment." [57] Punishment is a satisfaction of the law, since the contradiction between the law and the particular action is thereby annulled; but "the trespasser is not reconciled with the law," [58] for either he remains hostile to it as something external and alien to himself, or it is internal, troubling his conscience and causing him to feel alienated from himself. In either case the punishment does not heal the alienation.

Such is the punishment that is consequent upon the violation of a law, but "punishment represented as fate is of a quite different kind," [59] and reconciliation is even more difficult to attain. Punishment, as already seen, is a result of a particular event in which a 'disunion' has occurred between the individual's behavior and the law; but regarding fate there is no question of an opposition between some universal command and a particular inclination and action of an individual. Fate is more general: it is "unbounded like life itself." [60]

The punishment that is the result of a violation of some law comes from something outside the individual, something that is independent of him and set over him. Fate, on the other hand, is something fixed by his own nature, is regarded as being against him, but not above him. The fear of fate is different from a fear of punishment, for this latter fear springs from an opposition to an alien law, so that it is a fear of something alien; but in the case of fate it is life itself that is seen to be hostile. Fate involves a sense of separation between the individual and life, and so the fear of fate is not a fear of something alien, but "a fear of separation" in the sense of a fear of being cut off from the realization of the enjoyment and fulfillment of life because one's own actions might turn against one and be felt to work out against one's own interests. [61]

Reconciliation is dependent upon a recognition of this 'lost life' and of the possibilities of 'life', and upon a longing for this deficiency, this loss of life, to be compensated:

> When the trespasser feels the disruption of his own life (suffers punishment) or knows himself (in his bad conscience) as disrupted, then the working of his fate commences, and this feeling of a life disrupted must become a longing for what he has lost. The deficiency is recognized as a part of himself, as what was to have been in him and is not. (*ETW*, 230–31)

The way to rise above fate and to achieve reconciliation is through love. Reconciliation is not to be seen in terms of the overcoming and mastering of something alien; rather, it is "a return to life," a sense of the rediscovery of life, which "is love." [62] Love overcomes the fate that arises as a result of the deed of another person and one's own reaction to it, for love issues in forgiveness, and thus we are able to rise above our judgments of others and our claims against them; and in the forgiveness of others we find a growth of life in ourselves, for love involves the recognition of the humanity of the other—we see the other as a person like ourselves, and thereby develop a sense of union with the other rather than alienation. Love also overcomes the fate that arises as a result of one's own inner feelings of inadequacy and error, for through the growth of love a return to "a situation of wholeness" is made possible.[63] But this love, which makes possible the forgiveness of another or the return of a man 'to himself', cannot be commanded: Hegel saw love very clearly as something primarily characterized by spontaneity.

This fact, Hegel said, is borne out in the teaching of Jesus. Jesus "placed reconciliation in love and fulness of life, and expressed himself to that effect on every occasion with little change of form." [64] The main form that this expression takes in the Gospels, according to Hegel, is the promise of the forgiveness of sins. "Wherever Jesus found this attitude—*Lebensfülle*, the 'fulness of life' that gives one a sympathetic understanding even of those who injure one—he could confirm the 'faith' of whoever had it by assuring him that his sins were indeed forgiven." [65] The degree to which one possesses this *Lebensfülle* in oneself determines the degree to which one can enter into a meaningful relationship with another person, and also determines the degree to which one can perceive this *Lebensfülle* in another.[66] Hegel continued to illustrate this interpretation of the Gospels by citing examples where this perception of *Lebensfülle* is lacking.[67] But it is only Jesus who fully displayed that *Lebensfülle*, that wholeness of life that comes through love and is able to rise above fate and bring reconciliation to situations of alienation. And it is this *Lebensfülle* that enables the realization of unity, even the unity of the infinite and finite: "To love God is to feel oneself in the 'all' of life, with no restrictions, in the infinite. . . . Love alone has no limits." [68]

The Religious Teaching of Jesus

In this essay Hegel continued the theme of his interpretation of Jesus, though turning now to his religious or theological teaching. Just as Hegel had presented the moral teaching of Jesus as having transcended the level of reflection on which Jewish and even Kantian morality was expressed, so now he presented the religious teaching of Jesus as transcending that level on which all the traditional religious dogmas are formulated. Hegel's endeavor was to demonstrate the superiority of love in religious understanding to all religious dogmas formulated on the level of reflection: the reflective understanding is characterized by the concept of a sundered world, whereas love is the spirit that heals and overcomes divisions.

A very great problem for the communication of a religious understanding is the difficulty of language that is geared to the level of reflective understanding. This problem was particularly acute for Jesus, who confronted the very core of Judaism:[69] for while, "to the Jewish idea of God as their Lord and Governor, Jesus opposes a relationship of God to man like that of a father to his children,"[70] the attitudes of obedience and authority were so strong in Jewish culture that they had even penetrated the understanding of such an intimate relationship as that between a father and his children.

The common understanding of the paternal relationship is a product of reflective thinking that divides life into particular things standing in relation to each other as subject to object, and thus Jesus' description of God as 'Father' was open to the interpretation of God that was compatible with the usual reflective thinking, perceiving God as a being external to and above the living world of people and so an object of faith. But Hegel interpreted Jesus as meaning something quite different, namely, that "the divine is pure life,"[71] and therefore the divine must not be conceived of in terms of the reflective understanding: the divine should not be conceived or spoken of as something objective, but must be seen as being free from all opposition. In other words, God is not a separate, distinct entity standing against the world; rather God is "the wholeness of life", the origin or fount from which all separate lives spring.[72] "God is spirit"[73] that permeates all things and unites all things into a living whole.

Therefore, our knowledge of God is through the discovery of the presence of God in ourselves, while also perceiving that the divine presence is not confined to our finite selves. The divine 'other' is an infinite life that is present in each finite being, and in which each conscious finite self can recognize itself. This self-recognition is crucial to Hegel's understanding of God as 'spirit'.[74]

The problem of reflective thinking and language is well illustrated by the prologue of the Fourth Gospel and the question of the divine-human relationship as expressed in Jesus. In Hegel's view, "both [God and the Logos] are one,"[75] and the finite beings of the created cosmos are manifestations of the one infinite life of God. Each finite part "is just a whole, a life. And this life . . . is life ($\zeta\omega\eta$) and life understood ($\varphi\omega$s[light], truth)."[76] On the level of reflection the life and light appear as an external ideal to which one can point and in which one can have faith; but life and light are, in fact, in the human order, in every individual person as well as in nature—and this truth is recognized only by rising above the level of reflection through a growing self-consciousness of life in oneself, of being a manifestation of it. Only in Jesus, however, did 'life' achieve a complete self-consciousness, and thus he was the 'light' to the world.

This relationship of Jesus to God is strikingly expressed by the term 'Son of God', particularly as contrasted with the other term 'Son of Man', and Hegel understood it to be an illustration of his own interpretation of this relationship.

> The relation of a son to his father is not a conceptual unity (as, for instance, unity or harmony of disposition, similarity of principles, etc.), a unity which is only a unity in thought and is abstracted from life, not opposite essences, not a plurality of absolute substantialities. (*ETW*, 260)

The term 'Son of God' is indicative of Jesus' "oneness with God, who has granted to the son to have life in himself, just as the father has life in himself." [77] Regarding the term 'Son of Man', Hegel said that this does not mean 'son of mankind', for one is not the son of an abstract universal; the term simply means that Jesus is the son of 'a man' as is every man, so that "the Son of God is also son of man, the divine in a particular shape appears as a man." [78] But what was seen in Jesus is indicative of humanity and indeed the whole living order of things (Jesus is the light of the world); it demonstrates the presence of the divine infinite in the finite, and this presence "is life itself." [79]

The 'true' understanding of the relation of Jesus to God, Hegel said, cannot be achieved as a matter of reflective knowledge. The traditional dogma—that the person of Jesus is a joining of two natures, divinity and humanity, in one individual—is a product of reflective thinking. But in maintaining the total difference of the two natures while asserting their absolute union, reflection destroys the intellect, for it is impossible for the intellect to grasp it; thus, on the level of reflection it is more logical to deny the union, and that is why the Jews accused Jesus of blasphemy. The recognition of divinity in a man—Jesus' relation to God as son to father—"can be truly grasped only by faith." [80] But it must be understood that by 'faith' Hegel did not mean ordinary belief, an intellectual assent to some external ideal with which a subject-object relationship of dependence is possible. Here 'faith' is the culmination of various levels of faith; it is the recognition of the presence of the divine in oneself and at the same time discovering the divine in the whole without restriction. This is the consciousness or awareness that is achieved on the level of 'life', and so it is achieved only by a transcending of the reflective attitude that perceives the world in terms of restrictions and separations— and this transcending is accomplished through love, for only love recognizes the divine life (love) that permeates all reality; or, as Hegel said in this essay, "Spirit alone recognizes Spirit." [81]

Thus, it is on the level of life that all alienation is healed, since the reflective consciousness of a sundered world is transcended and replaced by a consciousness of the wholeness of life. Through love one discovers the divine presence in oneself and so becomes aware of that presence permeating all things, and from this comes the consciousness of the union of the whole—that while one's individuality is not annihilated, one is really a 'part' of the whole, and yet not a part, since an individual is only truly an individual life to the extent that he is at one with the infinity of lives that, though outside him, are not separated from him because all are united in the whole through the principle of love.

The Fate of Jesus and His Church

In the last essay of these manuscripts Hegel returned to the question he had first discussed in the "Positivity" essay, namely, the fate of Jesus and his church. But whereas the earlier presupposition—that Jesus' teaching embodied the Kantian rational moral ideal—had now been abandoned in favor of the interpretation of Jesus' religion being one of reconciling love, Hegel continued to regard the reaction of the Jews to the message of Jesus as the initiating factor in the determining of the fate of Jesus and his church. Jesus was the one in whom there was the perfect consciousness of the divine life within him, and so he was "the light individualized in a man"; but, except for a small group who attached themselves to him, the Jews did not even possess a spark of that light, for it had been extinguished by their being totally preoccupied with their fate—as Hegel says, they "were too self-satisfied in the pride of their servitude to find what they sought in what Jesus offered." [82]

The message of Jesus was an open confrontation with the Jewish fate, but the obvious misunderstanding and rejection of his message on the part of the vast majority of his fellow countrymen had inevitable consequences: Jesus "restricts himself to working in individuals and allows the fate of his nation to stand unassailed, for he cuts himself off from it and plucks his friends from its grasp." [83] The message of Jesus was the message of love and the highest kind of freedom that flows from love, but such a gospel was quite foreign to the Jews, whose law had penetrated and distorted every human relationship; and so Jesus, being unable to impart to his society the new life that flowed from his message, chose not to enter any natural relations, but to withdraw with individuals "to train them, to develop in them the good spirit which he believed was in them, and thereby to create men whose world would be his world." But the message of Jesus demonstrated the inevitability of being unable to escape fate, for "the fate of Jesus was that he had to suffer from the fate of his people." [84]

Similarly, though by a different process, the disciples of Jesus also were subject to fate: while, like Jesus, they were separated from the world, they were able to enter into a close relationship with each other built upon their mutual love. Also, their association with Jesus gave them a new understanding of life—a recognition of spirit—"He was their living bond; in him the divine had taken shape and been revealed. . . . His individuality united for them in a living being the indeterminate and the determinate elements in the [entire] harmony." [85] But the death of Jesus changed this, and the disciples lost their faith in the new life in which the separation of reality and spirit was broken down.

In Hegel's view, the Resurrection provided the image for which the Christian community was looking: it provided an object—the risen and ascended Lord—in which their love could be objectified and thus form the focus of a religion. While Hegel did not regard the Resurrection as a historical event, he did regard it as the beginning of the fate of Christianity. The Christian group felt the need for such an image; but, Hegel said, this "sad need . . . is deeply connected with its spirit and its spirit's fate." [86] Hegel regarded the tragedy of the Christian community as originating in their failure to allow their mutual love to become the source of life and in the consequent objectification of love in an external image. Thus, love ceased to be that which bound them together, and that bond was found in a faith in their Lord, who then became an object standing over against them, whom they were to worship and obey, and about whom they had to believe certain doctrinal propositions.[87]

> But in the lifelessness of the group's love the spirit of its love remained so athirst, felt itself so empty, that it could not fully recognize in itself, living in itself, its corresponding spirit; on the contrary, to this spirit it remained a stranger. To be connected with an alien spirit, felt as alien, is to be conscious of dependence on it . . . it recognized it as set over against itself and itself as dependent on it. In its spirit lay the consciousness of discipleship and of a lord and master. (*ETW*, 294)

In this way the Christian community became caught up in a fate that stemmed from this fundamental attitude that views reality as a sundered world and perceives God as being separated from it and standing in opposition to it; so God may be present in an individual's thoughts, but he is divorced from, never present in, life itself. This fundamental attitude, so contrary to the message of Jesus but which

quickly developed in the Christian community, has had dire consequences for the history of Christianity in all its forms:[88] for example,
Hegel cited the Catholic Church as being marked by a sense of
servitude springing from a feeling of total opposition to God in all
actions and expressions of life so that man finds acceptance only
through servitude; and the Protestant churches as having had more
pious notions of the otherness of God, either stressing the sovereignty
and holiness of God so that the life of the world is an affront to
God and must be denied through various puritanical practices, or
stressing the benevolence of God from whom life comes as a favor
and gift.

> Between these extremes of the multiple or diminished conscious-
> ness of friendship, hate, or indifference towards the world, be-
> tween these extremes which occur within the opposition between
> God and the world, between the divine and life, the Christian
> Church has oscillated to and fro, but it is contrary to its essential
> character to find peace in a nonpersonal living beauty. And it
> is its fate that church and state, worship and life, piety and
> virtue, spiritual and worldly action, can never dissolve into one.
> (*ETW*, 301)

In concluding this examination of these manuscripts it may be
noted that there was still no clear understanding of the dialectic in
Hegel's works; but the seeds of that crucial Hegelian concept can
be recognized, for, with the emergence of his concept of the morality
of love, a significant new dialectical category had been discovered.
The notion of love is a dialectical one: it is not merely abstract,
derived through reasoning, but has definite historical dimensions.
Genuine love recognizes particular instances of separation and alienation and overcomes such instances, thus giving rise to the awareness and healing of further instances of alienation. Associated with
the notion of love, fate and necessity are also important categories
in the emergence of the Hegelian dialectic; and, as observed, it was
Hegel's historical inquiry into the degeneration of Christianity that
gave rise to these categories: given the historical circumstances of
Jesus' life, Hegel detected a certain inevitability in Christianity's
becoming 'positive', and Hegel came to regard alienation as part of
the human condition. His analysis of the history of the Jews and
the life of Jesus in "The Spirit of Christianity and Its Fate" revealed
his view that it is only the life of love that makes possible this
recognition and acceptance of alienation as part of the human condition and that enables a person to overcome it.

Two Fragments of 1800

Amongst his labors during his final year in Frankfurt was the writing of two essays that require consideration for an adequate understanding of the stage Hegel's thinking had reached by this time. The title, given by Nohl, to the first of these essays is "Fragment of a System,"[89] while the second was a new introduction to the Bern manuscript, the "Positivity" essay.[90] On the whole, these two works contain themes that were already very apparent in Hegel's Frankfurt period, so that no radical change is perceptible; but, looking back on these works, it is possible to identify definite indications of such a radical change being fairly imminent.

That which emerges most clearly in "Fragment of a System" is his as-yet-unchanged view of the relationship between religion and philosophy, which asserted the supremacy of religion. Indeed, "Fragment of a System" contains Hegel's most explicit expression of his view that religion annuls and transcends philosophy. The explanation of Hegel's position is to be found in his fundamental theme of unity that overcomes separation, and in the fact that he had not yet conceived of philosophy being anything other than what he will distinguish as the "philosophy of reflection". It is the reflective intellect, in Hegel's view, that can think only in terms of division and separation, and that therefore cannot achieve the required unity. This unity is, however, discovered in 'love' and 'life' that find expression in religion.

From the point of view of the reflective intellect, "the multiplicity of life has to be thought of as being divided against itself."[91] On the one hand, there is the conscious individual, "an organization" of "an infinite multiplicity" of elements. On the other hand, there is the world of which the individual is conscious, and that is also an infinite multiplicity composed of things from which the individual feels to be 'separate', for these 'other' things appear to be outside his own restricted sphere; and the life of this world is regarded as "an infinite life with an infinite variety, infinite oppositions, infinite relations."[92] Thus, the reflective intellect has two ways of viewing the world: either as an infinite multiplicity of finite individuals that are expressions of restricted, dependent life, or as an organized whole that is an expression of infinite life.

How, then, is the *unity* of the whole and the parts, the universe and the endless diverse multiplicity of which it is composed, to be understood? This infinite life exists only in the form of particular and determinate individual things—each of which is finite and transitory, and all of which are emphatically seen, on the level of reflection, as standing in a relation of separation to one another.

Reflection's concept of unity is that of the unity between finite things that is not restricted by the finite and transitory character that belongs to particular individuals. But Hegel perceived a more genuine unity, stating that each particular is truly an individual life only to the extent that he is at one with all other elements of the infinite life.

> The concept of individuality includes opposition to infinite variety and also inner association with it. A human being is an individual life in so far as he is to be distinguished from all the elements and from the infinity of individual beings outside himself. But he is only an individual life in so far as he is at one with all the elements, with the infinity of lives outside himself. He exists only inasmuch as the totality of life is divided into parts, he himself being one part and all the rest the other part; and again he exists only inasmuch as he is no part at all and inasmuch as nothing is separated from him. (*ETW*, 310)

Each individual life is dependent upon the whole. The living individual "is aware, therefore, both that he is a 'part' set against the whole of which he is conscious, and that he is 'no part', that everything of which he is conscious is essential to him and not really sundered from him." [93]

The problem, however, is that, on the level of reflection, this kind of unity of the infinite and the finite cannot be truly conceived or expressed without being caught in contradictions—for the reflective intellect cannot affirm the unity of the infinite and the finite without denying their distinction, nor can it affirm their distinction without denying their unity.[94] Thus, in this fragment Hegel said that it is not possible, on the level of reflection, to think this kind of unity— a unity that does not exclude distinction—and it is because of this that reason, or 'thinking life', "raises a relation between the multiplex elements which is not dead or killing, a relation which is not a [bare] unity, a conceptual abstraction, but is all-living and all-powerful infinite life; and this life it calls God." [95]

It was these considerations that determined Hegel's view of the relation between philosophy and religion. He regarded philosophy as the work of the reflective intellect, which, in its analyses, necessarily divided and separated things in thought. Therefore, the genuine unity of things could be found only in life, in the living process by which reason is raised from the finite to infinite life—as a result of which the separate partial character of the finite is transcended, and this living process is religion, which thus supersedes philosophy.[96]

This concept of life is one of considerable significance in Hegel's development. As in "The Spirit of Christianity and Its Fate," Hegel continued to be concerned with the problem of a reconciling unity; but at the time of writing that manuscript Hegel's primary concept had been that of love as the means of achieving reconciliation in a unity that overcomes separation, whereas now he has expanded love into the concept of life, which, while being in no way in conflict with love, does represent a greater depth of his understanding of reconciliation. Reconciliation was now being presented by Hegel, with more precision, as the realizing of a unity of opposites in which differences are not annihilated.[97] It is surely not that love does not admit such a unity—indeed, it could be said that it is only such a unity that truly expresses genuine love[98]—but that Hegel saw all that was suggested by love being taken up, expanded, and deepened in the concept of life that would more adequately express his deeper notion of unity as the reconciling, without the annihilating, of opposites. It is a unity that is grounded in the process of life itself: as the life of each finite individual has an internal unity, so all finite things, which are themselves life, are united from within by infinite life that is the living unity of the whole.[99] That this infinite life, which is called God, is no mere conceptual abstraction is indicated by Hegel's stating that it must also be defined as spirit *(Geist)*:

> We may call infinite life a spirit in contrast with the abstract multiplicity, for spirit is the living unity of the manifold if it is contrasted with the manifold as spirit's configuration and not as a mere dead multiplicity; contrasted with the latter, spirit would be nothing but a bare unity which is called law and is something purely conceptual and not a living being. The spirit is an animating law in union with the manifold which is then itself animated. *(ETW, 311)*

Here, then, is another indication of the emergence of that which was to be Hegel's most fundamental concept, *Geist*. But it was in the challenging environment of Jena and through the influence of Schelling that this concept developed, for Hegel had yet to make other profound changes in his thinking, in the light of which the concept of *Geist* was to mature. That these changes were in process, however, as his Frankfurt period came to an end is further indicated by the last of his Frankfurt writings.

New insights that he had gained at Frankfurt led to his rewriting the introduction to the "Positivity" essay, in which it became apparent that he had finally broken with the Enlightenment criticism of religion.[100] A concept of the positivity of religion that depends on the reflective intellect's general concept of nature is to be rejected. Such a concept of positivity presupposes that there is only one natural religion, namely, that which is in accord with the general concept of human nature, and concludes that any religion that is consistent with and serves the needs of national and individual variations in human nature is a positive religion.[101]

But Hegel argued here that the general concept of human nature can no longer be regarded as adequate: "The general concept of human nature admits of infinite modifications; and . . . human nature has never been present in its purity. . . . But the living nature of man is always other than the concept of the same." [102] Therefore, "the universal concepts of human nature are too empty to afford a criterion for the special and necessarily multiplex needs of religious feeling," [103] and the only criterion of judgment regarding the positivity of religion is whether it meets the needs of particular expressions of human nature in specific circumstances. If a religion does achieve that, it cannot be described as positive, and only *becomes* positive when forced upon people for whom it is no longer meaningful. The positivity of religion is therefore a relative matter: what is quite satisfactory and compatible in one circumstance will become positive in another.

> The question whether a religion is positive affects the content of its doctrines and precepts far less than the form in which it authenticates the truth of its doctrines and requires the fulfilment of its precepts. Any doctrine, any precept, is capable of becoming positive, since anything can be proclaimed in a forcible way with a suppression of freedom; and there is no doctrine which might not be true in certain circumstances, no precept which might not impose a duty in certain circumstances, since what may hold good universally as truth unalloyed requires some qualification because of its universality, in the particular circumstances of its application, i.e., it is not unconditionally true in all circumstances. (*ETW*, 171–72)

This is a clear indication of the change in Hegel's thinking since he wrote the original essay in Bern. Hegel had now thrown overboard, as Lukács states, the assumption that "certain attitudes, religions and institutions were marked from the outset with the stain of positivity, whereas others were metaphysically and absolutely free from such stains." [104] Religion and theological dogmas that originally were a response to a need of human nature, even though they may now have been discarded, can be seen as having been, in their origin, natural and indeed inevitable;[105] but this is something that the reflective intellect cannot perceive.

Regarding the purpose that he wished to pursue here, Hegel said this essay would not be concerned with the question of whether Christianity contains positive doctrines, but only with the question of whether "it is a positive religion as a whole." [106] However, though he was occupied with Christianity, and therefore was supposed to be occupied with the 'positivity' of Christianity 'as a whole', he did not discuss this question. He merely made the assumption that Christianity is not a positive religion as a whole in order to demonstrate that a changed situation can cause a nonpositive religion to become a positive one. It turns out, therefore, that to argue this point was his *actual* purpose in this essay.

Hegel's argument is that the religion of Jesus was not positive, but that the circumstances in which he was placed caused it to become positive. Those circumstances were such that Jesus had no option but to appeal to messianic expectations, and this gave rise to the disciples propagating Jesus' teaching, not because of the truth and goodness of the teaching, but because Jesus taught it—they founded their faith on the authority of Jesus.

But Hegel saw very profound difficulties in this 'positive' approach to religion. It "betrays a humble modesty and a resignation which disclaims any native goodness, nobility and greatness in human nature." But human nature must possess some native goodness and sense of the divine, for without it there could be no response to Jesus' teachings; and it is not 'positive' to presuppose "that everything high, noble, and good in man is divine, that it comes from God and is his spirit." But such a presupposition does become 'positive' if it is assumed that "human nature is absolutely severed from the divine, if no mediation between the two is conceded except in one isolated individual, if all man's consciousness of the good and the divine is degraded to the dull and killing belief in a superior Being altogether alien to man." [107]

In this way Hegel presented the question of positivity as ultimately coming down to the "metaphysical" question of "the relation between the finite and the infinite." This was a most fundamental issue for Hegel, and one with which he was vigorously wrestling at this time, and it is the question that will be carefully investigated in the final section of this work. Just how Hegel was to resolve this matter in his own philosophy depended on important new developments and radical changes in his thinking that occurred at Jena.

Chapter 4
The Jena Period
The Concepts of the Dialectic and Geist, and the Superseding of Religion by Philosophy.

The modification that occurred in Hegel's view of religion is a symptomatic aspect of the development of Hegel's thought during his sojourn in Jena. This change was complex in its evolution, but the result may be stated simply: the view that had emerged in his Frankfurt writings, that philosophy must be superseded by the higher state of religion, was reversed so that philosophy, or "Absolute Knowledge", becomes the ultimate in our understanding of reality. But the occurrence of this modified perspective can be understood only in the context of other aspects of his philosophical development. Important Hegelian concepts that were budding during the immediately preceding years now began to blossom out into their mature form: the Jena years saw the development of his idea of necessity coupled with a more fully fledged historical approach; they saw the unfolding of a more explicit concept of contradiction, a concept that was important in the development of his view of dialectics, for it involved a discernment that saw in each finite thing and in each historical situation contradictions that inevitably brought about the emergence of change; and those years also witnessed the appearance of the concept of *Geist* at the apex of his philosophy.

Hegel arrived in Jena in January 1801 to take up a teaching position in the city's university, where his former fellow student and friend, Schelling, had held the chair of philosophy for nearly three years. Hegel's arrival in Jena was significant for two reasons: first, it coincided with an important philosophical development that was evolving in Germany and that was represented by the debate occurring between Fichte and Schelling; and secondly, his move to Jena gave Hegel the opportunity to become directly caught up in the controversy. His involvement not only revealed his views that were already in advance of his contemporaries,[1] but also resulted in the greater maturing of his thought.

The philosophical development that was occurring at the beginning of the nineteenth century was the emergence of German idealism, arising out of the current concern that centered upon the Critical Philosophy of Kant. Hegel immersed himself in this philosophical development and publicly entered into, and contributed to, the process by the production of two essays within his first eighteen months in Jena. In July 1801 Hegel completed his first published work in philosophy, "Differenz des Fichteschen und Schellingschen Systems der Philosophie," [2] in which he sought to discuss exactly what the title suggests, though with the obvious intention of presenting Schelling's system as the superior one. Then, precisely a year later, his second essay, "Glauben und Wissen," [3] was published as volume 2, number 1 of the *Kritisches Journal der Philosophie*, which Hegel was coediting with Schelling. In these two essays Hegel really declared his perception of the contemporary philosophical needs: just as in the first essay he argued for Schelling's superiority because of his considerable advance on Fichte's subjectivity and failure to achieve the desired unity, so in the second essay Hegel critically dealt with the whole range of "the reflective philosophy of subjectivity" in its Kantian, Jacobian, and Fichtean forms, which maintained the distinction between faith and knowledge, and thus also retained God as an unknowable, transcendent Other—quite contrary to Hegel's desired unity.

It was Fichte who, Hegel noted, in spite of a fundamental agreement with Kant, provided the first significant break with Kantian philosophy, and hence gave birth to German idealism. An important point at which Fichte was influenced by Kant was in the area of morality and the recognition in ourselves of an important principle, and thus it was this fundamental role of the self that Fichte adopted from Kant and made it central to his own philosophy. But there was a second side to this relationship between Fichte and Kant that indicated that Fichte had not just reinterpreted Kant's philosophy but had really developed an independent system. The chief source of Fichte's disagreement was the dualism involved in the Kantian philosophy. Epistemologically, Kant's view involved the dualism between reality and appearance, with the consequent agnosticism about reality that could never be known. Morally, Kant's view involved the dualism between the rational self, which recognizes the duty to adhere to the a priori moral imperatives, and the natural self, which is governed by inclinations that are constantly in conflict with duty. Fichte proposed that the best way to overcome the Kantian dualism and its consequent agnosticism about reality and moral conflict was to develop a consistent idealism.

Here, then, was a definite formulation of idealism, and this significant split with Kantian philosophy was one with which Schelling was in accord. Schelling had been with Fichte for a time in Jena until a charge of atheism forced Fichte to resign his professorship in 1799, and the relationship between the two men had been one of agreement in their common opposition to Kant. But below the surface of this united front there was the potential for disagreement, which began to emerge particularly after the appearance of Schelling's first systematic work, *System of Transcendental Idealism*, in 1800.

Such an idealism was to be developed, however, in the light of the obvious advance in philosophy achieved by Kant through his critical inquiry into the faculty of human reason. In his analysis of human experience, Kant had correctly identified the active, contributory role of reason, while maintaining the effect of the independently existing world of objects, the things-in-themselves. It was this double-sided explanation of experience that Fichte wished to overcome; his way was to eliminate the unknowable thing-in-itself as a factor in the explanation of experience, and to retain reason as the fundamental principle of explanation.

In following this path of idealism Fichte thus turned to reason—or, in his own terminology, the I or ego—as the first principle of philosophy,[4] and experience is seen to have its origin in the self. But account has to be taken of the apparently independently existing world of objects: on the level of conscious experience that independent existence seems irrefutable, and the self or ego, which is a self-conscious self, can achieve self-consciousness only when opposed by a nonself. There must be a nonself opposed to the knowing, conscious self, and independent of the finite self that is apprehending it. Hence, the second basic principle of philosophy is that "a not-self [is] opposed absolutely to the self."[5] However, idealism would collapse unless this nonself has its source in the pure, transcendental, absolute ego—which posits in itself not only the finite, divisible nonself, but also the finite, divisible self.[6] While Fichte asserts that this absolute ego can be known only by intellectual intuition, it is the ground of his idealism, the source of all existence—not an object of any kind, for it transcends objectification; not even an active thing, for it is activity, a doing, which posits both the finite, divisible self and the finite, divisible nonself.

Thus, there were two sides to the relationship between Schelling and Fichte. On the one hand, there was the fundamental agreement about idealism as the most consistent form of philosophy and thus as a definite advance on the Kantian critical philosophy; but on the other hand, there was the basis for significant disagreement about the kind of idealism that was being advocated.[7]

Schelling's philosophy evolved through different periods of development, but at this period he was developing a philosophy of identity (Identitätsphilosophie) as an expression of the fundamental identity in all that is taken to be real, which is perceived by intellectual intuition and stated in the basic principle that "what is real is also ideal, and what is ideal is real." The problem is that from the viewpoint of finite consciousness the subject and the object are seen to be distinct; therefore, there is required another kind of intelligence through which this unity will be recognized, and it is this capacity that Schelling called intellectual intuition. "This intuition is the faculty by means of which man arrives at a true understanding of objective reality; it reveals that objective reality (nature) and human knowledge are but two arms of the same river and man becomes conscious of their identity through the act of intuition."[8] This Identitätsphilosophie consisted of, and was articulated in, two parts: a philosophy of nature (his Introduction to the Outline of a System of the Philosophy of Nature, in 1799, although this was preceded by earlier drafts) and a transcendental philosophy (his System of Transcendental Idealism in 1800).

Schelling's philosophy of identity is grounded in his concept of the Absolute in which the ideal and the real, subjectivity and objectivity, are ultimately one. Therefore, he understood the two parts of his Identitätsphilosophie to be mutually complementary, manifesting from two different starting points, the nature of the Absolute as identity of subject and object, the ideal and the real. These two complementary approaches to understanding reality as Absolute were Schelling's answer to what he perceived as the unsatisfactory one-sided subjectivity of Fichte's transcendental self.

The philosophy of nature is an analysis of the real (objective) world that uncovered the ideal (the subjective) in the real, for the analysis endeavored to show nature as the self-objectification of the Absolute. The influence of Spinoza is evident in Schelling's terminology. Nature, as a system of particular objects, is natura naturata, the product of the self-manifestation of the Absolute; nature, as that productive process, is natura naturans, the evolving self-expression

of ideal nature; and nature is both product and productive process—
it is a dynamic relation between *natura naturata* and *natura naturans,*
a relation that ultimately is one of identity. Further, nature is an
organic unity: the identity, of which Schelling spoke, is an organic
unity.[9] He took up what he considered to be Fichte's advance on
Spinoza—the elimination of any notion of nature as dead, lifeless
substance—but Schelling then acted to deal with Fichte's failure to
use this advance adequately: Fichte did not recognize the dynamic,
self-evolving character of nature, and this Schelling stressed in his
description of nature as a "universal organism," not an instance of
mere mechanism.

The system of transcendental idealism is Schelling's attempt to
consider reality from a different standpoint, starting, where Fichte
started, with the ego, a knowing intelligence. If knowledge is to be
possible, Schelling argued, a condition must be found for uniting
subject and object, declaring their ultimate identity; and that condition
is self-consciousness, the ego. This is the departure point in the
system of transcendental idealism, and it is not the individual self,
but "the act of self-consciousness in general." [10] And it is this "one
absolute act" that is the ground of all reality, for that act is the
Absolute's production of itself as objective being.[11] Just as an individual self has the capacity to reflect upon itself, and so create itself
as object upon which it may reflect, so Schelling spoke of the Absolute
as self, which, in an act of self-reflection, produces itself as object
to itself. So he endeavored to move away from the one-sided subjectivity of Fichte's philosophy by developing a philosophy that
presented nature as the real reflecting the ideal, and the ideal being
uncovered in the real.[12]

Nature, thus is perceived as a self-contained system, the condition
of its being not lying outside it, but residing in the self-reflective act
of the ego, the Absolute, the identity of the ideal and the real, of
subjectivity and objectivity.[13] Indeed, this identity, according to Schelling, is such that all difference and distinction vanish.

Although, in correspondence at the end of 1800, Fichte showed
awareness of—and uneasiness about—Schelling's views, the debate
between them was not public, and they were generally regarded as
being in agreement. But Hegel arrived in Jena in the midst of this
debate, and the work that he did in the first six months clearly
highlighted the differences between Schelling and Fichte. This was
the purpose of the "Difference" essay, which also provided an
indication of Hegel's relationship with Schelling—as well as some
insight into Hegel's own reflections on the nature and purpose of
philosophy, reflections that naturally arose out of his discussion of
these two philosophical systems.

Hegel's attraction to Schelling's system is apparent from his presentation of it as the superior form of idealism, while his response to Fichte's subjective idealism was one of equivocalness. What attracted Hegel most to Schelling was Schelling's "attempt to view nature and history as a single unified dialectical process. This answered to the deepest intellectual aspirations of the young Hegel," [14] as well as providing a more adequate basis for a philosophy that, in Hegel's view, would meet the needs and satisfy the hopes of the times.

These needs and hopes Hegel understood in terms of the overcoming of all dichotomies through the search for a philosophy of identity. The goal of such a search could not be realized, he believed, on the basis of Fichte's work, even though that work had represented a considerable advance—and this is the cause of Hegel's equivocal attitude toward Fichte. For some time Hegel had identified a basic weakness in Kant's philosophy to be the division between the subjective and the objective resulting from the Kantian distinction between noumena and phenomena, although the irony was that Hegel recognized that, in dealing with that same distinction—in his deduction of the categories—Kant had discovered the principle of authentic idealism, the rational self. This Kantian achievement, however, had lost its power because of Kant's sharp and fundamental division between Reason and nature, and the same sad result was to be found in Fichte. Fichte had brought out Kant's discovery of the principle of authentic idealism "in a stricter and purer form," [15] and Hegel was full of praise for Fichte because of this advance. But he, too, in Hegel's view, was guilty of abandoning this principle: the finite, divisible ego remains opposed to the finite, divisible nonego, and the Ego in which they were supposed to be united is still transcendent 'other'. Hence, Fichte's principle is never realized, but remains only 'an ought'.[16]

Where Fichte achieved only an *ought,* Schelling presented an actual unity, and this was the reason for the superiority of Schelling that Hegel perceived. It was the vision of an overarching unity—of a living wholeness and identity—that inspired and motivated Hegel, and it was Schelling's philosophy, especially his philosophy of nature, that most closely approximated the realization of this vision.[17] It was therefore particularly in the sphere of the philosophy of nature that Hegel became a disciple of Schelling at this time and worked in collaboration with him, for it was chiefly in Schelling's view of nature as an organic unity that Hegel found a true philosophical basis for a systematic unity. This was the aspect of Schelling's philosophy on which Hegel concentrated in the "Difference" essay, and this, in turn, is indicative of the enthusiasm with which he took up Schelling's treatment of nature.

Indeed, it is especially because of this that it can be said that "their collaboration in Jena was the point at which the paths of two important minds *crossed*." [18] "Crossed" accurately describes the relationship between them, for in the early Jena years they shared a deep interest in a philosophy of nature; but previously their interests had not coincided, and Hegel's fundamental concern with social issues had already produced a more profound understanding of social philosophy and the problems of dialectic than Schelling had acquired; and later their interests were to diverge again and culminate in Hegel's severe criticism of Schelling and Schelling's subsequent bitter hostility. But for the present, this criticism did not explicitly emerge: it was a time of philosophical experimentation for Hegel, who was striving to work out his own system of philosophy that would meet the contemporary need he felt most strongly—"the need for a philosophy that will recompense nature for the mishandling that it suffered in Kant and Fichte's systems, and set Reason itself in harmony with nature, not by having Reason renounce itself or become an insipid imitator of nature, but by Reason recasting itself into nature out of its own inner strength." [19]

Encouraged and assisted by Schelling's quest for an *Identitätsphilosophie*—and by Schelling's philosophy of nature in particular, which indicated to Hegel that his own vision for philosophy was achievable—Hegel spent the Jena years bringing his philosophy to a maturity that was introduced to the reading public by the *Phenomenology of Spirit*. This maturing was realized partly through the influence of Schelling, but also in tension with him, for Hegel was never without reservations about Schelling's philosophy.

The Concept of the Dialectic

In a famous formulation in the "Difference" essay Hegel declared that "the Absolute itself is the identity of identity and non-identity." [20] Obviously this was of crucial importance as an expression of his understanding of the Absolute, for which the term *Geist* came to be the most satisfactory; but his formulation was also central to the emergence of Hegel's full recognition of the concept of inherent dialectic, as were the ideas of fate and necessity.

These latter concepts first appeared in the course of Hegel's historical inquiry into the degeneration of Christianity, where he detected, given the historical circumstances of Jesus' life, a certain inevitability in Christianity's becoming 'positive'. Also, Hegel had spoken of the "naturalness and inevitability" of a religion arising whenever it meets a particular need of human nature;[21] though he saw it as equally inevitable that a specific expression of religion should be discarded as human need changes. This was Hegel's view of the inevitability within the historical process—an inevitability that is due to the fact that division *(Entzweiung)*, even though it takes different forms at different times, is present in "the culture of the [any] era, it is the unfree and given aspect of the whole configuration";[22] and from these inevitable divisions there ineluctably emerges a greater degree of harmony in a succeeding epoch. However, not only should such a process be seen as inevitable, Hegel was now speaking also of its essentiality. For example, the breakdown of the great unity, which he believed had existed in the civilization of ancient Greece, was inevitable because of the 'division' that existed within it, namely, the parochialism that was a feature of the unity of the polis; the breakdown was also essential because without it man could not have realized his potential as a free rational being.

Similarly, in his assessment of the contemporay philosophical situation that he presented in the two essays of the early Jena years, Hegel argued along these lines. In the "Difference" essay he recognized the inevitability and essentiality of the appearance of Fichte's subjective idealism, even though he was extremely critical of it. Historically, Hegel argued that Fichte's philosophy was an inevitable consequence of Kantian philosophy, resulting from the endeavor to overcome the problems of that philosophy; but it is equally true that the Fichtean philosophy must give way to that of Schelling because of the inconsistencies involved in the former.[23] Lukács offers the view that this historical analysis "represents an enormous advance in his own development, one which clearly points to the mature Hegel of the future." [24] It is an advance that is also reflected and further refined in the second of these two essays, "Faith and Knowledge," in which he gave an analysis of the philosophies of Kant, Jacobi, and Fichte. In relation to Enlightenment thought, which absolutized the opposition between the finite and infinite and posited an incomprehensible "Supreme Being" as an object of faith beyond the world of experience, these three philosophies are "the completion and idealization." But the philosophy of Kant was necessary because, in systematizing, with such genius, this opposition between finite and infinte, knowledge and faith, Kant clearly demonstrated the consequence of this position, and thus opened the possibility of this position's being transcended. Furthermore, however, while these three philosophies share this fundamental principle of "the absolute antithesis of finitude and infinity" as "common ground," they "form antitheses among themselves, exhausting the *totality of possible forms of this principle"*: Kant's philosophy "establishes the objective side"; the philosophy of Jacobi "is the subjective side; while Fichtean philosophy is the synthesis of both." [25]

> In Kant, the infinite concept is posited as that which is in and for itself and as the only thing philosophy acknowledges. In Jacobi, the infinite appears as affected by subjectivity, that is, as instinct, impulse, individuality. In Fichte, the infinite as affected by subjectivity is itself objectified again, as obligation and striving. (*FK*, 62)

Thus, Hegel argued that, while these three philosophies were confined to the principles of Enlightenment thought, they also possessed elements that were opposed to that thought, and in this way, not only complete the philosophy of subjectivity and reflection, but also open the possibility of the limitations of that thought being overcome.

Indispensible to Hegel's thinking on these matters was his arrival at his view of *contradiction* as the most profound principle of all things and their movement, that is, the principle of the dialectic. Any two things stand in contrast to each other, as subject and object or as two different objects, and through the contrast there is an awareness of opposition between them; even the reflective intellect perceives the relation between things in this way. But that is the only way in which the reflective intellect can perceive it, so that the division and opposition become absolute and rigid. On the other hand, Hegel saw it to be necessary to transcend the reflective attitude, to suspend the rigidity of opposition, and to perceive the relation between things not as separated objects but from the standpoint of the totality of life by which the unity of all things is grasped, thereby locating the apparent opposition of the other within the self. However, this means that contradiction is found in all experience, and therefore what Hegel meant by *contradiction* was that "opposition has become internal to each term (each term contains its opposite within itself). Contradiction is thus *contradictio in subjecto*, and that is why the subject *develops.*" [26]

Therefore, Reason is not

> altogether opposed to opposition and limitation. For the necessary dichotomy is One factor in life. Life eternally forms itself by setting up oppositions, and totality at the highest pitch of living energy *(in der höchsten Lebendigkeit)* is only possible through its own re-establishment out of the deepest fission. What Reason opposes, rather, is just the absolute fixity which the intellect

gives to the dichotomy; and it does so all the more if the absolute opposites themselves originated in Reason. (*Diff.,* 90–91)

According to Hegel, then, opposition and limitation is "One factor in life," though it is to be understood in the reflective sense of one thing being separated from and therefore 'opposed' to another as if a barrier *(Schranke)* or emptiness existed between the two. However, to rise above the reflective view of rigid opposition—as can be achieved by the speculative attitude—is to see opposition internalized in each thing, and so to perceive the continuity as well as difference. Thus, if one factor in life is 'opposition' or 'contradiction', life itself is 'unity' or 'identity'. Continuous life allows for relative oppositions (relative because they are only products of reflection), but it also overcomes them; opposition and unity are thus interdependent. To grasp the concept of unity or identity is to perceive that 'separated' things are not really separate, just as instants of time or points of space are not really separate, and if treated so, break out of their separation and "seek reconciliation". This seeking reconciliation is the causal element of the development of each thing toward a greater realization of its nature.

What is true of all things is true, for Hegel, most profoundly of the totality of life. "Life is itself this dialectic," Life is Reality, and "Reality is Development." [27] Hegel's philosophical understanding of the Absolute is that of the unity of infinite Life and finite life, the unity consisting in the fact that finite life is the self-externalization of infinite Life. This externalization is a 'grief' in infinite Life, for it is an alienation of itself, but it is to be perceived purely "as a moment of the supreme Idea," [28] for infinite Life returns to itself in fulfillment of itself and in unity. That Hegel understood his view of the Absolute to be of God, the divine Absolute, is clear from the language he used: the death of Christ must not be understood merely in the sense of the death of a historical person, but in the philosophical sense of this externalization and alienation—the harshness of God-forsakenness—of the divine Absolute; and the resurrection of Christ must also be understood in the philosophical sense of the Absolute's rising to itself in unity and totality to achieve the realization of its nature, which is its complete freedom. What

must be re-established for philosophy [is] the Idea of absolute freedom and along with it the absolute Passion, the speculative Good Friday in place of the historic Good Friday. Good Friday must be speculatively re-established in the whole truth and harshness of its Godforsakenness. Since the [more] serene, less well grounded, and more individual style of the dogmatic philosophies and of the natural religions must vanish, the highest totality can and must achieve its resurrection solely from this harsh consciousness of loss, encompassing everything, and ascending in all its earnestness and out of its deepest ground to the most serene freedom of its shape. (FK, 191)

The consequences of this dialectic of alienation and the overcoming of alienation belonging to the nature of the divine Absolute are both numerous and fascinating for the concept of God. In order to accommodate those consequences—to purify and deepen the concept of God—Hegel favored the use of the term *Geist* (Spirit) to speak of God.

The Concept of *Geist*

At the outset of Hegel's Jena period one can see the reappearance of the Frankfurt concern about the need to overcome separation and division, but now he specifically said that this is the fundamental purpose of philosophy: "Dichotomy (*Entzweiung*, division) is the source of *the need of philosophy*," and he suggested that the formal task of philosophy is the cancellation of division.[29] This is so because the task of philosophy is to discern the inherent unity of all things that results from the cancellation of division; to discern that this unity is one in which separation has been overcome, but also that it is not a unity—as Hegel was now formulating more precisely— in which opposition is annihilated. Hence, in a very explicatory formulation, Hegel declared that "the Absolute itself is the identity of identity and non-identity; being opposed and being one are both together in it."[30]

This was a definitive statement of his perception of the Absolute as it came to be expressed in Hegel's concept of *Geist* that emerged in the early Jena period; and this emergence occured through his systematic elaboration of his concept of Life that was being notably influenced by Schelling's philosophy of nature. His concepts of identity, continuity and infinity, and development became crucial to Hegel's notion of Life, and he found these in Schelling.[31] Schelling was captured by a strong enthusiasm for nature as the embodiment of Spirit, so that the different forms of nature are all expressions of the same cohesive force, Absolute Spirit. Thus, Schelling's philosophy asserted the ultimate unity, and hence the identity, of subject and object: it grasped that the object is not an alien being opposed to the subject but is an expression of the subject.

The nonrecognition of such a unity was a fundamental inadequacy that Hegel perceived in the philosophies of Kant, Jacobi, and Fitche. Kant's critical philosophy, for example, maintained a distinct division between subject and object by his uncritical dualism of phenomena and the unknowable noumena, with the result that "the whole task and content of this philosophy is, not the cognition of the Absolute, but the cognition of the subjectivity." [32] Therefore, in Fitche's philosophy, the problem that Hegel saw was not in the solution Fichte proposed to this Kantian dualism, namely, the identity of subject and object, but it was in Fichte's failure to carry out this solution: "the principle of identity does not become the principle of the system; as soon as the formation of the system begins, identity is abandoned." [33] Consequently, it was here that Hegel found the superiority of Schelling, for "the principle of identity is the absolute principle of Schelling's system as a *whole*. Philosophy and system coincide. Identity does not lose itself in the parts, still less in the result." [34]

The presence of this absolute principle of identity in Schelling's philosophy was quite fundamental for Hegel, and its absence from those other philosophies was both a consequence and cause of other crucial inadequacies to be found in them. It was a consequence of those philosophies sharing the Enlightenment error of reducing Reason to mere intellect and of distinguishing between faith and knowledge. When Reason is reduced to intellect, the Absolute is said to be beyond the grasp of Reason, which can have positive knowledge only of the finite and empirical, so that the Absolute is 'a beyond' in which one can only have faith: God is unknowable and is therefore an empty concept, and all that Reason can know is that it knows nothing save that it knows nothing; it must take refuge in faith.[35] The effect of this is that, because Reason is so confined to the finite in these philosophies, they turn out to be forms of "an idealism of the finite" and their fundamental principle is "the absoluteness of finitude." [36] Furthermore, the only notion of infinity of which the reflective intellect is capable is one in which the infinite is absolutely opposed to the finite, yet is nothing more than the totality of the finite.[37] But in Hegel's view this is not a true infinity, for what those philosophers did not see is that "if infinity is thus set up against finitude, each is as finite as the other." [38] True infinity, for Hegel, is that in which the absolute opposition between the infinite and finite is abandoned and is replaced by the notion of continuity.

It is not that Kant's philosophy did not contain the potential for rising above these antitheses, for his solution to the problem, 'How are synthetic a priori judgments possible?', really depends on "the original, absolute identity of the heterogeneous" subject and predicate. But in Kant this identity has been sundered, "and appears as separated into the form of a judgment, as subject and predicate, or particular and universal. . . . In the judgment the absolute identity is merely the copula 'is', without consciousness. It is the difference whose appearance prevails in the judgment itself." Consequently, what is foremost in Kant is not the identity, but the antithesis, and in such a way that identity confronts the difference as its opposite.[39]

Therefore, Hegel considered that "the original synthetic unity," on which the synthetic a priori judgments depend, was not conceived by Kant as original at all, but only "as produced out of opposites." Whereas for Hegel, what is required is the assertion of "a truly necessary, absolute, original identity of opposites"[40]—an identity that is the identity of the identity and the difference between subject and predicate—an identity that will enable the most crucial and fundamental concept for Hegel, namely, of the Absolute itself as "the identity of identity and non-identity; being opposed and being one are both together in it."[41]

Hegel vigorously opposed the philosophers whose position involved what he considered to be rigid antitheses, permanent divisions, that led them to deny themselves the contemplation of the infinite and eternal, supposing it to be forever beyond reason. This, he argued, reduced religion to a mere longing: its chief aspect was feeling, and thus it was only subjective; and its longing was not to be satisfied, for it sought the Absolute, but was given only finitude.[42] In contrast to this, it was Hegel's view that, rather than perceive the infinite and the finite as being completely divorced and in absolute opposition, with knowledge being confined to the finite, it is the task of reason and philosophy to comprehend the infinite in the finite, the eternal in the here and now, to recognize the spirit in *this* world: "The task of philosophy consists in uniting these presuppositions: to posit being in non-being, as becoming; to posit dichotomy (*Entzweiung*, division) in the Absolute, as its appearance; to posit the finite in the infinite, as life."[43]

These concepts of identity, becoming, and appearance—which Hegel was convinced needed genuinely to be incorporated into a philosophy as principles on which it was based—were, he discerned, so presented by Schelling. It already has been observed that Hegel found Schelling's system to be superior to that of Fichte, primarily on the grounds that "the principle of identity is the absolute principle of Schelling's system as a *whole*"; but furthermore, in Schelling's philosophy of nature the concepts of development (becoming) and appearance were of utmost importance. There is a continuity in nature through the development from lower to higher forms, though each higher form is marked by the emergence of something new that, in turn, throws light on the lower forms. Nature is the self-objectification, the appearance, of the finite Absolute, and in the development of nature Schelling held that the activity that is at the basis of nature and that develops itself (becomes itself) in the world of finite things is this infinite Absolute. This was the crux of Schelling's philosophy of nature that so significantly influenced Hegel, because it coincided with and extended his own thinking as he wrestled with the working out of a philosophical system.

This is not to say, of course, that he merely adopted Schelling's philosophy as his own, for he differed from it in significant ways, and it is in regard to Hegel's concept of *Life* that one can begin to grasp the uniqueness of the thought he was evolving. Hegel "is less concerned with life as a biological concept than as the life of mind and spirit. . . . He is more concerned with human desire than with biological drives. If one were to characterize Hegel's philosophy as a whole, to express its origin and basic intuition, one would have to say that *it seeks to be the thought of human life*." [44] Hegel's concept of Life intrinsically involved the concepts of identity, dialectical development, and infinity. Life is infinite, and this infinity consists in the continuity and inseparability of the multiplicity and the totality of Life; and, because of continuity, each part contains its opposite in itself—that is, possesses contradiction—and that is why there is development that proceeds dialectically. Further, if this is true of each part, then because of the inseparability of the whole and its parts, it is also most profoundly true of the totality of Life: Life is characterized by dialectical development in which contradictions that exist in individuals, in relationships, and in society give rise to the emergence of a greater degree of harmony that is marked by a greater awareness of the identity or unity that exists between each individual and within the totality.

But Hegel never thought that this dialectical process issued in an identity or unity that was nothing more than an emptiness caused by the disappearance of all difference. He came to be convinced (by 1805–7, when he was writing *Phen.*) that Schelling's philosophy postulated such an emptiness, so that here was another point at which Hegel eventually sought to distance himself quite markedly from Schelling.

Important as the concept of Life was for Hegel, however, he went beyond it to the richer concept of *Geist*. This concept had appeared in his Frankfurt writings, but it was at Jena that *Geist* developed as the concept at the apex of his philosophy, embracing all that was involved in the concepts of love and life that had been such crucial determinants in the maturing of Hegel's philosophy. Life or Reality is Development, but in terms of the concept of *Geist*, this development is also the *self-discovery* of *Geist*.

As with the concept of Life, *Geist* is not to be thought of as an infinite Absolute that is beyond the finite particulars and beyond the divisions and oppositions that exist in the finite; nor is it an Absolute that preexists the finite world and from which the latter comes into existence.[45] But what Hegel was now finding to be the richer implications of the concept of *Geist*, in comparison with the concept of Life, was that discovering unity with the totality of life is not just uniting "with a larger current of *life*," but being united "with a cosmic spirit" :[46] nothing less is sufficient to satisfy the fundamental experience of spiritual relations and their development. This, however, is one of the great tensions in, and poses one of the great dilemmas about, Hegel's philosophy: what exactly is this notion of cosmic *Geist*, and how is it related to the more traditional views about God?

The latter question can most easily be answered by saying that the notion of *Geist* is related to the notion of God as a more purified and deepened concept of the Absolute than is presented in the traditional view of God. It is most clear that Hegel did not want to eradicate the concept of God from his philosophy; quite the contrary, for he himself declared the primary contemporary interest of philosophy to be "once again to place God absolutely to the front, at the apex of philosophy as the sole ground of all, as the single principle of being and knowing, after one has for long enough placed him *alongside* other finite entities or completely at the end as a postulate from which an absolute finiteness proceeds." [47]

So many religious presentations of the concept of God were inadequate. This was true of the Religions of Nature and Religion in the form of Art,[48] but it was also sadly true of contemporary Christianity, in which the truth of God was so misconstrued as to retain the inadequate view of God as an 'Other'—alongside of, and separated from, the world of finite actuality, but on whom that finite world depends as its source or first cause; also, a perfectly good God who is opposed to a world that has become corrupt and evil. However, that the traditional and popular form of Christianity should present that kind of understanding of God was a matter of great sadness because, in fact, Christianity—which Hegel regarded as the Absolute Religion—was a religion in which the truth of God, in its fullness, had been revealed:

Absolute religion is this knowledge that God is the depth of the spirit which is certain of itself. Thereby is he [God] the self of all. He is the being [*Wesen*], pure thinking; but if externalized from this abstraction, he is an actual self. He is a man, who has common spatial and temporal existence. And this individual is all individuals. The divine nature is not any other than the human. All other religions are imperfect. . . . The absolute religion is the depth which has come to the light of day. (*Jenaer Realphilosophie*, 266–67)

In absolute religion the depth of the concept of God had come to the light of day because it was the religion of incarnation,[49] by which the opposition between God and nature is overcome, and indeed, declared to be null; and the world of actuality, which is thought to be evil and separated from God, who is good, has been shown to be not so by God's becoming man. This principle of incarnation, "the sacrifice of Divinity," [50] is the fundamental, universal truth of the nature of God, not just a truth of God confined to a historical moment. However, that historical moment—the life of the divine man, and more particularly, the sacrificial death of that man—manifested this universal truth of God so that what is true in the case of this one individual could be seen to be true of all. Thereby the opposition between God and nature was declared to be negated: "Now that this opposition is itself nothing, and the evil, the reality for itself, is not so, but is universal, all this portrays itself in the self-sacrifice of the divine man." [51]

This truth manifested in absolute religion—this understanding of God—is most adequately portrayed in the notion of *Geist:* "That God is *Geist*, this is the content of this religion and the object of this consciousness." [52] Whereas the notion of *God* is so bound up with the many misconceptions of the Absolute, the notion of *Geist* frees it of those misconceptions, and declares the truth of the Absolute in depth. *Geist* expresses that truth to be that the Absolute is Spirit that comes to be, that becomes a self-externalizing (self-alienating), dialectical, self-becoming Spirit, which comes to know itself out of alienation—a process in which that which was alienated loses its appearance of alienation, and Spirit "knows itself as universal essence and universal reality." [53]

However, the fact that this truth of God, manifested in Absolute Religion, had been misconstrued to the point of being lost in traditional and contemporary religion led Hegel during this period to a new understanding of religion that indicated to him that religion will always be at risk in this regard because it presents its truth by means of representations (*Vorstellungen*). Therefore, Hegel concluded that the truth can be safeguarded only in the realm of speculative thought, philosophy: religion must be sublated; the religious notion of God must be sublated, and the speculative idea of *Geist* become the content of Absolute Knowledge.

The Superseding of Religion by Philosophy

The great originality of Hegel's work during his early years in Jena was the speculative attempt to conceptualize *Life* in terms of the dialectic. In Frankfurt, Hegel had not conceived of the possibility of such a conceptualization, for he was not aware of any potential conceptual thought beyond that of the 'understanding' and 'reflection', the inadequacy of which he proclaimed because they were modes of thought that were incapable of grasping the unity of things, being able only to divide into separate parts and perceive things in terms of subject and object. Hegel's great stress on the necessity to transcend the "partial character of the living being" therefore had to be satisfied in the living process of life, which was larger than thought and which thought could not comprehend, but which found expression in religion.[54] However, while at Frankfurt, Hegel had begun to show signs of this impending discovery that there was a possibility of conceptual thought beyond what he continued to call "imagination" and "reflection",[55] and this he pursued quite remarkably at Jena. "Thought and life are no longer to be separate domains, where life always outstrips thought and thought never comprehends life. The two terms are to be identified so that life is conceptualized as life and thought breaks with its traditional forms in order to grasp and express life itself." [56]

So, then, it was in *Thought* that Hegel now found the fully adequate expression of the unity of Life, but it was Thought raised to the level of *speculation* rather than reflective thought. The latter is aware only of dichotomies and an absolute separation: "Reflection cannot express the absolute synthesis in one proposition, . . . (it) must separate what is one in the absolute Identity," [57] and it is this separation that remains absolute for reflective thought. But this did not satisfy Hegel regarding the true nature of Reality, and this—the absolute Identity—is grasped only by speculative Thought: "In order to overcome these finitudes and construct the Absolute in consciousness, Reason lifts itself into speculation." [58]

Because it grasps the absolute Identity that is the fundamental truth of Reality, speculative philosophy is the only complete or absolute knowledge, that is, knowledge that comprehends the finite sublated in the infinite as an essential unity.[59] Moreover, it is absolute knowledge also because it comprehends the infinite as reflected in, for it externalizes itself in, the finite; and speculative philosophy itself is a self-externalization of absolute Reason, so that Hegel could say that the history of speculative philosophy is "the history of the one eternal Reason, presenting itself in infinitely manifold forms." [60] To rise to speculative philosophy, absolute knowledge was, without doubt, the great need that Hegel perceived, for philosophy must aim to present the things of the finite world as a continuity, as "internally connected," and thus "there necessarily arises the need to produce a totality of knowing, a system of science." [61]

Such *knowledge* would overcome all dichotomies, not least one that Hegel distressingly saw as a mark of the contemporary situation, namely, the dichotomy between faith and reason. This was a distinct separation that Hegel rejected, and he had been struggling to overcome it as well as that other dichotomy that gave rise to it, namely, the absolute opposition between the infinite and finite perceived by reflective thought, which therefore regarded the Absolute as a Supreme Being relegated to an unknowable beyond. On this view, 'knowledge' was confined to the empirical, finite world, and knowledge of the Absolute was unattainable—an unattainability that had the advantage, according to Kant, of making room for faith. For Hegel, however, this was entirely unsatisfactory: "in this relation or connection of the limited with the Absolute there is consciousness of their opposition only; there is no consciousness at all of this identity. This relation is called *faith*." [62] Such faith is grounded in subjectivity, for it springs out of a longing for what *ought* to be.

The solution of one of these products of reflective thought—the dichotomy between the infinite and finite—Hegel believed had been discovered in the concepts of *Geist* and the dialectic; similarly, the dichotomy between faith and knowledge is to be overcome by speculative thought, for "speculation constructs conscious identity out of what, in the consciousness of ordinary intellect, are necesarily opposites." [63] In speculative thought, therefore, faith and reason are reconciled and united, so that the "highest Idea," the Absolute, is not "the point where philosophy terminates in faith," [64] the point where reason dies; but rather, it is both the starting point and the supreme object and goal of philosophy.

It was this newly reached conviction, that one could attain to speculative thought in which the true nature of reality could be conceptualized, that brought about a reversal in the relationship Hegel perceived between religion and philosophy. Whereas in the Frankfurt writings philosophy had been superseded by religion as the living expression of the unit of Life, now philosophy came to occupy the highest place, for it was in speculative thought that Hegel was finding the fully adequate expression of the unity of Life. Religion, on the other hand, was no longer regarded by Hegel as providing the most adequate expression of these matters. Religious expression was confined to the form of figurative thought *(Vorstellendes Denken)*,[65] and so failed to reach the supreme level of absolute knowledge *(das absolute Wissen)* where truth is grasped in conceptual form.

Absolute religion had, as its fundamental idea, the desired "intuition of the self-shaping or objectively self-finding Absolute" that externalizes itself in alienation and becomes itself out of its alienation: it is this dialectic of absolute *Geist* that provides the unity or identity of all things. This truth of absolute *Geist* is to be found in the absolute religion, the Christian religion, in its "intuition of God's eternal human Incarnation the begetting of the Word from the beginning," [66] for it was in Christianity that this concept first became manifested. Therefore, although Hegel changed his view, thereby placing absolute knowledge above religion in terms of the clarity of expression of this truth, it is not to say that religion did not attain to that truth. Philosophical thought sublates the Christian religion, elevating the same truth manifested in the religion of incarnation from the *Vorstellungen* of religion into the form of *Begriff*. Indeed, in his Jena essays, one can already find the view, which he was to develop later, that this intuition of absolute *Geist* is to be found not only in absolute knowledge and absolute religion, but also in art; what Hegel distinguished was the clarity of expression of that intuition that was to be found in each, and in this regard he indicated religion to be superior to art, but absolute knowledge, speculative thought, to be the means of greatest clarity:

In *art* this intuition appears more concentrated in a point, and consciousness is stricken down. This happens either in art properly speaking or in religion. In art properly speaking, the intuition appears as a work which, being objective, is enduring, but can also be regarded by the intellect as an external dead thing; it is a product of the individual, of the genius, yet it belongs to mankind. In religion the intuition appears as a living (e)motion *(Bewegen)* which, being subjective, and only momentary, can be taken by the intellect as something merely internal; it is the single individual. In *speculation*, the intuition appears more as consciousness, and as extended in consciousness, as an activity of subjective Reason which suspends objectivity and the non-conscious. Whereas the Absolute appears in art, taken in its time scope, more in the form of absolute being, it appears in speculation more as begetting itself in its infinite intuition. But though speculation certainly conceives the Absolute as becoming, it also posits the identity of becoming and being; and what appears to speculaton as self-begetting is at the same time posited as the original absolute being which can only come to be so far as it is. In this way, speculation can rid itself of the preponderance that consciousness has in it; the preponderance is in any case something inessential. Both art and speculaton are in their essence divine service—both are a living intuition of the absolute life and hence a being at one with it. (*Diff.*, 171–72)

Hegel believed that the time was marked by a great yearning for such a speculative system to be developed in detail. This was so because, in Hegel's view, Schelling's philosophy, which so far was the closest to this achievement, was only a partial development of such a system. But Hegel also was convinced that if such an achievement could be attained, then the time was ripe for a great response to, and a taking hold of, such a system: this was the hope that inspired him. Further, it was his belief that in the philosophy he was formulating, such a grasp of the truth was being expressed in conceptual form. However, ironically, Hegel's philosophy has continued to pose very great dilemmas that have given rise to many conflicting conclusions about his position. One basic dilemma concerns Hegel's understanding of the relation between God and the world, and this is the issue that, in Part 2, will be highlighted in the context of an exposition of Hegel's 'religious' philosophy, and that, in Part 3, will be systematically investigated.

PART II

Hegel's 'Religious' Philosophy

The Unfolding of Religion as Philosophy's Quest for 'Eternal Truth'.

Introduction

In his *Lectures on the Philosophy of Religion,* Hegel declared that "the result of the study of philosophy is that [the] walls of separation, which are supposed to divide absolutely, become transparent." [1] In many ways, these words capture the abiding purpose and primary thrust of Hegel's entire philosophical endeavor, and in so doing, they make apparent the fact that the underlying concern that motivated and shaped his philosophy was a 'religious' concern, and that the central thread of his major works therefore is aptly described as 'religious'. The primary thrust of Hegel's philosophy is the transcending of that which appears to be separating barriers so as to perceive the permeating unity and the overarching wholeness of all things. This oneness was perceived, by Hegel, to reside in the fact that all things are a manifestation of *Geist;* and *Geist* is to be understood as event, as life, movement, or process, from which nothing is excluded. This, says Karl Barth, is "Hegel's boldest and most weighty innovation," and it "is therefore absolute, it is God." [2]

Herein is to be found the reason why Hegel's philosophy can be deemed to be a religious philosophy, though the use of the term 'religious', like the use of the word 'God', must be carefully qualified. Hegel maintained a definite and important distinction between religion and philosophy, and to speak of his philosophy as religious cannot be taken to imply that that distinction may be disregarded, but it can be taken to imply that the basic dimension, the primary orientation, of Hegel's philosophy is a religious one in the sense that the quest of his philosophy, like the quest of religion, was the comprehension of the meaning of life and of reality in its totality. [3] Regarding religion, Hegel himself said that in it, "in the thought, the consciousness and the feeling of God," is to be found "the ultimate centre" of "all that has worth and dignity for man," for "God is the beginning of all things and the end of all things"; and "in religion man places himself in a relation to this centre, in which all other relations concentrate themselves, and in so doing he rises up to the highest level of consciousness and to the region which is free from relation to what is other than itself, to something which is absolutely self-sufficient, the unconditioned, what is free, and is its own object and end." [4]

If this, then, is the way Hegel perceived the function of religion, it is also the way in which he regarded the task of philosophy: indeed, religion and philosophy have a common object and share the same content,[5] and, in this sense, they are one. As religion comprehends the meaning of all things by means of the concept of God, in philosophy that comprehension is attained by means of the Absolute Idea, which "alone is *being*, imperishable *life, self-knowing truth*, and is *all truth*." [6] This truth is known in the process and movement of history, and this truth is identical with God; and so Barth can describe Hegel's quest as "theological",[7] and Black can similarly emphasize the close relation between religion and philosophy in Hegel by reminding us that "Feuerbach saw in Hegel's philosophy religion in disguise," whereas "Hegel saw in religion philosophy in disguise." [8]

However, the closeness of the relationship was not such as to admit a complete identity of religion and philosophy: there is identity of content, but a crucial difference in the mode of apprehension. In the final section of *Science of Logic*, for example, Hegel stated his clear view that the Absolute Idea presents *its existence* in different modes of determination—Nature and Spirit—and that art and religion are modes in which it apprehends itself, but that philosophy is "the highest mode of apprehending the Absolute Idea because its mode is the highest mode, the Notion." [9]

Nevertheless, it was not this difference in the level of comprehension of the truth that, in Hegel's view, accounted for the contemporary antagonism between religion and philosophy; instead, the antagonistic attitude was seen to be in the failure to appreciate the identity of content and the consequent appearance of separation between religion and philosophy and, indeed, all other forms of human consciousness. Hegel detected the common view that knowledge was attainable only through scientific investigation of the world, and that in religion it was merely feeling and faith that were operative; even pious people fell into a state of dualism, being prepared to admit that science discloses everything about the finite world, and leaving God as an infinite and eternal 'other', who is not necessary for an understanding about the finite world, and the experience of whom is reduced to our simple feelings.

But this divorce between faith and knowledge is false, and imposes an unnatural division upon the human spirit; according to Hegel, it is quite incorrect to suppose that religious faith and philosophical inquiry can coexist without also being firmly interrelated, and such a supposition forces the human spirit into the unnecessary dilemma of having to choose between a state of indifference toward religion, a rejection of the demands of reason in relation to religion—leaving religion simply to the domain of feeling, or a denial of reason's ability to know the truth at all.[10]

All this, however, Hegel found to be a product of the prevailing attitudes of the time, according to which it is not possible to attain knowledge of God or to assert any religious doctrines that possess definite content. The Age of Reason had produced a Theology of Reason in which religious content had been annihilated "and the absolute object reduced to complete poverty" : through its intention "to place God very high," by speaking of him as 'infinite' and 'supreme Being', the Enlightenment merely reduced the concept of God to something that is "hollow, empty and poor." [11] Even theologians, Hegel believed, had succumbed to this prevailing tendency, and had "done everything in their power to do away with what is definite in religion," reducing previously essential doctrines to matters of history—the thoughts of others, which do not belong to contemporary thought or bear on contemporary needs—and thus it becomes apparent that "such theologians have no concern with true content, the knowledge of God." [12]

This general intellectual character of the age had found its preeminent expression in the writings of Kant, and it is clear that Hegel's disenchantment with Kant (that had begun in Frankfurt and developed in Jena, replacing the close, though never complete, adherence to Kant in Bern) had, in Hegel's mature works, become a stringent criticism of a philosophy he regarded as inadequately based. This is not to say that Hegel discarded the great debt he owed to Kant— as, indeed, to the Enlightenment generally—in arriving at his insistence on the autonomy of human reason, for this insistence remained as a cardinal premise of his philosophy. But Hegel did come to criticize vigorously some very fundamental aspects of Kant's philosophical position. At its most basic level, this ciriticism was a profound attack on the inherent dualism in Kant's ontology, and it was prompted by Hegel's fundamental conviction that every dualism must be eliminated.[13] Kant's declaration of the genuine autonomy of human reason sprang from his assertion that human knowledge is dependent on and shaped by human reason, not on anything external to itself. This assertion involved his distinction between the thing-as-known (phenomenon) and the thing-in-itself (noumenon), the former being the sole content of human knowledge and being partially shaped by human reason. While this declaration of autonomous human reason was essential and something to be prized, Hegel found its Kantian form to be quite insufficient, for it entailed an unsupportable dualism and placed an unnecessary and misleading limitation on human knowledge by denying its capacity to grasp the noumena.

A similar difficulty was to be found, according to Hegel, regarding the relation of the finite to the infinite because, in Kant's view, human reason is confined to the finite, without the capability of coming to terms with the infinite. Kant, of course, stressed the necessity of *Vernunftreligion,* but the role of reason in religion that he admitted was restricted to 'knowing' that the subjective response of faith was rational, for human reason could never obtain genuine knowledge of the object of religious faith. In other words, Kant's reason "is conscious of its incapacity to grasp any reality outside (or above) itself."

But an autonomy that involved such a restriction was, for Hegel, a very spurious autonomy, and in contrast, the autonomy of Hegel's reason consisted in the fact that it "is 'conscious of being all reality', and thus is conscious that there is no reality outside (or above) itself for it to grasp." [14] In declaring knowledge to be a completely finite activity, Kant had been at one with the Enlightenment; but quite clearly, Hegel was desirous of going beyond such a position—first, because he found it to be a mistaken position, and secondly, because of the undersirable consequences it had for the philosophy of religion, in that it meant the reduction of the means of approaching God to only the approach through faith, and thereby divorced faith from reason.

Therefore, Hegel strove to surpass that Enlightenment position, to end the conflict between reason and faith and "to overcome the romantic religious intuitionism of a Jacobi or a Schleiermacher;" [15] and in doing so, he found that although Kant had not developed its implications, he (Kant) in fact had begun to offer a more adequate assessment of human consciousness. Kant's distinction between phenomena and noumena, although untenable, was nevertheless an awareness of real things that are objective to and unconditioned by human reason, and his faith-assertion of God was an indication of an awareness of the Infinite and Unconditioned Reality. The deficiency was that in Kant's philosophy human reason was capable only of knowledge that was subjectively conditioned, and was not able to affirm the reality of the Infinite that was 'known' only by faith. Hegel's aim was to overcome such deficiencies, to set aside the distinctions and conflicts such as were contained in Kant's philosophy, and the means he employed to accomplish this aim was the dialectic.

Through the dialectic, in Hegel's philosophy, the apparent distinction of the subject and object, and of the finite and infinite, is surpassed: through the dialectic the bonds of Kant's individual subjectivity are broken, for the relationship between subject and object comes to be seen as a dialectical unity grounded in the fact that "subject and object are both manifestations of the same reality, each finding its fulfilment and clarification in the other";[16] and through the dialectic the separation of the finite and the infinite is transcended, for the relationship comes to be seen as a dialectical unity of finite and infinite grounded in the fact that "in the finite itself there is an infinite dimension, without which the finite does not make sense as finite. . . . The finite is real enough, and it is really finite . . . but it is real only as a 'movement' of the infinite." [17]

There is no undermining of the reality of the individual in Hegel's philosophy, for, indeed, he placed considerable stress on the distinct and definitely existing individual; but that is not all that can—or need—be said, since the distinctiveness is not absolute and the finitude of the individual is not unqualified. Hegel's whole approach is marked by his determination to avoid setting premature limits of any kind, because he asserted that there are no limits, that no individual is sufficient to itself or can exist for itself alone, and that the individual is not confined to the finite dimension. Each individual consciousness is capable of becoming aware of this, and it is only through such awareness that consciousness is fulfilled. This capability of consciousness is an inherent capacity to transcend all apparent separating barriers and to reach beyond supposedly limiting conditions, and so to "pass over" to its 'other', with which it thereby "becomes identical." Thus, consciousness becomes aware that nothing remains a single isolated individual, and that all reality is not just an aggregate of individuals, but is an infinite oneness that consequently can be known as Absolute Spirit. The process whereby this awareness is realized is the dialectical process in which "consciousness becomes . . . Spirit, and experiences the joy of finding itself therein and becomes aware of the reconciliation of its individuality with the universal." [18]

However, the dialectical process is not just the coming to this recognition by individual consciousness, for the life and movement— the total process—of all reality is also the self-manifestation or unfolding of, and the coming to fulfillment of, Absolute Spirit. It is only because this is so, in Hegel's view, that the individual has any reality: the finite individual has reality only as a 'moment' of the infinite universal; but conversely, the Universal or Absolute Spirit has reality only in and through finite particulars that are the concretization and self-manifestation of the Universal, and that are therefore stages or moments in the coming to self-knowledge and self-realization of the Absolute. Thus, the individual plays an essential and creative role in this process of self-realization—a dialectical process that results in the dialectical identification of the finite and the infinite.

The *Phenomenology of Spirit* is an account of Hegel's understanding of this process, and it is an account that goes to the very core of religion, for the process of dialectical identification of the finite and the infinite poses the most basic question of religion, namely, the nature of the relationship between finite particulars and the infinite Universal or Absolute, or, in religious terms, between the individual and God. According to Hegel, the separation of God and the individual is as spurious as the separation of faith and knowledge is delusive; and it is only when a recognition of this is achieved through the dialectical process—and also when, through the same process, all such separations are transcended—that the truth of reality is attained and the self-realization of Absolute Spirit is accomplished. It was Hegel's obvious intention in *Phen.* to facilitate this quest for truth: as Lukács says, the project Hegel set himself "was to provide ordinary consciousness with a ladder with which to ascend to the standpoint of philosophy." [19]

Thus, Hegel began where human beings are, with the forms of awareness or consciousness, and particularly with the most elementary form of awareness, "our ordinary consciousness of things [desiring] to take us from there to the true perspective of *Geist.*" [20] This viewpoint of ordinary consciousness is that of *Verstand,* which Hegel identified in *ETW:* its view of the knowing subject is as an individual finite person set over against the external world. But, in complete contrast, the perspective of *Geist* is that of love, about which Hegel also wrote in *ETW,* and which is the true goal of the process toward knowledge: it "shows us as vehicles of a spirit which is also expressed in the world, so that this world is no longer distinct from us." [21] Hegel's intention in *Phen.* was to show how it is possible to progress from the former to the latter; and as such, his work in *Phen.* possessed a very definite religious dimension.

The standpoint of philosophy is that which attains to a comprehensive grasp or knowledge of reality: but it is only truly 'knowledge' when that grasp is set in the framework of the totality, for, as Hegel said, "the True is the whole." [22] Having this in mind, the religious character of Hegel's philosophy becomes apparent when one also recalls his words, written elsewhere, namely, that "the aim of philosophy is to know the truth, to know God, for He is the absolute truth, inasmuch as nothing else is worth troubling about save God and the unfolding of God's nature." [23] This unfolding occurs within the dialectical process of the experiences of human self-consciousness through which alone the Absolute, God, comes to know Himself and to realize Himself as *Geist.*

Conversely, individual self-consciousness is truly fulfilled—becomes spirit—only when it knows the Absolute as infinite reality. Hegel's philosophy thus is about "a rise of thought to absoluteness or divinity,"[24] and it is this that gives his philosophy its religious dimension. While it is true that Hegel believed it necessary to go beyond—though not to forfeit—the religious standpoint, it is also true that it is, in Lauer's words, "essential to the integrity of human consciousness that it be religious, that it be consciousness of the absolute, the infinite, who is God."[25]

As Hegel saw it, the human consciousness could grasp God or the Absolute—there is no distinction between the Absolute known by the philosophical consciousness and the God known by the religious consciousness, and neither is there any disparity between knowledge and faith—and this grasping of the Absolute is realizable because finite reality is a self-manifestation of the Infinite, and finite human consciousness rises to the infinite; and the total process is a dialectic in which Spirit is coming to a self-realization as absolute Spirit. Further, it is in religion that human consciousness first comes to an awareness of the infinite and of consciousness' gradual "passing over into" the infinite.[26]

In the light of these features of Hegel's philosophy, it can be said, with Lauer, that "for Hegel religious consciousness is an essential stage in the march toward adequate self-consciousness, which is identified with adequate knowing. Unless in the process of its development consciousness becomes religious, the self of which it is consciousness would be only partially a self, not all that the self as spirit is."[27]

It can be said that in a very definite sense *Phen.* is representative of the whole of Hegel's philosophy:[28] it is a fascinating presentation of Hegel's conception of the whole dialectical process, and in it the essentiality of religious consciousness—not "as merely *one* of the stages in the spirit's advance, the penultimate one," but as "the phenomenology of religious consciousness [that] recapitulates the whole of the spirit's advance"[29]—becomes quite conspicuous. Therefore, while it is true that *Phen.* contains only an introductory presentation of Hegel's philosophy of religion and that a later and fuller formulation is to be found in *LPR*, it is expedient, legitimate,[30] and extremely utilitarian to examine Hegel's philosophy, for the purpose of perceiving and identifying the extent of its religious dimension, in the context of the whole dialectical process as presented in *Phen.* It is only in grasping the dialectical movement of *Phen.* that one can understand that, for Hegel, thought is not philosophical if it is not also religious.[31] Further, it is in *Phen.* that Hegel conspicuously revealed the dominant theme, which is clearly a religious theme, of his entire philosophy, namely, that "in thinking I lift myself up to the Absolute above all that is finite, and am infinite consciousness, while I am at the same time finite consciousness." [32]

Chapter 5
The Structure of *Phenomenology* *of Spirit*

This profound work, completed in haste in October 1806 (although he decided subsequently to write a preface, which was not completed and sent to the printer until February 1807), is often difficult to understand, though one can agree with Taylor when he says that in it "we have the most powerful and exciting of Hegel's works." [1] Its profundity and its difficulty, its power and excitement lie in the fact that it is so exceptionally inclusive in the material it embraces; and yet, always, it is geared to Hegel's primary concern about the problems of the age and the emergence of a new historical epoch characterized by a harmonious unity.

In the preface Hegel stated that the time was ripe for the "elevation of philosophy to the level of science," and it is quite clear that he believed that his own age was a time of transition and that the dawn of a new epoch was imminent:

> It is not difficult to see that ours is a birth-time and a period of transition to a new era. Spirit has broken with the world it has hitherto inhabited and imagined, and is of a mind to submerge it in the past, and in the labour of its own transformation. Spirit is indeed never at rest but always engaged in moving forward. (*Phen.*, 6)

He likened his own age to the gestation period in which there is quiet, gradual growth—"quantitative growth"—but just as this is followed by the birth—"a qualitative leap"—when new life emerges, so, too, "the features of the new world" would soon come into the light of day. It was in the context of such an understanding of the times that Hegel approached the writing of his first major work, which was to be a deeply probing and critical work, one which would provide the philosophical foundation for the new epoch that was about to dawn.

But the newly born child is not yet the mature adult, and neither will the imminent new era immediately be a perfect realization of the ideal harmonious unity. A 'voyage of discovery' is required in order to achieve that knowledge of the truth which enables the attainment of this unity; and it is a voyage of discovery or an 'ascent to absolute knowledge' that is marked by a gradual, but inevitable, move toward systematic understanding.[2] Indeed, to facilitate such an ascent to absolute knowledge determined Hegel's approach in *Phen.*, which was to develop a methodology by which the standpoint of knowledge could be acquired.

As the breadth of his careful and detailed description of this journey unfolds, it becomes apparent that this work is not like any other philosophical work. It is unique, says Shklar, largely because of its daring, which consists in the fact that "Hegel undertook to explore in a single work every conceivable [type of] human experience that could be thought of as knowledge."[3] The undertaking of this exploration is vital because, in Hegel's view, it is through these experiences that the Absolute comes to self-knowledge. The extent of this exploration is also important because it reflects Hegel's abiding interest in social and cultural issues. This is quite clear from the fact that when he came to consider social consciousness, he seems to have got caught up with the fascinating movement of history[4] as he moved from a description of one form of social consciousness to another, showing how he saw the inevitable subsuming of one into a higher form until finally, with equal inevitability, we come to absolute knowledge where there is attained the true understanding of consciousness as self-knowing *Geist*. And, for Hegel, this understanding is the true perspective of *Geist*—a perspective that transcends all distinctions, for it recognizes the individual consciousness as a vehicle of *Geist* that was thus conceived of as the all-embracing unity, the cohesive force by which would be realized the unity of identity and nonidentity.

As Hegel's analysis and methodology unfold in *Phen.*, it becomes clear that it was built upon, as Lukács says, "a synthesis of the systematic and historical approach." Indeed, Hegel's interest in, and the importance he placed upon, history is so significant that Lukács says that Hegel's "historicism determines both the method and the structure of *Phen.*" He goes on to quote Engels as providing a clear and succinct formulation of the fundamental method of *Phen.*: " 'one may call it a parallel of the embryology and the paleontology of the mind, a development of individual consciousness through its different stages, set in the form of an abbreviated reproduction of the stages through which the consciousness of man has passed in the course of history.' " [5]

It does seem that here Engels has summed up that which provides the fascination of *Phen.* The voyage that is being charted for human consciousness is also the route along which humanity has evolved, so that the mapping of the road involves not only systematic analysis but also historical description, for "what Hegel is concerned with in *Phen.* is the acquisition by the individual of the experience of the species." [6] Hegel himself clearly stressed the importance of this relationship between the experience of the individual and that of humanity as a whole:

> The individual whose substance is the more advanced Spirit runs through this past just as one who takes up a higher science goes through the preparatory studies he has long since absorbed, in order to bring their content to mind: he recalls them to the inward eye, but has no lasting interest in them. (*Phen.*, 16)

Thus, the experiences of the individual consciousness in its process of development are also those of humanity in its evolution—and not just theoretical experience, but the whole of experience,[7] and it is "a development, a process of maturing which ends with an understanding of the purpose and significance of the voyage." [8] But this voyage—this process of maturing and development of human thought—is one whose destination is not arbitrary, for each stage in this journey of human consciousness is "appointed for it by its own nature," [9] and the whole journey is "an unfolding of our potentialities which we are spiritually self-driven to realize." [10]

However, the structure of *Phen.* is not simply determined by the experiences of individual consciousness and of humanity in society and history. Certainly those experiences were there to be described, but Hegel obviously shaped that description in "a creative act of remembering," as is observed by Shklar, who also successfully discerns the broad sweep of that creative act: "In the course of this fantastic project Hegel moved from an account of Everyman's simple awareness of knowing something to his realization that he must know himself if he is to know what knowledge is. From seeking this self-knowledge the individual is ineluctably driven to seek knowledge of what man generally, what humanity, is. That knowledge eludes him. Hegel then followed all the religious, ideological, theoretical, moral, cultural and historical dispositions of the mind that prevent it from reaching its end. Yet these failures are intellectually creative and instructive and in reviewing them we are led step by step to the door of truth." [11]

Having thus sketched the broad sweep, in more detail the structure of *Phen.* can be seen to reflect the double-sided nature of Hegel's subject of thought. In it he presented his penetrating perception of both the evolution of individual consciousness and the evolution of humanity in society and history: thus, *Phen.* is about the evolution of the human spirit in individual consciousness and in social consciousness—an evolution of the human spirit that is the increasing of its awareness (however vague) of what it is to be spirit. But *Phen.* also discloses a parallel development—the dialectical movement of the journey toward the comprehension of *Geist,* the emergence of the consciousness of absolute *Geist* that Hegel presented through the progressive stages of religion and philosophy and without which all that spirit is could not be realized.

In a sense *Phen.* could have begun with any one of these three aspects of the evolution of the human spirit—individual consciousness, social consciousness, or consciousness of *Geist:* time and again, in Hegel's presentation of each form of consciousness, the same basic patterns are reflected. But, in fact, Hegel began with the evolution of the human spirit in individual consciousness because he was concerned to begin where the individual, who is the basic unit of society and the highest form of the manifestation of *Geist,* finds himself.

The Evolution of the Human Spirit in Individual Consciousness

Consciousness

In his analysis of the evolution of individual consciousness, Hegel's starting point was the ordinary experience of the individual in everyday life, namely, the immediate awareness of an external object (an 'other') that comes through sense impressions. Human existence implies consciousness, and Hegel began with a study of this in its most elementary form—what he simply called "consciousness" in the form of "Sense-Certainty," where the quest for certain knowledge is thought to be achievable by means of sense-impressions.

The knowledge or knowing which is at the start or is immediately our object cannot be anything else but immediate knowledge itself, a knowledge of the immediate or of what simply *is*. (*Phen.,* 58)

Here 'knowledge' is of something that terminates at the known object: all discourse is about the thing—the 'this'—not the knowing subject—the 'I'—that consequently gets absorbed by the object.

Hegel's analysis of "Consciousness," however, includes a demonstration that this mode of experience, like any other, contains elements that undermine its confidence in its ability to perceive "the real", and that therefore force the search to proceed to ever higher modes of understanding. The advance to these higher modes is thus an internal process of experience and is not produced from without: if a person pays strict attention to the results of experience, he will abandon one type of knowledge and proceed to another.

For Hegel, progress in this journey is achieved by means of the dialectical movement, and initially, this movement is entered upon by asking, "What is the *This?*" As soon as one is required to say something about the particular of which one is aware, one realizes the universal character of language, for in order to describe the particular it is necessary to use words like *house* or *tree*, etc., and these are words that do not refer only to *this* particular but to many particulars that have certain features in common: thus the mind is forced to turn its focus from the particular to the general.[12]

The same point is concluded in regard to the knowing subject. According to Hegel's analysis, when pressed it becomes apparent that the 'I' is not a pure particular, but is universal, for it is governed by the same dialectical movement as the object. 'I' can be used not only by a particular individual I as a means of self-reference, but can be used by any individual. As the term 'this', so the term 'I' has a universal application. "Sense-experience thus discovers that truth lies neither with its particular object nor with the individual I."[13]

Sense-certainty, which began with the apprehension of a supposedly independent, external object, ends by demonstrating the reality of the universal as the true content of experience. So Hegel's analysis identified the inner contradiction of sense-certainty: that on which the certainty is founded is really unattainable. It is the presence of contradiction that is the driving power of the dialectical process, and thereby sense-certainty must pass over into "Perception" which

takes what is present to it as a universal. Just as universality is its principle in general, the immediately self-differentiating moments within perception are universal: 'I' is a universal and the object is a universal. That principle has arisen for us, and therefore the way we take in perception is no longer something that just happens to us like sense-certainty; on the contrary, it is logically necessitated. (*Phen.*, 67)

Perception, therefore, necessarily takes up the problem of universality. While, like sense-experience, it collects evidence from the object, the object is no longer apprehended as a 'This', but is comprehended as a 'thing' that possesses certain properties, and these properties are recognized as being held in common with many other things. Thus, the mind no longer regards itself as a mere receptacle of sensations, for it now grasps the objects through aspects they have in common, and this is an advance, for the mind is actively doing something and not just passively absorbing what comes to it from external objects. Furthermore, this grasping of the objects through aspects they have in common means that they are no longer being grasped in their own particularity and that the mind "thereby transcends the singularity [of the object]." [14]

However, Perception also gives rise to a contradiction, namely, the tension between, on the one hand, the thing's unity (it is *one* thing) and distinctiveness (it is *distinct* from other things), and on the other hand, its diversity (it is characterized by a multiplicity of properties) and universality (it has properties in common with other things). Consciousness comes to see that the thing itself manifests itself in this twofold way: the thing is of this twofold contradictory nature—being both one and diverse—"in and for itself"; but it is also this "for another", for "what a thing is 'for itself' is inseparable from what it is 'for another', i.e., in relation to other things and to their properties." [15] Yet, it is this being-what-it-is 'for another' as well as 'for itself' that is the destruction of the perception of the thing as an isolated, independent, self-existent 'one', and the presence of this contradiction necessitates the dialectical move into the sphere of "Scientific Understanding".

In the form of consciousness that Hegel called Perception the mind endeavors to grasp the 'thing', the object of sense-experience, by describing its properties. The ensuing contradiction demonstrates the self-destructiveness of this process of description, for it forces the mind to go beyond it, to analyze the evidence of the senses to discover some unobservable entity by which the contradiction of the descriptive process can be resolved and the thing ultimately explained.

Hegel here introduced, in the following way, the concept of 'force' as the means of explaining how the diverse and complex thing is held together as a self-determining unity:

One moment, then, appears as the essence that has stepped to one side as a universal medium, or as the subsistence of independent 'matters'. But the independence of these 'matters' is nothing else than this medium; in other words, the [unconditioned] universal is simply and solely the *plurality* of the diverse universals of this kind . . . the 'matters' posited as independent directly pass over into their unity, and their unity directly unfolds its diversity, and this once again reduces itself to unity. But this movement is what is called *Force*. (*Phen.*, 81)

This, Shklar observes, "is still a belief in knowledge as consciousness of objects lying outside us, but not as mere sense-evidence. That is an immense leap because the primitive hyper-empiricism of the natural mind and of common sense has been given up." [16]

However, the same difficulty that appeared on the level of Perception regarding the tension between unity and diversity was here identified by Hegel regarding a tension between appearances and forces. Once again, a dichotomy emerges. On the one hand, there is the observable diverse, changing world, which is taken as the effect of the inner forces, and is only those forces expressing themselves in an external way. On the other hand, there are the unobservable inner unitary forces, which are taken to be the cause of the multiplicity of external appearances, and yet these forces are nothing but those appearances. Just as on the level of Perception the essential truth of reality was identified as consisting equally of the contradictory concepts of unity and diversity, so here it is identified as consisting equally of the contradictory concepts of inner force and external appearances.

Therefore, again in keeping with the dialectic, an advance gives rise to a new problem of contradiction; and this is due, in this instance, to the fact that "the inner world is, for consciousness, still a *pure beyond*, because consciousness does not as yet find itself in it." [17] As this inner "supersensible world" is taken to be the "true world", the task confronting 'Understanding' is to endeavor to penetrate this 'beyond' to find explanations for "the absoulte flux of appearance". At this stage, such explanations take the form of laws, but it quickly becomes apparent that they do not really *explain* the nature of the world of appearances, for Law merely *describes* that world. Therefore, the laws of nature do not stand behind or above the changing world of appearances as stable explanations of that world, but are only descriptions of the processes of nature: in fact, 'Understanding' has not moved beyond the level of description, even though it displays an awareness of the supersensible.

The significance of this cycle of "Consciousness" lies in the fact that Hegel regarded it as "the primordial, the basic, the primary pattern of mind which is repeated over and over again, whenever the mind has to find immediate certainty." [18] This immediate certainty of consciousness is due to its view of the world as a totality of separate, independent objects, which exist per se and which are completely independent of the knowing subject. It is in the supposed remoteness and objectivity of the external objects and the facts about them from the living, knowing subject that the feeling of being secure in this certainty of knowledge lies. But according to Hegel, this attitude is "the utmost defamation of truth," [19] and therefore, the move beyond this cycle of consciousness to the stage where man no longer sees the world as objective and estranged but recognizes himself and his own life in it is of supreme necessity. So it is that the evolution of individual consciousness progresses from "Consciousness" to the stage of "Self-Cosciousness", where there is an awareness of the self that is mediated through the object, and where the quest for certainity is through self-knowledge.

Self-Consciousness

The transition to "Self-Consciousness" is indicative of Hegel's view that self-consciousness is the truth of consciousness: the knowledge of the other is seen as a self-knowledge. This is so in a radically different way from that of Kant, according to whom knowledge of phenomena, the external separated particulars, brings self-knowledge in the sense of knowing that the self imposes certain categories on external things in the process of knowledge. But in Hegel, recognition that knowledge of an other is self-knowledge is a recognition of the self's identity with the other, so that—although the way is far from complete as yet—the transition to "Self-Consciousness" is a movement that opens the way to a recognition of "universal life" in which there is "the identity of identity and non-identity".

This transition from "Consciousness" to "Self-Consciousness" is crucial for Hegel—"with self-consciousness, then, we have therefore entered the native realm of truth" [20]—and it represents a move from the level of epistemology to the practical and social level. The key concern of Self-Consciousness is with knowledge of the self that is mediated through the object, that is, a self-knowledge that comes through relationships with other objects (practical relationships) and other people (social relationships), and the dialectical movement will occur because of contradictions that emerge between what we actually are and what we are potentially.[21] Self-fulfillment is the attainment of that stage in which the self no longer regards the surrounding universe as something other, as a limitation; the human longing for integrity can only be frustrated so long as man sees himself as a finite being depending on other things in the surrounding world, but that longing finds fulfillment as man comes to recognize himself in the 'other' so that it loses its appearance as 'other', as man undergoes "transformations which will raise him to a grasp of the universal." [22]

The course of the transformations begins with self-consciousness in the form of "desire". The self is concerned still with external objects, but with the attainment of self-awareness he no longer regards them as independent objects, information about which the self receives passively, as in the stage of "Consciousness". Self-awareness can appear only when knowledge of the object includes a consciousness of a relation between the object and the knower, which, Hegel said, is first perceived as desire to subordinate the object to the wishes, and for the satisfaction, of the self. This 'cancelling' the object's otherness is part of the drive for self-integrity, and it totally reveals the self and makes him conscious of himself.

And self-consciousness is thus certain of itself only by superseding this other that presents itself to self-consciousness as an independent life; self-consciousness is Desire. Certain of the nothingness of this other, it explicitly affirms that this nothingness is *for it* the truth of the other; it destroys the independent object and thereby gives itself the certainty of itself as a *true* certainty, a certainty which has become explicit for self-consciousness itself *in an objective manner*. (*Phen.*, 109)

However, the basic desire of self-consciousness can be fulfilled only by another self-consciousness,[23] because recognition by an other is an essential element in the process of coming to self-awareness. Man desires more than the common capability of all animals to cancel the otherness of—and appropriate for himself—other objects, such as food, in order to satisfy his own needs and desires. Such objects are incapable of reciprocating: they are not able to negate or cancel the otherness of external objects, and therefore man cannot acquire self-consciousness through them. What is needed is a reciprocating reality—another self, capable of recognizing him as a person. Here two important Hegelian claims appear: first, about the nature of self-knowledge, namely, that the self needs to "be aware of himself as an object of possible awareness for other human beings";[24] and secondly, about the essentiality of mutual recognition, for man "*is* only by being acknowledged or recognized" by others.[25]

This mutual recognition is a vital point on the road to man's realization that the surrounding universe is not 'other'; mutual recognition, Hegel said, "brings us to the reality of *Geist*," for it is the point at which *Geist* first appears on the dialectical stage. Here recognition is not just the recognition of an object as active or productive or usable for a particular purpose; it is recognition of the other as a person—not just the simple awareness of the other's existence, but the recognition of the other "as an *independent and autonomous agent*." [26] The reciprocity of this recognition is also essential as the point at which *Geist* enters the dialectical process, for it involves the mutual awareness of relationships, the breaking down of separating barriers, and the healing of estrangement.[27]

Thus the movement of the self beyond sense-certainty, and even beyond the initial stage of self-certainty, eventuates: as the self of 'Consciousness' sought security in the passive certainty about external objects, and as the self of 'self-certainty' found awareness of itself in its desire for external objects, here the self actively aspires to the truth by facing "another human being in mutual recognition and communion." [28] The situation is a paradoxical or dialectical one: *Being-for-itself* is also *Being-for-another; "Self* needs the other in order to be itself." [29] Yet this paradox has within it the inevitability of experiences of "a divided self" that must be encountered along the way toward the full realization of *Geist*.

Such experiences begin, within the dialectic of self-consciousness, with the self's first spontaneous reaction when confronted by another. Being as yet without recognition of the universal, and aware of himself only as a particular individual, the self desires recognition by the other, and also desires to "supersede the otherness" of the other self in order to assert his own selfhood, while refusing to reciprocate that recognition. Conflict is inevitable because the other self approaches the relationship in an identical manner, and Hegel's view was that it is only through risking of life in the conflict that true freedom can be attained, for the one who is prepared to risk bare existence for the possibility of self-fulfillment through recognition by the other is the one who emerges as the master, while the one who is satisfied with mere survival emerges in servitude.

However, the paradox of this master-slave relationship consists in the fact that the master becomes locked in a position of supremacy that he wants only to maintain; but it is really one of dependence and unfreedom, and therefore of no fulfillment, for he is dependent on the slave both for his position of supremacy and for the products he enjoys. But those products, not being the result of his own work, do not reflect him and he cannot recognize himself in them. On the other hand, the slave is reflected in them, for they are the result of his mastery over raw materials, and he can therefore recognize himself in them. Also, the slave begins to grasp the universal: through his production of goods he begins to think in universal concepts, and through his fear of death he realizes the contingency of the particular self and so recognizes the lasting reality of the universal. Thus, the position of the slave—unlike that of the master—has the potential for improvement, and in this the slave has already won a certain freedom, for he has come closer to overcoming the feeling of the alien nature of things. Here is a crucial point in the Hegelian dialectic of human consciousness: the slave has begun to grasp that the objective world is really subjective.

However, because of the failure of both master and slave to achieve that self-fulfillment for which they were striving, consciousness seeks its independence and freedom, irrespective of actual circumstances, by retreating from the external world into an inner world of pure thought. This is the characteristic of Stoicism, which collapses in the contradiction of a pure thought that is unrelated to the world of experience. Yet, the response to this failure is one that proves to be imprisoned in a worse contradiction, that of the sceptical consciousness, which strives for independence and freedom by denying the *reality* of the world.

The master-slave relationship reappears, internalized in the individual, as "Unhappy Consciousness". Whereas in the master-slave relationship the requirements for the achievement of full self-consciousness were divided between the two individual consciousnesses, now "the subject has to accept the fact of inner division *(Entzweiung)*, in which the inner self itself is painfully divided into an ideal immutable and self-identical being on one side and one plunged in a world of confusion and change on the other." [30] Hegel's description of 'Unhappy Consciousness' throws light on some aspects of his opinions concerning religion, and therefore will be considered in more detail in another context. But in the broad sweep of the dialectical movement, it brings to a close the cycle of "Self-Consciousness" in which the subject has been brought to a realization of his universal nature. But again there is failure to discover an adequate resting-place in this search, and so it leads on to the third stage of individual consciousness, "Reason", in which the individual discerns the rationality of objective reality and gradually comes to the awareness that human society and history are the product of human activity.

Reason

In looking back to preceding stages of Hegel's phenomenological presentation of the dialectic, one can recall that in the various forms of "Consciousness" the individual was aware of an 'other', external objects; and that in the various forms of "Self-Consciousness" the individual became aware of himself, but only as being in opposition to other things that he desired and upon which he could work. But the failure of the individual thereby to achieve self-fulfillment caused him to withdraw into himself, then to deny the reality of the other, and finally, in the case of the unhappy consciousness, to be convinced that "the in-itself is the beyond of itself." [31]

The problems of the cycle of "Self-Consciousness" were due to the individual consciousness being aware of the self only as an *individual* standing in a relationship of *opposition* to other realities. But in Hegel's analysis, these problems are overcome in the cycle of "Reason" because there is gathered up together the concept of universality, which was perceived in "Consciousness" in relation to external objects, and the awareness of the individual self, which was grasped in "Self-Consciousness", so that the finite subject rises to a concept of universal self-consciousness. Here self-consciousness

> discovers the world as *its* new real world, which in its per-
> manence holds an interest for it which previously lay only in
> its transiency; for the *existence* of the world becomes for self-
> consciousness its own *truth* and *presence;* it is certain of expe-
> riencing only itself therein.
>   Reason is the certainty of consciousness that it is all reality.
> (*Phen.,* 140)

Thus, Reason is the consciousness that knows itself to be all reality. This is the starting point of Reason, where men grasp the notion "that rationality, that is, the principle of their own thought, determines all reality, and hence they are certain to be 'at home' in the world." [32] The apparent relationship of opposition, of which the individual consciousness was aware in the previous cycle, now disappears, and it becomes one of acceptance—a positive, rather than a negative, relationship[33]—and there is "a confidence that the world is rational and can be rationally understood. There are no incomprehensible mysteries, nothing that is in principle beyond the reach of rational understanding." [34]

This starting point of "Reason"—that "Reason is the certainty of being all *reality*"—was described by Hegel as Idealism. At first it is a mere abstraction, known only by philosophers: this reality is "a universal pure and simple, the pure *abstraction* of reality." [35] However, in positing such an *"abstract Notion* of Reason to be the True," this Idealism becomes involved in a contradiction, for "reality directly comes to be for it a reality that is just as much *not* that of Reason, while Reason is at the same time supposed to be all reality." [36]

Therefore, the truth of Reason, that it is all reality, cannot remain an abstraction, even though it may be known with certainty; it must be raised to the level of being known as a truth with real content.

The process whereby this abstract truth becomes concrete truth works itself through the three stages of the cycle of "Reason", which, in turn, repeat the movement of "Consciousness" and "Self-Consciousness", though at a higher level, and come, finally, to a synthesis in the single truth of the universality of Reason.

The movement begins with "Observing Reason", which reiterates the movement of "Consciousness" in that it is a stage in which a consciousness stands in a relation to a reality outside itself. However, it is the movement of Consciousness at a higher level, for consciousness is no longer merely affected by an external reality, but actively observes that reality, being conscious of itself as an active reason and of the external reality as an embodiment of reason.

The outcome of this stage of the dialectic, however, is the realization that the movement has been in the wrong direction. Reason will not discover itself in this relationship of consciousness to external things; it will continue to be the case that "Reason takes itself to be *all thinghood*," without becoming conscious of its infinitude, if "the self [remains] fixed as self, the thing fixed as thing, and yet each is supposed to be the other." [37]

Thus, the dialectic of "Reason" returns to the movement of "Self-Consciousness" in "The Actualization of Rational Self-Consciousness through its own Activity". It is, of course, self-consciousness at a higher level, for it is rational self-consciousness, and in this stage attention is turned away from reason's observation of the physical world to the rational activity of a self-conscious reason. At the beginning, individual self-conscious reason knows itself to be reason—but abstractly, and the dialectic here is the endeavor of the individual self-conscious reason to give itself content. The process is a search for recognition, and at this stage it is through the individual's self-affirmation in relation to others. This self-affirmation is by means of the individual's own activity, and it is apparent that this is the right direction to move in the quest for the universality of reason because this stage of "Reason" produces a recognition of reason in other self-conscious individuals. The individual self-consciousness attributes to others what it finds in itself; it is aware of something universal about itself in that it shares something with all humankind, and thus, "having raised itself into universality, it becomes *universal* Reason, and is conscious of itself as Reason, as a consciousness that is already recognized in and for itself, which in its pure consciousness unites all self-consciousness." [38]

Because that which "unites all self-consciousness" is seen to be "its own pure consciousness," the truth of Reason is pursued in rational individuality itself—hoping to find its fulfillment in itself in that which it shares with others—in the third stage of "Reason", "Individuality which takes itself to be real in and for itself". "In so doing, consciousness has cast away all opposition and every condition affecting its action, it starts afresh from *itself*, and is occupied not with an *other*, but with *itself*." [39] The end result of this process, however, is that the "individual self-consciousness, after making every possible attempt to find itself by looking only into itself, comes to the realization that this is not enough. The universal dimension of human spirit is not to be attained by simply generalizing what is essentially individual; rather, the individual is to be recognized for what it essentially is by turning to the subjective universal which is spirit." [40]

The Evolution of the Human Spirit in Social Consciousness

To this point in *Phen.*, Hegel's general procedure has been to describe what he regarded as the characteristic attitude or viewpoint at each stage, then to analyze it, identifying the inherent contradiction that is involved, and thereby demonstrasting how human consciousness is compelled to proceed to another stage that is seen to be more adequate. The methodological procedure continues as Hegel now launches into his descriptive analysis—in the section titled "Spirit"—of human history.

What marks the transition to this stage is that the individual is no longer the abstractly singular individual, but comes to the discovery of community. In the 'peculiar shapes' of Reason, the self-consciousness knows or seeks itself only in the immediate present, and so remains on the level of individual consciousness, with no interest in Spirit. But the transition point from individual consciousness to social consciousness has been reached. By means of the dialectical progress Hegel has traced the development of individual consciousness to the position where it can transcend its own individuality, comprehend itself as an expression of the human spirit, and thereby understand the significance of history as the manifestation and development of the human spirit.

Reason is Spirit when its certainty of being all reality has been raised to truth, and it is conscious of itself as its own world, and of the world as itself. (*Phen.*, 263)

Following the pattern of his threefold analysis in other sections of *Phen.*, "Spirit" is divided into three stages, and these coincide with what Hegel regarded as "the great crises and turning-points in human history and in the history of man's consciousness." [41] The three stages of "Spirit" are: A. "The *true* Spirit, the ethical order", in which he considered the communal society of the Greeks and its degeneration into the individualized society of the Roman Empire; B. "Self-alienated Spirit, Culture", in which he dealt with Western Christian society from the end of the ancient world through the feudal age, and the rise of the modern world to the Englightenment and the French Revolution; C. "Spirit that is certain of itself, Morality", in which his attention was given to his own post-Revolution era.[42]

The manner in which Hegel presented his concept of 'Spirit' in this section of *Phen.* involved a descriptive analysis of types of historical epochs—of peoples and states and their moral and political institutions—and a tracing through of the tragic failures of the human spirit in its endeavors to find fulfillment in the various types of historical epochs up to Hegel's own era. He sought to demonstrate how the necessary dissolution of ancient society occurred, how the contradictory forms of civil society came to constitute a higher stage of human development arising out of this dissolution, and also how the contradictions of civil society might be reconciled. However, although Hegel thus continued his methodological procedure, there is here, in one sense, a distinct change in his style, for he was dealing with real historical forms: "These shapes are distinguished from the previous ones by the fact that they are real Spirits, actualities in the strict meaning of the word, and instead of being shapes merely of consciousness, are shapes of a world" [43]

Hegel here became immersed in history, whereas in earlier stages of *Phen.* it was only a purely abstract analysis of historical epochs to which he alluded, with history being used to provide illustrations of what he regarded as novel and necessary developments of consciousness. For example, in this probing the unfolding of consciousness, the master-slave dialectic was significant in the development of Self-Consciousness; but in his examination of Spirit, his introduction of the "Noble and Ignoble Consciousness," though a return to the principles of the earlier master-slave discussion, is so no longer in an abstract manner, but in a concrete, historical context. Hegel was thereby illustrating a concrete interpretation of the master-slave dialectic and demonstrating how that dialectic functions in a historical setting.

This qualitative difference between these first two parts of *Phen.* can be summarized in Hegel's own words: "What observation knew as a *given* object in which the self had no part, is here a given custom, but a reality which is at the same time the deed and the work of the subject finding it." [44] And therefore such realities cannot be seen as external to the self: these "social standards must be viewed as capable of *entering into* the self's selfhood, i.e., as capable of *being appropriated by* the process of individual self-making. If incapable of being so viewed, they would necessarily be external to the self-making process; the social whole sustained by them would be indistinguishable from the natural whole; and the self about to achieve or augment its selfhood would be forced to tear itself loose from both. . . . The terms needed for the philosophic grasp of the nature and genesis of social standards, then, cannot be wholly other than those used in the preceding section." [45]

This becoming immersed in history leads on to the realization of the unity of subjective and objective reality in the absolute, in *Geist*. Indeed, the whole dialectical movement of *Phen.* is a journey toward the comprehension of *Geist*, toward the realization of this unity, and it is in 'Religion' that there is first displayed "the consciousness of absolute *Geist*".

The Evolution of Religious Consciousness: Consciousness as Self-knowing *Geist*

Before religious consciousness can emerge, the dialectical path had to lead to the discovery of community (which, in *Phen.*, Hegel found in the stage of "Spirit"), because religious experience, in all its expressions, is a corporate experience.[46] It is the religious consciousness that begins to grasp the goal of *Phen.*, for in it the consciousness of absolute *Geist*, as self-knowing *Geist*,, is first displayed. However, religious consciousness is not uniform in its comprehension of *Geist*: this perception is the product of an evolution of religious consciousness, and so the dialectical movement is presented as proceeding through diverse levels of religious consciousness to the ultimate level in "absolute" or "revealed *(manifest)* religion". Throughout the dialectic of "Spirit", the understanding of history was still that of the manifestation and development of the *human* spirit, whereas for Hegel the truth is grasped only when it is perceived as being also, and fundamentally, the manifestation and development of absolute *Geist*. This is the perception attained in *Manifest* Religion.

Thus, religion was presented as occupying a crucial role in the whole dialectical process: religion was the necessary next step beyond "Spirit" ("spirit, i.e. as immediate spirit, which is not yet conscious of spirit"), in that while it presupposes insights gained throughout the preceding stages of consciousness, it is the totality of those insights and more; it is the pure recognition of self in the other, which has been implicit in previous stages but not realized. Those previous stages had culminated in "Spirit in the form of Conscience", in which spirit is certain of itself and finds freedom in itself; but even in that highest moment of "Spirit" there is still an awareness of conflict between the world of the universal, of spirit, and the world of actuality. It is only when human consciousness is religious that this conflict can be resolved because religious consciousness recognizes them as not two worlds, but one and the same world; yet, not all levels of religious consciousness achieve this recognition, for there is only a gradual coming to this recognition throughout the dialectic of religious consciousness, and it is not attained until the highest level of that dialectic, namely, "Manifest Religion." [47]

However, religion is only the penultimate stage in the dialectical movement: *Phen.* clearly reflects Hegel's mature view of religion— that religion is not the highest expression of truth—which he had reached earlier in his Jena years. Even at the highest level of religion the consciousness of absolute *Geist* that is reached is said to be inadequate: the attainment is oblique because, in Hegel's view, all levels of religious consciousness find their expression only in terms of *Vorstellungen*, and the grasping of the truth of *Geist* is attained with clarity only in the next and ultimate stage of the dialectic— Philosophy or "Absolute Knowledge".

Thus, having started with the ordinary individual consciousness of things as objects, in *Phen.* Hegel has traced his own vision of the movement of consciousness—always, and in his characteristic fashion, presenting "the spontaneous development of an experience as it offers itself to consciousness and in the way that it offers itself." [48] It has to be agreed that there is no single way of describing the sequences of *Phen.*: despite his great historical interest, those sequences certainly may not be described as consistently chronological. *Phen.* is a "creative act", an "intelligible reordering". But "the principles of ordering differ. One, the movement from sense-perception to self-consciousness, is borrowed from Kant. Sometimes Hegel depended on chronology. And occasionally, when he discusssed moral attitudes, the pattern is psychological. In every case, however, Hegel has invented the links that tie his models of thought together. It is history as art, but since he does not defend his decisions they do seem arbitrary, though not random. The ordering is always made to seem plausible, even though there is no evidence to prove its necessity or advantages over other possibilities." [49]

Hegel, however, was confident that he was engaged in the unfolding of the natural movement of consciousness, which is a progressive rise of spirit governed by the dialectic that is lived and experienced by ordinary consciousness. For Hegel, it was this that determined the structure of *Phen.*[50] It was the dialectic together with the Hegelian notion of contradiction that played a vital role in the movement of *Phen.*: dialectical change occurs in consciousness because things-as-thought are permeated by contradiction, and it is important to understand precisely what Hegel meant by it. The development of consciousness occurs throughout *Phen.* because each stage, up to and including the penultimate stage of Religion, breaks down in some form of contradiction and is consequently replaced by a new stage of development. This breaking down of the old position and the emergence of the new always involves a certain negative aspect, in that consciousness gives up views about life and the nature of reality that it held to be true; and furthermore, such a transition is not achieved without the experience of conflict, doubt and despair.[51] However, what is involved in this conflict and the 'giving up' is only partially grasped if it is seen purely from a negative viewpoint,[52] for it must be perceived in the light of Hegel's use of *aufheben*, which provides the key to fully understanding his idea of the nature of dialectical progression.[53] Then the journey of consciousness can be seen to progress as each particular stage is negated through the realization of contradictions involved in it, and consciousness is driven to resolve such conflicts by 'giving up' views that are seen to involve contradiction, though not in the sense of totally discarding, but in the sense of taking up and uniting the contradictory element with newly perceived elements in a higher level of understanding.[54]

In summing up the structure and movement of *Phen.*, one can turn to some introductory words of Hegel himself: This exposition:

> can be regarded as the path of the natural consciousness which passses forward to true knowledge; or as the way of the Soul which journeys through the series of its own configurations as though they were the stations appointed for it by its own nature, so that it may purify itself for the life of the Spirit, and achieve finally, through a completed experience of itself, the awareness of what it really is in itself. (*Phen.*, 49)

The transversing through these stations is the movement of spirit from one kind of knowledge to another; it is the journey of human experience, which sets off from a position of security based on a supposed certainty, but quickly moves on from this position as the superficiality of the certainty is realized—and thus the route to real knowledge, the quest for truth, is embarked upon. The stations encountered along the journey are the changing recognitions in the relation between consciousness and its objects. The journey that individual consciousness is to traverse is also the long and troubled historical process of humanity, one in which individual consciousness advances from 'Consciousness' to 'Self-Consciousness' and then to 'Reason', and one during which substance is being transformed into subject. However, the occurring of this transformation is also the process by which *Geist* comes to self-realization and fulfillment: the initial stages of individual consciousness are those in which consciousness is regarded as being confronted by an objective and fixed world—both nature and human society—that is a world of particularity and plurality; but by the process of interacting with this world, consciousness advances to more mature stages in which particularlity and plurality are progressively interpreted as universality and unity. Thereby substance is being transformed into subject, *Geist* is coming to fulfillment. The path of this process is the route of *Phen.:* to follow it is to sense the amazing comprehensiveness of Hegel's vision of life and to become aware, not least, of Hegel's conviction of the essentiality of the religious dimension of life as Spirit.

Chapter 6

The Role of Religion in Hegel's Philosophy

The treatment of religion in *Phen.* is marked by a daunting complexity and yet also a fascinating attractiveness, and this is indicative of the role of religion in Hegel's philosophy. Hegel regarded religion as "consciousness of *absolute Being*", and therefore, since the whole dialectical movement of *Phen.* is a journey toward the complete comprehension of absolute Being, one can say that it is religious consciousness that begins to grasp the goal of the entire *Phen.* But of course religious consciousness is not uniform in its level of comprehension of the Absolute; and Hegel reflected this by the dialectical movement proceeding through diverse levels of religious consciousness, just as that movement proceeds through diverse levels at every stage of the development of consciousness through various cognitive and social attitudes.

It is these numerous and diverse stages of the development of consciousness in *Phen.* that give to this work its great complexity and also its stimulating fascination, and that indicate the intricate and interrelated, as well as the penultimate, role of religion. It has already been observed that in Hegel's philosophical formation the chief motivating concerns were the realization of the rational autonomy of individual consciousness, the recognition of the wholeness and oneness of reality, and the attainment of these potentially contradictory goals through the proper understanding and function of true religion, the Christian religion. Now, having turned to *Phen.*, it can be said that this work superbly reflects these Hegelian concerns, and demonstrates with considerable clarity Hegel's conviction that, without religion, autonomy and wholeness cannot be achieved—all that the absolute, *Geist*, is could not be realized.

It has also been noted that *Phen.* is about the evolution of Spirit in individual consciousness, in social consciousness, and in consciousness as self-knowing *Geist*, and that, in a sense, because the same basic patterns are reflected in each of these three aspects of the dialectic of Spirit, *Phen.* could have begun with any one of them. There are obvious reasons why Hegel began precisely where he did, but his manner of presentation, with the constantly repeating basic patterns, does suggest a methodological difficulty—which both Fackenheim and Christensen identify—and also suggests another point about the role of religion in Hegel's philosophical method.

The methodological difficulty is to be found in the fact that the standpoint from which Hegel viewed every stage of the dialectical progress to absolute knowledge was the absolute standpoint itself—which was also the goal of the dialectical progress. Viewed from such a standpoint, each of the stages along the dialectical road was seen "as necessarily pointing beyond themselves to absolute knowledge"—hence the basic pattern: each stage is replaced by a 'higher' stage—"and only as he reaches absolute knowledge does he justify the standpoint from which he has done his viewing." [1]

It is true, as Fackenheim further observes, that "the gap between viewing and viewed standpoints must gradually narrow," [2] but the adoption of the viewing standpoint must also allow the preservation of the forms of human life that are represented by the viewed standpoints, and for this to occur there must necessarily be a bridge between the viewing and the viewed standpoints. In an important sense, the role of religion in *Phen.* can be seen as such a bridge.

In the first three sections of *Phen.*—"Consciousness," "Self-Consciousness," and "Reason"—Hegel presented his endeavor to trace the development of human consciousness to the state of rational autonomy, a development which can be described, in Fackenheim's terms, as a "double process of self-making and self-knowing." [3] Yet, such a development does not, and cannot, occur in the self's solitary isolation, but only in the context of some social and historical process. It has already been observed, through quotations from Hegel and Fackenheim, that these processes cannot be simply external to the self, but it must also be noted that neither can they be regarded simply as a collective product of individual selves. They must be represented by "the concept of a social whole" that is "somehow more than the individual selves which compose it," and yet that "can be more only if it allows self-hood full scope, i.e., if it includes or leaves room for it." [4] However, it is in this leaving room for selfhood that social and historical processes are exposed to being transformed by the self-asserting activity of individual selves, and thus there must be recognized an inextricable link between the two— a "spiritual bond between them [that] must be a tension as well as a union." [5]

So it can be seen that Hegel's presentation was designed to show the interrelatedness of the dialectic of human consciousness and the dialectic of human society and history: they stand in a mutually effective relationship with each other, and each dialectic consists of stages which recapitulate attitudes of corresponding moments of the other dialectic—though the dialectic of society and history is not merely the "collective product" of the dialectic of consciousness, for it goes beyond it and places the latter in "a richer and truer context".

However, it was Hegel's claim that the whole dialectical process of *Phen.* culminates in the point—which is also the viewpoint from which the whole process is being presented—at which there is the complete grasping of the absolute, Spirit; and this would remain quite unattainable if the dialectical process were confined to the development of human society and history, for "a history as thus far understood . . ., itself finite, could only produce . . . spiritual standpoints themselves confined to finitude, and philosophy, if possible at all, would share this finitude." [6]

It is in the dialectic of religious consciousness that there occurs the dimension of the infinite, and it is this that makes religion not only part of the dialectical process that was presented in *Phen.*, but also that which bridges the gap between what was presented and the viewpoint from which it was presented. The capacity of religious consciousness to provide such a bridge resides in the fact that religion appears as the natural progression beyond "Spirit" in the general dialectic, for "religion is the perfection of Spirit," [7] and in it the human consciousness progresses beyond the finite dimension to an awareness of the dimension of the infinite.

Furthermore, a consideration of the essential role of religious consciousness in the whole dialectical process of *Phen.* cannot be complete without noting that religious consciousness does not just appear as the next, or one more, stage in the spirit's advance, but that—as Lauer rightly suggests—"the phenomenology of religious consciousness recapitulates the whole of the spirit's advance." [8] Hegel offered a very distinct dialectic of religious consciousness, and that dialectic begins with the same kind of primordial attitude that is the hallmark of "Consciousness", namely, an attitude in which there is the immediate awareness of reality as object. As expressed in religious consciousness, this attitude displays itself in the understanding of absolute Being as an external and alien object, and in the concept of a fundamental distinction and separation between life and religion. As it progresses toward its culmination, religious consciousness passes through a variety of stages in which are reflected the same kinds of attitudes and insights found in the dialectic of consciousness—through the stages of "Consciousness", "Self-Consciousness", and "Reason"—and in the dialectic of human society and history—the stage of "Spirit"; and this is naturally so, for religious consciousness is not merely a new stage of the dialectic that emerges only at the completion of these other stages, but rather, the dialectic of religion, as a progressive revelation of spirit to itself, is evolving throughout the entire progression of the human spirit. This point, which is absolutely crucial to the manner in which Hegel's philosophy will be presented in this section of this thesis, is no doubt most aptly expressed in Hegel's own words:

The idea which a man has of God corresponds with that which he has of himself, of his freedom . . . when a man knows truly about God, he knows truly about himself too: the two sides correspond with each other. At first God is something quite undetermined; but in the course of the development of the human mind, the consciousness of that which God is gradually forms and matures itself, losing more and more of its initial indefiniteness, and with this the development of true *self*-consciousness advances also. (*LPR*, vol. 1, 79–80)

So it is that, in each moment of its dialectical development, the human spirit assumes a particular form that reflects the stage of development reached in its comprehension of *Geist*; and therefore in the dialectical development of religious consciousness there are successive explicit forms of religion that are appropriate to each particular stage of its evolution, and that have an affinity with the form taken by the corresponding moment in the dialectic of individual and social consciousness. While the whole dialectic of religion adds the awareness of the infinite to the development of human consciousness, it is only in its culminating stage—that of Manifest Religion—that religious consciousness achieves the discernment of the oneness of reality that, for Hegel, was the most fundamental truth.

The place of religion in Hegel's philosophy seems to be most expressively indicated by Hegel himself when he said that from the viewpoint of religion, the moments of the dialectic of individual and

social consciousness in relation to the dialectic of religious consciousness can be described as "only predicates of the Subject." [9] In other
words, it is when consciousness is religious consciousness (i.e., consciousness of absolute Being, especially in the discernment of it as
Geist in Manifest Religion) that the various stages of the development
of consciousness—as individual and social consciousness—lose their
partiality and consciousness becomes a consciousness of self as spirit,
a "consciousness of being all reality."

Religion in General

As Hegel presented it, religion appears as a natural and necessary
progression in the dialectical development of human consciousness,
for without that progression the development of human consciousness
would not achieve an awareness of spirit, of what it is to be spirit,
and would remain only "as immediate Spirit, which is not yet
conscious of Spirit." [10] The dialectic of human consciousness through
the various cycles of "Consciousness", "Self-Consciousness", "Reason", and "Spirit" is a development that is confined to the finite
dimension, and, as such, cannot rise to the truth of absolute Spirit;
it is, then, religion that is presented as the essential means "of rising
up to the True," for "religion is a departing from sensuous, finite
objects." [11] This is, for Hegel, the essential role of religion in general:
it enables human consciousness to rise to the truth of absolute Spirit.

But as has been observed many times already, religion itself,
according to Hegel, does not achieve the complete grasp of the Truth:
religion in general is of course only manifested in specific religions,
but not even the highest religion attains to the most complete grasp
of the Truth, let alone the less developed forms. Nevertheless, every
form of religion represents some grasping of that dimension of reality
which is described as "absolute", and it is this development from
one form of religion to another that constitutes Hegel's dialectic of
religion.

In a sense, each different form of religion, each specific kind of
religion, can be regarded as a moment "of religion in general": the
general notion of religion "contains the whole nature" of religion,
and the nature of religion is "the consciousness of Absolute Being,"
which is "the self consciousness of Spirit." [12] But religion in general
finds expression only in definite historical religions that develop in
human history, and the nature of these specific religions obviously
reflects some aspect of the notion of religion in general, though they
do not fully express the notion: as Hegel said, "the reality has not
as yet come to be equal to the notion" [13]—not, at any rate, until

the ultimate stage of the dialectic of religion is reached in "Manifest Religion". However, in possessing some aspect of the notion, the characteristics of each finite religion through its entire history can be said to be determined by "the determinateness of the notion itself, which can at no stage be absent"—a point that leads Hegel to add that "the thought of the Incarnation . . . pervades every religion." [14]

The totality of existence *(Dasein)* is to be understood as the nature of Spirit coming forth into existence, unfolding itself, and so bringing about the realization of the notion of itself. Just as each stage of the dialectic through "Consciousness", "Self-Consciousness", "Reason", and "Spirit" is a reflection—in terms of the development of individual consciousness and of social and historical consciousness—of a particular stage and the unfolding of the nature of Spirit, so each stage in the dialectic of religious consciousness—each specific religion—is a corresponding reflection of a particular stage of Spirit coming to consciousness of itself. In Hegel's words, religions "are determined by means of the notion. Their nature and succession are not determined from without, on the contrary, they are determined by the nature of Spirit which has entered into the world to bring itself to consciousness of itself." [15]

Within the dialectical movement from one religion to another Spirit is striving to achieve a correspondence between the character of the specific religion and the notion, but the various religions—from the Religions of Nature to those of Israel, Greece, and Rome—fall short of this: they "are not in fact as yet the true religion, and in them God is not as yet known in His true nature, since there is wanting to them the absolute content of Spirit." [16] The culmination of the dialectic of religious consciousness—in "Manifest Religion"—sees the correspondence of the content of the specific religion with the notion, for it is the attainment of the absolute content of Spirit. Furthermore, that culmination also brings about the final rising above *(aufgehoben)* the finite: whereas other moments of the dialectic of religion had achieved some awareness of an 'absolute' dimension of reality, the perception of it had confined it to either a solely naturalistic basis or a solely personal basis. But the culmination of the dialectic of religious consciousness achieves the recognition of identity (as the identity of identity and nonidentity) between all reality and absolute Spirit, with the consequence of also transforming into a unity any disunity perceived between the dialectic of individual, social, and historical consciousness on the one hand and of religious consciousness on the other:

As we now know that Spirit in its own world and Spirit conscious of itself as Spirit, or Spirit in religion, are the same, the perfection of religion consists in the two becoming identical with each other: not only that religion concerns itself with Spirit's reality but, conversely, that Spirit, as self-conscious Spirit, becomes actual to itself and *object of its consciousness*. (*Phen.*, 412)

However, this is to be attained only in the culmination of religious consciousness, which, in *Phen.*, Hegel has traced in terms of his analysis of its progress through three main stages—namely, "Religion of Nature", "Religion of Art", and "Revealed (Manifest) Religion".
The first form of religion is marked by an immediateness, where "Spirit knows itself as its object in a natural or immediate shape." [17] Here the awareness of absolute Spirit comes through the immediate experience of nature, and it is an awareness that the gods are something natural: intellectually it is a finding of absolute Spirit in natural things, though the human consciousness contributes nothing to this awareness of Spirit. The second and higher form of religion is one where the human consciousness expresses its awareness of absolute Being in forms of art that are expressions of the self, and thereby the self becomes conscious also of itself;[18] but this form of religion is also inadequate, because "the only divine presence in the work of art is what the human artist puts there." [19] The third and highest form of religion is a reconciliation of the two preceding forms, for it "overcomes the one-sidedness of the first two; the self is just as much an immediacy as the immediacy is the self." [20] Here absolute Spirit is immediately present and known as self, and self is recognized in that which is immediately known. The following quotation indicates the way in which Hegel saw the first two forms of religion being reconciled in the third, and how these forms correspond to the moments of the general dialectic of *Phen.*:

If, in the first reality, Spirit in general is in the form of consciousness, and in the second, in that of self-consciousness, in the third it is in the forms of the unity of both. It has the shape of being-in-and-for-itself; and when it is thus conceived as it is in and for itself, this is the Revealed Religion. (*Phen.*, 416)

The task now is to follow Hegel in turning to an examination of the specific dialectic of religious consciousness, and, in doing so, to notice the demonstration of his view that the pattern of the progress of religious consciousness through its various forms reflects the different levels of the dialectical progress of the human spirit. This reflection of the human spirit's progress in the progress of religious consciousness is due to the "essential principle of religion", namely, that religion is the "self-consciousness of Spirit". The dialectical progress of the human spirit from "Consciousness" to "Spirit" is the development of the human consciousness to an awareness of itself and then to an awareness of itself as spirit in the social and historical consciousness; and the dialectical development of religious consciousness is a progressive awareness of the divine spirit, culminating in the recognition of reality as a manifestation of the divine spirit.

In the light of this Hegelian recognition of reality, it means that the development of human consciousness to its own self-consciousness as spirit is also the development of divine spirit to its being present to and conscious of itself. However, as this "essential principle of religion" has "already come to light", Hegel is now concerned to examine the determinate forms of religion that appear at successive stages in the development of religious consciousness.

Chapter 7
Religion of Nature

The various determinate forms of religion that have emerged in the course of human history reflect different levels of experience and awareness of the divine by the human spirit, and conversely, the differences between one religion and another are determined by differences in the level of awareness of the divine spirit.[1] However, while there are these very real differences between religions, there are common features that were mentioned by Hegel: one is that these diverse religions all employ images or representations in order to express the awareness of the divine that has been achieved; the other is that, when the diverse religions are considered as a whole, there can be observed a common aim toward which the total progression of religious development is moving, namely, "to supersede this cardinal distinction" between consciousness and self-consciousness, so that the manifestation of the divine that is an "object of consciousness" can be seen to have "the form of self-consciousness."[2]

However, the use of images and representations in religion and the extent to which this cardinal distinction is transcended are integrally related. In the lower forms of religion God is 'represented' as an object of consciousness and is not yet experienced as "self-conscious spirit" manifested in reality and present in the self-consciousness of the human spirit. In order that this experience of God may become actual and God cease to appear as "something [merely] thought of, something alien to the self's knowledge," on the one

125

hand, it requires "the act of self-consciousness; and on the other hand, the lower determination must show itself to be reduced *(aufgehoben)* to a moment of the higher and to be comprehended by it." [3] Thus, in the process of religious development (i.e., in transcending the distinction between consciousness and self-consciousness, and in coming to the actual presence of God in the religious experience) the self comes to regard "the determination of the object as its *own*, [and] consequently beholds *itself* in that object" [4]—and thereby the lower determination of religious consciousness, which experiences God as an object presented to consciousness, is surpassed.

It is, however, with this lower determination of religious consciousness—the most primitive expression of religion, in which God is experienced as an object presented to consciousness—that Hegel began his descriptive analysis of the dialectic of religion. These primitive manifestations of religion are the religions of Nature, which were said to express "the unity of the spiritual and natural," [5] and Hegel was quite insistent in his distinguishing religion of this kind from that which, in his time, was usually referred to as 'natural religion' in contrast with 'revealed religion'. That kind of natural religion was seen to consist of that which "man is capable of discerning and knowing of God by his own unassisted powers"; but in Hegel's view, that meaning of the term 'natural religion' is "a wrong expression." [6]

On the other hand, Hegel readily agreed that, historically, natural religion (in the alternative sense in which he used the term) was the earliest form of religion; although, in opposition to those who said it is "the true, the finest, the divine religion," he declared it to be "the most imperfect religion." [7] The former view was based on the concept that natural religion was "a true original religion in the state of innocence" that obtained before the Fall: in such a state of universal harmony man stands in a perfect relationship with God, and so beholds God in an immediate manner, [8] giving rise to such true 'natural' religion. Hegel, of course, rejected such an interpretation of natural religion, but he did not summarily dismiss the concept of universal harmony as one that was totally without truth; and similarly he did not display a complete disdain for the idea of a fall from an original harmony and goodness.

The idea of a "harmony which has not yet passed over into division or dualism" Hegel acknowledged to be "in entire agreement with the Notion;" [9] and the idea of the Fall conveys the truth that man, in his evolution as a free being, had to come to "the light of consciousness and the awareness of good and evil." But it is a very different thing, Hegel believed, to assert that this state of unity was an actual historical condition that humanity once enjoyed, and to assert that at some point of time humanity 'fell' from a state of goodness; yet, the concept of natural religion as an original true religion is really dependent on such assertions, and thus cannot be sustained, but in fact must be declared to be the most primitive and imperfect form of religion.

In turning to a closer consideration of the Religion of Nature, Hegel described its specific character as generally "the unity of the Natural and Spiritual," in the sense that God "is posited as something natural." [10] But the immediate natural forms that are known as God are particular existent things—this heaven, this sun, this animal, this man—and are not to be thought of as nature in its organic totality, or even as, for example, man in his universal essentiality. Therefore, the beginning of the religion of nature is to be located in the concept that "spirit is found in an immediate, particular mode of existence," [11] though it is not to be thought that in the Religion of Nature natural objects are worshipped as God. Such a thought is distinctly excluded by the Religion of Nature's presenting the spiritual as that which is highest for man, for this indicates that it is the 'spiritually natural' and not just the 'physically natural' that is the true object of the Religion of Nature: "it is the religion of the Spiritual, but in its condition of externality, naturalness, immediacy." [12] Furthermore, a truth that is presented to consciousness by the Religion of Nature is that God always belongs to the present; and this religion can therefore continually be a reminder that the idea of God as an abstract Being beyond the present should be abandoned.[13]

In anticipating the dialectic of the "Religion of Nature", Hegel said that in the first form of that religion—that is, immediate religion or religion at its most primitive level—Spirit is still thought of as natural, for the distinction between Spirit as universal Power and as particular, contingent, transitory, and accidental forms of existence has not yet been made; and man has, at this stage, no Power higher than himself. Such a distinction "forms the second stage within the religion of nature," for it is only "with the entrance of thought that more worthy conceptions of God first appear." [14]

Such a statement, however, readily calls to mind another Hegelian assertion that has already been acknowledged as crucial to the scheme of this exposition, namely, that "the idea which a man has of God corresponds with that which he has of himself." [15] Therefore, before exploring the dialectic of the Religion of Nature, it is apposite to return to Hegel's analysis of the corresponding stage, the most elementary level, in the development of human consciousness, and to find there the basis of that correspondence, namely, significant features that are also present in the elementary level of religious consciousness.

Consciousness: From Confidence to Dilemma

As there is "immediate religion", which is religion at its most primitive level, so Hegel had identified knowledge of the most immediate kind, which is found in human consciousness at its primary and most rudimentary level.

This, as already observed, is consciousness in the form of "sense-certainty"—the immediate awareness of the world that comes through sense-experience, and an awareness that carries with it a confidence that one has immediately achieved knowledge of the truth of things as they really are.

However, this claim to have 'grasped' the particular is deceptive, and the confidence is short-lived. Any attempt to 'grasp'—to describe—the particular can be done only by means of general terms, and such descriptions do not capture the particularity of the object. Thus, the particular proves to be elusive, and in trying to grasp the object, we succeed only in showing "the fleeting, unseizable nature of the particular, and we can recover it and hold it before our gaze, as it were, only by subsuming it under a universal." [16]

The implication of this is that "it is in fact the universal that is the true [content] of sense-certainty," and that the relation between consciousness and its object is found to be the reverse of what it appeared at first.[17] Thus, the first stage of the journey of consciousness revealed an astonishing discovery: while the certainty of sense-experience has not yet been undermined, that certainty is seen to be grounded, not in the object, but in the subject, and the essential content of that certainty is, not the particular, but the universal.

Hegel then took up this matter of universality in his analysis of the next level of Consciousness, "perception", where the problem posed was that of the ambivalence between the unity and the diversity of the thing. The diversity consists in the fact that the thing is characterized by a multiplicity and complexity of properties and relationships, yet it is a unity in that it "presents itself purely as a One." [18] It is seen as 'one' in opposition to other things that are equally characterized by different combinations of diverse properties. But the particular set of properties is not arbitrary and exchangeable, for it is determined by what the thing is in itself;[19] and this also determines what properties the thing excludes, for it excludes those properties that contradict the thing being itself. However, neither the unity nor the diversity of the thing is due to the perceiving consciousness, for the thing itself "contains in its own self an opposite truth [to that which it has for the apprehending consciousness]." [20]

In the subsequent level of consciousness, the solution posited for the contradiction between diversity and unity is that diversity belongs to the world of sensory appearance whereas unity springs from some entity or entities that lie behind the observable world. The result of such a solution, however, is that reality is split into two dimensions. On the one hand, there is the force that is beyond or behind the observable properties of the thing, and it is this that is taken to be "the real"; and on the other hand, there is the thing of sensory experience whose mode of existence is now taken to be mere appearance.[21]

This notion of an inner reality behind mere appearances is clearly reminiscent of the Kantian dualism of noumena and phenomena; but it can serve equally to portray the religious dualism of God and the world, where God is wholly separate from, but makes intelligible, the diversity and conflicts of the world of sensory experience. But Hegel was equally desirous firmly to reject the one as he was fully to abolish the other.

Thus is can be seen that already *Phen.* has manifested a number of Hegelian concepts that are crucial to his philosophy in general, and not least to his philosophy of religion. But most significantly, in each of the three stages of the cycle of consciousness Hegel identified the emergence of a contradiction between opposites— particularity and universality, unity and diversity, appearance and reality—but consistently, "Hegel's theme has been the recognition that opposites coalesce," and rather than maintaining that opposed concepts are "simply abstract and separated opposites," he has claimed that "each is intelligible only in the light of the other."[22] This is vital for Hegel's whole philosophy: for him it involves the superseding of the characteristic attitude of *Verstand* whereby opposed concepts are taken to be alternatives, or at least, one is taken as being more fundamental than the other. In other words, says Norman,[23] Hegel rejected all forms of reductionism: he denied both empiricism—which says that everything is reducible to, or can be understood in terms of, the world of sensory experience—and supernaturalism, which says that everything is reducible to, or can be understood in terms of, a supersensible world.

But equally it is true that Hegel denied the dualist view: "He does not simply assert that, for example, there are *both* particulars and universals. . . . It is for him essential to understand the opposites not as separate entities but in their interconnection."[24] The significance of this for Hegel's philosophy of religion is such that on the most fundamental religious question Hegel was in conflict with the traditional theistic view, which maintains the dichotomy of God and the world.

However, the dialectic has barely begun: this awareness of "the *supersensible* or the *inner side* of objective existence" is, at this

rudimentary stage in the dialectic of human consciousness, merely
an awareness of the universal, without any hint of selfhood, and is
therefore "a long way still from being Spirit that knows itself as
Spirit." [25] Those features that make this true of the level of consciousness are reflected in the dialectic of the rudimentary stage of
religious consciousness, the Religion of Nature.

The Dialectic of the Religion of Nature

God as Light

The first form taken by religious consciousness is that of the
"Religion of Light", which Hegel took to be represented by early
Zoroastrianism.[26] In contrast to *LPR*, in *Phen.* Hegel was not attempting to examine the details of Zoroastrianism, but was presenting
it as being representative of a *type* of religious consciousness that
takes "the 'shape' of 'shapelessness' . . . this 'shape' is the pure all-
embracing and all-pervading *essential light* of sunrise, which preserves
itself in its formless substantiality. Its otherness is the equally simple
negative, *darkness*." [27] This religious consciousness corresponds to the
immediate form of spirit that manifests itself in the light of the rising
sun.

We can also recognize another important aspect of Hegel's thought
operating here, namely, that absolute Spirit 'leaves' itself as it is *an
sich*, and enters into estrangement, manifesting itself in nature; and
this concept is expressed when Hegel described this first manifestation
of spirit in the light of the rising sun as "the immediate, first
diremption *[Entzweiung]* of self-knowing absolute Spirit." In this
manifestation Spirit becomes aware of "itself in the form of *being*";
it is knowledge of the most immediate kind, which assumes "the
determination which belongs to *immediate consciousness* or to *sense-
certainty*" [28]—namely, knowledge of something 'out there', known
immediately as 'other'. But it is not exactly the same as sense-
certainty, where objects are seen simply as "filled with the contingent
determinations of sensation"—for here, where "Spirit beholds itself
in the form of *being*," "it is being that is filled with Spirit," [29] fittingly
represented by the "formless indeterminate substantiality" of Light.[30]

However, just as in the case of "sense-certainty", where the particular object proves to be unreachable and there is an attempt to
grasp the thing by describing its properties in the subsequent stage
of "perception", so here the formless substantiality of light is totally
indeterminate and therefore inadequate as a manifestation of the
inner nature of spirit. In Hegel's words, "the content developed by

this pure *being* . . . is, therefore, an essenceless by-play in this substance which merely *ascends,* without *descending* into its depths to become a subject and through the self to consolidate its distinct moments";[31] or, as Taylor explains, "this substance is not yet subject, for we have seen that subjectivity has this necessary structure whereby its external reality expresses its inner nature." [32]

Therefore, the dialectic must proceed, and this indeterminate manifestation of Spirit must "determine itself as being for self and endow its vanishing 'shapes' with an enduring subsistence." [33] The first stage of religious consciousness to give expression to a more particularized form was perceived by Hegel to reside in those religions where plants and animals are regarded as objects of religion.

Plant and Animal

In itself, self-conscious Spirit is a "unitary nature" *(Einfachheit),* and this is reflected in Spirit's manifestation of itself in the light of the rising sun; but that manifestation is in the shape of a formless substantiality, and that mere formlessness is changed into a manifestation of Spirit in specific forms as Spirit "determines its unitary nature as a manifoldness of being-for-itself." Here Spirit, manifesting itself, is "being-for-itself" in a most primitive form, as "it falls apart into the numberless multiplicity of weaker and stronger, richer and poorer Spirits." In the dialectic of religious consciousness, this is "the religion of spiritual *perception,*" and takes the form of 'Pantheism'.[34]

In the more lengthy treatment in *LPR,* Hegel spoke of Pantheism as a "consciousness of a substantial Power", by means of which all particulars—which are only "accidental" and "mere negatives"—subsist.[35] And Hegel elucidated his conception of what is involved in this stage of religious consciousness by speaking of the perception of infinitude in the finite (that is, in finite objects, such as plants and animals): "in the external manifoldness of the finite object, we at the same time behold the inner infinite unity, divine substantiality." [36]

The advance made by religious consciousness from its most rudimentary stage, which was marked by a consciousness of Spirit as a mere "formless indeterminate substantiality", is that now it is a consciousness of the universal in the particular, a consciousness of infinite unity, as manifested in the manifoldness of the finite, and as that which is the subsistence of everything. Indeed, to this consciousness the Infinite itself "becomes so really present in finite existence, the God becomes so present to it in this particularized existence, that this existence is not distinct from God, but rather is the mode in which God exists." [37]

Hegel found that this advance in religious consciousness was "a matter of the history of religion," but indeed, that this was so only because of something far more profound: first, that "it is necessitated by the notion." [38] It has been noted repeatedly, and Hegel said again in this section of *LPR*, that in his view the different religions are expressions of a stage in the "process of the unfolding or development [of the notion] which is Spirit," so that each determinate religion "is not merely this external form, but is what is innermost in the determining Spirit. It unites both in itself." [39] But secondly, the advance in religious consciousness is due also to the nature of thought: it is man alone, as a thinking being, who has religion, and this progression in religion to the consciousness of the universal, the Infinite, is identical to the dialectical development of human consciousness generally. "We think of an object; in doing so, we come to have its law, its essence, its universal element before us";[40] and so, from the finite as the point of departure, religious consciousness comes to an awareness of the Infinite.

However, this is still far short of the full realization of the Notion, for while this form of religious consciousness has raised ordinary things of sense-perception to "beings of spiritual perception," this is really of no avail. "The dispersion [of Spirit] into the multiplicity" of forms has only negative results in that the religious consciousness expresses itself also in a multiplicity of forms, each perceiving God in a different way under different forms, and there consequently occurs hostility among them, as each regards the other as following a different god: "the *actual* self-consciousness of this dispersed Spirit is a host of separate, antagonistic rational Spirits who hate and fight each other to the death." [41] The significance of this point, Lauer suggests, is that "it says a great deal about human spirits at this stage of their evolution. In particular it says a great deal about human activity which manifests itself as *destructive* before it is channelled and becomes *constructive*." [42]

In the stage of "perception" in the general dialectic there emerged a tension between unity and diversity, the unity of the perceived object as opposed to the diversity of its attributes; and similarly, in this stage of the dialectic of religious consciousness there is an underlying tension between the unity of the self-conscious Spirit and the diversity of forms in which Spirit manifests itself. But the hostility that exists in this religious consciousness is due to the failure to perceive the unity of Spirit in the diversity of forms and to the consequent acceptance of one form as the whole truth of absolute Spirit. Of course, such hostility is self-destroying and inevitably means a move in the dialectic, "and through this movement of the Notion Spirit enters into another shape." [43]

This new shape is one that reflects a greater awareness of the individual, as distinct from Pantheism, in which the concrete individual is said to be merely vacuous. In that previous form of religious consciousness unity was achieved, according to Hegel, by the mere disappearance of differences—it was a "negative unity" that submerged the "Many in the One". But in this next shape, into which Spirit enters, "the determinate in general is taken up into infinitude, the form is commensurate with the substance, the infinite form is identical with the substance, which determines itself within itself, and is not merely abstract Power." [44] Yet, of course, this stage is really only the beginning of that process of the greater awareness of the individual without which Spirit cannot come to self-realization; and while it is certainly not as discernible here as in the culminating form of religious consciousness (the Manifest or absolute Religion), and not even as discernible as in the intervening stages of "Religion in the form of Art" (or, in *LPR*, "Religions of Spiritual Individuality"), nevertheless, at least elementary forms of that process are discernible here.

According to Hegel's description in *Phen.*, the next and higher stage of religious consciousness is achieved by the activity of the self being constructive and producing, by means of his own labor, images or representations of those things that are seen to be manifestations of Spirit. Of course, such objects produced by the labor of the self are really reflections of the self,[45] but as yet the self remains unaware of this fact, and we have moved only to the religion of the artificer, not of the artist.

The Artificer

The religious consciousness of the artificer shows itself in the products of architecture and sculpture that the artificer feels impelled to make[46] in order to shape images of his god that were previously, but no longer adequately, found in nature. By so doing he "is already on the road to a higher conception of God since a transformed reality yields us an image closer to that of Spirit than some simply natural being. But in wrestling with his material the artisan is at first not aware that the only adequate image which can satisfy his search is that of free subjectivity. He struggles through a number of intermediate stages . . . . before he finally comes through to the clear representation of spirit which he seeks, viz., the human form." [47]

The first of these intermediate stages is expressed in the building of pyramids and obelisks, but the inadequacy of this artisanry lies in the fact that although the artisan has produced them himself by his own labor and these products are therefore expressions of the spirit of the artisan, his spirit is not made manifest in them, and he remains anonymous in his own work. This artisanry is therefore "lifeless", for the work accomplished "is not yet in its own self filled with Spirit." [48] The work of the artificer takes on "a more lifelike form" [49] in the next stage when he takes plant life, no longer regarded as sacred, and uses it as "an ornament" (as in the architecture of Egyptian columns), for in doing this the artificer is employing his own imaginative concepts to a greater extent and thus is expressing more of himself in his products. Similarly, the artificer is expressing himself in those products for which he uses the forms of animal life, and he shows that he no longer simply identifies human and animal life "by constituting himself the productive power in relation to it and knows himself in it as in *his* work." [50]

The human form is separated more clearly from animal form in those products of artisanry in which the god is represented by a half-animal and half-human form, which Hegel took as being indicative of a growing awareness of self.[51] But again there is inadequacy here in that these forms do not express their inner meaning in any clear way to the external world: "it lacks speech, the element in which the meaning filling it is itself present." [52] The products of the artificer are not adequate to allow the inner meaning to come out, and conversely, the inner meaning—the self-consciousness of spirit— has not yet found an adequate mode of representation. In Reardon's words, "it still is no more than an external and superficial universality, capable of expression only in the materialistic imagery beyond which the religious sense of this ancient people could not advance. For the spiritual as such it was unable to comprehend." [53] The dialectic of religious consciousness therefore must pass on to the point where both the outward expression and the inner meaning are combined in the "Religion of Art", or, in the more embracing term of *LPR*, the "Religion of Spiritual Individuality".

Before leaving the artificer, however, it is important to see how, in *Phen.*, "Hegel is trying to draw out the parallel between primitive religion and primitive (objective) consciousness." [54] The religious consciousness of the artificer corresponds to the "scientific understanding" in the dialectical cycle of "Consciousness" in which consciousness goes behind the simple evidence of the senses to discover some unobservable entity, some force and governing laws, as an explanation of the observable objects, and this gives rise to a dichotomy by which reality is split into two dimensions, an inner reality and mere appearances. We have just seen how Hegel identified a similar dichotomy in the religious consciousness of the artificer: just as consciousness in the form of scientific understanding produced laws to explain the objects of sense perception, so here the artificer constructs his products with scientific precision as representations of the religious consciousness that had focused in the sensory objects of nature; but those products, Hegel said, are inadequate as expressions of the inner meaning of the religious consciousness, so that this stage merely ends in a dichotomy between the inner reality and the external appearance.

And just as with consciousness in the form of scientific understanding, so here in the religious consciousness of the artificer the dichotomy is due to the failure of consciousness to recognize that its product is a reflection of itself, and that thus it can find itself in what it produces. Therefore, as in the case of scientific understanding where consciousness, in recognizing itself behind the appearance of things, discovers that the truth of understanding is self-consciousness, so religious consciousness, through the intermediary stages of the artificer, has reached the point where it can discover itself in what the artificer constructs, thereby bringing the divine and human spirit closer, though still very vaguely, together. In Hegel's words, the artificer "has worked himself up to the point where his consciousness is divided against itself, where Spirit meets Spirit." [55]

Chapter 8
Religion in the Form of Art

The dialectical transition to "Art Religion" is parallel to the transition from "Consciousness" to "Self-Consciousness" in that a new truth emerges, namely, that in the 'something other' we discover ourselves. In the general dialectic of consciousness this discovery of self comes through the developing awareness that our understanding of the given objects of perception is dependent on the scientific laws that we 'produce' as explanations of the observed phenomena. In the case of the dialectic of religious consciousness this discovery of self comes through the developing awareness that the products of the artificer are a reflection of himself, and this awareness is reflected in the shape of those products, which changes through the various stages of the artificer—as Hegel has specified—until this awareness of self blossoms out into a full realization and the work of the artificer becomes that of the artist, a "spiritual worker".

Spirit has raised the shape in which it is present to its own consciousness into the form of consciousness itself and it produces such a shape for itself. The artificer has given up the *synthetic* effort to blend the heterogeneous forms of thought and natural objects; now that the shape has gained the form of self-conscious activity, he has become a spiritual worker (*Phen.*, 424)

In turning his attention to art in this context it is quite clear that Hegel's "interest is not primarily classical art but the religious consciousness which expresses itself in art. Having traced the movement of the divine presence from a formless cosmic force, through differentiated forms of life to the work of men's hands, he now turns to the creative work which is most clearly infused with man's creative spirit, the works through which both the divine and the human spirit speak—more authentically than in the works of nature alone." [1]

However, by the time Hegel delivered his lectures on philosophy of religion he had engaged in an extensive treatment of art as a matter in its own right, so that his discussion of this form of religion in *LPR* was no longer as intertwined with art as in *Phen.*, and the result was that the breadth of material in *LPR* was much more extensive under the more embracing title of "The Religion of Spiritual Individuality".

The transition to the sphere of spiritual individuality is a change to a 'higher' and 'deeper' moment in religious consciousness, moving beyond the naturalistic basis of the previous moments. What comes into view here is "the consciousness of the Divine" in "the free form of subjectivity", by which is meant "that the Divine is determined on its own account as subjectivity." [2] The perception of this leads to the diminishing of the element of naturalness and immediacy, and the emergence of "inherently universal ends". Such ends are manifested only in particulars, but particulars are no longer perceived as merely particulars, for they are manifestations of the Universal; and the Universal is spiritual subjectivity, which "is the absolutely free power of self-determination"—a determination that must be in accordance with some end, though not an end that is external to subjectivity, for subjectivity is "nothing else than the Notion, and has no content but the Notion." [3] The historical emergence of this religious consciousness occurs when people "have reached that stage in the development of self-consciousness" in which they become genuinely personal (or, as Hegel said, they "come to the region belonging to the realm of Spirit" [4]), and the gods whom they worship are also genuinely personal—being active as founders of corporate human life in society and families, as originators and protectors of laws of morality, freedom, and justice, and as the inspirers of art.

Even though Hegel was convinced of the necessity of ancient Greek society passing away and being replaced, one is reminded of the great fascination which that society held for Hegel in his youth and continued to have throughout his life; and one readily perceives that in the culminating work of his developing years, *Phen.*, "Art Religion" is Greek religion—that kind of religion in which Spirit finds "the consciousness of its Absolute". In Hegel's view, the quality of Greek society was comparable to, and was reflected in, the superiority of the expression of its religious consciousness over those other lower expressions of the religious consciousness that have already appeared in Hegel's dialectic. The "Religion of Light", in which there is a consciousness of an irreconcilable opposition between infinite and finite spirit, portrays that kind of social spirit that was represented in Oriental Despotism. The religion that focused on the life of nature broke up into hostile sects, each of which perceived the truth residing in its particular form of religious expression, and this was a portrayal of that unsocial spirit that was represented in "the restless destruction of hostile peoples". In contrast, the social spirit represented in Greek society was that of "the free notion, in which hallowed custom constitutes the substance of all"; it is "not merely the universal substance of all individuals," for it is one of real individuality, "known by the individuals as their essence and their own work." [5]

Thus, what occurs in the process of *Phen.* is that "between natural religion and the Christian religion there surges this art-religion which is the self-consciousness of spirit as *finite humanity*";[6] and in this stage of religious consciousness there is a reiteration of the achievement realized in the cycle of "Self-Consciousness", namely an awareness of self.

Self-Consciousness: The Discovery of Self

Through the cycle of "Consciousness" truth was thought to be found in an object outside us ('something other' than consciousness itself), and certainty was seen to be acquired through knowledge of this 'something other'. However, this certainty has been eroded and has given rise to the new truth that in 'knowing' the 'something other', we in fact know only ourselves: "Certainty about the other becomes self-certainty."

This new truth is achieved through the emergence of the individual as self-consciousness within this stage of the dialectic. It is a growth in knowledge of oneself, the coming to consciousness of self, whereby the individual consciousness becomes conscious of itself as an individual self. The achievement of self-consciousness is a vital step in the whole dialectic of individual consciousness: self-consciousness is the truth of consciousness, in the sense that consciousness finds its fulfillment only in self-consciousness (because its true nature is that of self-consciousness); and self-consciousness is necessary for the emergence of further stages in the dialectic, because it is only through the coming to consciousness of self that there occurs the evolution of Spirit in individual consciousness, in social consciousness, and in consciousness as self-knowing Spirit.

Furthermore, self-consciousness emerges through the individual consciousness recognizing itself in an other—at first, a separated other, but as the dialectic of self-consciousness unfolds, the separation is transcended, opening the way to a recognition of "universal life" in which there is "the identity of identity and nonidentity". There is, in this recognition, profound implications for Hegel's philosophy of religion, and especially for his concept of God.

To illustrate this point, one can say that the transition to "Self-Consciousness" means that Hegel's solution to the opposition between finiteness and infinity arose out of a radically new concept of infinity. That concept "consists not in the absence of external limits but in the absence of *internal* limits. A finite entity becomes an element in an infinity, in this sense, not by being endlessly repeated but by being understood in its relations to all the other entities with which it is connected . . . the emphasis is on the existence of an interconnected system." [7]

This new concept of infinity is consistent with those implications already mentioned for religion, namely, that any religious notion of an 'infinite beyond' set over against the finite "is just as limited and one-sided as the finite. The important way in which our knowledge *can* go beyond the finite is by abandoning the attitude which says that 'everything is what it is and not another thing', and by understanding its objects as elements in a whole." [8] The possibility of the interconnectedness of the whole transcending the appearance of separation, the recognition of which is true knowledge, is opened up by the transition to "Self-Consciousness".

However, in order to proceed with Hegel's analysis of the unfolding of religious consciousness, one can note again that there are parallels with the unfolding of individual consciousness. In the dialectic of individual consciousness, the stage of "Self-Consciousness" is marked by the growth of the individual consciousness' awareness of itself as an individual self—and this is reflected in the dialectic of religion, which at this stage, in *Phen.*, is simply called "Religion in the Form of Art".

The Dialectic of Religion in the Form of Art

In Art-Religion Hegel turned to an examination of the religious life of ancient Greek society, and the warmth of his regard for that society is well established. It was a society that Hegel interpreted as having been characterized by a definite communal sense and a harmony between the individual and the community.

Somewhat paradoxically, however, Art-Religion, which characteristically portrays this social spirit, develops into its completed form only when the naive trust of the individual in the security of this communal life has been undermined.[9] This is so because that which Hegel regarded as the essential element in the development of Art-Religion in a completed form is also that which made inevitable the decline of "Ethical Life". This element is the growth in knowledge of oneself, the coming to consciousness of self, and when this occurred the confidence in the harmonious society was destroyed. Such a society really did not contain the principle of pure individualism: it was a society "in which the self does not know itself as a free individuality,"[10] for the stability of the society consisted in "the firmly established distinctions" amongst the populace and the corresponding functions to be fulfilled.

This carefully defined plurality of distinctions and functions resembled the plurality of qualities by which objects can be defined: consciousness first knows the object in its particularity, and then, through the perception of its qualities, in its universality; so here the individual was known in his universality through his place in the harmonious society, but awareness of his particularity emerged as the individual developed a trust in self and certainty of self.[11] The dialectic thus moves on to the inevitable breakdown of the harmonious society, and the spirit that bound the society together now comes forward as "self-consciousness grasping itself as essence."[12]

It is the emergence of the individual as self-consciousness aware of itself as essence *(Wesen)* that is reflected in Art-Religion, or what, in the more concentrated discussion of religion, Hegel called "Religion of Spiritual Individuality."[13] It is the religion in which "the consciousness of the Divine" is that of "free subjectivity."[14] God is "the Essence" or "absolute Power", and this is "the Power which determines itself from within itself";[15] and this introduces the concept of the Universal and determinative action according to ends—not external ends, but ends that are an "inner self-determination"—for this is "directly involved in the conception of free subjectivity,"[16] and it means that at this level of religious consciousness God becomes known as Spirit.

Of course, this knowledge of God as Spirit does not emerge full-grown, but must develop through a number of stages of the dialectic of religious consciousness: as Hegel said, "the subject may certainly pass for being Spirit so far as ordinary thought is concerned, but it is not itself true Spirit."[17] So, in *Phen.*, the dialectic of Art-Religion passes through the three stages—of "the abstract work of art", "the living work of art", and "the spiritual work of art"—culminating in that subjectivity whereby Spirit is no longer represented by nature; nor is it located in an immediate substantial existence, but is represented in a pure art form,[18] the crowning appearance of which Hegel located in Greek drama, especially the tragedy. On the other hand, in *LPR*, where his attention was obviously concentrated on religion, Hegel's presentation of this level of religious consciousness was more widely embracing, with the dialectic of "Religion of Spiritual Individuality" including not only Greek religion, which he called the "Religion of Beauty", but also the preceding "Religion of Sublimity" (Jewish Religion) and the succeeding "Religion of Utility" (Roman Religion).

The Jewish religion was presented as containing the conception of God, the Absolute, "as the one subjectivity . . . which is universal in itself" and is "consciously known as a personal One"; and so, while religion is thereby "conceived of as the religion of Spirit," it is so conceived of only in the region of Thought, and therefore it is not the most absolute form of the religion of Spirit.[19] Indeed, Hegel regarded the religion of the Jews as being only one stage above the religions of Nature, and certainly as a lower form of religion than that of the Greeks. Although Jewish religion is in the "region of free subjectivity", the essential characteristic of free subjectivity has not appeared, for God is perceived merely as the external, absolute Lord who exercises dominance over his creation, which is totally 'other' than himself.

In Greek religion, however, is to be found an expression of the "Religion of Humanity and Freedom":[20] in the religions of Nature, Spirit is represented in a natural, immediate way, while in Jewish religion Spirit is elevated completely beyond the natural; but in the form of religion, to which we now turn, the relation between Spirit and the natural world is that of inner mediation, so that "the sum and substance" of this phase of religion may be expressed as follows:

> God is in His own nature the mediation which man expresses. Man recognises himself in God and God and man say to each other—That is spirit of my spirit. Man is Spirit just as God is Spirit. He has also, it is true, finitude and the element of separation in him, but in religion he discards his finitude since his knowledge is the knowledge of himself in God. (*LPR*, vol. 2, 223–24)

It is this relation that Hegel presented as crucial to freedom; but nevertheless, this form of religion "is infected with the element of immediacy and naturalness, and thus we shall see the Human existing in God under what are still natural conditions." [21] Therefore, in spite of Hegel's continued high regard for the 'attractiveness', 'grace', and 'charm' of Greek religion, he did not find it to be the absolute form of religion: in those natural conditions the determinateness in which the Divine is perceived takes on manifold shapes, various natural outward forms that are "imagined by self-consciousness as something divine, and this divinity accordingly stands over against self-consciousness." [22]

In *Phen.*, which is providing the basic structure for this discussion, those manifold shapes were presented according to the familiar threefold dialectic.

The Abstract Work of Art

The dialectic of Art-Religion begins with the work of art that is most "immediate" and therefore "abstract and particular". Being the most "immediate and objective phase" of Art-Religion, this is the least adequate expression of self-consciousness, and the inevitable movement away from this to more adequate expressions of self-consciousness in the shape of the art forms issues in the use of language, in the hymn and the oracle, and in certain cultic practices. [23]

As the most immediate, objective, and abstract work of art, Hegel nominated the statues that were the products of Greek sculpture and by which the Olympian gods were portrayed. Of course, this is a more satisfactory expression of religious consciousness than was discovered in the work of the artificer, for here Spirit is being depicted in human form. That which the understanding could grasp of Spirit in the more primordial forms, where Spirit was represented in imitations of nature, is taken up and preserved in this more developed form—which "bears within it the shape of the self", which is a creation of the active consciousness, and in which, therefore, consciousness can discover itself in a way that it could not previously. Whereas the later stages of the artificer's work produced a mixture of human and animal form, here the human form is the one used to portray the god, and at most an animal form is used alongside the human, but no longer having any value of its own. "Religion has passed from the vitalistic to the anthropomorphic stage—with the help of sculpture," [24] thereby indicating a sense of the divine that is not that of a totally other, mysterious, and incomprehensible being.

There are two aspects of the essential being of the god portrayed in the statue, namely, "the universal existence of Nature" and "self-conscious Spirit": as the statue takes a particular shape, "its existence is one of the elements of Nature," and "its self-conscious actuality is an individual rational Spirit." [25] But, as it stands, the statue-god has to be seen as failing to meet the needs of religious consciousness. On the one hand, it takes on the appearance of a static object that destroys rather than portrays the living vitality of nature from which it was hewn; on the other hand, it takes on the appearance of a static object set over against the people whose god it is, and it appears to be beyond the restlessness of the ongoing life of the community whose self-conscious spirit is supposed to be expressed in it. The statue-god lacks all self-consciousness. In the creation of the statue the self-consciousness of the artist is involved, but that self-consciousness does not get depicted in the work,[26] for once the work is completed it becomes a dead object with which he cannot identify except through the gladness he experiences because of the admiration of others. Yet he does not find therein the pain of self-discipline or the exertion and strain of his work: he realizes that he himself is responsible for this statue-god, which does not even portray all that was involved in the work of creating it. The statue is not a spiritual being because, in this "initial duality" of spirit, the unity of the two "contrasted characters of *action* and of being a Thing . . . has not yet come about." [27]

Thus Hegel offered the motivation for the next dialectical step. "The work of art therefore demands another element of its existence, the god another mode of coming forth than this, in which, out of the depths of his creative might, he descends into the opposite, into externality." [28] This higher medium of expression is *language*, which is a product of human life, but also is "an outer reality that is immediately self-conscious existence." It is an expression of individual self-consciousness, but also has a universal character in that it communicates a meaning to many others. "The god, therefore, who has language for the element of his shape, is the work of art that is in its own self inspired":[29] here pure activity is not apart from the being of the thing as it was when the god was portrayed in the statue. Hegel suggested two forms that language takes as a medium of religious activity. First, the hymn, which is a form of devotion that can express the religious consciousness of the individual and also create the awareness in the individual of being at one in this consciousness with the community.[30] Taylor makes the point that the hymn "is closer to representing the God qua self-conscious subjectivity. We can see here . . . how for Hegel religion treats of more than the conceptions of God in theology; here we are dealing with God as lived in the community." [31] Secondly, the óracle, which is thought to be a form of divine utterance using human words, though it takes on the appearance of "the language of an *alien* self-consciousness," [32] because the Notion of the god (which "implies that he is the essence of both Nature and Spirit, and therefore has not only natural but spiritual existence as well") [33] has not yet been realized in religion.[34] Furthermore, the oracle, which is "the utterance peculiar to the god who is the Spirit of an ethical nation," [35] is taken to be an announcement to particular circumstances, but it has to be interpreted by the individual, who can make of it whatever he wills. In *LPR*, one can detect, in one of Hegel's comments about the oracle, a suggestion of the same point that he had already made about the slave: it is man who, though from a position of ignorance, must interpret the general divine revelation and act in accordance with it, and in his interpretation and action, which he knows to be his own, "he knows himself to be responsible." [36] Nevertheless, man is still very much in an unsatisfactory stage of religious expression, for whereas the statue, which appeared as a static 'thing', was too objective and lacked all self-consciousness, language, which appears as impermanent, lacks sufficient embodiment, being "too much shut up within the self." [37]

It is the unity of these two aspects—the external embodiment and the internal self-consciousness—that Hegel was seeking, and so he turned to the religious cult as the achievement of that unity. In the cult Hegel discovered what he regarded as "an essential dimension of religion . . . Cult is that dimension whereby men strive to become one with God. For all religion contains some inkling that it is the self-consciousness of universal *Geist*, hence that the finite consciousness is both separate from and at one with the infinite one it worships. Hence the necessity of overcoming the separation and returning to the underlying unity. This is the role of cult." [38] Or, in Hyppolite's words, "worship culminates in the living unity of the divine and the human, of *essence* and *self-consciousness*. In worship, human self-consciousness draws nearer to the Olympian god who was hovering beyond it, but conversely, in man, the abstract god obtains consciousness of himself. . . . The divine does not fulfill itself without man's help, and man discovers himself only by elevating himself to the divine." [39]

The example of the religious cult that Hegel cited here is the sacrifices of the Greek religions, for in the act of sacrifice the double-sided process, which is involved in the achievement of the essential dimension of religion, is exhibited. The sacrifice begins with the offering of some possession, an animal or fruit of the earth; this is "superseding the actual . . . and raising it into a universality" [40]—it symbolizes the individual spirit setting aside his finitude in order to be at one with the infinite. But that which is offered is also a symbol of a god, and so the offering is also "superseding the *abstraction* of the divine Being *[des Wesens]* . . . and making it actual" [41]—it symbolizes Being 'sacrificing' itself, going into estrangement in embodying itself in finite things. "Both these movements are necessary, for finite spirit can only become the adequate embodiment of infinite *Geist* by overcoming his particularity. The sacrifice of our own to the gods is our act of giving up our particularity; but the god's descent into the victim, and the return of the victim to us for our consumption, is the stepping of the infinite into finite embodiment." [42]

Thus, Hegel's essence and goal of religion is captured in this cultic sacrificial act; and yet, even so, he identified an inadequacy. Hellenistic religion, in the end, must be succeeded by Christianity, which Hegel regarded as the ultimate form of religion. The problem with the Greek sacrifices was that the real meaning of the act was in the devotion that accompanied the act, and this devotion was "not objectively produced," [43] for the act was not lasting and disappeared. This caused an endeavor to give the cultic devotion "an enduring objective existence," which took the form of the temple in which the sacrifices were offered and which therefore came to be seen as an embodiment of the presence of God: "a dwelling and adornments for the glory of the god." [44] Like the statue, the temple is a product of the artistic work of man; but unlike the statue, which takes on the appearance of an external and alien object, the temple is a center of human activity, which takes the form of elaborate decorations and ceremonies. This activity is something the people do repeatedly, so it is not external and alien, and therefore is something with which they can identify. It is a living work—but it only just achieves that status, for all too easily this human activity can become stereotyped, and hence give rise to the need for more spontaneous and creative forms of worship, which will therefore be more truly living works of art in which the life of the people is more creatively expressed.

The Living Work of Art

Hegel described the living work of art as the expression of a people formed into a community in which there is a greater consciousness of the religious and political life of that people. "That nation that approaches its god in the Cult of the religion of art is the ethical nation and knows its state and the actions of the state to be the will and the achievement of its own self." [45] This self-consciousness of the nation portrays itself in the religious activity of the Greek Mystery Religions, in which the Absolute is known as spirit *"immediately united* with the self" so that the self-consciousness of the people finds itself at home with the Absolute when it appears. In the more spontaneous and enthusiastic activity of the Mystery Religions the self knows "itself to be one with the divine Being [*mit dem Wesen*]." [46]

But again Hegel identified an inadequacy: "what is disclosed to consciousness is still only absolute [i.e., abstract] Spirit which is this simple essence, not Spirit as it is in its own self; in other words, it is only *immediate* Spirit, the Spirit of Nature." [47] In the feasting of the bacchanalian revel the life of absolute Spirit is recognized as embodied in the bread and wine, things of nature, and the self recognizes itself in those things as its own possessions that it offers—as in the case of the Greek sacrifices Hegel discussed earlier.[48] But there he identified the inadequacy in terms of the temporary spasmodic nature of the sacrificial activity; here, he identified the inadequacy in terms of the recognition of Spirit still only in things of nature and not yet in humanity—in flesh and blood. The next step toward this is when a people "produce a work that confronts it, as in the previous case the statue confronts the artist; as a work, moreover, that is equally complete, but not, however, as an intrinsically lifeless, but as a *living*, self." [49]

The Festival of the community, which man gives in his own honor, is the supreme instance Hegel cited where "man thus puts himself in the place of the statue as the shape that has been raised and fashioned for perfect free *movement*, just as the statue is perfectly free *repose*." [50] But, inevitably, the community's recognition of itself in the Festival becomes focused in the individual who emerges with the greatest prowess, the champion-athlete who is honored as "being, in place of the god in stone, the highest bodily representation among his people of their essence [*ihres Wesens*]." [51] However, this also is rapidly described as falling short of Hegel's ultimate requirement, and so must give way to another stage of religion in the form of art.

In the case of the feast the self is "beside itself"; in the festival the self is still only aware of "spiritual essence in corporeal beauty": a due balance and equilibrium between self-consciousness and spiritual Being is still lacking, and the quest for that element which will achieve this—an "element in which inwardness is just as external as externality is inward" [52]—once again returns to language, though it is language not in the form of the hymn or the oracle, but in the form of literature, which Hegel described as "Spiritual Work of Art".

The Spiritual Work of Art

Hegel considered language to be "the most significant form of human expression," especially in the form of literature, where "the spirit of man shines through with unmistakable clarity." [53] Hegel also considered literature, especially that of ancient Greece, to be a religious phenomenon, for it is the medium whereby man can express his sense of union with the divine. It was in classical Greek literature—in the epic, the tragedy, and the comedy—that Hegel found this expression of the religious consciousness, for such expression can emerge only when the period of the warring tribal deities has been transcended and they "coalesce into a single spirit." [54] This, in turn, is possible only when a multiplicity of individuals are purposefully bound together in a community without losing the sense and importance of their individuality. "This first alliance is, therefore, more an assembly of individualities than their domination by an abstract thought which robs the individuals of their self-conscious participation in the will and deed of the State." [55]

Of course, this process of development from a multiplicity of individuals to a united community in which each person remains conscious of his individuality is a gradual process, but one Hegel found to have been accomplished in ancient Greek society; and similarly there can be identified a number of stages in the process of the development of religious consciousness in the society of classical Greece—the warring tribal gods were first brought together into the Pantheon of Olympian gods out of which there emerged the consciousness of a god who is the god of the community. The moments of this development, which have appeared already in the previous sections of Art-Religion, now reappear and are reexamined in "The Spiritual Work of Art."

The Epic is the first kind of literature in which is portrayed, though not in the fullest sense, the universality of the gods—"universal at least in the sense of *completeness*, though not indeed as the universality of *thought*." [56] The epic takes up again the level of religious consciousness that is also manifested in the cultic sacrifices, namely, the problem of the unity of the divine and human: in the epic "there is in general *presented* to consciousness what is *implicitly* accomplished in the Cult, the relation of the divine to the human." [57] The real concrete individual in the epic, the minstrel, through the story that he sings, relates humanity—which appears in the shape of the heroes of the story—to the gods, the divine figures; but all that is being created is only a 'representation' of the divine-human relationship. The minstrel is the only concrete individual in the epic, and he is really outside the story; and the main characters, the heroes and divine figures, lack concrete reality, and are portrayed in such a way that the divine-human relationship cannot have any real unity. "The earnestness of those divine powers is a ridiculous superfluity, since they are in fact the power or strength of the individuality performing the action; while the exertions and labour of the latter are an equally useless effort, since it is rather the gods who manage everything." [58]

Also, there is a contradictoriness about the nature of the gods: on the one hand, they are external and unchangeable, above the transitoriness and conflicts of the world; but on the other hand, they are particular gods who stand in a relationship of conflict with each other. Their contradictory nature, their superhuman power in contrast to their particularity and determinateness, means that in the end the gods, as well as men, cannot escape the grip of "the irrational void of Necessity". "Above gods and men alike hovers the abstract unit of the *event*, the movement of time which is stated in the objective rhythm of the poem and in the impersonality of its language. *Destiny does not yet know itself as self.*" [59] The force of necessity appears to be above—controlling—the content of the story, while the language of the minstrel is outside the story; both are divorced from the content, but both "must draw nearer" to it in a higher kind of language.

It is in this higher language, that of Tragedy, that "the dispersed moments of the inner essential world and the world of action," [60] are drawn closer together. The irrational necessity—the Notion "as yet unconscious of itself" [61]—is more closely linked with the content in that there is no longer a mere submission to fate, but an attempt to work it out, realizing that it is the necessary consequent of his own action, that is, the Notion is becoming conscious of itself.[62] Also, the language is more closely linked with content in that it is no longer the impersonal speech of the outside narrator, but that of the self-conscious individual who is acting it out on the stage. "The hero is himself the speaker, and the performance displays to the audience—who are also spectators—*self-conscious* human beings who *know* their rights and purposes, the power and the will of their specific nature and know how to *assert* them." [63]

Just as religious consciousness was expressed in the statue produced by human labor, so that consciousness is expressed in an actual human being, the actor, playing the part of the hero, and representing every man; thus, religious consciousness is no longer being projected into an external object but is located in humanity itself. "Ultimately, in tragedy the religious consciousness of the community is brought to the surface in the actions and sufferings of the hero, the reflections of the chorus and the emotions of the spectators . . . here . . . the previously abstract relationship of the divine and the human, the family and the state, the female and the male, is concretized, and the confusing multiformity of divine beings shrinks to a small number of divine powers more nearly individualized and thus recognizable as personal." [64] This, of course, marks a step forward in religious consciousness, but disadvantages remain: the representation of the gods onstage is one that turns trust into mistrust, for the gods' speech is double-tongued and equivocal, causing uncertainity and confusion in man, who is left uncertain about what he should do; moreover, the actors are only 'representations' of the gods and of every man, and the relationship between gods and men is not raised above one of deception and mistrust. This mistrust is firmly based "in the antithesis of the certainty of itself [the knowing consciousness] and objective essence";[65] that is, as argued elsewhere in *Phen.*, absolute laws, taken in isolation, can be used to justify any action, thereby causing confusion and a reluctance to act because of fear that any action will destroy the absolute. Hence, the laws have to be more specific—the gods have to take certain shapes, and so, in the Tragedy, the characters representing the gods are limited to the divine law governing the home and family and the human law governing the polis.

But this division into "two individual shapes" occurs only "in the element of universality" in the laws themselves for the actual self-consciousnesses—real human beings—have to act in accordance with them, and this means trying to harmonize them; yet, inevitably, there are conflicts between obligations imposed by the city and the family. It is these conflicts that cause what Hegel called "the de-population of heaven": the family and civil laws, the embodiments of the gods, are undermined as the conflicts bring about changes in social life. This is so because of the parochiality of family and state ethics of the particular polis—reflected in the parochial characters of the Tragedy—which therefore express only part of the universal; but the universal is *seen* as being identified with them and hence is reduced to a parochial universal, which is thought to also go under in the face of a necessity (fate) that cannot be understood.[66] What is needed is for the individual consciousness to recognize his parochial nature and become conscious of himself as an individual in charge of his own destiny, though also aware of being in a wider universe.

> The self-consciousness of the hero must step forth from his mask and present itself as knowing itself to be the fate both of the gods of the chorus and of the absolute powers themselves, and as being no longer separated from the chorus, from the universal consciousness. (*Phen.*, 450)

"The religion of art thus ends in the triumph of the self-conscious whose certainty of self makes it master of all its surveys; all universality returns to it, and it recognizes no essence outside itself." [67] This is the condition of the free universal individual whom Hegel located in the *Comedy*, which portrays the weakness of the gods and of men in sharp contrast to their pretensions. The masks of the actors in the Tragedy symbolized their pretense to be something they were not and to present the gods as powers in themselves and not merely projections of human qualities.

> The pretensions of universal essentiality are uncovered in the self; it shows itself to be entangled in an actual existence, and drops the mask just because it wants to be something genuine. The self, appearing here in its significance is something actual, plays with the mask which it once put on in order to act its part; but it as quickly breaks out again from this illusory character and stands forth in its own nakedness and ordinariness, which it shows to be not distinct from the genuine self, the actor, or from the spectator. (*Phen.*, 450)

The separation of the divine and human, which was portrayed in both the Epic and the Tragedy, has now been overcome, but at the complete expense of the divine and the ethical world, for all that remains is the human and contingent. This is the state of the self certain of itself, a state in which the self resides in contentment— the self is the happy consciousness. "It is the return of everything universal into the certainty of itself which, in consequence, is this complete loss of fear and of essential being on the part of all that is alien. This self-certainty is a state of spiritual well-being and of repose therein, such as is not to be found anywhere outside of this Comedy." [68] But this condition of the human spirit also corresponds to the stoical attitude, for this self-certainty of spirit has been achieved only by a retreat into the self.[69] Yet, "since man as *Geist* must have an external embodiment to be, a self-certainty which is not expressed in external social and political forms is nothing worth. . . . His self-certainty is a retreat to an inner citadel, that of I = I, which cannot ultimately be defended, and which hence leads to the unhappy consciousness." [70]

Thus, this self-certain spirit turns out to be the opposite of what it at first claims to be: it represents itself as being happy consciousness, but in fact is unhappy consciousness, "the consciousness for which 'God himself is dead'. Thus it is the arena for a higher form of religion, Christianity. But in this dialectic of Greek comedy, we find a thought which continually reappears in Hegelianism: man is the truth of the divine, but although each time he reduces the divine to himself, each time he loses the movement of transcending himself, he loses himself. Hence the harsh phrase: 'God himself is dead'." [71]

A Transition

It has been apparent on many occasions that Hegel felt a great attraction for ancient Greek society, which he obviously regarded as a society of great beauty. In *Phen.* Hegel located "True Spirit, the Ethical Order" in that society, and this was very reminiscent of his youthful interest in—and idealization of—the ancient world, especially Greece, as the supreme example of culture and enlightenment. Yet, in spite of this fascination ancient Greece had for him, he recognized it as transitory and as necessarily having to pass away— and, for him, this necessity was due to the growth of the universal consciousness that emerged during the history of Greek society.

Hegel presented that world as the realization of Spirit in the actual social world: the unique happiness of that society resided in the development of the human sense of oneness both with the Absolute and with the society. In that period people felt at home in their society, for they saw themselves as dependent on it and yet at the same time they believed the very ethos of their society was embodied in their own activity. Through this affinity with society they also felt at one with the divine, since God was identified as the god of the people of the city, and this sense of oneness with the divine was indicated by the representations of the god in statues shaped in the human form. However, it was this sense of affinity with both the divine and society that contained the condition that brought about the negation of this affinity: that condition was parochialism. But to grasp Hegel's understanding of this dialectical process, one must explore a little further his concept of the harmony between the individual and the community as the essential characteristic of the ancient polis.

The community was one of two focal points upon which life in the polis centered,[72] and life in this community was governed by Human Law, which was composed of the commonly recognized conventions and established laws that were given particular expression in the governing body. Over against Human Law, known through its open manifestation in the life of the society, there was Divine Law, more obscure and not consciously known, but representing the underlying force in the life of the Family—"the *natural* ethical community"[73]—which was the second focal point of life in the polis.

The presence of the two laws, governing the community and the family respectively, is the factor that, in Hegel's analysis, becomes that which undermines the ethical world of the ancient polis. In other words, the polis had within itself that which brought about its dissolution. In principle, the two laws were apparently complementary and in harmony, and this complementary aspect was reflected in the primary concerns of the two sexes: men were concerned mainly with the human and the social, women with the divine and familial, and both were necessary for the well-being and preservation of the other. But this apparent harmony was illusory: even in principle this was so because human law was not truly universal, for it consisted of the conventions and laws of one particular polis, and so was really parochial; though it was in practice that the lack of harmony between the two laws became fully apparent, for whenever he acted the individual could not avoid identifying himself with one law or the other. It was this individual action that brought out the conflict between the two laws, and it was this conflict that led to the breakdown of ancient society.

So the harmony of the Ethical Order, the ancient polis, was destroyed by the contradiction inherent in it, and gave rise to a new form of social life; in the process, the parochialism was transcended through a true awareness of the universal and of particulars, including the self, as embodiments of the universal. Similarly, at the level of religion, the process is repeated: in the dialectic of religious consciousness Hegel presented his perception of the emergence of self-consciousness' affirmation of itself, which both brought to fruition the great qualities of Greek religion and gave rise to those conditions that brought about the collapse of Greek society.

In the society "the individual was actual and counted as such merely as a blood-relation of the family," [74] but by the inevitable activity of the individual affirmed itself as self-consciousness. The new society therefore has to be one in which greater emphasis was given to the individual's force and rights, so that, though it was more universal in extent, it was a soulless community because there was much more individuality: it was a community "whose simple universality is soulless and dead, and is alive only in the *single* individual *qua* single." [75]

Historically, this was the Roman Empire, which Hegel described as the world of "Legal Status". It was a society in which "the universal being thus split up into a mere multiplicity of individuals, this lifeless Spirit is an equality, in which all count the same, i.e., as *persons*." [76] On the one hand, it was a society that recognized the equality of citizens in that all were accorded legal rights as private persons; but on the other hand, it was a society based on external power—it was a vast and powerful empire, authority over which was concentrated in one man, the emperor, who in a sense was merely an individual citizen like everyone else. But he exercised a "destructive power . . . against the self of his subjects, the self which stands over against him. For his power is not the *union* and *harmony* of Spirit in which persons would recognize their own self-consciousness. . . . They exist, therefore in a merely negative relationship, both to one another and to him." [77] The content of the social life resided in this authority, which thus appeared as an alien authority, and the individual consequently existed in a society that did not reflect him at all. Thus, the individual was situated in a condition of alienation, and in order to maintain a sense of integrity, the individual retreated into himself.[78] This was the age of Stoicism.[79]

The stoical attitude is one that takes flight from actuality into a feeling of self-sufficiency, of complete independence, existing only for itself. "It is absolutely for *itself*." [80] But, as with stoicism in the abstract, so in the concrete world: the evolution of stoicism leads to skepticism, the denial of external reality, a position that, again, cannot be maintained. In life in Roman society one was very dependent on one's rights as a citizen, and the whole society revolved around an external authority centered in the emperor; it was therefore impossible to consistently maintain a denial of external actuality. The conflict that emerges in the skeptical attitude causes the overthrowing of such an attitude, and the individual is forced to acknowledge his condition of alienation: man becomes self-estranged spirit.

Life in the Roman Empire was reflected in Roman religion, which in *LPR* Hegel described as the historical appearance of the "Religion of Utility". A common, but thoroughly superficial, view is to identify Roman and Greek religion; but, while there were particular gods that were common to both religions, there were many other gods and ways of worshipping that were peculiar to the Romans—and most importantly, there was an essential difference between the spirit of the two religions. In Roman religion, even in those deities that were the same as the Greek, "the beautiful free individuality of the Greek gods" was missing: the beautiful, free, universal, and moral spirit of the "Religion of Beauty" was replaced by the self-seeking of the Roman worshippers with their gods of practical utility.[81] The many deities of the "Religion of Beauty" were indicative of the concept of *many* 'families' that constituted Greek society, but the Roman people were the *universal* family,[82] the people of the Empire; and while the deities of the former were particular ends, reflected in the diversity of that society (though in accordance with wisdom in general), the deities of the latter merely represented human ends and needs or fortunate events and circumstances, being in accordance with one dominating end, namely, the State.

Herein lay the universality of this religion, but it was only of an abstract kind: the State was not yet in the form of a rational organization, and conformity to the State was still conceived as something external, not internal. Indeed, if it had been so, it would have represented the peculiar nature of God; but God was not yet the true fullness of himself, and therefore the State was not a rational totality, but "merely a kind of dominion or sovereignty, the union of individuals, of peoples held together by some bond under one Power." [83] Roman religion culminated, therefore, in the cult of the emperor, climaxing in the divinization of the state and the suppression of the individual—which was the very opposite of that human self-confidence to which this society and religion owed their origin.

Nevertheless, Hegel found that the Roman world constituted "the supremely important point of transition to the Christian religion," [84] and it did so in both a positive and negative fashion. Positively, Roman religion did represent some advance on the "Religion of Sublimity" and the "Religion of Beauty"—first, because the single end of the former and the particular ends of the latter were "broadened out so as to form a universal end," [85] and secondly, because this universality, the Idea, was totally determinate in the Roman world, thus showing that at this stage of the religious spirit it had been perceived that the Idea must be fully represented by reality.[86]

What remained to be done, however, was that "the determinateness should be taken back again into the Universal . . . that the Idea as such may get its complete determination in itself." [87] This was not achieved in the "Religion of Utility", though: the determinateness that was realized there—even though an absolute determinateness— was still finite and empirical, appearing "as a particular immediate person"; and just because it was also seen as absolute, it became "the most evil and the worst." [88]

This, then, was the negative fashion in which Roman religion prepared the way for absolute religion: the one universal end of the "Religion of Utility" was the Roman State, an abstract Power, in the face of which "the happiness and joyousness of the beautiful life and consciousness of the religions which went before" were crushed into a uniformity that did not permit individuality and that created only "tremendous misery" and "universal sorrow," [89] from which reconciliation seemed impossible. Yet, it was precisely this world that "was to be the birth-throe of the religion of truth," for the unhappy self-enslavement in that world could result only in a stoical escape from the world, and thus demonstrate the complete futility of religions of finitude to achieve ultimate reconciliation. That could be achieved only by the finite individuals being set free, though not in order to be external to the Universal, but to be "taken up into the infinite universality of Thought." [90]

In contrast to Roman religion, this is achieved in the Christian religion,[91] which was a bringing together of "the Oriental principle of pure abstraction"—the idea of the One for itself—and "the finitude and particularity of the West." [92] In Fackenheim's words, "Jewish painful service of the infinite God in the fininte world, philosophical flight from this godless world to a worldless God; Roman unhappy self-enslavement in a godless world: these are all needed if the world is to become ripe for the Christian redemption." [93]

Chapter 9
Absolute Manifest Religion

In the dialectic of religious consciousness that so far has been experienced, Hegel said, "Spirit has advanced from the form of *Substance* to assume that of *Subject*";[1] but this advancement must come to fruition in Absolute or Manifest Religion, where Spirit is both Substance and Subject. It was inherent in the stage that had been reached that this fruition must be realized, for this stage was characterized by "the extreme of the Self", and obviously, in Hegel's view, that could be no resting-place for religious consciousness. The self cannot consistently deny the outside world, for it cannot avoid being dependent on it, but the finite self is not able to provide a meaning for the world and for itself within it, and consequently feels abandoned in a foreign world and therefore is ultimately an unhappy consciousness, which is "the tragic fate of the certainty of self that aims to be absolute."[2] The divine has been completely humanized— the only 'absolute' that remains is the finite spirit certain of itself— and the past representations of the divine in substantial form exist only in the conscious memory: Spirit as subject and Spirit as substance have not been united, but "the grief and longing of the Unhappy Self-Consciousness" is in fact the birth pang of that unity coming into being.

The advancement of Spirit from substance to subject has involved the complete humanization of the divine so that the divine appeared as nothing but self-consciousness; and Hegel felt assured that the inadequacy of this necessitated a return to Spirit in the form of substance in that the divine be grasped as something more than just the self. But this return to Spirit in the form of substance must not be a return to Natural Religion, thereby losing the insight of Spirit as subject; indeed, a return to that position is no longer possible because "something has been gained . . . which is that this cosmic spirit has no locus of self-consciousness, no other vehicle, than ourselves as finite spirits. He lives in and through us. We are his embodiment." [3] This gain cannot be lost, and so the stage has been reached where the true union of these two sides of Spirit can arise in the appearance of the incarnate God.

It is in the incarnate God[4] that this double movement of Spirit is revealed: the giving up ('kenosis' or emptying *[Entäusserung]*) of Spirit in the form of substance—as a distant 'other'—expresses that it "is *in itself* self-consciousness"; and the emptying of Spirit in the form of subject—as self-consciousness—expresses that it "is *in itself* the universal essence." [5] The incarnate God expresses the union of God and man, for absolute Spirit has assumed the shape of self-consciousness, alienating or giving up itself to take on the form of a definite self-consciousness—a real human being—who is an object of the immediate experience of seeing, hearing, and feeling. It is not the product of imagination or thought, nor is it the product of human labor: "on the contrary, this God is sensuously and directly beheld as a Self, as an actual individual man; only so *is* this God a self-consciousness." [6]

This dialectical transition of religious consciousness to Absolute Religion, where the true union of the double movement of Spirit becomes obvious, reflects the transition to the third cycle of consciousness, "Reason", which is described by Hyppolite as "the dialectical synthesis" [7] of the preceding cycles of "Consciousness" and "Self-consciousness". Therefore, before exploring the dialectic of Absolute Religion, it will be helpful to turn aside briefly to specify the parallel between "Reason" and "Absolute Religion".

Reason: The Discovery of the Universal

There is an identifiable parallel between the transition to Absolute Religion and the dialectical emergence of Reason. The cycle of "Reason" emerged because the individual self-consciousness failed to achieve self-fulfillment while standing in a relationship of separation from, and opposition to, other realities; and it gave rise to a concept of universal self-consciousness through the individual discovering the truth of self in himself, in his reason, which he recognized also in others. That failure of individual self-consciousness in the second cycle of human consciousness, which gave rise to the cycle of "Reason", is similar to what has just been noted about Hegel's observations concerning the second moment of the dialectic of religious consciousness; and so that dialectic progresses to "Absolute Religion", in which the individual discovers the truth of self in himself—in Absolute Spirit, which is manifested in himself and in all reality.

The starting point of "Reason" was the awareness that "Reason is the certainty of being all *reality*." It was arrived at through the dialectic.

This starting point of "Reason" was described by Hegel as 'Idealism'. It has been arrived at through the dialectical progress through the various stages of the cycle of "Consciousness"—"in which the essence of the True had for consciousness the determinateness of *being*"—and through the various stages of the cycle of "Self-Consciousness", "in which it had the determinateness of being only *for consciousness*." [8] But in the cycle of "Reason", the truth of "Consciousness" and the truth of "Self-Consciousness" "reduced themselves to a single truth, viz., that what *is*, or the in-itself, only *is* in sofar as it is *for* consciousness, and what is *for* consciousness is also *in itself* or has *intrinsic* being." [9]

It was in the dialectical cycle of "Reason", therefore, that Hegel discovered the expression of what for him was the crucial notion, namely, that in-and-for-themselves existence and self-consciousness are truly the same being. It is this same oneness of being that is the truth of Absolute Religion, and this is the point at which this stage of religious consciousness corresponds to the third cycle of individual consciousness, even though the specific working out of the characteristic three dialectical stages of "Reason" do not have any particular relevance to the dialectic of religion. [10]

Nevertheless, the truth attained at the climax of the evolution of the human spirit in individual consciousness—in the cycle of "Reason"—is repeated at the climax of the evolution of religious consciousness—in "Absolute Religion"—though here that truth is perceived at a higher level. That is because here the truth is grasped in terms of the manifestation and development of absolute *Geist*.

The Dialectic of Manifest Religion

The simple yet crucial content of Absolute or Manifest Religion is that divine Being "essentially and directly has the shape of self-consciousness." In this religion there is both the recognition of divine Being—in immediate present existence—as self-conscious Spirit, and divine Being's consciousness of itself as Spirit.[11] According to its general notion, religion "is consciousness of absolute essence"; but in other forms of religious consciousness there is seen to be a finite relation of mutual exclusion between consciousness and absolute essence, and even in Christian theology the objective is usually regarded as knowledge of God as an Other.[12] However, in absolute religion the notion of religion is truly realized, for here consciousness and essence are recognized as one Whole—as Spirit—that is both the content and object of religion, and "the unity of [the] idea which we call God with the conscious subject" is realized.[13]

If the object of religion appears to consciousness as an 'other', as something alien, then it is taken for granted that there will also be something that is concealed from consciousness. But this 'secrecy' disappears in absolute religion—where absolute Being appears to consciousness in the form of self-conscious Spirit—so that everything alien is removed, for "consciousness knows itself immediately in the object, or is manifest to itself in the object." [14]

If absolute Being is known only as "the Good, the Righteous, the Holy, Creator of Heaven and Earth, and so on," then this is merely attributing predicates to a subject, and, so long as it is only the predicates that are known, "their ground and essence, the Subject itself is not yet revealed." [15] But absolute Being is truly revealed when it takes on the shape of self-conscious Spirit, and it is this revelation that is the crucial content of absolute religion: "in this religion the divine Being is *revealed*. Its being revealed obviously consists in this, that what it is, is known. But it is known precisely in its being known as Spirit, as a Being that is essentially a *self-conscious Being*.[16] It is because divine Being is essentially self-consciousness that it reveals itself in the shape of self-consciousness (in order to be "identical with its self-consciousness"),[17] and thereby human consciousness can know itself as being in absolute Being.

Thus it is in the content of absolute religion (i.e., consciousness' recognition of the divine as self-conscious Spirit in the form of a real human being in which consciousness can know itself, and divine Being's revelation of itself in the shape of a self-consciousness in which it becomes conscious of itself as self-conscious Spirit) that the unity of the divine and human is beheld: in *the* particular self-consciousness, "Spirit is known as self-consciousness, and to this self-consciousness it is immediately revealed, for Spirit is this self-consciousness itself." [18]

In Hegel's philosophy of religion, the absolute religion's notion of absolute Being is that of Being that does not 'remain above' as a mere abstraction or is not "characterized in a merely one-sided way as object," but instead "opens itself out for an Other"—though without going out of itself, for indeed it is the Other: "it breaks itself up within itself, and makes itself an object for itself. Its content is therefore a content which is identical with itself, because it is the infinitely substantial subjectivity which makes itself both object and content." [19] Furthermore, this is not just a momentary or contingent truth of absolute Being, but is its eternal, essential characteristic: "this differentiation of the infinite form, the act of self-determination, the being for an Other, and this self-manifestation is of the very essence of Spirit. Spirit which is not revealed is not Spirit." [20] It is the life of Spirit to appear to itself or manifest itself: "this is its only act, and it is itself only its act. What does God reveal, in fact, but just that He is this revelation of Himself." [21]

However, Hegel admitted that this self-manifestation, as "an actual self-consciousness," may appear to imply that, in so manifesting itself, absolute Being has "come down from its eternal simplicity"; yet, Hegel argued that the opposite is the case, for "by thus *coming down* it has in fact attained for the first time its own highest essence." [22] This is so because it is in existing as an actual self-consciousness that the notion of Being—Being as it is in instelf—reaches its completion: it is both "the absolute *abstraction* which is *pure Thought* and hence the pure individuality of Self, . . . [and] the *immediate* or *being.*" [23] It is not only a remote absolute existing in abstraction, but it is also there in its immediacy as an existent self-consciousness.

> Thus the lowest is at the same time the highest; the revealed which has come forth wholly on to the *surface* is precisely therein the most *profound.* That the supreme Being is seen, heard, etc. as an immediately present self-consciousness, this therefore is indeed the consummation of its Notion; and through this consummation that Being is immediately *present qua* supreme Being. (*Phen.,* 460)

This fulfillment of the notion of absolute Being is that it is known as self-conscious Spirit—"Substance becomes Self". This unity of substance and self first became known in the initial and much narrower experience of individual consciousness as it moved from sense-certainty to understanding; but "what was for us must also be for the consciousness of spirit and for its immediate consciousness." [24] This is realized in Manifest Religion, which knows God as Spirit and also as an existent self-consciousness, as pure essence and also real existence, as a universal self and also an individual 'this'. It was toward this vision of the essence of absolute Being that "the hopes and expectations of preceding ages" were directed, and are now realized in knowing the revelation of "what God is" and in the joy of self-consciousness seeing itself in absolute Being.

The joy of self-consciousness resides in the knowledge of what God is, namely that he is self-conscious Spirit, that "He is for an Other," that he "posits or lays down (setzt) the Other, and takes it up again (hebt es auf) into His eternal movement." [25] Thus, there is the concept of 'reconciliation' in absolute religion, which Hegel therefore called "the religion of Truth and Freedom". For Hegel, truth is attained when "the mind does not take up an attitude to the objective as would imply that this is something foreign to it"; and freedom, while requiring this essential characteristic of truth, is attained through the realization that this truth is not something static, "which simply is, [but that], on the contrary, it is activity." This is the process of Reconciliation, which means that different forms of existence that appear to stand in opposition to each other—God and the estranged world—recognize themselves, find themselves and their essential nature, in the other. [26]

> All that we mean by reconciliation, truth, freedom, represents a universal process, and cannot therefore be expressed in a single proposition without becoming one-sided. The main idea which in a popular form expresses the truth, is that of the unity of the divine and human natures; God has become Man. This unity is at first *potential* only, but being such it has to be eternally produced or brought into actual existence; and this act of production is the freeing process, the reconciliation which in fact is possible only by means of the potentiality. (LPR, vol. 2, 347)

This is the truth attained by absolute religion, and it is also the absolute truth that is the result of the whole of philosophy. The reason why absolute religion must be supplemented by philosophy, however, is that religion fails to express the truth with complete clarity. But Hegel was convinced that the content of absolute truth was attained at this ultimate level of religious consciousness, and in *Phen.* he therefore considered, at comparative length, the various moments in the content of this religious consciousness. Of course, the details of these moments were elaborated to a much greater extent in *LPR*, where he treated them under the threefold classification of "the Kingdom of the Father", "the Kingdom of the Son", and "the Kingdom of the Spirit", thus reflecting the triadic manifestation of absolute Spirit as:

> eternal Being in and with itself, the form of Universality; the form of manifestation or appearance, that of Particularization,

Being for another; the form of the return from appearance into itself, absolute Singleness or individuality.

The divine Idea unfolds itself in these three forms. Spirit is divine history, the process of self-differentiation, of separation or diremption, and of the resumption of this; it is divine history, and this history is to be considered in each of these three forms. (*LPR*, vol. 3, 2)

The Kingdom of the Father

When Hegel spoke of "the Kingdom of the Father", he was speaking of God as he "exists in a pure form for the finite spirit only as thought." [27] This is the true notion of God, absolute Spirit *an sich*, or God as eternal Idea in his essential existence, regarded abstractly only in the realm of thought; and, so perceived, he is other than—before and outside of—the world,[28] existing only for thought as "the Idea in its eternal presence . . . whose fundamental characteristic is the untroubled light, self-identity, an element which is as yet unaffected by the presence of being other than itself." [29]

Although in itself abstract, existing only as thought, the Notion (*Begriff*) occupies a crucial place in Hegelian philosophy, for it is that which is the essential nature of the thing, that which is "the dynamic inner principle which guides [the thing's] development." [30] Therefore, in Hegel's analysis of absolute religion, that level of religous consciousness where truth is attained, what he said about the notion of God is central to the understanding of Hegel's 'religious' philosophy, for it expresses the essential nature of God—absolute Spirit *an sich*—and is that dynamic inner principle that guides the development of absolute Being to its fulfillment as self-conscious Spirit.

Here again we find the familiar—or more correctly, it should be said that here we find the most fundamental—threefold pattern, for Hegel asserted that absolute Being *an sich* (in its true Notion) is constituted by three distinct moments: namely, "essence, being-for-self which is the otherness of essence and for which essence is, and being-for-self or the knowledge of itself *in the 'other'.*" [31] There seems to be a very apparent and intentional parallel here between this notion of absolute Spirit and the Christian doctrine of Trinity according to which God is known as Father, Son, and Spirit; and this parallel becomes even more explicit when Hegel refers to "the otherness of essence" as "the Word" *(Wort)*, which is identical in meaning to the New Testament concept of 'Logos'.[32]

Hegel's distinguishing of the three moments in the pure notion of absolute Spirit needs to be further explored, and the parallel with trinitarian theology noted in more detail. Absolute Spirit, in its pure notion, is Spirit as 'substance' conceived of essentially "in the element of pure thought"; it is "immediately simple and self-identical, eternal essence." [33] But if it is conceived of only in such an abstract way, it would be "Spirit only as a form of empty words," an abstraction found in essence *per se* (found "at the heart of the Absolute"),[34] which is 'negativity'. Negativity, in Hegel's usage, is a lack of certain essential qualities, a falling short of perfection or wholeness; hence it is that which is the driving force in the dialectical movement. So Hegel said that absolute Spirit in its mere abstraction as essential Being is negativity; the Absolute does not consist in being merely an abstraction, but in being "what is actual", and so it expresses itself as a self-consciousness in its 'Word'.

> The Universal is . . . an inner movement, and its nature is to differentiate itself within itself, and thus to preserve within itself the element of difference, but yet to do this in such a way as not to disturb the universality which is also there. Here universality is something which has this element of difference within itself, and is in harmony with itself. (*LPR,* vol. 3, 9)

A word is a means of communication; it is an expression of a self-conscious individual, and, as such, contains something of that self; a word is something that the self sends forth from himself and that becomes an 'other', in which, because it is an expression of the self, the self can be recognized; and also the self can recognize himself in his spoken word. Similarly, Hegel said, absolute Spirit knows itself in its Word, its other, and this knowing itself in the other is a return to itself—a return that is the third moment of the pure notion of absolute Spirit. And thereby distinctions, which are identified in thought, between 'absolute Spirit' and 'Word' are at the same time dissolved: "In this *simple* beholding of itself in the 'Other', the otherness is therefore not posited as such; it is the difference which, in pure thought, is immediately *no difference;* a *loving* recognition in which the two sides, as regards their essence, do not stand in an antithetical relation to each other. . . . otherness itself, i.e. the supersession of the pure Notion that is only thought," lies in the very notion of Spirit.[35]

However, what is thus known of absolute Spirit by means of speculative knowledge, on the level of notional thought, is represented in the pictorial language of religion, on the level of representational thought, by Christian trinitarian theology.[36] This doctrine of the Trinity is fundamentally a theology of the nature of the being of God—God as he is in himself—as the Hegelian notion of absolute Spirit is a notion of Spirit *an sich.* But the pictorial language of

religion employs the natural relationship of father and son to represent
the relationship between the essential being of God and His Word,
which "goes forth" from himself: the Father is the "eternal Being"
who "*begets* for itself an other", the Son; and further in trinitarian
thought, the theology of the Holy Spirit concerns the unifying force
in the relationship of Father and Son, so that here Hegel found the
parallel with his own thought of Spirit's return to itself in its 'other'.

It is difficult to avoid the parallelism between Hegelian thought
and trinitarian theology, but equally one cannot avoid certain questions about this parallelism, namely, questions concerning the manner
in which this parallelism emerged in Hegel's philosophy and concerning the nature and extent of the parallelism.

Regarding the former, Lauer acknowledges that there is no cause
for surprise to find that Hegel has fitted the trinitarian doctrine to
his own system, but he adds that "it is just as plausible . . . to say
that he fitted his own system to his interpretation of Trinitarian
[doctrine]." [37] One is bound to point out, however, that from a
historical, developmental viewpoint this does not seem to be just as
plausible: from the exploration into Hegel's *ETW* it has been seen
just how his system evolved, and how his concept of love provided
the crucial starting point and pattern of his system in which all
divisive distinctions were to be taken up into a unity and wholeness;
and from this it seems correct to suggest that it was trinitarian
terminology that came to be incorporated into his system, rather
than vice versa. However, one cannot be dogmatic on this point,
because trinitarian thought would obviously have been an integral
part of the intellectual atmosphere in which he developed. All one
can really say is that there is a definite intertwining relationship
between Hegelian thought and trinitarian theology.

In turning to the question of the nature and extent of this relationship, one comes up against Hegel's claim that the absolute religion
is the Christian religion, but also against a weight of opinion that
asserts that they are not the same in content, and that trinitarian
thought provides an obvious example of this dissimilarity. McTaggart
is one who argued that Hegel's presentation of the notion of absolute
Being is not the same as the orthodox Christian conception of the
Trinity: McTaggart argued that the Hegelian conception departed
from the orthodox conception of three coequal Persons, for—according to the former—with its concept of a dialectical process within
absolute Being, it is only the Holy Spirit who is truly God.[38] However,
this kind of criticism depends on the projection of rigid distinctions
into the notion of absolute Being—distinctions that were anathema
to Hegel—and it illustrates the very dangers of which he warned.
According to Hegel, trinitarian theology is expressed in pictorial

language on the level of representational thought, so that although it has the true 'content', its form is defective and it therefore does not have the 'necessity' of speculative thinking.[39] The consequence of this kind of defective form—as the history of Christianity has conclusively illustrated—is that the distinctions for thought become rigid and the form in which the thought is expressed becomes static and stereotyped. The form, then, is sought to be retained at all costs, and this necessarily is at the expense of the dynamic truth of the content.[40] It is this dynamic element, however, that was so essential in Hegelianism: Spirit is life, movement, and eternal Process; "God is Himself just this entire act." [41]

This is the most important aspect of Hegel's thought that has to be grasped here, and when it is, the kind of criticism of which McTaggart is representative must disappear; for while one could lift certain words out of the Hegelian text that would seem to make this criticism plausible,[42] that criticism depends on the reading into Hegel of a rigidity of the distinctions to which he was quite opposed.[43] This is why he said that the natural relation of father and son, used figuratively in the context of trinitarian theology, "never entirely corresponds to the truth that is sought to be expressed";[44] and similarly, this is why he was critical of the implied numerical distinction in the divine nature that is part of so much orthodox language.[45]

For Hegel, God is "Beginning and End," and when he said that God is "the end only," he was not speaking of the end as distinct from the beginning but the end as totality, for "it is as totality that God is Spirit." However, although McTaggart's point—that for Hegel only the Holy Spirit is truly God—can be discarded, it still has to be admitted that the general point that the conceptions Hegel expressed regarding "the Kingdom of the Father" are not strictly compatible with the doctrine that has impressed itself as Christian orthodoxy; though one can agree with Whittemore in saying that what "Hegel has shown is that one basic Christian doctrine can be reinterpreted in such a way as to accord with the requirements of Reason. But this is not the same thing—although in the final analysis it may prove to be something of much greater importance." [46]

The notion of absolute Spirit that, according to Hegel's analysis here, contains these three moments—Essential Being, Self-Expression or Word, and Self-Knowledge or its return to itself—will remain, however, a mere abstraction unless it is also the first moment of another threefold dynamic, of which the other two moments are the Notion's necessary embodiment in reality and the return to itself out of this estrangement. The necessary embodiment is, representationally, Hegel's "Kingdom of the Son".

The Kingdom of the Son

Here we pass from the consideration of the Notion in abstract universality and infinitude to a consideration of its determination in the specific form of finitude.[47]

The first moment in the pure notion of absolute Spirit is described as 'Essence' *(Wesen)*, and we have seen that this was said to be only an empty abstraction unless it is 'self-moving' and 'goes out' of itself and 'returns' to itself in the other two moments; indeed, for Hegel, it is this 'self-moving' of Spirit as *Wesen* that expresses "absolute Being as Spirit". But we have also seen that even the notion of 'self-moving' Spirit, if it remains a mere abstraction, is also nothing but an empty phrase, essentially potentiality only, and therefore the abstract notion of self-movement or self-existence in another needs a real expression: "In the element of pure thought, being-other is not really posed; nor is alienation . . . as yet complete. Hegelian philosophy does not deduce the world from the logos. Logos and nature mutually require each other." [48] The merely abstract Spirit, then, "becomes an 'other' to itself, or enters into existence, and directly into *immediate* existence." [49] This is what the religious community describes, in pictorial language, as the creation of the world, and what, in the realm of speculative thought, is absolute Spirit's own becoming 'other', its real self-estrangment.

> What in the first stage represented God's Other or object, without, however, being defined as such, now receives the character or determination of an Other. Considered from the first standpoint, God as the Son is not distinguished from the Father, but what is stated of Him is expressed merely in terms of feeling. In connection with the second element, however, the Son is characterised as an Other or object. (*LPR*, vol.3, 4–5)

So, in what religion represents as creation, and speculative knowledge presents as Spirit's becoming 'other', there is a real opposition of nature between Spirit as pure notion and the world. Concerning those moments of the Notion, Hegel said there is "the dissolution of their simple universality and the parting asunder of them into their own particularity";[50] and without this dispersion, this alienation, "the absolute is not for-itself and is not spirit." [51]

This self-movement of absolute Spirit—which necessarily must be recognized as one movement—is its becoming 'other', and in its being 'other', Spirit returns to itself; that is, it knows itself to be self-conscious Spirit.

Eternal Being, in-and-for-itself, is something which unfolds itself, determines itself, differentiates itself, posits itself as its own difference, but the difference, again, is at the same time eternally done away with and absorbed; what has essential Being, Being in-and-for-itself, eternally returns to itself in this, and only in sofar as it does this is it Spirit. (*LPR*, vol. 3, 35)

This process of becoming 'other', this act of unfolding and determining itself, is not something that is extraneous to the nature of absolute Spirit, but belongs to its very notion; and it is for this reason that, although it is clear that Hegel here was expounding a doctrine of creation, it is commonly said that the view of creation in Hegel's absolute religion is not compatible with Christian orthodoxy for which creativity is a contingent, not an essential, aspect of the divine Being. This suggested incompatibility assumes greater probability when one considers the orthodox tendency to sharply distinguish and separate the divine life from the life of the world, and then compares this with the Hegelian denial of such separation and division.[52] For Hegel, the life of the world is the divine life in the mode of appearance; it is "the appearing of God". In Hegel's view, what is taken to be Christian orthodoxy is really a misconception that is the consequence of religious thought being expressed by means of *Vorstellungen* and confined to the level of *Verstand*. Similarly, the question about the world being eternal or having a beginning in time—and the assumption that if it is eternal it must be uncreated and exist immediately for itself—are indicative of thinking at this level; whereas for Hegel, the real truth is that the world is a posited moment in the eternal process of absolute Being.[53]

This creation, this self-othering of absolute Spirit, can be spoken of as a totality in terms of the appearance or manifestation of the Absolute or God. But this creation is a complex diversity: it is a diversity of natural things, which are "a revelation of God" and by means of which man can "see God."[54] Yet, it is in man, as a self-consciousness, that absolute Spirit most fully reveals itself as self-conscious Spirit; it is man, therefore, who is able to know Spirit; and it is through men, as finite individual selves, that absolute Spirit discovers itself as self-conscious Spirit in its 'other'.

Thus, one is confronted with the question of the nature of man, and immediately Hegel presented the dichotomy that man is by nature both good and evil.[55] Man is by nature good because he is potentially Spirit, rationality, having been created—as expressed by *Vorstellung*—in the image of God. However, initially the individual Self "is not yet Spirit *for itself*"; as such, the individual Self might be in a state that "can be called 'innocent'," a state referred to in traditional Christian theology as 'original righteousness'—though in Hegel's view it is a state that hardly can be called 'good'. In order that the individual Self may become Spirit it must become conscious of itself as an individual self-consciousness; "it must first become an 'other' to its own self, just as eternal Being exhibits itself as the movement of being self-identical in its otherness." [56]

In the early stages of *Phen.* Hegel argued that the individual's coming to self-consciousness involves 'otherness', for it is the affirmation of the self against other finite selves that is essential to self-consciousness; and there Hegel was asserting that this kind of affirmation marks the emergence of evil and brings man to the acquisition of the knowledge of good and evil.[57] Again, the *Vorstellungen* of religion provide a representation of this in the form of the biblical creation and garden narratives, which use the mythological description of a contingent event at the beginning of human history to present what for Hegel is a general and necessary truth about human development.

Thus, the problem that Hegel found here with religious consciousness is that it had not come to terms with the general and necessary nature of this development, because it tended to think too literalistically of those narratives and to accept the Fall as a contingent historical event that could—and should—have been avoided.[58] This, for Hegel, is merely an example of the kind of falsity that arises when thought remains at the level of *Vorstellungen*. The truth, in Hegelian terms, is that 'the Fall' is nothing other than man's necessary expression of himself as a subject who possesses will; and while this has a negative aspect, namely, the emergence of evil that results from the opposing of finite will to universal Spirit, it also has a positive and equally necessary aspect, namely, as an essential step toward reconciliation. It is this because, on one hand, it is that which characterizes man as a spiritual being and so distinguishes him from the beasts (thus, without it man would not be truly man);[59] and on the other hand, it is that which enables Spirit's self-knowledge, for, in becoming spiritual being, man has become self-conscious spirit,[60] a finite self-consciousness, in whom alone absolute Spirit is able to come to the self-realization of himself as self-consciousness and as spirit. Thus, the presence of evil is part of the self-movement of absolute Spirit.[61]

There is, however, in man a certain contradiction or incompatibility: as self-conscious spirit, he is at the level of a spiritual being; but as a finite self-consciousness, he opposes himself to universal Spirit, and so appears to be in a state of disunity with that with which he ought to be in unity. The one-sidedness of the religions that have already appeared rendered them incapable of adequately overcoming this estrangement;[62] yet the deepest need of Spirit is for reconciliation, and this need can be satisfied only by "the consciousness that this opposition is not the truth, but that, on the contrary, the truth consists in reaching unity by the negation of this opposition. . . . The subject must come to be conscious that this opposition is not something implicit or essential, but that the truth, the inner nature of Spirit, implies the abolition and absorption of this opposition." [63]

Since other religions have been unable to make possible the achievement of an awareness of this truth, one is confronted by the supreme importance and essentiality of absolute religion. The earlier appearing religions failed to make this truth known because they tended to stress the opposition and separation between the finite self-consciousness and absolute Being, having a strong bias to one or the other side of the opposition. It therefore becomes clear, according to Hegel, that an awareness of the truth—that Spirit implies the absorption of this opposition—will be made possible only if it is manifested in a specific human life:

> If Man is to get a consciousness of the unity of divine and human nature, and of this characteristic of Man as belonging to Man in general; or if this knowledge is to force its way wholly into the consciousness of his finitude as the beam of eternal light which reveals itself to him in the finite, then it must reach him in his character as Man in general . . .; it must come to him as representing Man in his immediate state, and it must be universal for immediate consciousness.
>
> The consciousness of the absolute Idea, which we have in thought, must therefore not be put forward as belonging to the standpoint of philosophical speculation, of speculative thought, but must, on the contrary, appear in the form of certainty for men in general. . . . Thus unity must accordingly show itself to consciousness in a purely temporal, absolutely ordinary manifestation of reality, in one particular man, in a finite individual who is at the same time known to be the Divine Idea, not merely a Being of a higher kind in general, but rather the highest, the absolute Idea, the Son of God. (*LPR*, vol. 3, 72–73)

The most superb feature of the Christian religion is this declaration of the truth of reality: namely, that absolute Spirit is essentially embodied in immediate finite individuality—its 'other'; that in this 'other', Spirit remains self-identical; and that the finite is thereby known to be transfigured as the manifestation or incarnation of Spirit. But the special appearing of the divine Spirit in the form of immediacy is most adequately represented only for others, and thereby known, in human form which is the spiritual form; and it is an appearing that "can only take place once" because God as Spirit "contains in Himself the moment of subjectivity, of singleness," and because a multiplicity of such special manifestations would cause the Divine to be known only abstractly.[64] In order for man to grasp the truth of the incarnation of Spirit in the whole finite reality, it must be demonstrated for him in one specific human life. It is this feature of Christianity that makes it, in Hegel's view, the absolute religion.

An obvious question that emerges here is that of how Hegel distinguished between this unique revelation of Spirit to consciousness, and Spirit's incarnate presence in the whole finite world—especially in man as a spiritual being. There is no doubt that for Hegel the truth grasped in absolute religion is that of this universal incarnation of Spirit, and it is also true that Hegel believed that this truth was originally grasped through the historical reality of a unique manifestation of Spirit in a real concrete human being who could be seen, heard, and touched—the man "crucified under Pontius Pilate." The decisiveness of this event in human history is that it was the vehicle whereby the realization that incarnation is universally true was achieved[65]—though one must add the necessary observation, as Findlay does, that "the realization rather than the vehicle remains the important thing for Hegel." [66] It was Hegel's *belief* that this realization originated from this particular vehicle—that was his Christian faith; but his philosophical position did not depend on *this* vehicle, for philosophically, it was the realization that was essential, and the vehicle by which it was achieved was irrelevant.

One is left, therefore, with these two Hegelian assertions about the nature of the truth revealed in absolute religion: there is the fundamental matter of human consciousness coming to realize the universal incarnation of Spirit; but there is also the matter of there having been a decisive event that enabled that realization, namely, the appearance in human history of the unique God-Man in whom absolute Spirit "externalizes itself and becomes the 'I' for consciousness." [67]

But the manner in which Hegel regarded the uniqueness of this God-Man is not easily discernible. He clearly stated that there are two different ways of looking at this historical manifestation, for one can regard it as the appearance of an ordinary man, or one can look at it in a spiritual way and discover an individual who possesses divine nature, thereby canceling the concept of God as a Being beyond this world.[68] It is the latter view that recognizes the uniqueness of this God-Man, but it is what Hegel regarded as the basis of this recognition that causes the puzzle. It does seem, however, that two things can be said: first, Hegel placed considerable emphasis on the teaching of Jesus, declaring that Jesus lived "only for the truth and the proclamation of the truth"; and that in doing so, he proclaimed a "revolutionary teaching," an example of which is found in the 'Sermon on the Mount', some of the words of which "are amongst the grandest that have ever been uttered." To the quality of the teaching one has to add its impact, and the strength of this was made possible because he appeared "when the common people were in perplexity and helpless." [69] Secondly, the uniqueness of the God-Man, for Hegel, was based in his death, which made possible and began "the conversion of consciousness."

Again Hegel recognized two ways the death of Jesus can be conceived of: as a natural death caused by injustice, hate, and violence; or the higher way, as the confirmation of the belief that in Jesus the divine nature has been revealed. Since "it is the lot of finite humanity to die, death is the complete proof of humanity"; and therefore the death of shame and dishonor that Jesus suffered reveals him as one in whom "humanity was carried to its furthest point." [70]

But there is also a further aspect of the death of Jesus that emerges: namely, it declares that "God has died, God is dead"—which is "the most frightful of all thoughts, that all that is eternal, all that is true is not, that negation itself is found in God." Yet, in spite of this frightful aspect, essential truths are expressed. The divine nature, infinite Spirit, can never be fully expressed in the finite, and that is why the finite must die; but negation, otherness, human finitude, and frailty "is consciously known to be a moment of the Divine nature," so that that nature is revealed as not existing in any one particular individual only, but as being universally manifested in the finite.[71]

If in the first division of the subject we conceived of God as He is in pure thought, in this second division we start from immediacy as it exists for sense-perception and for ideas based on sense. The process is accordingly this, that immediate particularity is done away with and absorbed; and just as in the first region of thought, God's state of seclusion came to an end, and His primary immediacy as abstract universality . . . was annulled, so here the abstraction of humanity, the immediacy of existing particularity, is annulled, and this is brought about by death; the death of Christ, however, is the death of death, the negation of the negation. We have had in the Kingdom of the Father the same course and process in the unfolding of God's nature; here, however, the process is explained in so far as it is an object for consciousness. (*LPR*, vol.3, 92)

So then, just as Hegel stressed the necessity of the special incarnation of absolute Spirit as a real historical event in order to enable the realization of the truth of the universality of the externalization of Spirit, so he stressed the cruciality of going beyond that actual historical event if the truth revealed by that event was to be truly grasped. The necessity of moving beyond the actual event lies in the fact that so long as awareness of absolute Spirit is linked with the immediate experience of an individual existent, spirit is equated with *this* self-consciousness—it is individual and exclusive, and the universal self-consciousness of Spirit is not grasped. As yet, Spirit does not have the form of its notion—that is, the form of universal self[72]—and the manifestation of Spirit in the unique individual self-consciousness is still seen as a manifestation in an 'other' self-consciousness, and so the incarnation of Spirit in every self-conscious individual is not yet grasped. Lauer says that so long as "the self-consciousness which knows God is only the self-consciousness of the individual God-man, God is there, it is true, in concept, but the implications of the concept have not been worked out." [73]

So long as "the *immediately* present God" is particularized in the sensibly perceptible man Jesus, the universal identity of absolute self-conscious Spirit with individual self-consciousness is not explicit, and so the particular man must pass away—"his *being* passes over into *having been*" [74]—and this is the significance of the death of Jesus. The unity of God and man having been presented, the immediate sensible experience had to pass away so that we could grasp the truth that God is not confined to any one particular individual, but is universally incarnated in finite subjects—the truth "that the human is God as immediate and present." [75] Hegel found this truth reflected in the Christian doctrines of Resurrection, Ascension, and Pentecost; and so, for Hegel, Jesus' dying, his rising to life, his ascending, and the coming of the Holy Spirit all belong together; for Hegel, it is "*death* of the individual and *resurrection* of the universal." [76]

For an expression of Hegel's interpretation of the Crucifixion, Resurrection, Ascension, and Pentecost one can profitably turn to Taylor: "What they reflect is that the unity of God and man cannot be consummated in an individual. For there must always be an opposition between the universal spirit and any particular embodiment. This opposition is resolved . . . when the particular embodiment passes away. Hence the individual must die. But in this case, Christ's death also signifies the transformation of this unity between God and man from a particular to a universal fact. That is why the death and resurrection are indissolubly linked to Ascension and Pentecost, for the whole meaning of the death lies in the coming of the spirit whereby the locus of Incarnation shifts to the community, the 'body of Christ'." [77]

The Death and Resurrection of Christ is the passing from the immediate present of the self-conscious individual to his coming to life again in the spirit of the community, "as universal self-consciousness". This time, in Findlay's words: "The death involved is a death to particularity, which presumably here covers both the particularity of sense and the particularity of interest and impulse, and a resurrection to universality. It is also the death of all imaginative religious representations, and a resurrection to a more inward, notional form of religious experience. The death of the Mediator must be appropriated by the religious community: His independent, objective self-consciousness must be set aside, and transformed into a universal self-consciousness. With this dissolution of the Mediator in the communal consciousness will also go the death of the divine Essence, as something abstract and apart: we must learn to sing, not despairingly, but exaltingly, that God himself has died." [78]

So then, in Hegel's presentation, what has occurred in the individual life of Jesus is the focusing of the whole dynamic movement of absolute Spirit: the first moment in the dynamic of Spirit, the Absolute in its essential nature, inherently involves the second moment, Spirit becoming its 'other', which is intensely focalized in the life of Jesus and symbolically represented by the theology of Incarnation; and in the Death and Resurrection of Jesus we see the third moment of Spirit, its return to itself in its 'other' as universal self-conscious Spirit. But what has been made manifest in the life of Jesus has to be made real for the community: "the movement that took place in Christ *must now be executed in the midst of the community* and must become *its own* movement instead of being alien to it." [79]

> It is with the consciousness of the Spiritual Community, which thus makes the transition from man pure and simple to a God-man, and to a perception, a consciousness, a certainty of the unity and union of the Divine and human natures, that the Church or Spiritual Community begins, and it is this consciousness which constitutes the truth upon which the Spiritual Community is founded. (*LPR*, vol. 3, 99)

The Kingdom of the Spirit

The truth, then, for Hegel is that absolute Spirit is *self*, or *subject*, and that this is so not just for one individual self by whom this truth was first manifested, but it is true universally—and "this is the life of the community *(Gemeinde)*." [80] This is what Hegel called "the

Kingdom of the Spirit", because in it "we have the consciousness that Man is implicitly reconciled to God, and that this reconciliation exists for Man." [81] This third sphere of absolute Spirit is that unity of Individuality *(Einzelheit)* that is accomplished through the 'other' of Spirit—"the many individuals confronting it"—being brought back "into the unity of Spirit," into the "Spiritual Community *(Gemeinde)*, and exists here as real, universal self-consciousness":[82]

> This region is accordingly the Kingdom of Spirit, implying that the individual is of infinite value in himself, knows himself to be absolute freedom, possesses in himself the most rigid fixedness and maintains himself in what is absolutely an Other. Love harmonises all things, even absolute opposition. (*LPR*, vol. 3, 102)

What characterizes the formation of the Spiritual Community is that the truth that was manifested externally in history becomes a truth that is known inwardly and with certainty.[83] It is a truth by which the individual subject knows absolute Spirit as present in his own existence, and his existence as a moment in the infinite and eternal Spirit. But it is also a truth by which the subject "yields up its particularity and individuality," and finds true meaning and worth in the universal and nonexclusive Community, in which all are equal—for it is characterized by that "unity in the Spirit," "the love, in fact, which is just the notion or conception of Spirit itself." [84] It is a unity in the spirit that is born out of a realization that the reconciliation between the finite and infinite has been accomplished, and not just as something far off in a past historical figure, but as a present reality through which the oneness of all finite life is fulfilled, transcending without destroying the particularity of each individual.

> Spirit is infinite return into self, infinite subjectivity, not Godhead conceived of in ideas, but the real present Godhead, and thus it is not the substantial potentiality of the Father, not the True in the objective or antithetical form of the Son but the subjective Present and Real. (*LPR*, vol. 3, 107) [85]

It is because the Christian religion contains this truth that Hegel described it as "the religion of Spirit"; but it contains this truth only because such truth was once represented as something historical, manifested in a particular individual, and also because it has been spiritually comprehended by the Spiritual Community that has thus come into being.

This, Hegel observed, is precisely the process that operates in the acquisition of all knowledge: our acquaintance with some physical law comes about through the inductive process, which has sensory knowledge as its starting point; but absolute knowledge consists in the comprehension of the law as being true in its own nature.[86] Similarly, the true content of Christian faith appeared in the life of a single individual, and not only did the real significance of that life have to be perceived, but the eternal nature of the truth thus manifested also had to be comprehended. It was the Spirit that taught the significance of that individual life,[87] but only after the immediate presence of that individual had ceased to be; then that particular life did not remain a mere historical event, but the religious significance of it was apprehended by Spirit. Then, and only then, through the Spirit, could the universal and eternal nature of that significance be grasped—as present and available for the individual in the present.[88] This is the faith of the Spiritual Community that came into being through Spirit's making that truth presently available to each individual member.

The ongoing existence of the Spiritual Community, as "the expression of what the Spirit has discovered," presupposes that discovery of truth as something that is actually present. It is this truth that constitutes the doctrine of the Spiritual Community, although the Community, because of the presence of Spirit within it, is also the authority whereby this doctrine "is further developed and gets a more specific form." [89] Each individual member of the Community becomes a partaker of this truth, though at first as something that is external to the individual and presented in the form of authority. This, Hegel observed, is the manner in which all truth initially comes to men, even truth about the material world. But it must not remain so. The child who "is not yet realized Spirit," who "has only the capability . . . of becoming Spirit," must become Spirit: the truth, which is at first only external, must become something that is known inwardly; it must become "identical with his Self," so that it "becomes his act of will, his Spirit." [90] It follows that "what we have here is the consciously felt presence of God, unity with God . . . the feeling of God in the heart," so that God is "no longer for the individual something beyond this world." [91]

However, there can be no doubt that this Spiritual Community (*Gemeinde*), which is primarily an inward reality, is not, for Hegel, to be identified with the Christian church in history. The Spiritual Community will always show itself in some form of worldly existence—and this, for Hegel, is the Christian Church—but in that worldly existence the truth will always be distorted, for in being expressed in *Vorstellungen* it admits "disunion" and "differentiation" in a variety of forms, culminating in the representation of divine Being still as an Other.[92]

In this context in *Phen.* Hegel found it appropriate to recall the dialectic of sense-certainty: "the superseded *This of sense* is, in the first place, the Thing of *perception*, not yet the *universal* of the Understanding." [93] What Hegel meant by this is that as in immediate sense experience the sense-certainty about the object must give way to the perception of a 'thing' as a collection of universal properties, so here the death of Christ is the end of consciousness' immediate sensory experience of the presence of God in this individual person; and the Resurrection, Ascension and Pentecost are the transition to the perception of the presence of God in the community *(Gemeinde)*. But this is not yet a proper understanding of the universal, for here universality exists only by representation in the life of the community *(Gemeine)*.[94] Here, as in the perception of the 'thing' as a collection of diverse universal properties, so the representation of Spirit, while being true in content, is defective in form, for self-conscious Spirit is perceived as being expressed in diverse moments such as in the distant past life of Jesus: the unity of God and man is confined to the life of a past individual, and the bridging of the gulf between God and man is seen to be dependent on the sacrificial death of that individual and will not be fully realized until some time in the remote future. In fact, therefore, religious consciousness still perceives God as a 'Beyond' in unreconciled estrangement *(unversöhnte Entzweiung)* from the 'Here'.[95]

What has to be comprehended is the great totality and unity of all that is: that the death of Christ was not just "the death of the God-man but also the death of the abstract God whose transcendence radically separated human existence from the divine essence." [96] What has to be realized is that the Death and Resurrection of Christ not only has significance as aspects of a particular life history, but fundamentally, that in the whole Christ-event there took place the focusing of the entire dynamic movement of absolute Spirit, which 'others' itself and 'returns' to itself, knowing itself as universal self-conscious Spirit. It must further be comprehended that this movement of Spirit is also the movement of every self-conscious spirit, who thus exists in the unity of universal self-conscious Spirit, a unity that is not removed to some future time but is constantly being lived and renewed every day.

The *death* of the divine Man, *as death*, is *abstract* negativity, the immediate result of the movement which ends only in *natural* universality. Death loses this natural meaning in spiritual self-consciousness, i.e. it comes to be its just stated Notion; death becomes transfigured from its immediate meaning, viz. the non-being of this *particular* individual, into the *universality* of the Spirit who dwells in His community, dies in it every day, and is daily resurrected. (*Phen.*, 475)

"But as yet the religious community is only an imperfect form of absolute knowledge. Even though in this community representation comes back into self-consciousness, this return is not actual for it; it still represents the return to itself in such a way that the reconciliation that the community embodies does not appear to it as *its* work; the community is indeed truth that knows itself, but it is not conscious of producing this truth. Production of truth as a development of the self belongs to absolute knowledge." [97] While religious consciousness possesses the truth of the unity of the Divine Man, it does not know it and hence does not fully live it; and it is for this reason that Hegel regarded religious consciousness as not completely escaping that from state of unhappy consciousness.

Manifest *(offenbare)* Religion in Actuality: Revealed *(geoffenbarte)* Religion

Hegel repeatedly spoke of absolute religion as manifest religion *(die offenbare Religion),* the religion in which 'what God is' is simply and openly manifest. "It is the religion which derives its fulness from itself, which is complete in itself" in the sense that it is "the religion which has itself for its content, its fulness." In itself—according to its Notion—Hegel said religion is "the consciousness of absolute Essence" ; and whereas in most expressions of this consciousness, the content—absolute Essence—is perceived as being in a relation of exclusion and separation to consciousness, in absolute religion, consciousness and content are one, for it is the religion in which God is manifested to Himself, and knows Himself, in the finite spirit, and so it is the religion in which infinite Spirit and finite spirit are known as inseparably connected.[98]

However, Hegel recognized that this religion, as it is actually known, is not fully comprehended as manifest religion, but is reduced to the level of understanding where it is seen to be the religion that has been revealed *(die geoffenbarte Religion).*

This religion, which is manifest or revealed to itself, if not only the revealed *(offenbare)* religion, but the religion which is actually known as a religion which has been revealed *(geoffenbart)*; and by this is understood, on the one hand, that it has been revealed by God, that God has actually communicated the knowledge of Himself to men; and, on the other hand, that being a revealed religion, it is a positive religion in the sense that it has come to men, and has been given to them from the outside. (*LPR*, 335) [99]

By the use of the past participle, *geoffenbart*, Hegel has cleverly indicated his meaning. Absolute religion is, in truth, manifest religion, in which finite consciousness and absolute Being are known as inseparably one; but in fact, the way this religion comes to individuals inevitably involves the marks of positivity—it appears as a truth that has once been revealed by God and comes to each individual from outside himself, being presented in the first instance through "education, training, definite teaching," its truth being "simply given." This, of course, is no different from the way in which other things, such as the law of freedom, come to us; and it is necessarily the case that manifest religion, possessing as it does a historical outward form, will always possess an element of positivity. However, just as the law of freedom ought to come to be accepted not simply "because it is actually there, but rather because it is the essential characteristic of our rational nature itself," so, too, this religion—although it has the appearance of positive elements—must come to be known as openly manifest: the truth of Spirit must be known inwardly, "for what is spiritual is higher than what is outward, its truth can be attested only by itself and in itself, and demonstrated only through itself and in itself." [100]

Hegel, however, did not find any genuine expression of this openly manifest religion. Certainly Christianity possessed the truth of Spirit within it, but the actual historical forms of Christianity really remained in the condition of positivity without attaining that inwardness in which the truth of Spirit is truly manifest. Hegel's conviction on this matter is well indicated in two sections in *Phen.*, in which he discussed the "Unhappy Consciousness" and the "Believing Consciousness".

Religious Consciousness as Unhappy Consciousnesss

The unhappy consciousness is the divided or sundered consciousness; it is the consciousness that has not yet grasped the unity of universality and particularity, of identity and diversity; it is the consciousness that feels a separation between the particularity of the self and the universality of the essence of life; and therefore it is the consciousness that aims at something beyond itself. The unhappy consciousness is "inwardly disrupted"; it is the consciousness whose essential nature "is for it a *single* consciousness," but that always has "in the one consciousness the other also," for it "itself *is* the gazing of one self-consciousness into another and itself *is* both." [101] But it is not yet this unity, and because both are seen as being completely opposed, consciousness takes one to be essential, and the 'other'—the pluralistic, variable, and contingent world—to be inessential, and seeks to liberate itself from this changing world by escaping into the unchangeable of which it is aware and which it identifies with itself. However, consciousness cannot escape this world, for it finds that it is caught up in this changing world, is subject to it, and depends on it for its existence; and so consciousness' sense of its own essentiality gives way to the sense of "its own nothingness," and it becomes conscious "of itself as a particular individual." [102]

Consequently, consciousness projects the Unchangeable *(das Unwandelbare)* into a 'Beyond' set over against the world of diverse and changing things. But there is no positive achievement here, argued Hegel; rather, only a negative one, for the immutable has been reduced to an opposing particular. "For consciousness to look for itself in another, then, is to go nowhere, since the other is only a projection of itself. Worse still, by representing the other, the immutable, to itself, it makes the other simply into another particularity, so that the other is pictured as both *outside* and *particular*, and what is achieved is a unity '*in which the difference* of both is *still* dominant'." [103]

Consistent with his repeated manner of analysis, Hegel identified three different ways by which individuality can be linked with the Unchangeable.[104] First, there is the form in which individuality "appears to itself as opposed to the Unchangeable," where the Unchangeable is known "only as the alien Being who passes judgment on the particular individual." The second way occurs where "consciousness learns that individuality belongs to the Unchangeable itself, so that it assumes the form of individuality into which the entire mode of existence passes." [105] The difference between this first and second way, for Hegel, is the difference between Judaism and Christianity: in the former, there is the consciousness of man and God being opposed, the consciousness of the particular lacking the essence of its life, which could be found only in a transcendent Unchangeable Being who is always a 'Beyond'; in the latter, there is the consciousness of man and God being united, the grasping of the Beyond being united with subjectivity, that is, the consciousness of the Unchangeable, the essence of life, being joined with a particular self-consciousness and being present as a historical figure.[106] Having thus become aware of the genuine reconciliation of particularity and the Unchangeable in the historical figure, there emerged the possibility of the third stage, in which the particular consciousness discovers itself as a 'particular' in the Unchangeable and so reaches the truth of the unity of God and man, for it "becomes aware of the reconciliation of its individuality with the universal." [107]

Naturally, for consciousness to achieve this third stage would be to experience "the joy of finding itself" in the Unchangeable, an achievement that would mark the transformation of the unhappy consciousness into the happy consciousness. But of course, Hegel did not consider this transformation to have occurred in the religious consciousness, which he continued to liken to the unhappy consciousness. As Hegel saw it, Christian consciousness has not been able to discover the implications of the awareness of the genuine unity of God and humanity that was manifest in the historical person, Jesus; it has not been able to experience the joy of discovering itself in absolute Spirit and thus of attaining the truth of the unity of God with every being. This is so because Christian consciousness sees this unity posed only in the one historical person, and it does not see the universal meaning of the Incarnation. The unhappy result is that "the beyond not only persists, but really is more firmly established." [108] If, on the one hand, the 'Beyond' has been brought closer, on the other hand, it remains in confrontation with the individual; and furthermore, because it is identified with a particular individual, it inevitably and increasingly becomes a thing of the past, thus remaining in fact just as remote. All hope of the individual becoming one with the divine still remains "a hope, i.e. without fulfilment and present fruition," [109] and consciousness has not been liberated from its unhappy state.

But this does not mean that there is no striving to realize this hope, and Hegel proceeded to analyze ways in which he detected that this consciousness endeavored to attain oneness with the objective reality that it perceived to be over against it; and, of course, as Hegel regarded the unhappy consciousness as being characteristic of the historical expressions of religious consciousness, his analysis contains many allusions to historical forms of Christianity.

When the Unchangeable is taken to be incarnate, it seems as "an object for pure consciousness" to be "present in its own proper nature." [110] However, this cannot be so, for the presence of God in a historical figure is not God as he is in himself; the truth of God manifest in Jesus has to be thought through conceptually so as to internalize the truth that has been revealed externally, and to universalize that truth that has been revealed in individuality. But this is what consciousness fails to do: consciousness has not made the presence of God its own, for the Unchangeable, God, is still thought of as essentially an individual existent; consciousness does not know that "its object, the Unchangeable, which it knows essentially in the form of individuality, as *its own self*, is itself the individuality of consciousness." [111] So consciousness remains unhappy consciousness because its essence remains a 'Beyond' for it. It fails to grasp conceptually the relationship between the immutable and the particular consciousness, and so it devotes itself to a kind of thinking about real thought, a mere state of devotion *(Andacht)*, which focuses itself on external ceremonies such as the "chaotic jingling of bells", the "mist of warm incense", and a kind of "musical thinking".[112] But an awareness of God through such externals is nothing more than emotional feeling, a certainty of "being known and recognized" by a God who is a particular "being out there"; it is not a grasping of God as he is in himself—in the Notion.

Hegel located the inadequacy not in the ceremonies themselves,[113] but in the attitude of which he takes them to be symptomatic in this instance—namely, the attitude that, devoid of the truth of incarnation, strives for unity with an external, remote God through devotional acts. So, religious consciousness remains unhappy consciousness: in failing to internalize the universal truth of incarnation, it attempts to 'picture' the Unchangeable 'out there', and in consequence, the relationship with God is emotional and results in what is really a separation from God.

This religious consciousness is also divided in its attitude toward reality, which, on the one hand, it takes to be "intrinsically null"; but on the other hand, it takes it to be "a sanctified *world*." [114] As the latter, it is a symbol of the divine through divine intervention, especially in the Incarnation,[115] but also in the sacraments,[116] in which, through the authority given to the priesthood to pray for the sending down of divine grace, physical elements are seen to become vehicles of the presence of God—but they are not seen to be such vehicles in themselves, for they are thought to need to be 'changed' by the intervening power of God.

The sense of the nothingness of reality in the face of the universal, and the unworthiness of the self before God, is also displayed in the ascetic attitude and practices that have the consequence of making the drives and needs—which are part of one's existence as a physical being—not a source for the enjoyment of life (which they ought to be), but a cause of unhappiness. In the more extreme forms of asceticism, they are "the object of serious endeavour, and become precisely matters of utmost importance"; and by a consequent preoccupation with them, the ascetic becomes imprisoned by those very things that he believes to be evil, and that therefore he is supposed to be striving to conquer. Thus, "we have only a personality confined to its own self and its own petty actions, a personality brooding over itself, as wretched as it is impoverished." [117]

Nevertheless, this feeling of the need to deny oneself springs from the consciousness of a relationship with the Unchangeable, though it is the kind of relationship that is seen to depend upon a mediator, a "conscious being" who brings about a presentation of the two extremes to one another. Again, Hegel's language makes it fairly apparent that he has in mind the mediating role of the church's priesthood; and his argument is that the presence of such a mediator has a destructive effect on the individual consciousness, for it "frees itself from action and enjoyment so far as they are regarded as its own." [118] The mediator presents itself, and is accepted as "having a direct relationship with the unchangeable Being"; hence individual consciousness surrenders its own freedom of choice and decision making to the mediator, and seeks from the mediator a release from the sense of guilt. Consciousness' abandoning itself as a free specific will shows itself first in the quest for advice from the mediator on matters of justice and goodness, and the ready acceptance of that advice; secondly, in the abandoning of its independent thought by doing something quite "foreign to it, a thinking and speaking of what is meaningless to it" [119]—an agreement to something it does not understand, that was symbolized in the use of Latin in the church's liturgies that are imposed by the church; and thirdly, in consciousness' surrendering of itself, at least symbolically, in handing over, by means of fasting and almsgiving, the products of its own labor and enjoyment.

According to Hegel's observation of these matters, they are further testimony to the religious understanding of the separation between infinite Being and finite humanity, and thus testimony to the failure of religious consciousness to grasp the true notion of Spirit that is really manifest in the Christian religion.

Religious Consciousness as Believing Consciousness

This Hegelian conviction, that the historical expression of Christianity had fallen short of the truth that had been lived and taught by its founder, was first expressed in *ETW*, and it subsequently remained a firm conviction. It was in the piety of Catholicism that had developed as an expression of the Christian consciousness in the medieval church that Hegel found his primary example of the divided or unhappy consciousness. In another section of *Phen.*, "Faith and Pure Insight," he turned his attention to another, equally inadequate, form of Christian consciousness—namely, the stress on Faith, which found forceful expression in the Reformation and with which he was familiar in the Lutheran Church of contemporary Germany.

In seeking to discover the difference that Hegel identified between these two expressions of Christian consciousness, one must note that Hyppolite suggests that in Hegel's early writings the use "of the term 'objectivity' in the sense of 'positivity' foreshadows a difference between unhappy consciousness and faith." [120] That use of the term objectivity in regard to religion was descriptive of the religion that was alien to the people, imposed from without on the basis of some external authority, and was divorced from the spirit and needs of the people. In contrast, 'subjective' religion was essentially personal and a matter of direct experience.

However, there cannot be a strict parallel drawn between this distinction and that between unhappy consciousness and faith. The religion that is indicative of unhappy consciousness, like subjective religion, is essentially personal, for it is an expression of a subjective piety.[121] But, unlike the earlier reference to subjective religion with which the individual felt at one and in which he found liberation, the unhappy consciousness is a condition of the individual self-consciousness that is certain of itself in relation to other things and beings that it takes to be beyond and opposed to the self; therefore it is a consciousness that feels a separation between the particularity of the self and the universality of life, and thus it is a consciousness that aims at something beyond itself.

On the other hand, the consciousness of faith is a consciousness of objectivity; like the earlier term 'objective religion,' it is the acceptance of an externally given belief in a Being remote from the world. Now there is also this sense of remoteness in the religion of unhappy consciousness, and that is why the strict parallel with the earlier distinction cannot be drawn—Hegel's conception of subjective religion was not one that admitted a sense of remoteness; but in the consciousness of faith all suggestion of subjectivity has disappeared. Hegel himself, in the later section of *Phen.*, sums up the distinction he saw between the unhappy consciousness and the believing consciousness:

> In the ['unhappy' consciousness, the content] has the character of a content produced from consciousness for which Spirit yearns, and in which Spirit cannot be satiated or find rest, because it is not yet *in itself* its own content, or is not the Substance of it. In the 'believing' consciousness, on the other hand, the content was regarded as the selfless *Being* of the world, or as essentially an *objective* content of picture-thinking, of a picture-thinking that

simply flees from reality and consequently is without the certainty of self-consciousness. (*Phen.*, 464)

Both involve the sense of disunity. The unhappy consciousness is a description of the individual consciousness, which is self-aware and is certain of itself in its particularity over against the universality of the 'other', of which the self is not certain, and with which it strives for union, being not yet its own. Of course, this consciousness is not to be equated with medieval Christianity; it is just that Hegel found that expression of Christianity (or at least some aspects of it) to be the most apt example of this consciousness.

On the other hand, the believing consciousness is a consciousness of the objectivity of its object as something that is externally given, that is, a Being that is a 'Beyond' in relation to the world. The consciousness of faith is therefore an escape from the world, and the historical example cited by Hegel is found in the world that followed the collapse of the Middle Ages. But, again, it is important to realize that such historical examples are not to be overstressed, because one can find these different attitudes appearing repeatedly in different historical eras: what Hegel was doing was using these historical examples to illustrate the consciousness he was seeking to describe.

Hegel's presentation of the believing consciousness is that it is one that has faith in a Being beyond the world of reality; it is the attempt to transcend the alienation of the world by a retreat into a Beyond, a suprasensible world, into which the self projects the unity—which it desires, but does not find in this alienated world.[122] As faith in a Beyond, however, this believing consciousness carries within itself its own alienation, and Hegel was quite adamant that it is not to be thought of as the authentic religious consciousness: "it is not the self-consciousness of absolute being as it is *in* and *for itself*, not religion, that is here dealt with but Faith, so far as this is a *flight* from the real world and thus is not *in* and *for itself*. This flight from the realm of the present is, therefore, in its own self dual-natured."[123]

Hegel's discussion of the believing consciousness is set in the context of the struggle between Faith and Reason.[124] Reason or 'pure insight' also is a flight from the world of alienation, but a flight into the self as the only significant reality; it is an attempt to overcome alienation by the self penetrating everything that appears as other and alien and reducing it to itself. This retreat into the self is, on the one hand, in sharp contrast to believing consciousness, which is a flight into a Beyond; but, on the other hand, they have certain basic similarities in which they both hold the same truth. Both see the values of "the World of Culture" as being rather superficial, even though apparently sophisticated; and both consequently feel alienated and seek to withdraw from that world in search for self-realization in that which is affirmed by the innermost depth of consciousness as the only significant reality. In this both are identical, but their ultimate vision of this significant reality is in sharp opposition—for one, it is a Being beyond the present world; for the other, it is the self—and on the basis of this difference, they strongly oppose each other, the more so because of the basic similarity between them.

The defect of believing consciousness, in Hegel's opinion, is that the object of its faith is present as a Beyond, as a content that is estranged from self-consciousness, and so Reason could find in the object of Faith "an inconceivable world . . . , a world alien to reason, a being-other whose otherness is irreducible." [125] In contrast to Faith, Reason—which Hegel regarded as having achieved its greatest strength in the Enlightenment—asserts the absolute freedom of the human spirit, and so purposes to liberate it from the shackles of the irrational content of Faith. Any such imposition on human consciousness as the external content of Faith is a mark of positivity, and it is this that Reason denounces. This conflict between Reason and positive Faith had permeated the atmosphere of his student days, and it had become one of the fundamental problems for the young Hegel. He was convinced of the Enlightenment's assertion of the autonomy of human reason, and he accepted the truth of much of the criticism directed against religious faith; but he was not an uncritical man of the Enlightenment, and in *Phen.*, in discussing the philosophic implications of the reason-faith conflict, in the light of his conception of "religion as a moment of absolute Spirit," he saw that "the Enlightenment's critique, although correct, appears as merely negative," and that the Enlightenment had failed "to grasp the content of faith and discover its speculative meaning." [126]

First, the purely negative attitude of the Enlightenment was displayed in its attack on the object of believing consciousness—an attack that was so blindly negative that it resulted in contradictory accusations. On the one hand, it accused the believer of inventing his object;[127] on the other hand, it attacked the object of belief as something imposed on the believer by a deceptive priesthood, and as therefore being external and alien to the believer.[128] But here the Enlightenment showed itself to be foolish, even absurd, for it contradicted itself in that it also claimed that consciousness cannot have anything imposed upon it by an external source.

Secondly, the Enlightenment's failure to grasp the content of Faith was displayed in its reduction of the religious object to nothing but a finite thing, thereby attacking every aspect of belief as mere superstition. Such an accusation was based on a number of allegations: the Enlightenment took the absolute Being of Faith to be nothing but "a piece of stone", "a block of wood", or "a piece of dough"; [129] it alleged that Faith based its certainty on the external grounds of some particular historical evidence; and it dismissed cultic practices as foolish, superstitious activities on the part of the believer. However, in these allegations Hegel again found the purely negative attitude of the Enlightenment toward belief: it destroyed religious symbolism, showing itself to be "incapable of comprehending the *ground* of belief";[130] it completely misunderstood belief when it took external evidence as the sole basis of belief,[131] and it failed to distinguish the goal of achieving "the superior consciousness" of freedom (which Reason itself seeks) from the means pursued to achieve it, and thereby Reason was again trapped in contradiction.[132] Furthermore, the foolishness of the Enlightenment's attack on Faith was demonstrated by its accusation that Faith is foisted on the believer by an external authority, such as deceiving priests, for Hegel contended that the consciousness of a people cannot be deluded on such a fundamental issue, for here "consciousness has the immediate *certainty of itself.*" [133]

The disappointing consequence of this negative and foolish attitude toward Faith was that the Enlightenment failed to come to grips with the real defect of Faith, namely, the projection of absolute Being into a Beyond, away from the present world; and it also failed to recognize its own similarity with believing consciousness. Both search for "the knowledge of that essential being in which consciousness has the immediate *certainty of itself*"; and whereas the believer finds it in a remote absolute, the Enlightenment man finds it equally in an absolute, but his absolute is reason. The similarity between Faith and Enlightenment meant that the latter's critique of the former was really a critique of itself.[134]

Nevertheless, the fact was, in Hegel's view, that the Enlightenment had had a very significant effect upon Faith. Under attack from Reason, believing consciousness had reacted strongly by attempting to prove the content of Faith, thereby demonstrating that it had come to accept the intellectual framework of the Enlightenment that was built on the cult of Reason. Evidence of believing consciousness being won over to the ways of its opponent was provided by the believer's desire "to appeal to historical evidence in order to get that kind of foundation, or at least confirmation, of its content." [135] Similarly, evidence was provided by the believer—in the Protestant tradition, which Hegel knew and on which his discussion largely concentrated—denying the importance of religious symbolism, being unable to comprehend—within the intellectual structures of the Enlightenment, which he had come to accept—the "unity between the divine and the merely external." Thus, believing consciousness was "forced to an even more 'spiritual' religion in which the things of God are more clearly separated from this world." [136]

On the Enlightenment view, the only knowledge open to human reason is knowledge of the finite, and on the acceptance of such a view, the subsequent 'enlightened theology' took one of two forms. On the one hand, it was argued by such theologians as Storr, Hegel's teacher at Tübingen, that man's knowledge of God comes only through revelation—the content of which was divinely given and was not open to the scrutiny of the human mind, which is bound to the world of finitude. On the other hand, there was the deistic view that limited man's understanding of God to the mere knowledge of his existence, which human reason can attain through the arguments of natural theology and morality. But human reason can know nothing of the nature of God—God is totally separated from the world, and is nothing more than a mere abstraction; God is an absolute Being who exists absolutely, but about whom nothing else can be said, an absolute Being who turns out to be "a *vacuum* to which no determinations, no predicates, can be attributed." [137]

In Hegel's opinion, such a 'theological' view was really no different from the other typical Enlightenment concept of the world, namely, materialism. In the characteristic materialistic view of the time, there is some absolute essence, Matter or Nature, that underlies the changing particulars of the sensible world. But this essence, or substratum, is a mere abstraction—void of all content, Hegel argued, for nothing further can be said about it. Therefore, in both cases, whether it be the absolute essence of God or of Matter, the Enlightenment view results in an absolute that is a mere characterless abstraction; and when there is coupled with this the Enlightenment ethic—namely, utilitarianism, which denies any intrinsic value to things—there has emerged what Hegel regarded as "an impoverished world view," the "dullest philosophy that ever was." [138]

The Hegelian Answer: The Truth of Manifest (*offenbare*) Religion is expressed in Philosophy

In Hegel's view, there could be no alternative but to transcend such a world view offered by Enlightenment man; and, in the striving to achieve this, Hegel presented 'Faith' as having the dialectical advantage. 'Reason' is locked into an insurmountable finitude, which it regards as the sole context of human experience and with which therefore it is satisfied. But in contrast, Faith is dissatisfied with finitude—this is the dialectically important difference between Faith and Reason[139]—and it therefore longs to discover and be united with the infinite. The sense of difference, detachment, and distance from God has to be overcome in the principle of identity as contrasted with the principle of duality. This was Hegel's constantly recurring theme: just as he firmly denied Kant's thesis that man can know only phenomena, so he denied the assumed divergence between, and radical otherness of, the finite and infinite. He saw the relationship between God and man "as an *essential* one, requiring no fantastic leap towards the unknown (and/or unknowable) 'beyond'. God and man no longer seem to confront one another as estranged and alien others, from opposite sides of an unbridgeable ontological chasm, but are viewed as having an intrinsic unity." [140]

However, not all endeavors at demonstrating this truth were successful in Hegel's view. Hegel's contemporary, Schleiermacher, for example, sought to give expression to the principle of identity in order to make possible a new understanding of religion and to satisfy the longing for knowledge of, and union with, God; but Schleiermacher's approach was by means of intuition and the feeling of absolute dependence, and Hegel was extremely critical of intuition and feeling as the basis for truth. To base truth on mere feeling is to lock it into the realm of subjectivity, for it means that the individual subject cannot really get beyond himself: "What has its root only in my feelings is for me alone; it is mine, but not its own, it has no independent existence in and for itself." [141] Therefore, Hegel saw this position to be just as empty as that of the Enlightenment, against which it was reacting;[142] and consequently, it appears to be necessary "to show that God is not rooted in feeling merely, is not merely *my* God." [143]

Hegel did not doubt that the truth of God, of absolute Spirit, is represented by religion, though only in Manifest *(offenbare)* Religion, which alone reveals absolute Spirit as immediately present and known as Spirit in whom the individual spirit can recognize itself and with whom it can feel at one: thus, absolute Spirit is known as universally present in, and at one with, reality. Yet, the fact is, Hegel asserted, that even in this highest form of religion—the one in which the truth is contained—that truth is obscured through the form of religious representation. And this obscurity can be replaced by clarity, Hegel argued, only at the level of absolute knowledge—philosophy, which can therefore be said to present the truth of Manifest Religion in its most clear and distinct form:

> At the present time it is philosophy which is not only orthodox, but orthodox *par excellence;* and it is it which maintains and

preserves the principles which have always held good, the fundamental truths of Christianity. (*LPR*, vol. 2, 345)

Hegel was absolutely convinced that the proper relation between Faith and Reason was not that of separation—an idea that Kant helped to promote and that was subsequently developed to its extremity by Kierkegaard—but rather that of coalescence. Thus, Hegel could assert repeatedly, and without any divergence, that the content of religion in its highest form and the content of philosophy are identical: they both contain the truth of absolute Spirit; but they differ in the form of the presentation of that truth, with the philosophic form being the most adequate to demonstrate the rationality of the content and to sustain the Community, which is the locus of actual Spirit.[144]

It must now be asked, How is one to react to this Hegelian position?

Lukács is representative of a number of commentators when he refers to the "double movement in Hegel's philosophy," the "negation and reinstatement of religion." [145] He reminds us that it was Feuerbach who first observed and criticized this aspect of Hegel's philosophy, and he says that Feuerbach's chief point—that Hegel first negates and reinstates Christian theology—undoubtedly applies to *Phen.*, particularly if we bear in mind the conclusions Hegel reached concerning believing consciousness. However, it seems to me that such a criticism can be directed at Hegel only if one in fact fails to grasp Hegel's own chief point about religion. The forms of religious consciousness that Hegel had negated in his analysis of "Unhappy Consciousness" and "Believing Consciousness" are certainly not expressions of what he took to be authentic religion: authentic or absolute religion is Manifest *(offenbare)* Religion, and the inadequacy of those various forms of religious consciousness that Hegel has negated lies in their failure to comprehend the implications of Manifest Religion.

The apparent failure of Feuerbach and Lukács to grasp what Hegel was doing could possibly stem from their basic disagreement with him. Feuerbach wished to reduce absolute spirit to human spirit, arguing that the absolute was nothing but a projection of the human spirit; but Hegel, while he wished to maintain a sense in which the absolute is identified with human subjectivity, said the "Absolute Being is at the same time in and for itself," [146] i.e., not just in the sense that the Absolute is "in and for itself" for the believer, but "in and for itself" for itself.

It is for this reason that Hegel presented religion as a bearer of the truth; but what Hegel supposedly 'reinstated' is not the foregoing inadequate forms of religious faith, but rather the absolute Manifest

Religion (and it is not a reinstatement within Hegel's system, but a dialectical progress), in which the quest of the human spirit attains, though still not with complete clarity, the truth that reality is a manifestation of absolute Spirit.

An entirely different assessment of Hegel's position is the assertion that, although Hegel repeatedly presented the Christian religion as the absolute religion, his interpretation of Christian beliefs from his viewpoint of speculative knowledge or philosophy, really amounts to a rewrite that "leaves out the very essence of Christian faith, or indeed of any faith relating to the God of Abraham." [147]

While there will be occasion to consider the Lukács—Feuerbach assessment, the main thrust of Part 3 will be to make an evaluation of this other assessment by means of examining in considerable detail Hegel's treatment of one doctrine, namely, the doctrine of God.

PART III

Ambiguity of Hegel's 'God':

A Systematic Investigation

Introduction

One fact about Hegel's position, which the foregoing analysis has sought to make clear, is that he invariably asserted the identity of content in both absolute religion and philosophy. But whereas religion presents that content by means of *Vorstellungen* only, philosophy presents it in thought, and by this means the truth of the content is fully grasped. The content, nevertheless, remains identical: it is nothing less than the process of reality itself—it is 'the absolute Spirit' *(der absolute Geist)* or, to use the religious *Vorstellung*, as Hegel frequently did, it is 'God' *(Gott)*. Nothing could give a clearer indication of the religious dimension that pervades Hegel's philosophy. Yet, one can also point to the fact that his philosophy, like religion, is about the achievement of reconciliation *(Versöhnung)*, since his abiding concern was to discover the way to overcome alienation—which he perceived as resulting from a finite understanding of reality as being divided into individual parts, separated from and opposed to each other. If this alienation is to be overcome, Hegel believed, it is necessary to rise above the finite through speculative thought: only a total world view can provide the means for rising above the one-sidedness of the finite, and so heal the sense of separation and alienation.

This latter observation explains the former: given Hegel's desire for a secure basis of reconciliation, it is not surprising to find that his concept of absolute Spirit or God occupied the central place in his philosophy.

In any system of religious thought the concept of divine Being is the focal point and determining feature of the religion; and in Hegel's philosphy, which possesses such a pronounced religious dimension, his concept of God as absolute Spirit is fundamental to an understanding of his philosophy in general and his philosophy of religion in particular.[1] In any system of religious thought a hope of reconciliation will be closely related to and dependent on its doctrine of God; and in Hegel's philosophy the fulfillment of his quest for reconciliation is grounded in the concept of divine Being, who "is the beginning of all things, and the end of all things," the point from which "all things proceed" and to which "all return back":[2] indeed, "God is Himself all content, all truth and reality."[3] Given

such a concept of divine Being, Hegel's philosophy exuded a confidence that the unity of all things resides in God, who is Universal
and self-subsisting, One and the only true reality.

> God is universal, concrete, full of content, [by which it is implied]
> that God is One only, and not one as contrasted with many
> Gods, but that there is only the One, that is, God. . . . God in
> His universality, this Universal, in which there is no limitation,
> no finiteness, no particularity, is the absolute Self-subsisting
> Being, and the only Self-subsisting Being; and what subsists has
> its root, its subsistence, in this One alone.
> God is the absolute Substance, the only true reality. All else,
> which is real, is not real in itself, has no real existence of itself;
> the one absolute reality is God alone, and thus He is the absolute
> Substance. (*LPR*, vol. 1, 92)

This understanding of God as the one true reality is the belief of
religious consciousness, and at the level of religion this concept finds
expression both in theological formulations and in devotional practices, which, in Hegel's opinion, lead to the distortion of the truth
of this concept. But Hegel was aware that, when taken in an abstract
way, at the level of speculative thought, this understanding of God
may possibly be equated with Spinozism; and, believing such an
equation to be a misrepresentation of the truth, he carefully sought
to avoid it. Indeed, as will be noted in some detail, Hegel frequently
distinguished his own position from that of Spinoza, and he did it
by means of his concept of Spirit, whereby he asserted that God is
not only Substance, but also Spirit: "God is Spirit, the Absolute
Spirit." [4]
Through this concept Hegel excluded from his own philosophy
any idea of God as fixed, static substantiality, and affirmed the notion
of the movement and activity—the process—of God as living Spirit.
According to the Hegelian concept, Spirit, in its pure eternal life, is
characterized by the rhythm of the threefold movement of Universality, Particularity, and Individuality: it is the very nature of living
Spirit, "just because it is living, to be at first only potential," that
is, in its Universal aspect; but it also belongs to the nature of living
Spirit to go forth into existence, to manifest itself in Particularity—
"to have itself as object." Indeed, Spirit that does not so manifest
itself, "*is* not"; and yet, Spirit is not truly Spirit until "it exists for
itself as the negation of all finite forms, as the absolute ideality," as
Individuality. [5]
Because Hegel was convinced that this essential understanding of
the nature of God as Spirit is contained in what he called "Manifest

Religion", which he identified in Christianity, it is less than surprising
to have found that Hegel located the principal tenets of his philosophy
in the doctrines of the Christian religion. Indeed, it was the Christian
doctrine of Trinity—representing, as it does, the idea of God as
activity and movement—that provided the model for Hegel's doctrine
of God: "the nature of Spirit unfolds itself for rational thought,
inasmuch as it apprehends God as essentially the Triune God. . . .
Without the characteristic of Trinity, God would not be Spirit, and
Spirit would be an empty word." [6] Thus God, as Spirit, is Universality;
but this "is only the foundation, *one* moment in the determination
of God as Spirit," for God is only God insofar as he manifests himself
in his 'Other', the particular, and in love unites this Other to himself
in a complete Individuality. So then, "the Universality of God is not
in regard to the content itself to be taken as an abstract Universality,
outside of which, and as opposed to which, the particular has an
independent existence." [7]

Hegel fully realized the importance, for both philosophy and religion, of the manner in which God is conceived, for that, in turn,
determines the manner in which God's relation with the world is
conceived; and both questions are common to all philosophies and
all religions.[8] Thus, the insights into the nature of God, which are
grasped by Manifest Religion, immediately raise the question of the
relation between Universal and Particular, between God and the
world: as Hegel himself said, "religion in itself essentially involves
the relation of Man to God." [9] Yet, it is very apparent that at the
familiar level of religious consciousness there is a phenomenological
description of God expressed in superlatives that reflect a perception
of God as an ultimate Being who transcends the realm of ordinary
experience: through the natural tendency of the human consciousness
to distinguish, God is objectified, being presented as an object who
is 'out there', other than the world of actuality, so that a gulf of
separation and opposition is seen to pervade the relationship between
God and humanity, God and the world, the infinite and the finite.

> The 'reflective' understanding begins by rejecting all systems
> and modes of conception, which, whether they spring from heart,
> imagination or speculation, express the interconnection of God
> and the world: and in order to have God pure in faith or
> consciousness, he is as essence parted from appearance, as infinite
> from the finite. (*EM*, §573)

But here a paradox emerges, as Hegel so perceptively observed,
for this intended description of ultimacy does nothing but reduce
God to another finite Being alongside of the finite world:

They stand in a finite relation to each other, and so far they are themselves both finite, and thus consciousness knows the absolute Essence only as something finite. (*LPR*, vol. 2, 329)

However, Hegel recognized that this level of religious consciousness does possess some insight into the transcending of this sense of separation and opposition, for it has the conviction that the estrangement between God and humanity is overcome through the cultic practices of the religious life. For religious consciousness, it is as man worships God that he becomes aware that "the standpoint of separation is not the true relation," and therefore has to be nullified by the awareness of unity with God through worship. "The subject recognizes the absolute substance, in which it has to annul or lose itself, as being at the same time *its* essence, *its* substance, in which, therefore, self-consciousness is inherently contained. It is this unity, reconciliation, restoration of the subject and of its self-consciousness, the positive feeling of possessing a share in, of partaking of this Absolute, and making unity with it actually one's own—this abolition of the dualism—which constitutes the sphere of worship. Worship comprises this entire inward and outward action, which has this restoration to unity as its object." [10] Central to this idea of worship as the means of realizing unity with God is that it must not be regarded simply as a human act, nor even as a divine act in response to a human act, but rather that God himself is the initiator behind the human act.

Be that as it may, it was Hegel's purpose to transform this sense of unity—which is attained through the conviction that the fundamental gulf of separation between God and humanity is bridged in worship—into the knowledge, at the level of philosophic thought, of the essential unity between God and humanity, God and the world, the infinite and finite.[11] But it is precisely here that the real difficulty lies: How is this relationship to be thought? [12] How are we to think of God if not as an ultimate Being who is over against the world, separated from the realm of ordinary experience? That Hegel precludes our thinking of God in such a way is clear from the fact that such an understanding implies estrangement between God and the world—a fact that necessitated, for Hegel, its transformation into a doctrine of God that provides the means for grasping the underlying, fundamental unity of all things.

In seeking to describe what Hegel was attempting in this regard, one can take up the suggestion of Copleston and say that Hegel was endeavoring to make the transition from 'God' to *God*;[13] that is, he was aiming to transform the understanding of God as some kind of—namely, ultimate—Being (a view that emphasizes 'otherness' as the hallmark of the relationship between the divine and the world of humanity) into an understanding of God that is at the heart of his own philosophy, namely, a doctrine of God that declares the relationship to be that of a fundamental unity. As Hegel put it: "the Idea of Spirit means the unity of divine and human nature. But the divine nature itself is merely something which is to be Absolute Spirit, and thus it is just the unity of divine and human nature which is itself the Absolute Spirit." [14]

One can say that the Hegelian doctrine of God poses two fundamentally significant questions that are central to any discussion of Hegel's philosophy of religion. First, is it possible to classify Hegel's doctrine in terms of any one of the major traditional options, namely, theism or deism, atheistic humanism or pantheism? It frequently has been the case that interpreters of Hegel have placed his doctrine of God in the category of pantheism, while many others have wanted to classify it as atheism. The latter interpretation requires Hegel's use of the term 'God' being taken as an appellation for the totality of finite things; while to attribute pantheism to Hegel—in the sense of acosmism, in which he himself used the term 'pantheism'—is to declare finite things to be illusory. In both cases, what has been achieved regarding the God-world relationship is the elimination either of God (in atheism) or the world (in Acosmic Pantheism). Still other commentators endeavor to interpret Hegel as embracing a theistic view—a doctrine that essentially emphasizes the otherness of God in relation to the world.

In an exploration into these various interpretations, it will be argued here that neither the elimination of God or the world nor the maintenance of a separation of God from the world is consistent with Hegel's striving for a philosophy that declares that God and the world are a unity, that finite and infinite do not lie apart, but are held together in a tension in which they penetrate one another. Taylor agrees that Hegel's philosophy "is not a theism, but it is not an atheist doctrine either, in which man as a natural being is at the spiritual summit of things. It is a genuine third position, which is why it is so easy to misinterpret." [15] But just how precisely that genuine other position is to be described is a major difficulty to be explored here.

Admittedly, another possible interpretation would be a form of pantheism other than the acosmic form; or alternatively, it might be possible to discover, as some suggest, some other middle way by which to interpret Hegel's doctrine of God. Hyppolite, while denying that Hegel leaned toward humanism or mysticism, also says it is "impossible to accuse Hegel of pantheism," and he concludes that "Hegel's thought remains equivocal, and opens the way to the diverse interpretations." [16] Hartshorne, much more strongly, has said that Hegel is "a man who is and wants to be in a perpetual systematic muddle between classical theism, classical pantheism, and something like neoclassical theism, with a dose of humanistic atheism, or the self-deification of man, thrown in for good measure." However, one must agree with Westphal in rejecting this view as "misled" and in asserting that "Hegel's position is considerably less muddled. He clearly wants nothing to do with either the kind of transcendence affirmed in classical theism or the finitude affirmed by neoclassical theism. His position is and wants to be a systematic mediation between classical pantheism and humanistic atheism." [17] Similarly, Fackenheim, throughout his important work, suggests that Hegel's thought seeks to discover a middle way. He speaks of "the extreme care with which his thought seeks a middle between right- and left-wing extremes, of which one would destroy the actual world and the other, philosophical thought"; and of the "equal care" with which "Hegel's speculative transfiguration of Christianity" seeks "a middle which would preserve Christianity against two extremes equally destructive of it. One of these is a speculative pantheism which would dissipate the human into the Divine. The other is an atheistic humanism which would reduce the Divine to the human." [18]

But, as already noted, this kind of talk about Hegel's position being a mediation between extremes creates the difficulty of describing the nature of that mediation. Thus, after examining—and rejecting— a number of alternative interpretations of a traditional kind, it is intended, then, to explore the nature of this middle way, concluding that—as is frequently the case with middle ways—there is in Hegel, as Hyppolite observed, an element of equivocation; but suggesting also that, given the nature of Hegel's purpose, this was both intentional and inevitable.

Secondly, how is Hegel's philosophy of religion to be assessed in terms of 'orthodox' Christianity, given his formal claim to be a Christian thinker? Indeed, one can go further and couch the question in more general terms, asking whether or not religious beliefs are so transformed in Hegel's philosophy that they completely lose their religious character. Thus, the interpretation of Hegel's doctrine of God as one that seeks a middle way brings to light the most fundamental question concerning Hegel's philosophy of religion: Is it the case that religious beliefs become different doctrines? Hegel asserted that in absolute religion the true nature of the God-world relationship was grasped, but still expressed in the language of *Vorstellungen*—a deficient form of expression that, leaving the way open for the interpretation of a separation between God and the world, needs to be transformed into speculative philosophy.

But is it the case that this transformation of the form in which the content is expressed is of such a kind that the content itself is really transformed into a different content? Or, in Fackenheim's words, "how can philosophical thought emancipate itself from the religious form and yet recognize, preserve, and indeed itself presuppose the truth of the religious content?"[19] Fackenheim sees this question as identifying a dilemma that, he says, haunts Hegel's philosophy of religion, and which he poses in the following manner: *"Either the representational form of religion is essential to its content, and this is why philosophy requires religion (and the absolute philosophy the Christian religion) as necessary presupposition. But then how can philosophy transcend or transfigure the representational form without loss of the religious content? Or else philosophy does indeed achieve its unprecedented feat: but then was not the representational form all along unessential to the religious content?"*[20]

A further dimension is added to this dilemma when Fackenheim restates it in the following manner: *"Either God is ultimately other than man,* as is the religious testimony of the believer who stands in relation with Him. *But then religion is true in form as well as in content, . . . Or philosophic thought can become an absolute, all-encompassing self-activity. But then it discloses the illusoriness of the gap between the Divine and the human, and hence that—in the decisive respect—religion is false in content no less than in form."*[21]

These two questions, which form the subject matter of the ensuing discussion, are inevitably closely linked: Hegel's doctrine of God cannot be isolated from the way he saw the relationship between religion and philosophy. If Hegel did achieve a middle way in his doctrine of God, is the truth, thus expressed, retained in speculative thought? If speculative thought transforms religious representation, does that transformation mean that the doctrine of God is so changed that it no longer contains anything of the religious content?

As already indicated, the intention here, in relation to the question concerning Hegel's doctrine of God, is ultimately to explore the middle way Hegel seems to seek; and then, in relation to the question concerning the relationship between religion and philosophy, to conclude that not only was it not Hegel's intention to lose the religious content, but that his position does not even entail—unintentionally—such a loss.[22] But first, the task is to examine the more traditional interpretations of Hegel's doctrine.

Chapter 10
Two Contradictory Interpretations of Hegel
Theism and Atheism

From the very nature of the terms themselves, theism and atheism, it is apparent that they represent contradictory views about the nature of reality, and when used as descriptions of Hegel's philosophy they represent two interpretations that are in definite conflict. Yet, the fact that both have been employed in reference to Hegel is highly indicative of the equivocal nature of Hegel's position and the consequent uncertainty of interpretation.

Hegel as a Theist

Amongst the many and various interpretations of Hegel's philosophy of religion is that which would place Hegel in the category of those who uphold a doctrine of God as a transcendent Being. The first piece of evidence that one could seek to support this interpretation is the fact that Hegel sincerely regarded himself as an adherent of Christianity in its Lutheran (Protestant) tradition, and that belief in a transcendent deity was a fundamental tenet of the orthodoxy of that faith. But further evidence can be sought in Hegel's major works and in his published (posthumously) lectures. Of course, whether or not the evidence that is called forth from these works to substantiate this interpretation is being used in a justifiable manner is a matter that demands considerable inquiry; and it is an inquiry that appears to lead to the conclusion that the evidence, when used in this way, is really being misconceived and misused.

Evidence of Theism

From the context of his writing about absolute religion—in *Phen.*, *LPR*, and *Enz.*—there is material that can be, and has been, cited for the support of this interpretation of Hegel's thought. In each of these works Hegel spoke of absolute Spirit *an sich*—the pure Notion of absolute Spirit—exhibiting itself in three moments: namely, Universality, Particularity, and Individuality.[1] It is what Hegel said about this pure Notion of absolute Spirit that is crucial for a theistic interpretation, the important question being: Does Hegel impute to absolute Spirit *an sich* any transcendent reality? In answer to this question one can point out that Hegel said that "under the moment of Universality," absolute Spirit "is at first the presupposed principle," which is "creator of heaven and earth: but yet in this eternal sphere [is] rather only begetting himself as his *son*, with whom, though different, he still remains in original identity."[2] Similarly, in *Phen.*, he said: "Essence beholds only its own self in its being-for-self." And in *LPR* he spoke of "God in His Universality" as "this Universal, in which there is no limitation, no finiteness, no particularity, [and which] is the absolute Self-subsisting Being, and the only Self-subsisting Being."[3]

Furthermore, Hegel stressed that absolute Spirit is not to be understood as abstract Substance, but as Subject—the Notion of absolute Spirit will remain a mere abstraction if it is not also seen as the first moment of another kind of threefold dynamic:[4] thus, absolute Spirit is Subject as the source of action or movement. It is absolute Spirit to which is ascribed self-revelation: "clearly if the word 'Mind' *[Geist]* is to have a meaning, it implies the revelation of Him."[5] It is absolute Spirit that does not stay "aloof and inert," but is "creator of heaven and earth"; "the merely eternal or abstract Spirit becomes an 'other' to itself or enters into existence, and directly into *immediate* existence."[6] It is by this concept of absolute Spirit 'becoming an other to itself' that the implication of a transcendent reality seems to be strongly suggested: "the absolute, eternal Idea is, in its essential existence, in and for itself, God in His eternity before the creation of the world, and outside of the world."[7]

Furthermore, when one turns to two other sections of Hegel's works, where his focus was not upon absolute religion, similar expressions are to be found. In *SL*, and also in *EL* (an abridged revision of the former), Hegel presented, at the level of pure thought, the Absolute, to which he here gave the name 'the Notion' *(Begriff)*, the doctrine of which, he said, "is divided into three parts": namely, Subjective Notion, Objectivity, and the Idea.[8] Of the Notion as Notion, he said that it "contains the three following 'moments' or functional parts," namely, Universality, Particularity, and Individuality.[9] In fact, in introducing the Notion, Hegel spoke in the following significant fashion:

> The notion is not something which is originated at all. No doubt the notion is not mere Being, or the immediate: it involves mediation, but the mediation lies in itself. In other words, the notion is what is mediated through itself and with itself. . . . the notion is the genuine first: and things are what they are through the action of the notion, immanent in them, and revealing itself in them. In religious language we express this by saying that God created the world out of nothing. In other words, the world and finite things have issued from the fullness of the divine thoughts and the divine decrees. Thus religion recognizes thought and (more exactly) the notion to be the infinite form, or the free creative activity, which can realize itself without the help of a matter that exists outside it. (*EL*, §163, Zus.)

Additional references, supplying material that is suggestive of the transcendent reality of the Notion, can be indicated in the following examples: In *SL* Hegel referred to the *Logic* as "The exposition of God as he is in his eternal essence before the creation of nature and a finite spirit." [10] In *EL* he said that "Thought, regarded as an *activity*, may be accordingly described as the *active* universal, and, since the deed, its product, is the universal once more, may be called a self-actualizing universal";[11] and that "It is by the notion alone that the things in the world have their subsistence; or as it is expressed in the language of religious conception, things are what they are, only in virtue of the divine and thereby creative thought which dwells within them." [12] Then, at the important point of transition between Hegel's "Logic" and his "Philosophy of Nature", these indicative words appear: "Enjoying an absolute liberty, the Idea does not merely pass over into life, or as finite cognition allow life to show in it: in its own absolute truth it resolves to let the 'moment' of its particularity, or of the first characterization and other-being, the immediate idea, as its reflected image, go forth freely as Nature." [13]

A Discussion of Hegel's 'Theism'

Those commentators, who find in Hegel the religious philosophy of a theist, read this kind of evidence as being supportive of their interpretation, indicating Hegel's concept of absolute Spirit to be that of an active Subject, having transcendent and independent reality, and being the source by which all things have their subsistence. However, before proceeding to examine this interpretation in some detail, it is necessary to classify what is meant by 'transcendence' in order to know exactly what one is eliminating when one denies that Hegel can be categorized as a theistic philosopher.

Findlay, in dismissing as misconceived this kind of interpretation of Hegel, describes it by means of the term 'transcendent metaphysician', thereby giving to 'transcendent' a meaning akin to Kant's use of 'transcendental'—which is shown in his definition of 'transcendent metaphysician' as "one who deals with objects or matters lying beyond our empirical ken, or who fits together or transforms what we know or experience into some total view going beyond any individual person's knowledge or experience." [14] However, while I want to argue that Hegel was not a philosopher of transcendence in the traditional theistic sense, I believe that if the term 'transcendence' is to be applied according to Findlay's definition, then it is not possible to exclude the interpretation of Hegel as a philosopher of transcendence. Therefore, it is my own view that the kind of transcendence that one can exclude as a possible aspect of Hegel's philosophy is that traditionally understood as part of theistic doctrine. Fackenheim comes nearer to this sense of transcendence when, making use of Findlay's term 'transcendent metaphysician', he defines such an interpretation of Hegel as one "whose logic . . . describes an ontologically self-sufficient, transcendent realm." [15]

However, it seems necessary to be more precise than Fackenheim's definition, for the expression "an ontologically self-sufficient, transcendent realm" could refer, with equal correctness, to a deistic or a theistic philosophy; and yet it is completely inconceivable that the former could ever be attributed to Hegel. In other words, within the context of traditional doctrines of God, it is justifiable to discuss Hegel only in relation to theism, because a deistic interpretation of Hegel could find no supportive evidence at all and must be quickly dismissed; but Fackenheim's definition does not accommodate this distinction. Both deism and theism assert a transcendent Deity whose existence is quite distinct from that of all finite beings, for Deity possesses its own existence whereas it is the source, the external cause, of all that is finite. Such a Deity must be One, self-sufficient, infinite and eternal. But Deism is the more thoroughgoing view of transcendence: it is a doctrine that holds the Deity to be completely unrelated to the finite, except for the relationship of creator in the sense of first cause. In Deism the transcendent nature of God is thoroughly stressed to the complete exclusion of the concept of divine immanence, thus denying the possibility of God's involvement in, and his self-revelation to, the created universe, and also denying the knowability of God.

Now it is clear that every aspect of Hegel's philosophy protests that such a doctrine is un-Hegelian: Hegel thoroughly did away with that which is merely transcendent and unknowable. An unmistakable indication of this is his repeated attacks upon the rationalist theology of the Enlightenment, which took the deistic view of God as the unknowable Supreme Being.[16] With such a doctrine of God, Hegel argued, in place of absolute Spirit of the believing consciousness, the 'enlightened' reason had only an abstract absolute, a Supreme Being, that is merely "a *vacuum*," an "empty Being," that is unknowable and "to which no determinations, no predicates, can be attributed."[17] In addition to his attitude toward this deistic view, there is Hegel's constant assertion of the very opposite kind of view about absolute Spirit: "God posits or lays down the Other, and takes it up again into His eternal movement. Spirit just is what appears to itself or manifests itself; this constitutes its act, or form of action, and its life; this is its only act, and it is itself only its act. What does God reveal, in fact, but just that He is this revelation of Himself?"[18]

In the light of this kind of evidence, which is abundant throughout Hegel's works, and without the need to argue the matter any further, deism can be dismissed as a possible interpretation of Hegel's philosophy. But the question of theism is not to be so easily dismissed, and has to be more seriously considered as a possible Hegelian position within the category of a 'transcendent metaphysician'.

Theism does not make the sharp deistic divorce between God and the world, in the sense that the theist endeavors to hold the divine transcendence and the divine immanence in a careful balance, precarious though that balance may be! Theism is a philosophical system that seeks to maintain this balance by asserting that while God is other than, and transcendent from, the world he has created (in this, it is the same as deism), he is continuously active in the world, preserving and governing it, being in a personal relationship with it (this, of course, is denied by deism). The God of theism is ultimate reality, and thus is one, infinite, and eternal Being, who is personal and worthy of worship; God is infinitely powerful both in himself— as self-existent Being—and, consequently, in his relationship with the world, which he has created ex nihilo, and to which he reveals himself in that preserving and governing activity, on which everything in the world depends for its existence.

In this way, theism tries to maintain a deliberate balance between transcendence and immanence. But it is questionable whether such a balance can be maintained within the terms of traditional theism—indeed, Hegel definitely argued that it cannot—for there is much within it that indicates the ultimacy, rather than the abrogation (*Aufhebung*), of the apparent separation between God and the world, thereby revealing a difficult tension, not to say contradiction, within a theistic philosophy.[19]

In spite of its affirmation of the immanence of God, theism is fundamentally a philosophy of the otherness of God, in that it asserts a definite ontological distinction between an absolute God and a created universe. God is infinite and eternal, yet the world is finite and transitory; God is wholly immutable, yet the world is in constant flux; God is totally independent and self-sufficient in his Being, yet the world, in itself, is insufficient and fully dependent on an Other for its being. The notion of God, as the unchanging and impassible Being, stresses that Deity must be completely unaffected by any other reality and must lack all passion or emotional response. The notion that Deity is the Absolute Being has carried the implication that God is not really related to the world, in the sense that God's relation to the world—his creating and sustaining it and his immanence in it—does not really belong to his Being. But the world is related to God in that the relation to God is constitutive of the world, and some reference to its dependence on God is therefore necessary for an adequate account of the world. Yet, on the other hand, there is nothing about the world—not even the fact of its existence—that is constitutive of the Being of God, for God is totally independent of the world, and the God-world relationship is asymmetrical in kind, a relation that is purely external to God, that is what the Scholastics called the divine aseity.

The traditional theistic view of the self-subsistent, independent nature of God involves a difficulty in explaining why there should be a world at all, since God's creative and revelatory activity is quite inessential to his nature. In the final analysis, the application of the terms 'absolute', 'unchangeable', and 'impassible' to the divine character really says the same thing, namely, that the world contributes nothing to God and that God's influence upon the world is in no way conditioned by divine responsiveness to unforeseen, self-determining activities of created beings.

Hegel's response to the theistic description of God is, it seems, quite definitely negative: "God, the absolutely infinite, is not something outside and beside whom there are other essences"; indeed, "when we hear the Idea spoken of, we need not imagine something far beyond this mortal sphere. The idea is rather what is completely present: and it is found, however confused and degenerated, in every consciousness." [20] It appears to be the theistic version of religion that Hegel had in mind when he spoke of that view in religion that "is the consciousness men have of a Higher, of something beyond the present, outside of themselves, and existing above themselves; that is to say, consciousness finds itself dependent, finite, and in this its experience it is insofar consciousness, that it presupposes an Other, on which it is dependent, and which is held by it to be its true Essence, since it is itself characterised as the negative or finite." [21]

But this, said Hegel, is religion from the point of view of observation and reflection; and a true grasp of religion can be achieved only from the higher viewpoint of speculative thought, to which it is therefore necessary to rise: only then can a true understanding of the nature of the finite and infinite be gained. And Hegel undoubtedly asserted that in the gaining of that true understanding the traditional theistic separation and opposition of the finite and infinite will be overcome; and it is apparent that the rise to speculative thought will also bring about the transformation of other aspects of traditional theism, so that to speak of Hegel as a traditional theist really cannot be justified.

Hegel's discussion of religion clearly shows that for him there is a fundamental problem with the religious outlook commonly known as theism, and that he identified this problem as being caused by the viewpoint of *Verstand*, which he believed to be a determining feature of this religious expression. Precisely what Hegel thought of *Verstand* became apparent as early as *ETW*: it is the inferior level of understanding at which separation and alienation, division and opposition are seen to characterize the relationship between things, for the tendency of *Verstand* is to perceive things primarily in their finitude. This opinion of *Verstand* remained part of Hegel's philosophy, so that in *LPR* he could say that in senuous experience, at the level of ordinary consciousness, we see ourselves as finite and as standing in a relation to what is other than self, "the negative of myself," so that the relation is seen to be one of mutual exclusion. Indeed, mutual exclusion appears to be the characteristic of all living things, and consequently in all our relationships we see ourselves having "always to do with what is only single or individual," with that which is 'other'. "This is the standpoint of the natural Being, of natural existence." [22]

It is at this level of understanding, the viewpoint of *Verstand*, that the principle of noncontradiction and the concept of the mutual exclusion of opposites are regarded as having universal validity. Now it is natural for the human intellect to maintain these principles, asserting, as they do, that 'y' and 'non-y' are mutually exclusive and that the statements 'x is y' and 'x is non-y' cannot both be true at the same time. Therefore, the terms 'finite' and 'infinite' are taken to be mutually exclusive ('finite' meaning 'noninfinite'), with the consequence that the statement 'the world is finite' excludes infinitude as a quality of the world, and the statement 'God is infinite' excludes finitude as a quality of God, and that therefore the infinite God is other than the finite world—a Beyond.

This is the viewpoint of *Verstand*, which Hegel found to be the source of the difficulties about the traditional theistic doctrine of God.[23] A consequence of this doctrine is that it gives rise to the most deep-seated inconsistency: the infinite God of theism is really only another finite being alongside of, but excluded from, the finite world, which is thus the boundary of the supposed infinite.

> The finite relates itself to the infinite; each is exclusive with regard to the other. Considered more closely, the finite is regarded as that which is limited, its limit being the infinite.
> . . . Now if the finite is limited by the infinite and stands on one side, the infinite itself is something limited too; it has its boundary in the finite; it is that which the finite is not; it has something which is on the yonder side of it and is thus finite, limited. Thus we have instead of the Highest, something which is a Finite. (*LPR*, vol. 1, 185)

What we have, therefore, according to Hegel, is an unintended dualism, since the infinite absolute Being is reduced to a finitude, and correspondingly, the being of the finite is raised to absoluteness: "In Reflection, the finite stands opposed to the infinite in such a way that the finite is doubled." [24]

> Dualism, in putting an insuperable opposition between finite and infinite, fails to note the simple circumstance that the infinite is thereby only one of two, and is reduced to a particular, to which the finite forms the other particular. Such an infinitude, which is only a particular, is co-terminous with the finite which makes for it a limit and a barrier: it is not what it ought to be, that is, the infinite, but is only finite. In such circumstances, where the finite is on this side and the infinite on that—this world as the finite and the other world as the infinite—an equal dignity of permanence and independence is ascribed to finite and to infinite. The being of the finite is made an absolute being, and by this dualism gets independence and stability. (*EL*, §95)

This same awareness of the difficulties of the theistic position, and hence of the need to modify it, is displayed by Hegel in his "Lectures on the Proofs of the Existence of God." In the lectures on the Cosmological Argument "he is clearly trying to steer clear of a theistic interpretation of the proof which portrays God as creator, a being sufficient to himself and distinct from the world he freely creates";[25] and Hegel did try to "steer clear" because of the errors he clearly showed to be involved in the argument and in the theism it endeavours to support.

The starting point of the Cosmological Argument is the existence of the contingent world, from which the conclusion is drawn that an absolutely necessary Being exists: "*because* the One, the contingent exists, is, *therefore* the Other, the Absolutely-necessary, is, or exists." [26] The subsequent analysis of this argument led Hegel to the conclusion that it implies two contrasting propositions, one of which asserts that "the Being of the contingent is not its own Being, but merely the Being of an Other, and in a definite sense it is the Being of its own Other, the Absolutely-necessary." [27] It is this proposition that, for Hegel, possesses "the true meaning" of the argument; but contrasted with it there is another proposition—"the proposition of the Understanding *(des Verstandes)* "—which asserts that "the Being of the contingent is merely its own Being, and not the Being of an Other, of the Absolutely-necessary." [28]

Herein is to be found what Hegel identified as the fundamental error in the Cosmological Argument and the underlying difficulty of traditional theism. The starting point of the argument is that "the contingent *is*", but this really "is inherently self-contradictory," [29] because the very nature of the contingent is for it *not* to be. Yet, at the level of the Understanding, nothing seems more reasonable than to hold that any form of existence, including the contingent, "since it *is*, is its own Being, is in fact just the definite Being which it is, and not rather an other kind of Being! " And by that assumption of the Understanding, the contingent is "retained on its own account separately from the Absolutely-necessary." [30]

We thus have the underlying difficulty of theism: "so far as faith is concerned this contingent Being as something present to consciousness remains standing on one side confronting the other side, the Eternal, the Necessary in-and-for-itself, in the form of a world above which is heaven." [31] This position of faith arises from the fact that when, as in the Cosmological Argument, "we thus regard finite Being as standing in relation to itself only, it is merely for itself, and is not Being for an Other. It is consequently taken out of the region of change, is unchangeable and absolute." [32]

It well might be objected that Hegel's analysis of theism is false because theists do not assert the contingent to be unchangeable and absolute, for, indeed, they assert the opposite. But Hegel would reply that this is precisely the point, namely, that theists do emphasize the distinction between the contingent and the absolutely-necessary, ascribing opposing characteristics to each, and by so doing really establish the finite as standing in its own right,[33] and thus also reduce the infinite to just another finite.[34] Another consequence of theism follows from its implicit 'proposition of the Understanding', according to which "the Being of the finite is only its own Being, and is in no sense the Being of an Other," for "it is thereby declared that there is no possible way of passing from the finite to the Infinite, and therefore no mediation between them."[35]

It is this consequence that really highlighted for Hegel the difficulty of theism, and that calls to mind his criticism in *Phen.* of contemporary 'Faith', which caused nothing but sorrow and the longing for an absent and faraway God: the "believing consciousness" is one that has faith in a Being that is beyond the world of reality; it is the attempt to transcend the alienation of the world by a retreat into a Beyond, a suprasensible world, into which the self projects the unity that it desires but does not find in this alienated world.[36] It is a theological outlook that admits no "essential connection between the two sides"—that is, between the finite and the infinite, the contingent and the Absolutely-necessary—and any overcoming of this separation can only be "made in the form of a leap from one to the other."[37]

That religious Faith admits such a leap is due to the fact that in spite of the Understanding's assertion of "the existence of this absolute separation," "the heart of Man" will not admit the ultimacy of the gulf—such a gulf "does not exist for Spirit."[38] Therefore, according to theistic belief, the transition from the infinite to the finite is spoken of in terms of creation and revelation. It is clear in theism that there is nothing essential about this transition, thus emphasizing the separation between the infinite and finite, and what is given in revelation is seen to be something that comes from outside.

> The result of such a conception of religion is that the Divine content is regarded as something given independent of us, as something which cannot be known but is to be received and kept in a merely passive way in faith, and on the other hand it lands us in the subjectivity of the feeling which is the end and the result of the worship of God. (*LPR*, vol. 2, 331)

Worship is seen as the act of rising to God, in which belief senses the transition from the finite to the infinite: it is in the act of worship that the devout man can get rid of the senses of separation, for in that act he "sinks himself in his object together with his heart, his devotion and his will," thereby achieving the "feeling that the object is not foreign to consciousness." [39] But even this is not successful in the overcoming of the sense of separation, for here again that sense of something foreign is present, namely, in the feeling that in worship man cannot act of himself, but only in response to, and because of, "the grace of God which man has to acquiesce in as something foreign to his own nature, and his relation to which is of a passive sort." [40]

The inadequacy of such a conception of religion is due, according to Hegel's analysis, to the fact that it is religion at the level of the Understanding, which means that the religious content is not expressed in its true form. What is necessary, therefore, Hegel said, is the rise to the level of speculative thought, at which the true relation between the finite and infinite is perceived. Instead of the finite being seen as standing "opposed to the infinite in such a way that the finite is doubled," now it will be seen that "what is true is the indissoluble unity of the two"; in other words, that "the finite is but an essential moment of the infinite." [41] This does not mean that worship, for example, will be lost or made redundant, but that the true nature of worship will be discovered: in worship I recognize the Infinite, Absolute Spirit, and myself, whose finiteness and independence is thereby renounced, as being in a relationship of dependence on, and in an indissoluble unity with, the Infinite; and therefore, worship is no longer regarded as an act in which I, as an independent finite being, rise from myself to that which is an Other, the infinite God.

Here I am determined as finite in the true manner, finite as distinguished from this Object, as the particular over against the universal, as the accidental in reference to this Substance, as a moment, as something distinguished, which at the same time is not independent, but has renounced itself and knows itself to be finite. Thus therefore I do not go beyond the consciousness of myself, and this arises from the fact that the universal Object is now potentially thought and has the content within itself, it is substance in motion within itself, and as an inward process in which it begets its content, is not empty, but is absolute fulness. All particularity belongs to it; as universal it overlaps or includes me in itself, and thus I look upon myself as finite, as being a moment in this life, as that which has its particular being, its permanent existence in this substance only, and in its essential moments. (*LPR*, vol. 1, 197)

The same point is made in Hegel's discussion of the Cosmological Argument. No longer can that argument take the form in which it is expressed at the level of the Understanding, namely, *because* the contingent is, *therefore* the Absolutely necessary is. Rather, in its true form, the argument can be seen to be an adequate expression of the relation between the contingent and the Absolutely necessary, the finite and the infinite: "Not because the contingent is, but, on the contrary, because it is non-Being, merely phenomenal, because its Being is not true reality, the absolute necessity is. This latter is its Being and Truth." [42] Therefore, there is no *leap* from the finite world to the Infinite or Absolute, for the former is in the latter in the sense that the world is the activity of the Absolute and has its being in the Absolute. In Lauer's words, "there is a sense in which conceiving God is a passage from the world to God but only because God's relation to the world is God's own activity and finding God is finding Him in the world." [43]

The important question that must be asked is whether Hegel's account of religion at the level of Understanding is one that can be taken as an accurate and justifiable account of traditional theism. Hegel clearly labeled this form of religion to be dualistic: "The repetition which is involved in this conception of the ordinary division of the finite and the Infinite [is] that separation by which the finite is put on one side in an independent form, and the Infinite on the other in contrast with it, while the former is not the less asserted in this way to be absolute. This is the dualism which, put in a more definite form, is Manicheism." [44] But theists would strenuously deny that they are dualists; they would deny that they put the finite "on one side in an independent form," for they would assert the contrary to be the case, namely, that the finite is utterly dependent on the infinite and eternal God who, as creator and sustainer, is the source of all finite existence. Furthermore, no theist would want to protest at Hegel's reexpression of the Cosmological Argument or his description of the true nature of worship.

However, having said that, it remains true to assert that Hegel does distance himself from traditional theism. Taylor stresses this in relation to, for example, the concept of creation,[45] and Westphal sees it when, in commenting on Hegel's treatment of the Cosmological Argument, he says that Hegel was avoiding the theistic view, "which portrays God as creator, a being sufficient to himself and distinct from the world He freely creates"; and Westphal also says that one reason why Hegel was avoiding theism was his conviction that it establishes the finite as fixed and independent and thus is really "a kind of Manichaean dualism." But Westphal goes on to assert that, in saying this about theism, Hegel missed the point, for he overlooked "the fact that such an ontology [i.e., theism] places the world in an asymmetrical dependence relation to God." [46] Yet, it seems that Westphal has really missed the point of what Hegel was doing: it is not that Hegel was overlooking the "asymmetrical dependence relation" in which the world is placed to God by the theistic ontology, but rather that he was rejecting the notion of such a relationship.

In fact, Hegel was saying two things about the theistic concept of this asymmetrical relation. First, that in spite of its assertion that its ontology places the world in such a relation to God, theism really does not succeed in consistently maintaining that position because it establishes a gulf between the infinite and finite, and thereby the infinite is reduced to another finite, and the finite becomes "fixed, absolute, perennial", and thus also independent. Secondly, that the theistic concept of the dependence relation is not really asymmetrical because the true relation between the infinite and finite is not one of separation, but one of indissoluble unity in which the finite is an essential moment within the infinite, making also the latter dependent on the former; or, theologically speaking, in Hegel's words, "without the world God would not be God." [47]

Therefore, it can be concluded that there is no justification in interpreting Hegel as having accepted traditional theism as containing the true content of absolute Manifest Religion. Rather, it appears to have been his conviction that the theistic formulations of that truth had been so permeated by the concepts of the Understanding that aspects of the truth had been lost or misconstrued. The God of theism may or may not create the world and reveal himself, and he stands to the world in a relation of asymmetrical independence; but this understanding of God has to be transformed, in Hegel's view, into the truth contained in Absolute Religion, whereby it is manifest that "Spirit which is not revealed is not Spirit . . . God as Spirit is essentially this very self-revelation; He does not create the world once for all, but He is the eternal Creator, this eternal self-revelation, this *actus*. This is His Notion, His essential characteristic." [48]

This conclusion regarding Hegel's position in relation to theism, however, still leaves open the question of how Hegel's philosophy of religion is to be interpreted. Westphal says that anyone who views classical theism as dualistic—as Hegel does—is best defined as a pantheist,[49] and, while this is a popular view about Hegel, there are others, on the other hand, who regard atheism—the contradiction of theism—as the most accurate interpretation of Hegel's position.

Hegel as Atheist

The Meaning of Atheism

The answer to the question "Is Hegel's philosophy an atheistic philosophy? " really depends on what one takes as the definition of 'atheism'; and that, in turn, depends on the understanding of 'God' in the light of which the judgment is being made. At the most popular, yet superficial, level of understanding, 'atheism' is defined as the "disbelief in the existence of God";[50] it is the maintaining of the proposition that there is no God, in the sense that it is a "denial of God as an entity over and above the more familiar objects of experience." [51] Now it is quite clear that, given that understanding of 'God' as the assumption on which the definition of 'atheism' rests, then Hegel ought to be labeled 'atheistic': the concept of God as "an entity over and above the more familiar objects of experience" was, for Hegel, an absolutely spurious concept, a concept that, as Tillich says, "is the deepest root of atheism . . . an atheism which is justified as the reaction against the theological theism and its disturbing implications." [52]

Hegel appears to have perceived this danger inherent in the superficial concept of God, which he regarded, therefore, not only as a spurious concept, but also one that almost inevitably would give rise to the denial of God. Hegel did not embrace such a concept of God, and if this concept is the only standard of judgment, then he will be judged to have been atheistic. But, in contrast to this narrow understanding of the terminology, Tillich suggests that "God means depth" and that an atheist is one who could say in complete seriousness, "Life has no depth! Life itself is shallow. Being itself is surface only." [53] It is equally clear that, given this understanding, Hegel could never be called 'atheistic', for his philosophy is nothing if it is not a proclamation that Being is not 'surface' only, and if it is not an exploration into the depth of life.

However, in order to embark on a serious discussion of the question of Hegel's atheism—and there are those who seriously interpret Hegel in this manner—one must look elsewhere for an understanding of the terminology. Hegel himself defined atheism, in the context of "the relationship between God and the finite," as the view that "only the finite exists . . . , but God does not exist." [54] Feuerbach is one who admitted to such a denial of the existence of God, declaring that it follows from his doctrine "that there is no God, no abstract, disembodied being distinct from nature and man who decides the fate of the world and mankind as *He* pleases." [55] But Feuerbach did not stop with a denial as the heart of his atheism, for he said that "if atheism were a mere negation, a denial without content, it would be unfit for the people" because it would be "worthless." Therefore, true atheism must have positive content, it must be "an affirmation: it negates the being abstracted from man, who is and bears the name of God, but only in order to replace him by man's true being." [56] Now when Hegel is said to have developed an atheistic philosophy, it is an atheism of this Feuerbachian kind that is most frequently meant, and therefore it is appropriate to look briefly at Feuerbach's position of humanistic atheism.

Feuerbach occupies a significant and peculiar place in the development in German philosophy that converted idealism into materialism. As in Hegel, so in Feuerbach, the theme of self-alienation is a profound concern, and Feuerbach found the root of alienation in "man's projection of a part of his own being into another imaginary being, the fantasy which is God." [57] The evidence that the basis of religion lies in man's self-projection was found in the fact that the description of the attributes of God in orthodox theology is nothing more than the projection of human attributes, even though theologians, rather inconsistently, refused to admit that the subject of those attributes is also a human projection. It is this projection that is the basis of religion, and the reason for it is located in human feeling and desire, especially the desire to be and to have what one is not and does not have; in other words, "man believes in gods because he seeks help from them. What he is not himself but wishes to be, he projects into the being of the gods in order that he may get it back from them." [58]

As Feuerbach found human alienation to be the result of this self-projection, it means that alienation will be overcome only "by the removal of the supernatural and the recognition that the self is entirely in space and time." [59] What this means, in Feuerbach's own words, is that, seen from the true perspective, "theology is anthropology, that is, the object of religion, God, expresses nothing other than the essence of man; man's God is nothing other than the deified essence of man"; [60] it is only as a man understands that the term 'God' is merely a name for his own nature, which he has idealized and projected into a transcendent realm, that he will be able to recapture his faith in himself and overcome the self-alienation that religion involves. It was therefore Feuerbach's purpose "to transform theologians into anthropologists, lovers of God into lovers of man, candidates for the next world into students of this world, religious and political flunkeys of heavenly and earthly monarchs and lords into free, self-reliant citizens of the earth. . . . I negate the fantastic hypocrisy of theology and religion only in order to affirm the true nature of man." [61]

However, Feuerbach did not conclude from this view that religion had been a hindrance in human development; on the contrary, he regarded religion as having played an integral role in that process, because man's projection of himself into the notion of 'God' was essential to the emergence of human self-awareness—without that objectification of his nature, man would not have become aware of it as *his* nature. But with the achievement of that awareness, it becomes necessary to overcome religion, in the sense that religious language needs to be recognized for what it is, namely, a misappropriation of language when understood as referring to a transcendent deity, for it is in fact language describing the nature of humanity. In this way, Feuerbach's kind of atheism "was to be an internal threat to theology because it demythologized God from within religion, which was itself shown to be a true affair of the heart. It said that theistic language is not at all meaningless: it is full of meaning, but it is finally disclosed to be talk about man himself." [62]

This, of course, immediately brings Hegel to mind, and it is because this is so that it is understandable that some have interpreted Hegel's philosophy as atheistic. The most frequent interpretation along these lines is one that sees Hegel as anticipating Feuerbach: in other words, that what Feuerbach made quite explicit is really to be found implicitly in Hegel, and that Hegel's view about the relation between absolute religion and absolute philosophy was the same as Feuerbach's transformation of the theologian into the anthropologist.

Interpretations of Hegel as Atheistic

A very conspicuous example of the reading of Hegel along atheistic lines is to be found in Kojève's commentary, in which Hegel is quite noticeably presented as an implicit Feuerbachian. "For Hegel," says Kojève, "the real object of religious thought is Man himself: every *theology* is necessarily an *anthropology*," for while "religious Man believes that he is talking about God," he is "in fact talking about himself." [63] Kojève finds in Hegel's use of *Vorstellungen* in his treatment of religion a parallel to Feuerbach's notion of projection, stating that for Hegel the religious Man "substantializes and externalizes the *concept (Begriff)* of Spirit by *re-presenting (Vorstellen)* it to himself in the form of a Being *(Sein)* existing *outside* of Man and *independently* of his Action." [64] Thus, a theistic interpretation of Hegel is, for Kojève, "absolutely impossible," and an atheistic reading of Hegel is to be substituted as the accurate alternative.

Regarding *Phen.*, Kojève argues that if this work "has any meaning, the Spirit there in question is none other than the *human* Spirit: there is no Spirit *outside* the world, and the Spirit *within* the world—

this is Man, humanity, universal History." [65] So then, the absolute *Wesen*, of which Hegel spoke, is not God, but Man himself—not indeed as individual, but as "humanity taken in its spacio-temporal totality." [66] It is apparent, therefore, that Kojève presents Hegel as a humanistic atheist; but it is equally apparent that his presentation is transparently couched in the language of Feuerbach, thereby giving Hegel's philosophy the appearance of being much more neatly clear-cut than is justifiable.

However, there are other interpreters of Hegel who, while abstaining from such conspicuous use of Feuerbachian language, nevertheless propound a similar view along the lines of humanistic atheism. The key passage for those who adopt this interpretation, the passage that is regarded as containing Hegel's clearest statement of his position, is found in *EM:*

> God is God only so far as he knows himself: his self-knowledge is, further, a self-consciousness in man and man's knowledge *of* God, which proceeds to man's self-knowledge *in* God. (*EM*, §564)

Kaufmann's exposition of this passage is clearly indicative of the kind of understanding of Hegel that is being considered here. He says that the only cause of the misunderstanding of Hegel's view on these matters is "Hegel's occasional references to God." All misunderstanding would have been avoided, Kaufmann suggests, if, once Hegel had chosen the "eminently suggestive word" Spirit *(Geist)* as the key term in his philosophy, he had clearly stated "in God I do not believe"; but instead, he "could not resist equating" Spirit with God, and this is the source of confusion.[67] But in fact, the truth about Hegel, according to Kaufmann, is that it is man who is the true explication of spirit. "What does this mean," asks Kaufmann, regarding the passage from *EM*, "if not that God does not know himself until man knows him; and since 'God is only God insofar as he knows himself', God comes into being only when man 'knows' him?" Thus, Kaufmann concludes that Hegel's "religious position may be safely characterized as a form of humanism";[68] and such a conclusion is seen to be compatible with, and indeed implied by, Hegel's idea of the relation between absolute religion and philosophy: "in his [Hegel's] system Christianity was treated as an anticipation in mythological form—on the level of vague notions and feelings—of truths articulated in philosophy." [69]

In the Wofford Symposium, Shea compares Hegel to Marx, and suggests that, in the sense of atheistic humanism, Marx is clearly more, but not significantly more, "Promethean" than Hegel. For, whereas Marx "smashes all gods set above man," Hegel "melts and assimilates" such gods, with the result that one must conclude that both are to be identified as atheistic humanists, even though Hegel's approach makes this position less clear in his case. "To use a Hegelian metaphor Croce was fond of: Hegel melted down the statues of the old gods in the crucible of his dialectical imagination and cast out a radically new one: modern bourgeois man, as enshrined in his social, economic and political institutions." [70]

In contrast with these views of Hegel's philosophy, which are clearly identifiable as expositions that place Hegel within humanistic atheism, Findlay's position poses an interesting puzzle. Min presents the views of a number of expositors of Hegel,[71] including Kojève and Kaufmann, as well as Findlay; and, concerning all of them, he says that, while their views are not totally homogeneous, their broad characteristics are such that they can be regarded as presenting an 'immanentist' view. In this way Min links Findlay's interpretation with that of Kojève and Kaufmann; and similarly, Kaufmann himself, when declaring Hegel's religious position to be a form of humanism, does so in the context of quoting Findlay as referring to Hegel as "the philosopher . . . of liberal humanism." [72] Yet one also notices that six pages earlier Findlay declares that it is not possible to say "that Hegel is a mere humanist." [73] Findlay's position therefore poses a puzzle, suggesting a certain ambivalence, and consequently requiring a more detailed analysis.

It is obviously the case that Findlay strongly rejects any suggestion that Hegel is a 'transcendent metaphysician'. "There can be no doubt at all," he states, "that Hegel sees what is 'absolute' is nothing which lies beyond the experiences and activities of men." [74] Then, in concluding his exposition of Hegel, he declares that "despite much opinion to the contrary, Hegel's philosophy is one of the most anti-metaphysical of philosophical systems, one that *remains* most within the pale of ordinary experience, and which accords no place to entities or properties lying beyond that experience, or to facts undiscoverable by ordinary methods of investigation." [75] Expressed succinctly, "Hegel's system of thought is wholly 'immanent'." [76]

Findlay admits that Hegel does make use of the language of metaphysical theology (although he indulges in an understatement when he refers to this use as "occasional"),[77] but such usage is plainly nothing more than, he says, a "mere concession to the pictorial mode of religious expression";[78] and furthermore, Hegel made it quite clear that such language "merely says by way of imaginative representation what can be more clearly said in the notional diction of philosophy." [79] Hegel's use of *Geist* is indicative of this, says Findlay, for although Hegel often equates *Geist* with God in the sense that it is "the truth of everything in the world," it is not the case that *Geist* is to be understood, as God is understood, as "something which underlies the universe or is causally responsible for it." [80]

Similarly, in the case of the term *Idee*, Hegel spoke of it as existing like God "before the creation of nature and finite spirit", but in the language of speculative philosophy, *Die Idee* must be taken "in the sense of being the 'conceptual blueprint'" of the world, or "an abstract notional possibility." [81] So the Hegelian view of God is seen to exclude the concept of the existence of God as a transcendent reality, for the term 'God' is merely part of pictorial religious language, and Hegel is said to have assumed that it "will, when stripped of pictorial associations, reveal itself as meaning no more than the 'I' of self-consciousness, which is for Hegel also the element of universality and unity present in all thinking, which is inseparable from the finite particular self to which it may *seem* transcendent, but which uses the latter as the vehicle through which it achieves self-consciousness." [82] What is, for Findlay, the important and fundamental point about the Hegelian Absolute is that it could not *be* at all except through the medium of individual human spirits, for Hegel was "the believer in nothing that does not spring from the free, uncommitted, self-committing human spirit." It is for this reason that Findlay speaks of Hegel as one who "remains the philosopher of liberal Humanism." [83]

What then is to be understood by Findlay's assertion that Hegel is not to be seen as "a mere humanist," even though, as a philosopher, he "believes in no God and no Absolute except one that is revealed and known in certain experiences of individual human beings"? [84] It seems, by negating the idea of Hegel as a mere humanist, Findlay is making the point that the Hegelian Absolute cannot be regarded as being identified with Man himself, but that the Absolute is the element of universality and unity in the totality of finite existence. In other words, Hegel saw the facts of the finite world "in terms of a 'principle of Idealism', which . . . is a teleological or quasi-teleological principle, according to which things must be seen as if existing on account of, or as if tending towards, certain consummating experiences, experiences where there will cease to be a barrier between the self and other persons, or between the thinking mind and the world confronting it." [85]

This is one aspect of what Findlay describes as the element of universality and unity in the totality of finite existence; and also, specifically within human existence, that universality and unity is to be identified with the best in human experience, the 'absolute, infinite experience' within the whole range of human existence—for Hegel, it is "the absolute and 'infinite' sides of human experience" that are "the ultimate, and overreaching ones, for the sake of which the finite individual ones may be held to exist." [86] This absolute, infinite experience of human existence is expressed "in the creative activities and products of the artist, the faith and worship of the religious person, and the systematic insights of the philosopher." [87]

Now, when Min discusses these interpreters of Hegel, he groups their views about Hegel's Absolute under the heading of 'immanentist', by which he means the view that the Hegelian Absolute "has no reality of its own, its reality being exhaustively definable in terms of the totality of finite beings even if it could not be identified with any one finite being or even with all finite beings as an aggregate, and that it has no proper self-consciousness except insofar as it is mediated by the self-consciousness of finite spirits." [88] However, Min is correct when he says that not all the commentators discussed under this heading present homogeneous views.

On the one hand, there are those whose interpretation of Hegel seems really to amount to the belief that he anticipated Feuerbach in defining Man as the ultimate in the sense of Man's being "recognized and celebrated precisely in his actual humanness." [89] Kaufmann, for example, speaks of Hegel's religious position "as a form of humanism," and, more obviously, Kojève explicitly says Hegel's absolute *Wesen* is "humanity taken in its spacio-temporal totality." Including Shea as a further example of this kind of interpretation, one can observe that he says Hegel "melts and assimilates" "all gods set above man." If these views accurately reflect Hegel's position, then it can be said that he was affirming "that there is no measure other than man"; and while such an affirmation, as Welch indicates, does not necessarily "say that man is unlimited and not measured," [90] it is not altogether clear whether these interpreters of Hegel are excluding this infinite, unmeasurable, absolute element in human experience—Kojève, at least, certainly seems to imply that exclusion. Either way, however, the term 'humanistic atheism' remains an apt description of their view of Hegel's philosophy.

On the other hand, Findlay says that Hegel is not a mere humanist, for he obviously does not regard humanism as covering all that is to be said about Hegel's position. Not only does Findlay clearly admit the infinite immeasurable, absolute element in human experience, and not only does he admit Hegel's conviction of the experiences of the human spirit as "the ultimate and overreaching ones" in all existence, his interpretation really seems to be the only one of those mentioned here that matches the breadth of Min's definition of 'immanentist': namely, that the reality of Hegel's Absolute must be seen as "being exhaustively definable in terms of the totality of finite beings."

Two important points must be noted about this statement: first, it is the 'totality' as opposed to an 'aggregate' of finite beings, and this is a crucial Hegelian distinction that cannot be overlooked—for in Hegel totality contains the idea of continuity and interrelation, which is not conveyed by the sense of a mere aggregate. Secondly, it is 'finite beings' and not just 'human beings', and again this is an important distinction because Hegel's *Geist* is a *cosmic* force, not just in the human realm. It may be that those who see Hegel merely in humanistic terms can accommodate the first of these distinctions, but they cannot accommodate the second, and in that sense they are far too inadequate. Therefore, while Min's definition of 'immanentist' may be seen to embrace such interpretations—for human is included in the finite—it is really much broader, in a very crucial manner, than the humanistic interpretations,[91] and it can be said that Min is really applying his own definition too loosely in including such interpretations of Hegel under the term 'immanentist'. Of course, what all the interpretations discussed here—Findlay's included—have in common is the assertion that the Hegelian Absolute has "no reality of its own," and therefore they can all be commonly called 'atheistic' interpretations of Hegel.

A Discussion of Hegel's 'Atheism'

Is it accurate to describe Hegel's philosophy as atheistic? Feuerbach himself said it is not accurate: he asserted that one had only to scratch the surface of Hegel's philosophy to find the traditional theological position, and he spoke of " 'the nonsense of the Absolute'. The absolute spirit is 'nothing else than' the departed spirit of theology, wandering about like a ghost in Hegel's philosophy." [92] "Whoever does not surrender Hegelian philosophy does not surrender theology. The Hegelian doctrine that reality is determined by the idea is only the rationalistic expression of the theological doctrine that nature . . . was created by God." [93]

It has already been argued above that Hegel cannot be identified with this traditional theological position, but it is interesting to note that Feuerbach suggested, in these very definite terms, that Hegel could be so identified. Feuerbach's forcefulness here was probably due to his desire to differentiate himself markedly from Hegel: in other words, he saw his own position as very different from that of Hegel; and that is a conclusive point against those who wish to interpret Hegel as an atheist of a Feuerbachian kind.

However, the arguments in favor of Hegel as an atheist are more weighty than the attempt simply to present Hegel as a Feuerbachian. Hegel's position is declared to be atheistic primarily on the basis of

God, as spoken of by Hegel, being essentially dependent on humankind, in the sense that the Absolute could not *be*—could have neither existence nor knowledge of itself—except through the medium of individual human spirits. It is clear that Hegel argued that the Absolute knows itself *für sich* in human knowing, that finite knowing is God's self-knowing. On the atheistic interpretation, this is taken to mean that Hegel's God is nothing other than the finite, not in the sense of being identified with human beings themselves, but in the sense of being the element of universality and unity in the totality of finite existence.

Some attempts to free these Hegelian statements from an atheistic interpretation appear to be unsuccessful. For example, Min makes an attempt by posing a number of questions about such an interpretation: he asks, if the Absolute "could be conscious of itself 'only' in and through finite spirits, what or where would the Absolute have been, say, before the emergence of man in the evolutionary process? " Further, he asks, if "the Absolute 'comes into being' only when man 'knows' it, is it not attributing to man the function and power which Thomists traditionally attribute to God, namely, that of 'causing' the existence of something—in this case, God himself—through thought? " [94]

There is, however, a definite weakness in attempting to counter an atheistic interpretation of Hegel by means of such questions. For those who give an atheistic or immanentist interpretation of any kind, the questions are fundamentally irrelevant: it is only in and through man that the Absolute emerges, and it is meaningless to ask about the prior condition or whereabouts of the Absolute— simply to follow Schelling's "*Geist* sleeping in nature" would suffice; and similarly, it is meaningless to complain that man 'causes' God when God is not to be understood in the popular fashion.

On the other hand, more telling questions—which do lead one to see that an atheistic interpretation of Hegel is just as obscure, ambiguous, and inconsistent as a theistic one—can be formulated. For example, in the light of Findlay's view of the Hegelian Absolute as the "notional possibility" or "the conceptual blue-print" of the concrete world, one can ask, with Min, how then "could Hegel say that it is the 'self-thinking Thought', 'self-determining Concept', the Idea which 'alone is *Being*, imperishable Life, self-knowing Truth, and is all truth' ? " [95] Furthermore, the difficulties involved in taking Hegel's to be an atheistic philosophy also became apparent by exploring the implications of the notion of dependence: at the heart of an atheistic interpretation is the view that in Hegel's philosophy the Absolute *depends* "on finite beings in order to *be* and on finite spirits in order to be conscious of itself," and it is taken to be a dependence that implies that the Absolute is no 'more' than the self-sufficient finite. However, if it is as simple as that, in what significant sense could the Absolute be said to be 'absolute', 'universal', and 'Spirit' ? Again it is apt to support Min by asking, "would not the Absolute then be 'relative', 'finite' and 'particular' because limited by finite beings from outside? How could it 'posit' the world as 'its' world when it presumably depended so totally on the world? How could the world be, as Hegel repeats, the 'externalization' of the Absolute when this latter had no interiority of its own so to externalize? " [96]

In addition to the difficulties implied in these questions about the atheistic interpretation, there are other points, of greater import, to be made. Central to any atheistic interpretation of Hegel is the question of the nature of the transition from absolute religion, with its pictorial mode of religious expression, to absolute philosophy, with its speculative language; and this, in turn, involves the nature of the dialectical method. In order for an atheistic view to be correct, it would have to be the case that this transition involved the transformation of the religious content of 'God' into an Absolute that is exhaustively definable in terms of the totality of finite things.

But it is not at all certain that this is the case regarding Hegel's philosophy. In describing the basic characteristic of Hegel's dialectical method, Findlay says that "it always involves *higher-order-comment* on a thought position previously achieved," and that it is important to realize that this "always involves the possible emergence of definite novelties of principle, things not formally entailed by what one has done at the lower level. Sometimes these novelties are slight, mere affirmations or endorsements or particularly stressed versions of what one had previously thought; sometimes, however, they involve an ironical swing-over to what is contrary, . . . sometimes again they involve the making clear of a conceptual inadequacy, and the concealed need for some sense-making, saving complement. Sometimes still more remarkably, they involve a reversal of perspective which turns a problem into an explanation." [97]

Which kind of dialectical move applies to the transition from absolute religion to philosophy? Clearly, Findlay must see it as a move that involves "an ironical swing-over to what is contrary," one that "consists in finding absoluteness, finality and infinity *precisely* in what at first promised *never* to be so." [98] However, from Hegel's own discussion of the nature of religious *Vorstellungen*, it would seem to be more accurate to describe Hegel's final dialectical move as one that involves "the making clear of a conceptual inadequacy." Hegel's frequent declaration about the absolute religion is that it is not inadequate in content, for it possesses the true content; but it *is* inadequate in the form—religious *Vorstellungen*—in which that content is expressed. Therefore, the dialectical move from absolute religion to philosophy cannot be seen to be a move that involves the loss or negation of the true content, but rather it must be a move that involves the transporting of that content—expressed in the religious *Vorstellung*, 'God'—into the speculative language of philosophy in which it will attain a new expression in the true form: in the speculative concept of *Geist*. This point is clearly expressed by Hegel in the concluding paragraph of his discussion of the nature of *Vorstellungen*:

> And thus it is that idea melts into the form of thought, and it is this quality of *form* which philosophic knowledge imparts to truth. From this it is clear that nothing is further from the aim of philosophy than to overthrow religion, and to maintain forsooth that the content of religion cannot for itself be truth. On the contrary, it is just religion which is the true content, only in the form of idea or ordinary thought *(Vorstellung)*, and it is philosophy which must first supply substantial truth *(LPR*, vol. 1, 154–55) [99]

One may also consider the atheistic interpretation of Hegel's philosophy in the light of Hegel's reactions to what he regarded as the evils of his time and what he believed to be the necessary requirements to rectify those evils. It has already been established that Hegel regarded the Enlightenment as having done considerable "mischief" to religion and theology, in the sense that "they no longer possess a truth that is *known*, an *objective content*, a *doctrinal theology*." [100] It was not that the Enlightenment did not begin with a laudable intention; indeed, its purpose was to "attack error and superstition." But the unwelcome result was that God had been "deprived of all definite character, predicates and properties," and "lifted into a *beyond* where we cannot know Him," so that God had been "reduced to an abstraction void of all content—man can have no knowledge of what possesses *intrinsic* Being." [101]

This state of affairs, Hegel observed, has three consequences: first, the human spirit is "denied the capacity and the vocation to know the objective truth"; secondly, therefore, the activity of the human spirit is confined to the realm of contingent appearances, for "absolute Being is removed to an empty Beyond"; and thirdly, the basis of religion is thereby reduced to the region of feeling, where the spirit is forced to "take refuge in its quest for Truth." [102] Hegel regularly complained that it is not only philosophy, but also religion itself, that has made the assumption that man is incapable of knowing God into some kind of dogma; and the reason Hegel found this inadequate is that religion is forced to find its home in subjectivity—feeling is made "the seat and the source of the True." But this is a most unhappy consequence, for "if feeling is made into a principle that determines a content, all that has to be done is to leave it to the individual *which* feelings he will have." [103]

Therefore, Hegel firmly asserted that just as it was right to attack as one-sided the earlier natural theology that looked upon God as a remote object, so it is right to attack as one-sided the concept of religion as something that is only subjective. "If this substantial element remains shut up in the heart only it is not recognized as the something higher than ourselves, and God himself becomes something merely subjective." [104] And Hegel clearly saw that what follows from this state of affairs is the emergence of that critique of religion that subsequently was to be expounded by Feuerbach.

> The result has, in this case, been atheism. God would thus be an historical product of weakness, of fear, of joy, or of interested hopes, cupidity, and lust for power. What has its root only in my feelings, is only for me; it is mine, but not its own; it has no independent existence in and for itself. (*LPR*, vol. 1, 51)

That is why it is absolutely necessary "to show that God is not rooted in feeling merely, is not merely *my* God." [105] It is the case, Hegel said, that the human heart and feeling are vital to the religious experience, but it is another question completely "whether such a content as God, Truth, freedom, as simply felt is supposed to have its warrant in feeling, or whether such an objective content possesses its own inherent validity before it enters into one's heart and feeling." [106] It is this Hegelian stress, in the context of what is said about God and religion as well as about philosophy, on an "objective content" possessing its "own inherent validity" that marks Hegel out from any atheistic philosophy. It is *"a substantial, objective content for Truth"* that Hegel saw as the common need of both contemporary religion and philosophy: "What is a theology without a knowledge of God? Precisely what a philosophy is without that knowledge, sounding brass and a tinkling cymbal." [107]

The inherent validity of the objective divine content is apparent in Hegel's view that it is from God that knowledge of the divine begins: God reveals himself, and it would be sheer envy on God's part if he denied man a knowledge of himself, for "in doing so He would also have denied to man all Truth, for God alone is the True." [108] Now it is true that in Hegel *Gott* is *Geist*, and therefore whether what Hegel meant by God adequately coincides with the religious concept is a question for later attention. But here the point is that for Hegel *Gott* or *Geist* is known only through self-revelation, and the concept of revelation could not find a place in Hegelian philosophy if that philosophy were atheistic, because then there could be no suggestion of the inherent validity of the *objective* content of *Gott* or *Geist*.

Finally, one can look to Hegel's regard for the mystics as further evidence in support of a nonatheistic interpretation of his philosophy. This regard does not imply that Hegel himself is to be seen as a mystic—for, indeed, he was not—but his high esteem for their writings, in which, he believed, could be found a thorough grasp of the divine, is sufficient to clearly suggest that he should not be interpreted as a proponent of a contradictory, atheistic philosophy. A celebrated reference to the German mystic, Meister Eckhart, occurs in *LPR*, where again Hegel had been deploring the shortcomings of contemporary theology. Theologians, he observed, were so restricted by the culture of the times that they could allow only a doctrine of God that defines God "as something absolutely supersensible," for any other doctrine is suspected as a form of pantheism that expresses an affirmative relation with God "as mere ordinary abstract identity." The reason for this is that "people do not know how to get a knowledge of God as Spirit: Spirit is an empty idea to them, having merely the same meaning as motionless abstract Substance." [109]

On the other hand, Hegel also believed pantheism to be an unworthy view of God: it is a "conceiving of Spirit as devoid of Spirit," and even more so in the popular, though false (in Hegel's opinion), idea of pantheism in which "Spirit is to be taken only as the existent 'I', and this existent 'I' as the ultimate and true determination of self-consciousness, and even as absolute eternal Being." [110] However, the true relation of self-consciousness to God as Spirit is completely different: man becomes united with God only through the abrogation of the natural sense of separateness of the single individual self-consciousness.

> But the relation of self-consciousness to God as Spirit is wholly different from this pantheistic mode of conceiving the relation, since in such a relation it is itself Spirit, and since by the renunciation of the exclusive character which it possesses as immediate oneness or isolation, it places itself in an affirmative relation, in a spiritually-vital attitude toward God. (*LPR*, vol. 1, 216)

However, theologians frequently dismiss this as pantheism, since they are unable even to distinguish this view from what they mistakenly take for pantheism, let alone pantheism in its proper sense.

In doing so, they forget many doctrines of the church, such as the doctrines of Creation, of divine grace, of justification, and of the Holy Spirit—"such doctrines which undoubtedly have to do with the innermost depths of the divine Essence"; and so one has to look to the older theologians for "the most thorough grasp of divine depth." [111] The example of such a grasp that Hegel cited is that of Meister Eckhart's famous words from a sermon: " 'The eye with which God sees me is the eye with which I see Him; my eye and His eye are one. By a righteous standard I am weighed in God, and God in me. If God were not, I would not be; if I were not, then He were not. It is, however, not needful to know this, for there are things which are easily misunderstood and which can only be thoroughly understood in thought.' " [112]

This quotation, in which Hegel cited these words of Eckhart, is generally agreed to contain Hegel's view, but it has been variously interpreted. It is taken to support an atheistic view of Hegel, on the grounds that it asserts God's dependence on man in such a way that God and man are identified: man is self-sufficient, and the supposed 'more' or 'otherness' of God is nothing other than man himself. However, this is to take from the quotation an unwarranted sense of dependence, and one that is not consistent with what Hegel said throughout his writings on religion, and especially on Manifest Religion. The sense of dependence of infinite on finite that is contained in Hegel's position is "only the dependence that any whole has on one of its parts—that without this part it could not be a whole. The infinite is not identical with but is the ground of the finite, and the ground could not know itself as what it is (the ground) unless there was something of which it was the ground." [113]

The words of Eckhart are ones that, for Hegel, convey a "thorough grasp of the divine depth", and as such they must preclude an atheistic interpretation of Hegel. However, a further indication that this Eckhart passage has been variously interpreted was given by Hegel when he admitted that it was frequently taken by theologians to be pantheistic. It is not surprising, therefore, that just as some regard this Eckhart passage as atheistic and consequently take it to support their view of Hegel as atheist, so with this passage as a proof text, many have seen Hegel's own philosophy as a form of pantheism—what might be described as the contrary of atheism—and so it is this question that now must be given considerable attention.

Chapter 11
A Contrary View
Hegel as a Pantheist

The rejection of both theism and atheism as possible interpretations of Hegel's philosophy of religion leads the way to a consideration of pantheism as a viable alternative. However, whether pantheism can be regarded as the only possible alternative is a question that must remain open at this stage. In theism and atheism one finds two philosophies about the nature of reality that usually are taken to represent contradictory views—to be two opposing extremes—and therefore, apart from all the factors that have been considered, it would be completely out of keeping with Hegel's general philosophy for him to promote one of two extremes. Rather, the Hegelian way is to seek out the synthesis as the genuine alternative to the opposing extremes; and the question is whether or not Hegel's synthesis is to be described as pantheism.

The Meaning of Pantheism

The first difficulty is to determine an adequate definition of pantheism. It is a straight-forward task to state the familiar pantheistic expression—το ἐν και Παν—that God is the One and All; but it ceases to be straightforward when one endeavors to indicate the meaning of the expression, for it is shrouded in considerable ambiguity. Hartshorne observes this ambiguity when he says that pantheism can mean "literally almost anything you please and so nearly nothing. That is probably the chief reason for its popularity as a label for opponents. And it ought to be clear that to say, 'God is the all', means whatever one's view of the all implies." [1]

Hegel, while wanting to speak of pantheism in fairly definite terms, nevertheless would have agreed with Hartshorne's observations about the actual use of the term being distinctly ambiguous. There are three detectable ways in which 'pantheism' is interpreted: first, it is taken to mean that each existing finite thing is deified; secondly, that it is the integral totality of finite things that is the divine Being; or thirdly, that God is the substance or essence—the essential structure of being—of all things. Hegel was well aware of the frequency of the first interpretation: in a number of references to pantheism he observed that the pantheistic expression that 'God is the One and the All' leads to the idea that "every existing thing in its finitude and particularity is held to be possessed of Being as God or as a god, and that the finite is deified as having Being." [2] But Hegel was quite adamant that this is a "false" and "unworthy" idea that is wrongly promoted as the meaning of pantheism: no pantheist has ever advanced it, and the only people to whom "such an absurd idea" has ever occurred are the opponents of pantheism, of whom the contemporary theologians provided a typical example.[3]

The ancient and modern representations of pantheism were the eleatic system and Spinozism respectively, but because of the popular misconception of the meaning of pantheism, "it is preferable to use the expression 'the philosophical systems of substantiality' and not to speak of systems of Pantheism." [4] The essential characteristic of these systems, Hegel said, is a fundamental unity, the recognition of "the Absolute One as the truth" of existence; and the basic category employed by these systems is that of Being or Substance, so that "God is Absolute Being, an Essence, which exists absolute in-and-for-itself, and does not exist through an Other, but represents independence pure and simple." [5]

Thus, Hegel took pantheism to mean that God is Substance or Essence, where Substance is identified with, and is in no sense other than, the totality and unity of all existence. But having spelled out this view as to the true meaning of pantheism or the "systems of substantiality", Hegel rejected pantheism as being an inadequate understanding of reality because it contains two defects that were quite crucial to Hegel in the light of his own view of reality. These defects are the treatment of actual existence "as a nullity," and the absence of any sense of "dialectical development," which means, as Hegel repeatedly said, that pantheism does "not get beyond Being or Substance" : [6] in other words, it does not attain to the notion of spirit.

Interpretations of Hegel as Pantheistic

However, in spite of Hegel's fundamental, and frequently repeated, criticisms of pantheism, and his numerous denials that his own philosophy could be identified with that of Spinoza or any pantheistic system, almost immediately Hegel was suspected of—and sometimes charged with—having espoused pantheism; and it is this fact that can provide an account of much of the adverse reaction to Hegel in the nineteenth century. An early accusation of pantheism against Hegel's philosophy occurred during Hegel's lifetime, in the work of F. G. Tholuck, and although Hegel clearly and specifically defended himself against this accusation,[7] such charges against his philosophy continued after his death because they were reinforced by the views of that section of the Hegelian "left wing" that did not openly profess atheism.

A prominent member of that school was D. F. Strauss, who developed a pantheism that he regarded as the philosophy of Hegel: in his second major work, *Die christliche Glaubenslehre* (2 vols., 1840–41) Strauss "argued that Christianity was a stage in the evolution of a true pantheism that had reached its culmination in Hegelian philosophy." [8] Subsequently, this has been a fairly persistent kind of exposition of Hegel's philosophy, finding expression in the works of Dilthey, who "interpreted Hegel in the sense of a 'mystical pantheism'," and Lütgert, for whom "a sufficient indication of Hegel's pantheism was the statement that Hegel's dominant concern lay in the 'overcoming of belief in a God above and beyond the world'." [9]

In the Wofford Symposium, Barrett suggests a pantheistic interpretation when he says that Hegel, "with his stress on the finite's capacity to bear the infinite, definitely tends in the direction of their identification." However, in noting Fackenheim's point that the kind of identity Hegel had in mind is "an identity of inclusion, not an identity of equation," Barrett observes that there are points "where inclusion and equation tend to verge on each other," so that "a discontinuity between finite and infinite" cannot be established with clarity unless Hegel can be shown to have established safeguards "against confusion of the identity of inclusion with that of equation." Such a safeguard, Barrett suggests, would be the freedom of the infinite; but, in contrast to this, Hegel spoke of the necessity of the infinite, and hence does not escape the tendency to identify—in the sense of equating—the finite and infinite.[10]

Pannenberg also has difficulty with Hegel's idea of the divine necessity, and recognizes that this is the most telling argument in the support for a pantheistic interpretation of Hegel: "Thus from Hegel's assertion of the logical necessity of the creation of the world and the coming into being of evil as the self-assertion of finiteness, *the consequence is drawn* that in spite of all the distinctions which Hegel makes, the world must belong to the process of the self-realization of God, and that therefore Hegel's system is pantheist." [11]

An interesting comparison is found in a discussion of Hegel by F. La T. Godfrey, who argues that, properly interpreted, the content of Hegel's *Logic* must be regarded "as the thought of a divine creator"; and that while Hegel frequently spoke of the Absolute in terms of a creator, using the language of religion, Hegel did not rightly see these implications, for "his strict doctrine as a philosopher is a metaphysic which finds the Absolute in a monistic pantheism, in which God is the world force or spirit immanent in the world and coming to self-consciousness only in the minds of men who are conscious of it as the Absolute." [12].

Thus, in each case, these commentators conclude that Hegel's philosophy is accurately interpreted when it is read as a pantheistic system. But what can be said about such interpretations?

Hegel and Spinoza

Any suggestion that Hegel's philosophy is a form of pantheism clearly links him with Spinoza, and any search for similarities between the two philosophers naturally would be given further impetus by the fact that Hegel displayed a very high regard for Spinoza. This regard is obviously shown by the comparatively lengthy discussion of Spinoza's philosophy given by Hegel in *LHP*, in which he revealed the value he placed on Spinoza as the very fountainhead of philosophy: "thought must begin by placing itself at the standpoint of Spinozism; to be a follower of Spinoza is the essential commencement of all Philosophy." [13] Hegel said that Spinoza "carried on the Cartesian principle to its furthest logical conclusions," and therein is to be found the importance of Spinoza's philosophy, for in it the Cartesian dualism is set aside. [14] In Spinoza's system, the true is simply and solely the one Substance, for it is only this absolute unity that is reality, and it alone is God. The two absolutely distinct substances of the Cartesian system, thought and extension, are brought together in Spinozism by their becoming moments of the one absolute Substance. Herein lies the grandeur of Spinoza's philosophy, as Hegel perceived it: Spinoza restricted himself to the One; and this is the foundation of all philosophy.

> When man begins to philosophize, the soul must commence by bathing in this ether of the One Substance, in which all that man has held as true has disappeared; this negation of all that is particular, to which every philosopher must have come, is the liberation of the mind and its absolute foundation. (*LHP*, vol. 3, 257–58)

However, the praise of Spinoza does not mean that Hegel identified his own philosophy with that of Spinoza. Indeed, Hegel argued that there were fundamental weaknesses in the work of Spinoza. It may have been the case that Spinoza's strength lay in his stress upon the unity of absolute Substance and in his glimpse of the truth "that Being must be grasped as the unity of opposites" [15]—that is, the union of the two attributes, thought and extension, in the one Substance—but it is also the case that it is here that Hegel located his weakness, namely, in his failure to perceive the implications of this truth, that Being is the unity of opposites. This failure, in turn, was due to a further and more fundamental weakness, namely, his understanding of absolute Being in terms of 'Substance' rather than 'Spirit',[16] which meant that Spinoza was unable to progress beyond a rigid substantiality.

This inability was a cause of disappointment regarding Spinoza, because Hegel was of the opinion that the seed of such a progression was to be found in the first definition with which Spinoza's philosophy commenced, and yet he failed to bring that seed to fruition. Spinoza's definition of 'cause of itself' was the definition Hegel had in mind as the one that contained the clue to overcoming the rigidity of substance, for while cause and effect are usually taken as standing in opposition to each other, the notion of 'cause of itself' is that of "the cause which, while it operates and separates an 'other', at the same time produces only itself, and in the production therefore does away with this distinction." [17] *Causa Sui* is "its own effect, that is, the mediation which cancels itself. The unity implied in this latter characteristic belongs to an infinitely deeper and more developed form of thought than the abstract unity of Being, or the One. . . . *Causa Sui* is a very striking expression for that unity." [18]

It is therefore the expression that points the way to the overcoming of that persistence of opposition that characterizes the rigidity of substance. According to the customary usage of the terms 'cause' and 'effect', the cause is taken to refer to one entity and the effect to another, but Hegel argued that—taking the clue from the notion

of *causa sui*, which does away with the distinction and opposition
between cause and effect—it can be seen that any cause is inseparable
from its effect. The cause is cause only in relation to its effect, and
the effect is effect only in relation to its cause, and this means that
both the cause and effect are mediated through their 'other', which
thereby ceases to be an other—"for this which is supposed to be
an Other is of such a kind that the cause is first a cause in it, and
therefore in it simply reaches itself, and in it affects only itself." [19]
Spinoza's shortcomings lie primarily in the fact that he was not able
to develop the implications of his notion of *causa sui*, and so, with
him, substance remained rigid and unworkable.[20]

Therefore, although Spinoza attained the grand achievement of
perceiving the unity of the one Substance, he failed to grasp the
notion of mediation through an Other. In other words, he stopped
"short of defining substance as subject and as mind *(Geist)*," [21] and
consequently the unity of substance remained "abstract unity", "mere
identity", and substance was merely "the empty absolute". Spinoza
called this absolute 'God', which is thus the 'All'—not in the sense
of 'everything', but in the sense of "Absolute Being, an Essence,
which exists absolutely in-and-for-itself, and does not exist through
an Other, but represents independence pure and simple." [22] Therefore,
even though Hegel regarded Spinoza's notion of God as being rather
inadequate, he still concluded that those who accuse Spinoza of
atheism are greatly mistaken.

So, far from it being the case that Spinoza's philosophy is a version
of atheism,[23] Hegel in fact, asserted that with Spinoza the opposite
is the case. It may be the case that Spinoza's philosophy could be
described as atheism in the sense that "Spinoza does not distinguish
God from the world, the finite"; but this would really be "a misuse
of the term," for "Spinozism might really just as well or even better
have been termed Acosmism." [24] This is so because—rather than
treating the relationship between God and the finite in the way
atheism does, by denying the existence of God—Spinoza asserted
that God alone exists, and thus he really denied the reality of the
finite. So, Hegel continued, the consequence of Spinoza's view of
God as the one Substance is that finite individuality is lost: individual
things—the modes—are nothing in themselves, they are nothing
substantial; hence their apparent independent life is purely illusory.
What *is* is God alone, and all that we know of the world has been
cast into the abyss of the one identity, for the world is merely a
form of God.

> Spinoza maintains that there is no such thing as what is known
> as the world; it is merely a form of God, and in and for itself

it is nothing. The world has no true reality, and all this that we know as the world has been cast into the abyss of the one identity. There is therefore no such thing as finite reality, it has no truth whatever; according to Spinoza what is, is God, and God alone. Therefore the allegations of those who accuse Spinoza of atheism are the direct opposite of the truth; with him there is too much God. (*LHP*, vol. 3, 281–82)

As Hegel rightly said, Spinoza strove to overcome all forms of dualism, not least the traditional theistic dualism between God and the world. In Spinoza's philosophy, what traditionalists argued in the case of God, Spinoza argued concerning Substance, which he equated with God and Nature. Therefore, any external relationship between God and the universe was an impossibility, and so Spinoza was suggesting the necessity of relating God and the world by means of some bond other than that of 'causation', which was defined in such a way that the effect is simply external to the cause. But in so doing, he was posing another problem of how to define more exactly the sense in which God is the total Reality; and it was this feature of Spinoza's philosophy that prompted Hegel to describe it as an acosmism, since it does not mean that God is the world, but that God is the one and only substance.

According to Hegel's interpretation of Spinoza's acosmism, it contains both a positive and a negative element: "the negative element is the view that the world, the 'cosmos', does not exist; it is a mere phenomenon, lacking in true reality . . .; Spinoza's acosmism, seen from its negative side, is the denial of the real existence of individual things. Individuality, and indeed distinction of all kind, is obliterated; everything is thrown in an abyss of annihilation. The positive element in Spinoza's acosmism is the view that what does exist is God, to whom everything is reducible. Individual things are the 'modes' of God; fundamental differences of kind—in particular, the distinction between mind and matter—are seen as different 'attributes' of God." [25]

However, Hegel regarded Spinoza's acosmism as defective. Of course, this defectiveness does not lie in Spinoza's rejection of dualism and his asserting of everything as a unity in the sense that God is the one and only Substance that exists. The defectiveness is to be found in what Hegel took as the consequence of Spinoza's position, namely, that this unity is a completely undifferentiated unity in the sense that the individual is unreal. The fault here was due to Spinoza's concept of the individual, the mode, by which he meant "that which exists in, and is conceived through, something other than itself";[26] for the individual, so conceived, has no reality in itself: mode, said

Hegel, "is not conceived as reality, but through and in something else." [27]

The cause of this fault in Spinoza can be further identified as residing in Spinoza's method, which Hegel regarded as a weak point in his system. This weakness was caused by his commencing with formal definitions that merely were asserted without any examination as to whether their content is true. It was, then, observed Hegel, from these definitions that Spinoza, by means of axioms and propositions, claimed to prove a variety of matters: "Spinoza descends from the universal of substance through the particular, thought and extension, to the individual. . . . But the mode, under which head falls individuality, he does not recognize as essential; for it disappears in existence, or it is not raised into the Notion." [28]

It is Hegel's criticism that Spinoza did not maintain a firm grasp of the individual, for since the finite mode has no reality in itself, it is lost in the universality of Substance. But it is not in the universality of substance that Hegel found the fault; rather, it is in the rigidity of that substance, which was due, in Hegel's opinion, to Spinoza's geometrical method. What is vital for Hegel, in contrast, is the dialectical process, with its movement that he called "the negation of the negation", and it is this that Spinoza failed to grasp, Hegel believed, thus resulting in substance remaining as something rigid. Together with Spinoza, Hegel stressed universality, but in contrast to Spinoza, he presented the dialectical nature of universality by which individuality is derived from universality, in the sense that universality finds its expression in individuality, and individuality finds its truth in universality. But Spinoza did not derive individuality from universality, he simply asserted both, and defined individuality in such a way that it has no reality of its own, and so is lost in universality, defined as substance, which remains as something rigid.[29]

Spinoza's defect is therefore this, that he takes the third moment as mode alone, as a false individuality. True individuality and subjectivity is not a mere retreat from the universal, not merely something clearly determinate; for, as clearly determinate, it is at the same time Being-for-itself, determined by itself alone. The individual, the subjective, is even in being so the return to the universal; and in that it is at home with itself, it is itself the universal. The return consists simply and solely in the fact of the particular being in itself the universal; to this return Spinoza did not attain. Rigid substantiality is the last point he reached. (*LHP*, vol. 3, 260–61)

If there is a sense in which Spinoza can be spoken of as an atheist, it is, Hegel claimed, to be found at this point of rigid substantiality, in contrast to the dialectic of Spirit. In speaking of these systems—especially the Spinozistic system, which he called acosmical—Hegel said, "they are most accurately called systems which apprehend the Absolute only as substance," and he observed that "the fault of these modes of thought and systems is that they stop short of defining substance as subject and as mind *(Geist)*." [30] Yet, Hegel argued, God is truly conceived as Spirit, and the failure to grasp this truth, asserting, as Spinoza did, only that God is substance, can be regarded as a form of atheism.[31]

A determination of Hegel's position has to be seen, in an important part, in relation to Spinoza, because Hegel believed he had succeeded in his endeavor to distance himself from the Spinozist position. Of course, he could distance himself from that position only *as he understood it,* and while the question as to the correctness of Hegel's understanding of it is of no detailed importance here, it does have some bearing at this stage in our inquiry. One of the criticisms Hegel directed at Spinoza was that he denied genuine reality to finite individuals, and clearly Hegel did not wish to be guilty of the same error. Contrary to Hegel's assessment, however, many argue that Spinoza did not deny finite reality, but that he could avoid that denial, given his system, only by falling into a serious inconsistency. The question that can then be asked regarding Hegel is that, if he got Spinoza wrong and distanced himself from a position that was not Spinoza's, might he not have ended up with the same system—a pantheism—and be guilty of the same inconsistency? Therefore, a slightly diversionary consideration of Spinoza's position relating to these matters does not seem to be irrelevant at this point.

Spinoza made a distinction between *natura naturans* and *natura naturata,* but rather than being seen as representing a division of the whole of Nature, this distinction should be taken as representing two different ways of looking at the whole of Nature. *Natura naturans* is the infinite One regarded as creative activity, while *natura naturata* is the infinite One regarded as the passive actuality caused by that activity, and as such it is also an Infinite Whole of parts. But do these parts have genuine reality? And linked with this question is another, namely: Do the two descriptions of the one reality—as *natura naturans* and *natura naturata*—really amount to a contradiction? It is argued that either Spinoza remained trapped in a contradiction or else he must have mitigated it by the device of treating one side of his conception of reality as mere appearance, that is, treating the finite parts as having no genuine reality. While Spinoza asserted that both aspects of substance *must* be, he did not proceed to inquire whether both *may* be. Therefore, it can be argued, he was finally unable to stand the strain of the contradiction that thereby emerged, and he was forced to imply—though he never recognized—that one aspect is *less* true than the other, that in itself substance is merely simple, while the manifold concrete content and the differentiated attributes declared to inhere in it are only appearances created by the human intellect.

In Spinoza's view, finite modes are necessary modifications of substance, and thus all contingency is denied. His position therefore can be sharply contrasted with traditional theism, which emphatically asserts that God is logically and ontologically independent of the world, for without the world God would still be God. It is also apparent that in theism one can—and indeed must—speak of the priority of God as cause; but in a system such as Spinoza's, where everything is seen as necessary, it is no longer appropriate to speak in this manner, thus making apparent the distinction between Spinoza and the traditional theistic view.

In the Spinozan system, not only does the proposition 'particular finite things exist' necessarily involve the proposition 'God exists', but it is also true that the latter necessarily involves the former.[32] Therefore, as well as admitting a relationship of dependence between finite existing things and God,[33] it is difficult to see how Spinoza could avoid having to admit also the reciprocity of that relationship, so that God is dependent upon finite things. This he clearly would have wanted to avoid, but it appears to be logically inescapable that a thing cannot be logically independent of that which it necessarily involves. Similarly, there ought not be any suggestion of priority in the relationship between God and finite existing things. But the priority of substance was categorically set forth by Spinoza: "A substance is prior in its nature to its modifications";[34] and his 'proof' of this consisted in the argument that it necessarily follows from the appropriate definitions.

These matters indicate the paradox in which Spinoza was involved. Although he wished to deny the dualism of God and the world, it seems that he was not able to avoid language that is suggestive of two different realms, particularly in his talk about the priority of substance. Thus, apart from accusing Spinoza of a contradiction, the only alternative conclusion is one that provides support for the claim that in the end Spinoza was forced to reduce the finite particulars to the illusory. In this way it is possible to explain Hegel's interpretation of Spinoza along these lines.

However, in opposition to Hegel, one has to say that it does not seem to be a correct interpretation of Spinoza to argue that he denied the reality of finite modes—such an option does not appear to be a feasible one for Spinoza. There is a sense in which Spinoza would have wanted to insist that any general proposition like 'all X are Y' is about real individual X's, and to insist that the 'truths' that are expressed in his definitions and axioms must be true of real things— for a world of individuals not coming under the truths is inconceivable; but similarly, a world of truths without real individuals is also inconceivable. Parkinson agrees when he says that from an examination of the doctrine of modes in the *Ethics* and the definition of *natura naturata*, "it is hard to see how something can be said to follow from the necessity of the nature of God if that something is a mere illusion." Further, "Spinoza declares in *Ethics* I 30, that the intellect grasps not only the attributes of God but also the 'affections' of God, that is (*Ethics* I Def. 5) the modes. As the modes are grasped by the intellect, it follows that they have objective reality." [35]

Hallett also would agree, for he strongly denies that Spinoza reduced the finite durational world to pure illusion—such a reduction is "contradicted by many overt statements and by the whole tenor of his ethical doctrine." [36] However, this conclusion means that the question of Spinoza's being trapped in an inconsistency remains. Hallett's suggestion of a way forward concerning this problem is to assert that the relationship between the infinite and the finite can be explained in terms of a self-reflecting and creative unity. Hallett's suggestion is to see the relationship in such a way that each finite individual is a partial, finite expression of the infinite Whole, and to the extent that any such part does reflect the Whole it also reflects other finite parts. Above all, the Whole must be a unity. Each part must partially reflect the Whole; but each part cannot reflect it in such a way that the Whole is completely in each one. But not only is it a self-reflecting unity in this sense, it is also a creative unity— it is creative because the activity of creation "is the infinite self-manifestation of a being whose essence it is to express itself." [37]

However, there is still a puzzle concerning Spinoza: it appears that there remained in his philosophy elements of the theistic tension between transcendence and immanence, even though he was strongly motivated to avoid the difficulties of traditional theism. Yet, it seems that he was not really successful: substance is transcendent, yet immanent; the finite modes are essential, yet not of the essence of substance; nothing is contingent, everything is necessary, and so it would seem that substance cannot be independent of modes, yet substance is prior; substance is that which creates but must also be identified with that which is created.

It is important to stress that Spinoza was committed to upholding the two aspects of reality—*natura naturans* and *natura naturata*—but quite paradoxically, in the end, so long as the basic principle of the oneness of reality is maintained, one wonders how the inconsistency can be avoided, since neither of the two possible ways—denying the reality of the finite modes or admitting the 'otherness' of the absolute—seems to be open to him.

This is the paradox found in Spinoza. Spinozism and traditional theism are both founded on the same notion, namely, that God cannot in any way be genuinely related to others. However, while such a notion meant that classical theism was dualistic, Spinoza used it in an endeavor to overcome dualism, and thus developed a pantheism that he succinctly expressed in the formula *Deus sive natura.* Nevertheless, the Spinozistic paradox is that unless he denied the reality of the finite, he could not really avoid the suggestion that God is in some way 'other'. This is shown by the fact that he himself continued to use conflicting language: he did not avoid retaining some language of transcendence; he did not avoid speaking of the priority of God and thus did not escape the implication of the otherness of God, even if the priority is ontological rather than temporal; and, so long as he maintained the distinction of that which creates and that which is created (corresponding to the distinction between Substance and Mode), he could not avoid the self-contradiction that is involved in identifying the two. This seems to show the hopelessness of the endeavor to make a metaphysic by framing a conception of an Absolute Reality on which everything is dependent for its existence while denying the otherness of that Reality.

However, was not this also Hegel's endeavor? Many commentators regard Hegel as having failed to escape from the Spinozistic position— hence the interpretation of Hegel as being pantheistic. So, in this inquiry, it is necessary to ask how Hegel is to be assessed on this matter.

It has already been observed that in spite of his warm praise of Spinoza, Hegel directed a number of strong criticisms at him, and in so doing, he sought to distance himself from the Spinozistic position. It is apposite to this discussion to look again at two of these criticisms.

First, Hegel accused Spinoza of having a concept of substance that suggests substance is that in which all particulars are absorbed and obliterated: in Spinoza's philosophy, Hegel said, "there exists the One into which everything enters, in order to be absorbed therein, but out of which nothing comes . . . God alone is the positive, the affirmative, and consequently the one substance. All other things are only modifications of this substance, and are nothing in and for themselves." [38] Because the finite modes have no genuine reality, therefore, it means that the consequence of Spinoza's philosophy, so Hegel argued, is that the universal, in all its plurality and difference, is nothing but an illusion; and it was on this interpretation of Spinoza that Hegel based his description of it as 'acosmism'.

In directing this criticism at Spinoza, Hegel was following Fichte, and indeed was criticizing Spinoza in terms similar to those in which he criticized Schelling and other Romantic philosophers. Parkinson, who believes Hegel is mistaken in this criticism of Spinoza, says that Hegel allowed himself to be misled, and that his "attack on Spinoza is in effect an attack on a Schelling who is projected back into the seventeenth century." [39] It has been suggested already that there is ample evidence in Spinoza to refute this kind of accusation that Hegel directed against him, for, as Shmueli expresses it, Spinoza "often stressed the falsity of abstractness and the validity of concreteness. An adequate idea for him is always a concrete idea since it has its designation within a system. Ultimately substance is the most concrete." [40]

From the evidence, therefore, one cannot accuse Spinoza of holding the finite modes to be merely illusory, but, as Parkinson suggests, it is still possible "to argue that this is at any rate what Spinoza *ought* to have held" in order to achieve consistency within his philosophy.[41] Indeed, it is possible to imagine Hegel's agreeing that Spinoza would not have wanted to dismiss finite modes as mere appearances, and that there is evidence in Spinoza's works to support this claim.[42] Hegel's reply to this, indeed his real point against Spinoza, would be that in spite of what Spinoza may have wanted to assert about the reality of finite modes, it is an assertion only at the level of *Verstand*, whereas at the level of speculative thought it can be seen that in fact in Spinoza the finite modes are presented only as 'Nothing', because Spinoza has not attained to the true concept of the Absolute as *Geist*.

This is the second of Hegel's main criticisms of Spinoza, and it underlies the first. The fact that Spinoza perceived absolute Being as Substance rather than Spirit, Hegel said, meant that he did not progress beyond a rigid substantiality. It is this difference that he identified between himself and Spinoza upon which Hegel placed much emphasis,[43] for he was confident that in his own philosophy he had overcome the deficiency of Spinoza. What he believed is philosophically inadequate in Spinoza is that Substance has "no vitality, spirituality or activity";[44] it is a passive, immobile, and inert unity, which is always actual and fulfilled, and so is totally without any process of self-unfolding, becoming, or development.

The Spinozistic system's complete lack of any kind of dialectical development was due to the fact that although Spinoza correctly perceived that every "determination is negation", he overlooked what Hegel took to be the inevitable principle of "the negation of the negation", which, in turn, meant that Spinoza did not attain to the true concept of 'return' into the absolute. Hegel argued that Spinoza's concept of negation, whereby each finite particular is a negation, 'nothing', a mere modification of substance that has no reality of its own, means that his concept of the 'return' of the particular into the universal involves the dissolution of the finite in the absolute, which, with its lack of movement and becoming, is solely an infinite receptacle in which the finite particulars are merely contained.

> What we find regarding this particular then is that it is only a modification of absolute substance, which, however, is not declared to be such; for the moment of negativity is what is lacking to this rigid motionlessness whose single form of activity is this, to divest all things of their determination and particularity and cast them back into the one absolute substance, wherein they are simply swallowed up, and all life in itself is utterly destroyed. (*LHP*, vol. 3, 288)

In what Hegel took to be a sharp contrast to Spinoza, he emphasized reality to be a process, becoming, and development. Crucial to this thought is what he presented as the true concept of negation, namely, "the negation of the negation", whereby the perception of each particular as a negation is itself negated so that the particular is perceived as a finite being, positively possessing reality within the total embrace of the infinite. But the particular is not dissolved within the absolute, for while the reality of the particular is the self-unfolding of the absolute, the particular retains its reality, and itself contributes to the being of the absolute, which is thus seen to be the process of becoming. "The philosophic requisite is therefore to apprehend the unity of these differences in such a way that difference is not let slip, but proceeds eternally from substance, without being petrified into dualism." [45] This is what Hegel meant when he spoke of the Absolute as Substance disclosing itself as Subject or Spirit.

Again, is it the case that Hegel's interpretation of Spinoza is accurate and his criticism justified? It does seem that Hegel overstressed the difference between his own and Spinoza's philosophy, and that, in fact, the contrast between them is not as great since it is possible to identify in Spinoza the presence of the dynamic character of substance. This is apparent when substance is considered under the aspect of *natura naturans*, i.e., nature viewed as active, which brings out the free causative activity of substance or God. [46]

McMinn speaks of "the intrinsic dynamic of Substance", arguing that "Spinoza does not assume an abstract, passive, unreflective universal Substance; rather, his God, though Substance, is also active, concrete, conscious Spirit, which articulates Himself through His modifications in the finite world and thereby gives some reality to individuality." [47] Similarly, Shmueli says that against the Hegelian critique of Spinoza "one must emphasize that Spinoza's ultimate ground for identifying his substance with its attributes and the infinite intellect was his notion of substance as an activity and not as a static 'thing in itself' perceived by the intellect from the outside. Spinoza's substance stands for fulness of acts, for the active essence of God. Substance realizes itself not in a relationship of an object to its perceiver but in modifications of its attributes." [48] Further, as already noted, Hallett stresses the interpretation of Spinoza's substance as creative: the ultimately Real, he says, "is an eternal *creative* and *self-producing* unity," and "each finite part issues eternally from the undivided creative nature of Substance"; and the nature of Substance is truly described as creative because the activity of creation "is the infinite self-manifestation of a being whose essence it is to express itself." [49]

Now of course this kind of description of Spinoza's philosophy gives it the appearance of being Hegelian, since Hegel was quite insistent on "the infinite self-manifestation" of the Absolute; and so it begins to appear that there is no significant difference between Hegel and Spinoza on these matters. Hegel criticized Spinoza for reducing finite particulars to mere illusions; and while he might have acknowledged the evidence that Spinoza did admit the genuine reality of the finite, Hegel countered it by accusing Spinoza of failing to rise above the level of *Verstand*, and so failing to perceive the Absolute as Spirit, as dynamic process—thereby making the finite particulars mere modifications of the always actual and fulfilled substance, into which the finite is dissolved as 'nothing'.

But now it seems that evidence can be presented from Spinoza to counter this accusation, emphasizing Spinoza's substance as creative activity in contrast to rigid substantiality. And it is in the light of this evidence that the difference that Hegel asserted between himself and Spinoza on these matters begins to diminish.

Thus, the issue becomes the question whether Hegel, regardless of his own utterances, did succeed in distancing himself from Spinoza. There are two ways in which this matter may be approached: one may ask whether Hegel was in error in his interpretation of Spinoza, in order to discover whether Spinoza in fact did achieve that which Hegel accused him of failing to attain—especially the notion of the absolute as Spirit, which Hegel himself claimed to have attained; or one may ask whether Hegel was able to escape pantheism—a question which again focuses attention on the main concern of this inquiry—

in order to discover whether Hegel did achieve a position other than that of which he accused Spinoza.

It has just been observed that amongst those who have commented upon Hegel's discussion of Spinoza there is a strong opinion that Hegel was mistaken in his interpretation. What seems to be the case is that there is in Spinoza more of the dynamic aspect of Substance, which thus discloses itself as Subject or Spirit, than Hegel was able to recognize.[50] This aspect is especially noticeable in Spinoza's treatment of the theory of knowledge: the case for this is presented most strongly by McMinn, who argues that here Hegel was guilty of an inadequate observation, particularly of the modal character of the understanding. Hegel was correct, McMinn acknowledges, "in noting that the Understanding [in Spinoza] is a modification of Substance, an explicit expression of the attribute of thought. But his [Hegel's] assumption that the function of the understanding [in Spinoza] is *necessarily* an external thinking is incorrect." [51]

Indeed, Spinoza distinguished three levels of knowledge, the first of which might be described as external thinking, for it is the level of *imagination* at which our ideas are derived from sensation, and as such it is the level of inadequate ideas. But the next level, that of *reason*, is the level of adequate ideas, at which the understanding can rise above immediate and particular things and deal with abstract ideas that are not formulated by the understanding, but are concrete ideas of God.[52] As such, McMinn suggests "the adequate idea does not have its being or cause in the understanding. Its ontological status is determined rather by its source, viz., the infinite intellect of God; it is essentially in its epistemological function that it relates itself to the understanding. In reality, therefore, the adequate idea *in se* is the real unfoldment of Substance as the *infinita idea dei* or as Spirit, i.e., Substance disclosing itself as Subject." [53] Thus, McMinn continues, "the understanding demonstrates through its expression of the adequate or true idea its true modal character in that it becomes the essential individual expression of the universal, reflecting thereby the dynamic, if not the dialectic, of the Spinozistic impersonal system and refuting Hegel's charge that mode is illusion, merely a vanishing moment." [54]

But Spinoza's third and highest level of knowledge is *intuition*, at which the understanding can grasp the whole system of nature; it is an adequate knowledge of the essence of things that are ideas in God, and thus the understanding, in its finitude, expresses the infinite Idea of God. Therefore, McMinn argues, "the understanding, in its modal particularity, its finitude, is not God as such; but insofar as the universal mind *(infinita idea dei)* is in it in the fulness of the adequate idea, the understanding rises to the position of the universal, which in Hegelian terms is the third moment of the dialectic, the individual 'raised to the Notion'. From the inverse order, the universal, making itself particular in the understanding, yet at the same time remaining what it is *in se*, thus reveals or discloses itself as concrete Spirit." [55]

What this suggests is that there is in Spinoza evidence to support the claim that the Spinozistic Substance discloses itself as Subject or Spirit; but it does seem that this kind of presentation involves a spelling out of these aspects in a much more explicit way than they are in Spinoza himself, and it is, in fact, a spelling out that is done in the light of Hegel's philosophy. Nevertheless, it can be said that Hegel did fail to observe the dynamic, active aspect of Spinoza's Substance—which is a creative and self-reflecting, not a static, Substance. But having said that, it is also true that the dialectic is not to be found in Spinoza—McMinn himself speaks of "the dynamic, if not the dialectic, of the Spinozistic impersonal system"—and this is of notable significance in terms of Hegel's criticism. In spite of the dynamic, active aspect of Spinoza's Substance, because everything is eternally as it must be, and because particular events are simply finite modifications of Substance, there is no direction in which things are moving—there is no end, no purpose, no final cause.

In Spinoza, the truth is that all events are a continuous and necessary set of modifications of the eternal Substance, which simply *is*. But, for Hegel, this is not enough: it is not just a matter of the dynamic nature of things, for the greater depth of Hegel's perception of reality brought into crucial prominence the concept of specific *development*.[56]

It was Hegel, therefore, who clearly developed the concept of dialectical development and final cause. The infinite living substance becomes truly in-and-for-itself through the process of positing itself in its other, the finite, and through the finite negating itself as the finite and passing over into its other. The living substance "is truly realized and actual solely in the process of positing itself" in its other, the finite; and the finite is truly itself when it is the other, when it goes beyond itself and thus passes over into its essence and finds itself *within* the infinite. Of true reality, Hegel said, "only this self-*restoring* sameness or this reflection in otherness within itself— not an *original* or *immediate* unity as such—is the True. It is the process of its own becoming, the circle that presupposes its end as its goal, having its end also as its beginning; and only by being worked out to its end, is it actual." [57]

Therefore, it seems that one can conclude that Hegel was partly in error in his interpretation of Spinoza, for Spinoza did achieve more than Hegel admitted. But it is also true, as has just been observed, that Hegel added important concepts that do distinguish him from Spinoza. As far as the latter's position is concerned, it is quite apparent that he himself sought to establish a pantheism, in which he identified God with the whole cosmos: *Deus sive Natura* is his famous formula, which suggests that the two words are interchangeable, emphasizing not the *relation* between, but the basic *identity* of, God and the world.

However, it has already been considered in some detail how Spinoza got into difficulties and how he was not able completely to avoid language that is suggestive of the transcendent 'otherness' of God (e.g., that the source of adequate ideas is the infinite intellect of God). He thereby indicated the difficulty, if not the hopelessness, of the endeavor to establish a metaphysic by framing a conception of Absolute Reality on which everything is dependent for its existence, while denying the 'otherness' of that Reality by identifying it with all that is. As Shmueli observes, "the divergent elements of the monistic system burst apart. The tension between them remains even in what is seemingly a justified synthesis. There persists always the possibility of emphasizing one element of the synthesis over and above the other." [58] Nevertheless, the question that is of prime concern here is whether Hegel himself was able to escape pantheism: in other words, did he achieve a position other than that of which he accused Spinoza, and if so, was he any more successful in establishing a synthesis and holding the divergent elements of a monistic system together?

It is quite clear that both Spinoza and Hegel were motivated by a similar purpose. Both were moved to counteract systems of dualism and to establish the *unity* of reality; both were inspired to develop a philosophic system in which apparent irreconcilables were reconciled. Shmueli suggests their common purpose when he says that both "attempted to render a cognitive account of some basic mystical insights, particularly of the mysteries of identity-in-distinction and of the interpenetration of the divine and the human"; "both thinkers attempted to define an intuitional claim that the world is capable of being known as a single, ordered and continuous totality, since its substance is rational, coherent and all-encompassing." [59]

But not only did they share a common purpose, they also, Shmueli concludes, in spite of some differences, shared a common pantheism of the acosmic type, so that Hegel did not achieve a system other than the one he attributed to Spinoza. Furthermore, just as Spinoza failed to hold together the divergent elements of the monistic system, emphasizing one element of the synthesis over the other, so, too, did Hegel fail. While both insisted "that every philosophical flight from the world is a mark of failure," "neither could they stay with the world: they sought intensely to rise to eternity." [60] In some contrast to Shmueli's conclusion, other commentators, such as McMinn and Whittemore, while also asserting the similarity of the two systems of thought, prefer to speak of that similarity in terms of the systems being a form of panentheism.

The discussion of Hegel and Spinoza, as a means of determining the question of Hegel's alleged pantheism, has thus come to the point where it can obviously be recognized that there are similarities between these two philosophers; where it is apparent that Hegel firmly distinguished his own position from that of Spinoza; but where one also has become aware that there is strong opinion to the effect that it is the similarities between Spinoza and Hegel that are predominant, though that opinion differs as to whether both systems are thereby to be styled pantheistic or panentheistic.

It can be agreed, however, that Spinoza's intention was to establish a system that was typical of pantheism, and that in doing so, he encountered difficulties that produced certain tensions and ambiguities in his philosophy. The opinion that Spinoza was a panentheist can be based only on the argument that those tensions and ambiguities are such that Spinoza really failed to achieve the kind of system he thought he had produced and that he expressed in the words *Deus sive Natura*. Hegel certainly took Spinoza to have been pantheistic in an acosmic sense, and it is equally certain that Hegel intended to develop a system that would be distinguished from Spinoza's, and in which the failings of the Spinozistic pantheism would be overcome.

There have already emerged suggestions that Hegel in fact did achieve this; but if he did, what then is to be said of his system? The suggested 'panentheism' would seem to be a possible description of the Hegelian position, and so the stage has been reached where the search for a final answer to the question of Hegel's alleged pantheism must continue in—and can be answered only in the light of—an examination of the possibility of Hegel's panentheism.

Chapter 12
A Medial View
Hegel as a Panentheist

An exploration into Hegel's philosophy leaves little doubt that he was at one with Spinoza in the desire to avoid the dualistic consequences of theism; and Hegel was firm in the opinion that Spinoza's achievement largely consisted in the extent to which he was able to avoid the problems of dualism. But Hegel believed that Spinoza had fallen into a serious error: namely, that in the effort to avoid the sharp theistic distinction between God and the world, the infinite and finite, he had moved into the pantheistic position of conceiving the infinite-finite relationship in terms of an identity that, in Spinoza's case, was of such a kind as acosmically to deny the reality of the finite. While this criticism was unfair and unwarranted, Spinoza really escaped from such a philosophic state only at the expense of admitting—though not intentionally—certain tensions and ambiguities. However, whatever the criticisms one makes of Spinoza, Hegel would say that Spinoza's difficulties were due to the fact that his work is a philosophy of *Verstand*, and at this level of thought various systems, such as theism and pantheism, are seen to stand in an irreconcilable contrast to each other. It was Hegel's claim to have found the way to progress beyond this, and so to be able to express, for example, the divine-human, infinite-finite relationship in a way that reconciles the two antithetical concepts, theism and pantheism, at the higher level of speculative thought where absolute Being is known, not merely as Substance, but also as Spirit.

251

This Hegelian claim poses two important and related questions. First, was Hegel really successful in achieving his claim, or is it the case that, if he maintained talk about God, then it is not really possible for him to have avoided either a kind of traditional theism or Spinozistic pantheism? Secondly, is the only possible way of viewing Hegel's endeavor as successful to interpret it as a form of atheism, in the sense that his treatment of the God-world relationship, at what he claimed to be the level of speculative thought, really amounts to the elimination of the concept of God? Such an inter-pretation suggests that in seeking to overcome the problems of Spinoza, whom he agreed was a "God-intoxicated mystic," [1] Hegel translated talk about God into talk about absolute Spirit, so that, at the level of speculative philosophy, ultimate reality is spoken of as the all-comprehensive Life, and there is, consequently, a demythol-ogizing of the content of religious belief that really is nothing but the elimination of that content.

If these two questions are taken to be exhaustive of what can be asked about the possible Hegelian position regarding the God-world relationship, then the underlying assumption is that—broadly speak-ing—theism, atheism, and pantheism exhaust the possible viewpoints on this matter. Lütgert identified Hegel's dominant concern as the " 'overcoming of belief in a God above and beyond the world'," and took this to be "a sufficient indication of Hegel's pantheism." [2] Now it is clear that Hegel did wish to overcome such a theistic belief, but Lütgert apparently assumed that pantheism is the only other alternative for one who desires to maintain the concept of God; and Westphal suggests the same thing when he says that "one could do worse than defining as pantheistic those systems which view classical theism as dualistic." [3] It is, however, feasible to ask whether it is possible to suggest some other alternative; and if it is, then, with regard to Hegel, one also would have to ask whether it is possible to consider Hegel's philosophy as being compatible with it.

Regarding this matter of a possible alternative view, one can immediately nominate that which is known as *panentheism,* a position that insists that all things are *within* God, and a position that, apart from its obvious difference from atheism, also needs to be distin-guished very definitely from theism and pantheism. Then, regarding Hegel's position, one finds it described by Fackenheim as "a middle which combines a pluralistic openness with a monistic comprehen-siveness"; it is a middle that, being achieved as a result of the speculative transfiguration of Christianity, seeks to preserve Chris-tianity against two extremes equally destructive of it: namely, "the right-wing extreme of speculative pantheism which would deny the reality of the finite and contingent," and the left-wing or immanentist interpretation in which "the world of human experience *exhausts* Reality." [4] Thus, Fackenheim identifies the Hegelian mediation as being between pantheism and atheism, and—in apparent contrast to this—it has been suggested above, in the context of the discussion of the relation between Hegel and Spinoza, that the mediation is between pantheism and theism.

In yet another context, it can be suggested that Hegel's mediation is between theism and atheism; and none of these mediations can be dismissed as not applicable to Hegel, for one must take very seriously Fackenheim's description of Hegel's position as one of openness and comprehensiveness. This is entirely in accord with his dialectical thinking, according to which every stage in human thought possesses some truth, and that truth is not to be discarded or lost, but is to be absorbed into a higher level of thought in which more of the truth is comprehended. Accordingly, Hegel's philosophy of religion is to be described accurately as an endeavor to reconcile, at the higher level of speculative thought, the antithetical views of *Verstand*—theism, atheism, and pantheism—thereby retaining those aspects of the truth that are to be found in each: the theistic sense of divine otherness, the atheistic stress on the reality of the finite, and the pantheistic emphasis on unity so that all things are in God and God is in all things. Thus, Hegel can be seen to have evolved a philosophic position that is truly a genuine alternative. It seems there can be no question that this was Hegel's endeavor, and equally it seems there can be no question that he believed his goal had been achieved.

Although, therefore, there can be little doubt that Hegel's objective was the development of a mediating middle, the immediate question now concerns how that middle is to be specified, and whether one can turn to panentheism as the adequate specification of Hegel's position. The very nature of the term itself—panentheism—immediately alludes to the middle ground between theism and pantheism, and it does seem feasible to suggest that the Hegelian position may thus be specified. However, a greater understanding of the meaning and application of this term is necessary to determine whether the assumed feasibility of its use here is justified.

The Meaning of Panentheism

As in the case of the other examples of this kind of terminology, so also 'panentheism' is not easily given a precise meaning when one considers the various nuances implied by the usages of the term. However, panentheism has been defined as "the belief that the Being of God includes and penetrates the whole universe, so that every part of it exists in Him, but that His Being is more than, and is not exhausted by, the universe." [5] It is the view that God is in the world and the world in God, thus expressing the conception of the inter-penetration of God and the world, while also asserting that God is not exhausted by—or reducible to, or identified with—the world. Such a view upholds the reality of the finite (which is stressed by atheism) as opposed to the loss of reality of finite things (which Hegel said is the consequence of pantheism); it upholds the ultimacy and absoluteness of God (which is the stress of theism and pantheism) as opposed to the ultimacy and absoluteness of finite things (which is the assertion of atheism); it upholds the unity of God and the world (which is the stress of pantheism) as opposed to the separation from the world of traditional theism's God 'out-there'; but it also upholds a sense of the transcendence of God as encompassing, but surpassing, the finite (which is the stress of theism) as opposed to the identification of the world with God (which is the assertion of pantheism). [6]

Hegel regarded these other viewpoints about the God-world re-lationship as being philosophies of *Verstand*, and therefore as being unable to satisfy the reflective mind. This, however, did not amount to an assertion on Hegel's part that these positions had no validity at all: indeed, the objectification of God as a personal transcendent 'being-out-there' was, Hegel believed, a dialectically necessary stage in the process by which universal spirit comes to know itself in the human spirit; equally necessary in the dialectical process, as reactions to theism, are pantheism and atheism. But each of these positions is characterized by a one-sidedness that, Hegel stated, needs to be surmounted[7]—and although that surmounting is achieved in the absolute religion that contains the truth of the God-world relationship, because of religions' use of *Vorstellungen*, that truth is not fully grasped until it comes to be viewed from the higher vantage point of reflective thought. Hegel was confident that this had been achieved in his philosophy.

Whether that achievement can rightly be designated as a form of panentheism has yet to be fully explored, but the nature of Hegel's dialectical thinking—and the apparent mediating nature of panenthe-ism—does seem to make it possible that this term could prove to be an apt description of that truth of the God-world relationship that is attained in absolute religion and fully grasped in speculative philosophy. Of course, Hegel himself never used the term 'pan-entheism', and it is not possible to nominate a passage in which Hegel obviously stated the panentheistic position; all one can do is to say that panentheism seems to be consistent with Hegel's viewpoint and to explore the evidence and analyze the commentators' opinions that support this contention. If the evidence and the opinions are sufficiently weighty to give the required support, then clearly the earlier conclusions, that Hegel's philosophy cannot be identified with either traditional theism or atheism, would be further substantiated; but also the unresolved problem of Hegel's relationship to Spinoza's pantheism would be settled. So far, the questions relating to this last problem have proved to be difficult and complex in spite of Hegel's strong and often repeated assertion of the difference between his own philosophy and pantheism. But if Hegel's panentheism can be established, then these difficulties will be resolved and Hegel's own claim upheld. If, on the other hand, it cannot be established, then one would have no option other than to say that Hegel was unable to escape the pantheistic system.[8]

Evidence for Hegel as Panentheist

The exploration of the evidence must begin by noting Hegel's undeviating insistence upon the fundamental affirmation of true religion that God is unity or that God is One: "It is the result of philosophy, as it is already the belief of religion, that God is the One true Reality, and that there is no other reality whatsoever." [9] But, as Hegel soon observed, what is important is the character of divine unity: "the Unity of God is always Unity, but everything depends upon the *particular nature* of this Unity." [10] In this regard, Hegel spoke of God as Universality, the Universal in which everything that subsists has its root, the absolute reality or absolute substance that is the source of all that is real. However, Hegel immediately added, this is no abstract substantiality of the Spinozan kind, for "God is Spirit, the Absolute Spirit" that "posits or lays down (*setzt*) the Other and takes it up again (*hebt es auf*) into His (*seiner*) eternal movement." [11] Now this process of laying down the Other, of positing determinate beings, is not the creation of a finite world that is separated from God, for here is another aspect of Hegel's concept of the divine unity, namely, the unity of God and the world, the infinite and the finite: "What is true is the indissoluble unity of the two." [12]

Yet again the question of the nature of this unity is important: although it has been noted already that Hegel strenuously denied that this unity is a pantheistic identity, the question of how else it can be described remains. Hegel himself said, "the real infinite, far from being a mere transcendence of the finite, always involves the absorption of the finite into its own fuller nature." [13] Or again, "the unity of the finite and infinite . . . is . . . of such a kind that the infinite is the positing of itself as what is finite . . . it is the infinite, but it is this infinite only as the positing of itself *within* itself *(in . . . selbst)* as the finite, and the abrogation of this finite as such." [14] Evidence for these points can be found scattered throughout Hegel's works, but the following passage provides a succinct expression of them.

> This Universal is the starting-point and point of departure, but it is this absolutely abiding Unity, and not a mere basis out of which differences spring, the truth rather being that all differences are here enclosed within this Universal. It is, however, no inert, abstract Universal, but the absolute womb, the eternal impetus and source from which everything proceeds, to which everything returns, and in which everything is eternally preserved. (*LPR*, vol. 1, 95)

Hegel's use of the word '*in*' (within) to describe the relationship between the determinate, finite realities and the infinite or Universal is credibly suggestive of panentheism,[15] which describes this relationship in terms of all finite things being 'in' God and God embracing or encompassing all things. And, as Reardon states, according to Hegel's philosophy, the universe "must be conceived as existing *in* God," [16] which is one aspect of the panentheistic view.

However, there is another aspect of panentheism, namely, its involvement of the concept that God is 'more than', in the sense of 'not exhausted by', the 'all' of the created world: in other words, panentheism also involves a notion of divine transcendence (not in the sense of being separated from the world, but in this sense of not being exhausted by it), and it is this aspect that is not so readily identified in Hegel's philosophy. His use of '*in*' does leave open the possibility, but certainly does not necessarily imply it. All that one can derive from such words as '*in*' is a hint in the direction of panentheism. Yet, as Hegel never explicitly stated such a view, and as his philosophy is marked by an ambiguity about which commentators inevitably disagree, perhaps hints are all one can find.

It is obviously necessary, but no less valuable, to consider some passages that clearly indicate Hegel's view of that which, in traditional theology, is known as Creation:

> God creates the world out of nothing; that is to say, besides the world nothing external exists, for it is itself externality. God alone is; God, however, only through mediation of Himself with Himself. He wills the finite; He Himself posits it as an Other,

and thus Himself becomes an Other than Himself—a finite—
for He has an Other opposed to Himself. [The finite] is God's;
it is His Other, and exists notwithstanding in the definite form
of the Other of God. It is the Other and the *not* Other; it
dissolves or cancels its own self; it is not it itself, but an Other,
it destroys itself. By this means, however, the 'other-ness' has
wholly vanished in God, and in it God recognizes Himself; and
in this way He maintains Himself for Himself as His own result
through His own act. (*LPR*, vol. 1, 198–199)

Again, stressing that Creation is activity, process, movement, Hegel
continued:

Thus God is this movement within Himself, and thereby alone
is He the living God. But this separate existence of the finite
must not be retained; it must, on the contrary, be abrogated.
God is movement towards the finite, and owing to this He is,
as it were, the lifting up of the finite to Himself. In the Ego, as
in that which is annulling itself as finite, God returns to Himself,
and only as this return is He God. Without the world God is
not God. (*LPR*, vol. 1, 199–200) [17]

It is abundantly clear, as it has been noted already in an earlier
context, that Hegel was firmly dissociating his view from the traditional notion of Creation. He would have nothing to do with the
notion of a God who is a self-sufficient Being having no need of a
created universe, but who creates, out of nothing, a finite world that
is other than and separated from himself. Yet it might seem that
Hegel replaced this with an idea of God who is nothing but, and
is exhausted by, the 'all' of the world—that Hegel might just as
happily use the expression *Deus sive Natura* as Spinoza did; for
indeed, he said that it is equally true to say that God exists as finite
and the self as infinite as it is to say the reverse.[18]

But in saying that God exists as finite, Hegel was, in another way,
stressing the unity of God who includes the finite so that the finite
is not separated from God: "What is true is the unity of the infinite,
in which the finite is contained." [19] And in saying that the self exists
as infinite, he was again asserting the unity and stressing that the
finite has its 'essence' in the infinite, with the consequence that "the
finite 'is not' when it *is* really finite; vice versa it '*is*' when it '*is not*',
it is '*itself*' when it is the '*other*', it comes to birth when it dies."
"This 'true' finite, then, is not the finite which is *outside* the infinite,
but the finite *within* the latter." [20]

Hegel's meaning must be understood in the light of his fundamental affirmation that God is unity, and it is in this unity that all finite determinations subsist. God *is* also the movement by which the finite is negated as finite and "returns to Himself," and without which God would not be 'complete'.[21] Every aspect of this process is necessary to the nature of God. Indeed, this is the meaning of Hegel's words, "Without the world God is not God": without the process by which the finite is posited, without the finite as finite, and without the movement by which the finite is taken up again into himself, God would not be God. How different this is from traditional theism! Yet again Hegel's language—the use of the word 'without' *(ohne)*— although not necessarily implying it, does not preclude a notion of divine transcendence, for rather than forcing one to say that God is nothing but, and is exhausted by, the world, this terminology does allow—though again, does not force—one to suggest that God is not exhausted by the world, and therefore is, in that sense, transcendent.

One may also note the language Hegel used in speaking of the concept of God's revelation, and observe that precisely the same point can be made. This is because the creative process, by which God posits the finite, is God's revelation of Himself—so that just as Hegel spoke of the creative movement as God's essential characteristic, and could therefore say that God is that process, so, too, he spoke of God as being his self-revelation because self-revelation is God's essential characteristic.

> God as Spirit is essentially this very self-revelation; He does not create the world once for all, but He is the eternal Creator, this eternal self-revelation, His *actus*. This is His Notion, His essential characteristic. (*LPR*, vol. 2, 335)

Self-revelation, then, constitutes the being of God, for it belongs to the nature of God as Spirit to reveal himself; and it is through this revelation that not only man knows God but that God knows himself. God is his revelation: What God *is* is to reveal himself, and being revealed he *is*. This revelation of God is manifested in the eternal 'breaking out' of Spirit in the world, in finite individuals, and in the closing and opening of barriers between things in the world. But to recognize this nature and mode of revelation does not necessarily remove every concept of transcendence. Schmitz[22] reports that Albert Chapelle's[23] "chief concern seems to be with those who would charge Hegel with reducing God to man, the infinite to the finite, and the knowledge of God to the knowledge of man"; yet not so to reduce God is to admit an element of transcendence. Now the concept of transcendence, which at least is admitted by Hegel's use of revelation, is linked with the concept of the mystery of God. Of course, Hegel would not allow mystery to be thought of as that which is hidden, lying beyond the world in unknowable darkness, for God's self-revelation *in* the world is unrestricted and completely open. However, God as Spirit is totally open not just in the sense of unreservedly revealing himself, but also in the sense of being "the 'free' infinite," the potentialities of which are unlimited and cannot be 'gathered up' in the sense of being totally comprehended. Man's gathering up or comprehending of God "is always short of the 'free' infinite," and indeed, even "God cannot gather himself up . . . not by failure of knowing but by an excess . . . of presence." [24] It is in the inexhaustability of God as free infinite Spirit that a sense of transcendence may be recognized and be seen to be reflected in Hegel's language, which consistently speaks of revelation as God's revealing *of* himself.

Similarly, one can identify the same kind of standpoint in what Hegel said about religious experience. It is not the case that the relationship between the religious person and God can continue to be spoken of as an external relationship, as it appears in religious *Vorstellungen:* as a relationship between observer and observed, between finite humanity and an absolute Being who is beyond and totally other than the world. Such a notion has to be discarded in order to grasp the internal unity of the religious person and God:

> If observation would observe the infinite in accordance with its true nature, it must itself be infinite; that is, it must no longer be observation of the true object, but the object itself. . . . In like manner, religion is only for the religious man; that is, for him who at the same time *is* what he observes. There is no such thing as mere observation here: the observer is, on the contrary, in such a relation to the object, that his observation is not purely external; he is not a simple observer, is not merely in a negative relation to that which he observes. (*LPR*, vol. 1, 203)

Again, Hegel's stress on the unity as the fundamental affirmation comes out in such a phrase as that which says that the religious man *"is* what he observes"; but again it does not seem to be an identity that suggests the religious object is nothing but the totality (continuity) of observers, for Hegel could still go on to speak of a relation between observer and object. However, the relationship is one of identity-in-difference; it is not an external relationship, but an internal one. In a section in which he dealt with 'Cultus' and 'faith', Hegel said that "in devotion *(Andacht)* the subject does not maintain itself in its particularity, but only in its movement in the Object *(im Gegenstand)*, and only as this individual self-moving spirit." [25] And when he went on to criticize the theologians who could speak of God only as "something absolutely supersensible" and who misinterpret the conception of God that was being indicated by himself (Hegel) as the "mere ordinary abstract identity" of pantheism,[26] Hegel seems to have been excluding from his own philosophy the idea that the object of religious experience is abstractly identical with the 'all' of the world.

A further hint can be found in Hegel's obvious respect for the mystics, of whom Jacob Boehme received notable treatment in *LHP*, and Meister Eckhart was quoted with much commendation in *LPR*. Here the hint about Hegel's 'panentheism' is suggested by the fact that the thought of these two mystics contains very strong overtones of a panentheistic position.

Taking up the thought of Boehme first, one can find the suggestion of most of the main features of his world view in his description of his seminal mystical experience—an experience that occurred as he glanced at a pewter dish that reflected the sunlight, and in his consequent enraptured state he saw "the Being of all Beings, the Byss and Abyss; also the birth [or eternal Generation] of the holy Trinity, the descent and original of this World, and of all creatures through the Divine Wisdom." [27] The 'Abyss' is God considered as the *Urgrund*, the ground of all things, the undifferentiated Absolute that is "neither light nor darkness, neither love nor wrath, but the eternal One." Thus, Boehme represented God as unity: "God is the eternal Unity, the immeasurable one good, which has nothing after nor before him that can give him or bring him in anything, or that can move him; and is devoid of all tendencies and properties. He is without origin in time and in himself one only, . . . He has nowhere a place or position, nor requires such for his dwelling; but is at the same time *out of* the world and *in* the world, and deeper than any thought can plunge . . . for he is Infinitude . . . the unity of God cannot be expressed, for it is *through* everything at the same time." [28]

In this quotation from Boehme, the words italicized do appear to suggest the view that is now commonly known as panentheism: God is *in* the world, and *through* everything; but at the same time God is *out of* the world, although clearly not in the sense of 'separated from', so that there is strong reason for taking it in the panentheistic sense of God's not being exhausted by the world. This point seems to be confirmed when Boehme continued: "it is not the case, as Reason supposes, that God dwells alone above the stars, outside of the place of this world. There is no place prepared for him where he dwells apart, but his manifestation only is distinguishable. He is in, with and through us; and where in a life he becomes mobile with his love, there God in his working is revealed." [29]

Similarly, Meister Eckhart declared that God is Unity: "God is one in all ways and according to every reasoning, so that in him no plurality is to be found . . . he who sees any distinction clearly does not see God. For God is One." [30] And "the divine One is being— God and existence are the same—and it is from God that all things have their being . . . for how could anything be except from being, or be one except from the One and through One, or through unity?" [31] Yet, Eckhart also asserted that God is higher than or above being,[32] and in commenting on the statement " 'God is something that must transcend being, that by itself needs nothing and yet which all things need'," he said that "anything which has being, date or location does not belong to God, for he is above them all and although he is in all creatures, yet he is more than all of them." [33]

Now the obvious way in which this apparent contradiction is to be reconciled is to recognize that when he asserted that God transcends being, it is finite beings, which derive their existence from God, that God transcends—that is, God is not exhausted by finite beings, not even all finite beings, yet God is *in* all finite creatures, and apart from God there is nothing; nor is God 'apart from' anything. Here again is a position that is suggestive of the panentheistic view.

When one recognizes this point, it becomes all the more significant to notice that it is toward these views that Hegel directed some considerable praise. This is not to say that Hegel was without criticism of them, for, regarding Boehme, for example, he declared that his manner and system must be termed barbarous, and that he was unable to arrive at a free and systematic presentation of the Idea, for he could not express it in the form of thought.[34] But Hegel was still able to say that Boehme's fundamental idea is the comprising of "everything in an absolute unity, for he desires to demonstrate the absolute divine unity and the union of all opposites in God," and thus Hegel was led to declare that "the principle of the Notion is living in Him." [35]

As far as Hegel's regard for Eckhart is concerned, Blakney reports that "Franz von Baader writes 'I was often with Hegel in Berlin. Once I read him a passage from Meister Eckhart, who was only a name to him. He was so excited by it that the next day he read me a whole lecture on Eckhart, which ended with: "There, indeed, we have what we want!" ' " [36] This high regard for Eckhart is very evident in the famous passage in which Hegel quoted him; and the context in which that quotation appears is very significant to the present point of discussion. It occurs at the conclusion of a section in which Hegel has been criticizing contemporary theologians for their unsatisfactory concept of God, and for their inclination to label as 'pantheism' the "most thorough grasp of this divine depth" as represented in Eckhart.[37] It is certain that Hegel distinguished between Eckhart's standpoint and pantheism, and it is equally certain that he identified the true grasp of the divine depth with the former, so that there can be no doubt that Hegel placed himself on the side of the mystics as distinct from pantheism and the contemporary expressions of theism.

However, the conception of the God-world relationship that the mystics advanced is very much akin to the view that, in modern terminology, may be labeled 'panentheism'. That conception of the God-world relationship understands it as a unity of God and the world, though in the sense that the world is *in* God, and that God is not exhausted by, or reducible to, the world. In this understanding of the relationship, there is no suggestion that 'God' and the 'world' are terms that can be used interchangeably in the way that Spinoza used "God or Nature". Since it was this conception of the mystics that received Hegel's high praise and favorable commendation, one can agree with Mure: Hegelianism "is not mere humanism but a strenuous and uncompromising effort, which has no serious parallel, to rationalize and bring into the light the mystic union of God and man proclaimed by men such as Meister Eckhart and Jacob Boehme, to reveal it as union through distinction for which the whole world is evidence." [38]

This is not to say that Hegel identified himself completely with the mystics, but rather that he saw in the mystics the seeds of a truth about the relation between God and the world, the infinite and the finite, clearly exemplified in their mystical union between God and the human soul—a truth that, Hegel believed, needed to be given systematic expression at the level of speculative philosophy.

Opinions for Hegel as Panentheist

Having considered evidence that suggests the possibility of Hegel's position being described as panentheistic, it now is apposite to consider the views of commentators who argue that this is the most appropriate interpretation of Hegel.

This opinion is well expressed by Copleston when he says that "what Hegel endeavours to accomplish is to think the relation between the infinite and the finite in such a way as to allow the infinite to fill, as it were, all reality, while at the same time a distinction is preserved. If we take pantheism as representing the concept of identity and theism that of distinction, Hegel's aim is to show how the two concepts, which appear antithetical, can be reconciled at a higher level. All things are 'in God', moments of the divine life; but God, as the One, is not simply reducible to 'all things', to the Many." [39] However, Copleston is not content to say unreservedly that Hegel was a panentheist, but rather only that he was a panentheist 'by intention'. In other words, this is what Hegel *endeavored* to accomplish, though Copleston believes he failed to succeed because "the result of Hegel's reflections is so ambiguous that it is questionable whether it can be properly described as theism of any kind." [40]

This is a matter to which it will be necessary to return, but for the moment it will suffice to state Copleston's reasons for seeing panentheism as the correct description of the position Hegel intended to express. The fundamental feature of that position is that of a unity-in-distinction, and Copleston identifies three ideas "to which Hegel thinks that he has given expression," and that signify Hegel's intended standpoint. First, "the Hegelian Absolute is clearly not reducible to the human mind. For it is the One which, though not temporally prior to the Many, manifests itself or expresses itself in the world." [41]

Secondly, "the Absolute exists in and through the Many, immanent in them while comprising them within its own life." [42] Copleston takes the analogy of the national State to illustrate these points: the State is not reducible to any particular group of citizens, for the State, as an organic whole, endures in time, and also the State "does not exist apart from its citizens but in and through them, though at the same time it is more than the sum of them." [43]

Thirdly, while the Absolute is defined as 'self-thinking thought', "it must also be conceived as a dynamic process of self-actualization." So it is said that "the Absolute comes to know itself in actuality in and through the human mind as its vehicle," but "the divine self-knowledge is not reducible to any individual's knowledge of God; but the individual's knowledge of God is a moment in the process of the Absolute's return to itself in self-reflection." [44] These features of Hegel's thought provide Copleston with evidence for concluding that Hegel *intended* to give expression to a view about the relationship between the infinite and finite that was based on the conception of identity-in-distinction, and such a view can be spoken of as panentheism.

A second interpretation of Hegel along panentheistic lines is given by Whittemore. Unlike Copleston, who argues that (what might now be called) a panentheistic position was Hegel's unrealized intention, Whittemore sees Hegel as having clearly displayed that essential feature of panentheism, namely, the concept that the world is *in* God but that God is not reducible to the world. In other words, Whittemore asserts that Hegel did maintain a concept of the transcendence of God, not in the sense that God is separated from the universe, but in the sense that God encompasses though excels, absorbs though surpasses, the universe, for "transcendence is not connotatively synonymous with independence." [45] While presenting a number of passages from Hegel in support of his interpretation,[46] Whittemore readily acknowledges that there is nothing in Hegel that offers clear-cut evidence of panentheism, although he is convinced that the weight of the evidence is supportive of a Hegelian sense of transcendence.

Then, too, there is Hegel's description of the divine unity as Subject, which, in Hegel's own terms, is the crucial difference between his own and Spinoza's philosophy. But it is not Subject as ordinarily understood. "God as Subject does not mean, to Hegel, that absolute simplicity to which such qualities as Goodness, Might and Wisdom are attached by way of compliment. On the contrary, God as Subject is *aufgehoben*, is the unity of the process of its own becoming. More specifically, it is unity-in-difference, the mediation of the moments of its own self-determination, the eternal synthesis of itself. Most briefly, God as Subject is a *society* or *community* rather than an individual." [47] Using Whitehead's notion that every organism is a unity or nexus of 'actual entities' or 'actual occasions', and is therefore a society, since a society 'is a nexus with social order', Whittemore argues, in opposition to McTaggart, that "Hegel's Absolute is *implicitly* both society and person. Indeed, they demand this inference, for if Hegel's God as Absolute is *not* both society and person, it cannot be that *it is* Subject, Mind and Spirit."

So Whittemore argues! He is prepared to admit, however, that the demonstration of the personality of the Hegelian Absolute is not of primary importance for the case of Hegel's panentheism, for that case is basically "the case against pantheism," namely, that Hegel's philosophy contains a sense of the transcendent. It is just that Whittemore asserts that the easiest way to establish transcendence is to demonstrate the Hegelian Absolute as person, "since 'person', however defined, connotes some sort of transcendent unity." [48]

Another aspect of Whittemore's case for Hegel's panentheism is the kind of special significance Hegel attributed to the life of Jesus. "The meaning of His life is His witness in His teaching to the unity of Man and God," and "the signification of His death is its symbolization of the necessary return of Man out of finitude to union with God." This, Whittemore concludes, "is almost exactly what a panentheist would be expected to maintain." [49]

In summing up his case, Whittemore asserts that the total picture of the Hegelian religion is a picture that "is panentheistic rather than pantheistic because: (a) God as Spirit encompasses all things natural and divine; (b) God as Society is a unitary Whole internally transcendent of the totality of its parts; (c) God as Society is compatible with God as Person."[50]

A Discussion of Questions
Relating to Hegel as Panentheist

Now that evidence supportive of Hegel as panentheist has been presented and expository opinion favoring such an interpretation has been canvassed, it is imperative to consider carefully a number of crucial questions that are unavoidable in this kind of analysis of Hegel's philosophy of religion. But how can one appropriately approach this task? An apt way to begin is by raising the important question of the extent to which Hegel transformed religious belief.

To What Extent Did Hegel Transform Religious Belief?

It really is a matter of priority to pose this question regarding whether or not Hegel did transform religious belief into some different kind of doctrine, because if it is the case that he brought about that kind of transformation, then not only would the rejection of theism as a possible description of Hegel's position be confirmed, but also any suggestion of panentheism would be nullified. This would be so because the kind of transformation of religious belief that is usually suggested as occurring in Hegel's philosophy involves the elimination of the notion of divine transcendence in every form. Therefore, in the context of this inquiry, this question takes on great significance: does the dialectical move in Hegel's philosophy from absolute religion to absolute knowledge involve the discovery of a new and different truth? If one answers this question in the negative it is because one argues that the dialectical rise to absolute knowledge is a rise, not to a new truth, but to a new vantage point from which the truth, already contained in absolute religion, can be perceived with greater, even complete, clarity. On the other hand, an affirmative answer means that one understands Hegel to have been dissolving the content of absolute religion and expressing the truth in terms of a speculative-dialectical-pantheism, or even atheism.

It is, of course, the former answer that is in accord with what Hegel himself said on this matter: as already noted, Hegel repeatedly affirmed, firstly, that the content of absolute religion is the true content; but secondly, there is a necessity to go beyond the religious expression of that truth because the form of expression, *Vorstellungen,* is inadequate, and it is this inadequacy that causes the truth to be misconceived and misconstrued. Such misconceptions, in Hegel's view, take the form of the traditional theistic notion of God as separated from and independent of the world, which in turn gives rise to—in order to remove this notion of distinction—either the pantheistic notion of the identity of God and the world, or the atheistic view of the reduction of the divine infinite to the finite. But, for Hegel, each of these three positions involves a misconstruing of the true content that absolute religion possesses, and it is the dialectical rise to speculative thought, where the true content is perceived in its true form, that avoids the possibility of the misconceptions that arise from the deficient religious form of expressing the same truth.

There can be no doubt that this was Hegel's own view of what his philosophy involved, but exactly how one is to elaborate on the meaning of Hegel's intention is another matter. To turn to some examples of those expositors who seek to explain Hegel's philosophy of religion on these lines, one can note that Fackenheim's explanation of what Hegel meant by the difference between the Christian faith's expression of the truth and the expression of that same truth at the level of speculative thought is succinctly stated in the following passage: "They differ in that thought and speculation will grasp as one single activity what in faith and representation remains double. How is this possible? *Religious spirit—the heart—exists on the human side of the divine-human relationship. Philosophic spirit—speculative thought—rises to its divine side. What for Christian faith is free reception of the Divine by the human is for speculative thought divine activity in the human.*" [51]

There is, however, a difficulty with an explanation of this kind, even though there is a definite sense in which it accurately explains Hegel's viewpoint. It is accurate in suggesting that for faith and representation the divine-human relationship is understood in terms of a double activity, namely, divine initiative and human response; whereas in speculative thought this relationship is grasped as one activity, or, in other words, that the relationship is not perceived in terms of the external subject-object relationship (the human activity being seen as not other than or outside of the divine activity), but as one with the divine activity in that it is contained within the divine. There is no doubt that with this Hegel would have no quarrel.

On the other hand, the difficulty with Fackenheim's explanation is that it easily could be understood as suggesting that the truth of the divine-human relationship is a different truth from that which is understood by absolute religion. With this Hegel would have some quarrel! Hegel's conviction was that the truth at the level of philosophic thought is the same as the truth at the level of absolute religion. What is deficient about religion's grasping of that truth is that its mode of expression is *Vorstellungen*—an example of which would be talk about divine initiative and human response—which gives rise to the concept of the divine-human relationship as a double activity.

But this, in Hegel's view, is a misconstruing of the truth because of *Vorstellungen*, the language of symbol and myth, being assumed to be a literal expression of the truth; and in order to avoid such misconstruing, one must transcend the religious language of symbol and myth to reach the conceptual language of philosophy. But the truth expressed then is *not* a new and different truth. This is Hegel's position, and Fackenheim understands it very well; it is just that the terminology of his explanation, given above, seems at least to open the way to possible misunderstanding of the Hegelian position.

Christianity, centered on the person of Jesus and the doctrine of Incarnation, is, for Hegel, the absolute religion because it contains the truth of the unity of the divine and the human (indeed, the whole cosmos); but, being confined to the religious mode of expression, Christian faith has easily forgotten that truth, and it has become just like other religions in which the divine is perceived as something over against the human, to which the human must be subjected, as to an external and superior force. An inevitable—and certainly what Hegel regarded as contemporary—reaction is the stress on the autonomy of man and the sovereignty of human reason in all respects of life, with man being asserted as the bearer of universal reason, and thus as the source and measure of all things.

What is necessary, therefore, in Hegel's view, is the reasserting of the truth of the Christian or absolute religion, namely, the unity of the divine and human, of the infinite and finite: that the divine ground of being is the innermost ground of man himself, that the source of life, while it transcends man, is, at the same time, his own. But the difficulty with religion is that its truth seems to be imparted to us from outside, and the religious mode of expression encourages the conception of God's revealing himself to humanity as some external and superior being. It is like a law that, being imposed by an external authority, one must obey; but the law has validity for the individual only when it is recognized as rational and thus comes to have inward authority as well and most importantly. So, too, the truth of absolute religion must become internal, having an authority for our own reason;[52] and this, argued Hegel, is achieved only by transcending the religious language of symbol and myth in order to rise to speculative thought in which the same truth is grasped and given true expression.

Copleston deals very adequately with this point, clearly spelling out the distinction between the truth of the Christian religion and the religious consciousness' perception of that truth—a distinction that, as suggested above, Fackenheim makes, though not sharply and accurately enough—and summing up his argument by asserting that "Hegel does not separate the concept of truth from religious statements and attach it only to philosophical statements. Religious statements can be true. And when the philosopher expresses their truth in a different form, it is the same truth which he is presenting. That is to say, in Hegel's opinion the truth remains the same." [53]

This is the viewpoint that is being favored by this inquiry, but of course, it is not a view about Hegel's position that is commonly shared. There are many who argue, like Pomerleau, that "Hegel's conception of the Absolute is a far-cry from the Judaeo-Christian personal and transcendent God," [54] so that, in fact, the 'truth' contained in Hegel's philosophy is a new *truth:* indeed, to argue that Hegel adopted atheism or pantheism (entailing acosmism or not) is to argue that his own claim to have maintained the 'truth' of absolute religion is not borne out by the nature of his philosophy. It has already been argued that Hegel cannot be described as atheistic, but the possibility of pantheism still remains open, and, unless it can be shown to be undemonstrable, Hegel can no longer be said to have presented the same truth as absolute religion. Of course, it might be argued that that same truth was retained only if Hegel can be shown to have been consistent with traditional theism, and yet the position already adopted in this inquiry is that Hegel quite intentionally distanced himself from that viewpoint.

This in itself, however, does not necessarily invalidate his claim that the truth of absolute religion was being maintained. The suggestion here is that a position, which now might be named 'panentheism', is also consistent with that claim—indeed, it might be said to represent a restoration of forgotten aspects of absolute religion. However, the suitability of panentheism as a descriptive term for Hegel's position cannot continue to be entertained if the possibility of pantheism is not substantially removed. Therefore, further important questions remain to be explored.

Did Hegel Escape Acosmism?

The question that must now be asked is whether Hegel successfully escaped the charge of acosmism, which he consistently directed against Spinoza as the necessary consequence of the latter's pantheism. Any suggestion that Hegel also became ensnared in acosmism is founded on his frequent use of language that stressses the unity or identity of the finite and the infinite, of the human and divine. For example, in *Phen.* Hegel stated that *"in themselves"* the divine Being *(das gottliche Wesen)* and human nature "are not separate." [55] Throughout Hegel's works there is to be found something that is crucial to Hegelian thought, namely, the ontological concept that the finite is 'nothing' in itself, but has as its essence and ground that which is 'other' than itself, the infinite: "When we say of things that they are *finite*, we understand thereby that . . . non-being constitutes their nature and being," and that they are truly 'themselves' when they are their opposite.[56]

Such language has frequently been taken as an indication that Hegel "called into question the status of the individual." [57] Indeed, Kierkegaard strongly opposed the Hegelian system with his own stress on the individual, firmly believing that Hegel had left no place for the individual being, for, at what he claimed to be the level of speculative knowledge, Hegel conceived of the finite individual as nothing but a determination or mode of infinite spirit, with the consequently perceived unity between the infinite and finite being one in which finite individuality is lost. Such a view is often seen to have been explicitly stated in words such as the statement that "the human is God as immediate and present," [58] or again, that "the main idea . . . is that of the unity of the divine and human natures." [59]

The specter of pantheism, and especially the more extreme acosmic form, has been seen to hang over the Hegelian system as a result of this assumed failure to place adequate stress on the individual. Of course, as Kierkegaard perceived, it is true that the former is a natural consequence of the latter; but it is true in Hegel's case, for example, only if—as Pannenberg rightly suggests—the unity of the finite and infinite, of which Hegel spoke, "is always a *negative* unity, an identity mediated by the negation and superseding of the finite." [60] If this is the meaning of unity that Hegel was espousing, then clearly those who interpret Hegel as adopting an acosmic position, involving a denial of the reality of the finite, have a strong case, and the argument for a panentheistic interpretation would have to lapse.

However, to interpret Hegel in an acosmic sense does seem to misrepresent his meaning in those passages that are taken as being indicative of it, and to overlook much evidence to the contrary. In the *Encyclopaedia*, while speaking about the meaning of unity, he categorically denied that it is "abstract unity, mere identity and the empty absolute," and he castigated those who can understand unity only as identity, likening them to physicists who apply only one mode of relation between properties and elements, namely, the relation of composition. From this 'shallow identity' the inference of 'shallow pantheism' is drawn;[61] but the contrasting sense of unity that Hegel promoted is 'concrete unity (the notion)', asserting "that each step in its [philosophy's] advance is a peculiar term or phase of this concrete unity, and that the deepest and last expression of unity is the unity of absolute mind *(Geist)* itself." [62]

Thus, the evidence from Hegel is that when he spoke of the unity of the infinite and finite he was not asserting a unity of simple identity, but rather a unity of the finite and the infinite in the sense that the finite is contained within, and is not separated from or outside of, the infinite. As Min expresses it, for Hegel, the relationship between particularity and universality "can only be *internal*, one of union, not separation." "The true relation between finite and infinite is an inseparable union, such that the finite shows itself as an essential moment of the infinite. Only thus is the finite a living, concrete, true infinity; only then is the universal a true, concrete universal comprising and spurring on the finite and particular from *within*." [63]

Thus when, in *LPR*, Hegel said that "the human is God as immediate and present," it ought not to be taken as indicative of a denial of the reality of the human—as a superficial reading may suggest; rather, it is a statement that can be accurately comprehended only in the context of his understanding of God as infinite Spirit, of which all finite reality, especially rational humanity, is a manifestation, and of the finite whose reality and process of development is grounded in and dependent on the infinite. In Lauer's words, God "is not the world, nor is the world God, but the world is God's appearing, God's activity of self-manifestation, an appearing which is completed in man. The world, and man in it, are real only to the extent that God is in them, and their true being is in God, which is but another way of saying that the finite is the appearing of the infinite and has its being in the infinite." [64]

Similarly, when in *Phen.* Hegel said that *"in themselves"* the divine Being and human Nature *"are not separate (nicht getrennt),"* it ought to be taken as a denial of the idea of a divison or separation between the divine and human such as characterizes the traditional concept of God, rather than as an assertion of the kind of simple identity of the infinite and finite that involves the negation of the reality of the finite. Furthermore, Hegel explicitly undermined the assertion of that kind of unity when he said, in that same work, that it is "an unspiritual way of talking" to say "that the divine Being is the *same* as Nature in its whole extent." [65] That was a Spinozistic kind of unity *(Deus sive Natura)*, and clearly it was not the kind Hegel wished his own philosophy to express for precisely the reason that he believed it necessitated acosmism.

The earlier discussion of this point led to the conclusion that Hegel overlooked Spinoza's definite stress on the reality of the finite, but it also led to the observation that Hegel well might have insisted that in spite of what Spinoza may have wished to assert about the reality of the finite, it can be seen, at the level of speculative thought, that in fact Spinoza presented the finite only as 'nothing' because he had not attained to the true concept of the Absolute as *Geist*, and so did not progress beyond a rigid substantiality. On the point that the reality and essence of the finite is grounded in the infinite, Hegel had no desire to differ from Spinoza. Hegel believed that the Cosmological Argument, properly understood—and he was confident that Spinoza had grasped it clearly—declared this truth that the finite has its being only in the infinite. But Hegel also believed it was necessary to go further—and this he was sure Spinoza had failed to do—and to grasp the other direction of thought represented in the Ontological Argument, which begins with the concept of God as infinite Being that, as Hegel perceived it, has being by particularizing itself in the finite—by negating its infinitude, as opposition to the finite, through its positing of finitude.

Thus, in Hegel, "the finite individual is restored to a place of meaning and importance which he seemed to be losing in the movement towards the Absolute Substance." For Hegel, both directions of thought are necessary for a grasping of the Absolute Spirit.[66]

It is in the Hegelian concept of *Geist* and of the dialectical movement that the fundamental difference from Spinoza is to be found, and the suggestion of Hegel's acosmism finally precluded. Unlike Spinoza, for Hegel the Absolute *Geist* attains to itself only in its other. The Absolute, by its very nature, 'passes over' into its other, the finite particulars. But these moments of particularity are not 'beyond' the infinite; rather, they are contained *within* it. Yet, the particulars are clearly characterized by oppositions and differences, which, though not ultimate, are definitely real—so that another feature of Hegel's concept of unity is that of unity-in-distinction. In Hegel, there is the sense of a primordial, ontological unity of Being; but there is no primal, static identity, as in Spinoza, for the primordial ontological unity manifests itself existentially in finite beings, which are characterized by a growing into ultimate unity through the dialectical movement by which each finite moment, within the infinite, is drawn—not in isolation but in its relatedness to other particulars— toward the fulfillment of its end. It is only through this dialectical movement that the Absolute attains to its true nature as *Geist*.[67]

The significant point here is that the nature of the dialectic is such that the reality of the finite particulars, their oppositions and differences, cannot be illusory; and furthermore, the dialectic is such that the reality of each particular's individuality is never excluded: the sublation of oppositions and differences does not mean that the real individuality of each finite moment is ever superseded in the sense of becoming mere nothingness, for it is dialectically taken up and preserved within absolute Spirit. Hegel condemned the loss of all individuality within the Universal as an abstract identity, as "the night in which all cows are black"; and such a position clearly is not one for which Hegel wished to be known.

Did Hegel Completely Escape Pantheism?

The foregoing discussion, with its conclusion that Hegel does escape the charge of acosmic pantheism, permits us to continue the exploration into the plausibility of retaining 'panentheism' as an interpretation of Hegel's position. However, rightly directed perseverence in this task requires one to follow the path of inquiring whether there linger any features of Hegel's thought that cause his philosophy to remain trapped within the pantheistic system. Though it may not be acosmic pantheism, it perhaps could be designated as another form of pantheism, such as "dialectical pantheism".[68] However, it is abundantly evident, as it frequently has been noted, that Hegel sought to dissociate himself from pantheism in *any* form. Pantheism in an acosmic form was anathema to him, and on this and other evidence it has already been submitted that such a pantheism cannot be accurately attributed to him. In addition, it has been noted that Hegel also argued that any philosophical position claiming to be a form of pantheism—though not the acosmic form, that is, one that seeks to imply "that the finite world possesses a genuine actuality and affirmative reality"—really "renders God completely finite, and degrades Him to the bare finite and adventitious congeries of existence."[69] Such a position was equally anathema to Hegel.

But in spite of Hegel's protestations and denials of pantheism, it is still argued by many that his own position was such that in fact he did not succeed in escaping pantheism. The case for this kind of exposition of Hegel is based on one or both of the following propositions. First, that Hegel did not admit that absolute Spirit or God actually does evince a transcendent aspect, and without a demonstration of transcendence, his philosophy is still within pantheism. Secondly, that Hegel asserted the logical necessity of the Creation of the world and the coming into being of evil as the self-assertion of finiteness, and without an admission of contingency in this regard, pantheism prevails.

These matters now must be considered in order to determine their feasibility and thus to determine whether Hegel remained trapped in pantheism.

The Hegelian Sense of Transcendence. First, is it true that Hegel did not admit a transcendent aspect of absolute Spirit? Many of the expositors of Hegel who would wish to reply in the affirmative have already been considered, and need not be reiterated; it will suffice to recall those views by means of one quotation: Hegel's "strict doctrine as a philosopher is a metaphysic which finds the Absolute in a monistic pantheism in which God is the world force or spirit immanent in the world and coming to self-consciousness only in the minds of men who are conscious of it as the Absolute." Hegel's is a theory in which "the religious consciousness is transcended in the mind of the philosopher, and the idea of the personal God of theism must be regarded . . . as metaphorical language." "The result is a form of pantheism which reduces God and man to an impersonal system of thought-content. This avoids a transcendent Absolute." [70] Thus, on this interpretation, the only transcendence that Hegel permitted is the transcending of religious consciousness by philosophy, for there is no transcending of the finite world by absolute Spirit.

Whittemore, however, is amongst those who propose an alternative exposition, the starting point of which is a determination of the meaning of transcendence. So long as 'transcendence' is taken in the traditional theistic sense of God as a self-contained being existing apart from the material world, there can be no possibility that Hegel admitted an aspect of transcendence. But Whittemore rightly suggests that this meaning is too narrow and restricting, for transcendence can also mean surpasses or excels, encompasses or absorbs; and when taken in this more complex sense, Whittemore argues, it can be seen that Hegel did maintain a concept of transcendence.[71] Whittemore is of the opinion that there is a weight of evidence in Hegel's works that supports this interpretation;[72] but he is particularly interested in, and deals extensively with, Hegel's description of the Absolute as Subject, and, as Whittemore sees it, consequently as Person. This description of the Absolute can be cited as evidence in favor of the case for panentheism on the grounds that the notion of Subject and Person implies some sort of transcendent unity that is not to be found in any form of pantheism[73]—indeed, it was the lack of a concept of the Absolute as Subject that Hegel believed marked the deficiency in Spinoza. It is for this reason that some attention will now be paid to this matter.

According to ordinary usage, the terms 'subject' and 'person' are employed to refer to particular individuals in a way that identifies an individual as finite and separate from other individuals; and to each individual certain predicates can be attributed for the purpose of description, while certain actions can be said to be performed by each individual. Now it is the notion of 'subject' that is a crucial one in Hegel's philosophy, and it is this notion that serves as his basic model for his concept of absolute Spirit or God: "everything turns on grasping and expressing the True, not only as *Substance*, but equally as *Subject*." And closely allied with this is his reference to God as "absolute Person" and his observation that such a notion is the true notion of God in Christianity.[74]

In considering these Hegelian statements, it must be noted that there is no way his description of absolute Spirit as 'Subject' can be taken in the ordinary sense of that term, according to which, Spirit, or God, as Subject could be defined by means of predicates, just like some natural object. Such a mode of description, Hegel said, is the way of the Understanding—the use of *Vorstellungen*—and it is defective because "predicates are only particular characterizations"; thus, it is necessary to assert that God must have an infinity of such characterizations, which, however, only "come to be in opposition or contradiction with each other." Also, given this way of defining God, God is thought of as the "essentially undifferentiated" subject to which these predicates attach—a thought that Hegel regarded as an empty concept of God; and further, it is a way of defining God that reflects the idea of God as a being apart from the world, as an Other, and thus as being limited. This explains why the predicates attributed to God become contradictory.[75] Therefore, when Hegel spoke of the Absolute as Subject, the ordinary understanding of the term must be disregarded, and be substituted by the Hegelian notion of subject.

The latter is not a notion of the isolated individual, but one that removes the sense of divisive barriers and rises above the idea of separateness to present the subject in its interrelatedness and continuity with all life, and to present the essence of subjectivity as genuine freedom characterized by total self-realization and rational self-awareness. This Hegelian notion emerged by presenting a conception of the human subject that is in the tradition, but also a development, of those who broke with the dominant Cartesian dualism. Hegel's theory of the subject "was radically anti-dualist" in that it "was a theory of self-realization," inheriting from Herder and others the Aristotelian concept of the subject "as realizing a certain form." [76] Like Aristotle, there was no suggestion of a Platonic view that such a 'form' existed separately from the individual subjects, for the reality of the form is not to be found anywhere else than in the individual. But unlike Aristotle—for whom the form was wholly determined beforehand—and Spinoza—for whom God is the substance of everything, which is thus predetermined—the late-eighteenth-century theorists, whom Hegel followed, added another dimension in that they looked on "this realized form as the expression, in the sense of clarification, of what the subject is, something that could not be known in advance." [77]

Indeed, for Hegel, the truth of the conscious self is in being a subject, which means that the essence of the self is to be understood in such a way that it is an active coming-to-itself and for-itself. This process of development was a vital part of Hegel's concept of subject—a process whose dynamism is impelled by the presence of conflict within the self and between selves and their surroundings. But Hegel saw that division is not the end of life, because the individual self is truly subject—truly comes-to-itself and for-itself—when his expression of life becomes a rational self-awareness of his real nature and is seen to be interrelated and continuous with all life.[78]

For Hegel, absolute Spirit *(Geist)*, or God, is to be understood as subject: the Hegelian notion of subject finds its chief exemplification in cosmic *Geist*. The continuity of *Geist* with all life is not to be found, as with a finite subject, in its interrelatedness with all life, but as infinite subject, in being that which underlies—the Source, or *Grund*—of all that is. But this underlying Spirit, permeating and giving form to the whole cosmos, does not have existence other than in its embodiment or expression in the cosmos, particularly in human, rational beings. The cosmos is the self-expression of Spirit, and it is necessarily and only in that expression that Spirit comes to self-awareness, especially in man's knowledge of Spirit. Unlike the finite human subject, which expresses itself and comes to self-awareness in its surroundings that are largely given, for Spirit, as infinite subject, nothing is given, since the universe is posited by Spirit as its own self-expression.

But, in sharp distinction from Spinoza, for whom God is the substance of everything and by which everything is wholly determined beforehand, Hegel's notion of *Geist* as Subject possesses a radical freedom: the nature of *Geist* is such that it "is only what it makes itself become," [79] expressing itself in its embodiment, the cosmos, according to its nature, which is characterized by rationality and love (in which its freedom is grounded), and thereby clarifying and recognizing itself in that self-expression by which its potential is realized. Thus, as in the case of a finite subject, there is in Hegel the notion of development in *Geist* as infinite Subject: that the fullness of its self-expression, the consummation of its potential, the total clarification of its nature, and its complete self-awareness are not determined beforehand, but are progressively achieved in and through the growth of the cosmos, especially in human growth in consciousness, both in one's individual and collective life, and in one's identification with the whole.

When Hegel also spoke of God (or *Geist*) as 'absolute Person' and observed that such a notion is the true notion of God in Christianity, it is possible to argue that such terminology must be seen to be metaphorical,[80] but Whittemore regards it as a true reflection of Hegel's position; and so, too, does Pannenberg, who says that from Hegel's references to God as absolute Subject "it is difficult to understand how anyone could overlook the idea of the personality of God in Hegel." [81] Both Whittemore and Pannenberg find a crucial passage in *LPR:*

> It is . . . the nature or character of what we mean by person or subject to abolish its isolation, its separateness.
>
> Morality, love, just mean the giving up of particularity or of the particular personality and its extension to universality, and so, too, is it with the family and friendship, for there you have the identity of the one with the other. Insomuch as I act rightly towards another, I consider him as identical with myself. In friendship and love I give up my abstract personality, and in this way win it back as concrete personality. (*LPR*, vol. 3, 24–25)

This passage is of considerable significance: it is based on Hegel's distinction between abstract and concrete personality, and it expresses his idea that the truth of the person does not lie in abstract individualization, that is, it does not lie in the person's isolation and separateness; but rather, this abstract personality is given up in friendship and love—the separateness is *aufgehoben*—and, in that giving up, personality is won back as concrete personality.

This same idea was expressed by Hegel when he spoke of the Ego "annulling itself as finite," [82] by which he meant that the individual self ceases to see itself as a separate individual, and extends its self-awareness to see its relationships with others in terms of a continuum. In pursuing this point it will be useful to take the individual person as an analogy. The individual comes to self-realization and fulfillment only through the process of living: it is through his diverse activities, which are expressive of what he is, that his potential is being actualized, that the clarification and his own awareness of what he is is being increased, and the recognition of whether his life is an adequate expression of what he is potentially is being attained. And it is through a growing consciousness of his interrelatedness and continuity with—rather than separation from—others, that his true nature as 'person' is achieved: as Hegel said, it is only in this way that personality ceases to be "abstract" and takes on the character of "concrete personality". But of course, in the case of finite personality, this achievement is only partial, and therefore it seems that Hegel could have had no referent for his concept of concrete personality if it does not refer to absolute Spirit or God: the finite individual is not wholly self-complete, and we are driven to the conclusion that individuality in the full sense belongs only to the Absolute.

Thus, as in the case of Hegel's treatment of subject, it now must also be said that his notion of concrete personality finds its chief exemplification in cosmic *Geist*, or God: as it is said of the individual that it is in identifying with the other and breaking down the sense of otherness that true personalness is won—"In friendship and love I give up my abstract personality, and in this way win it back as concrete personality"—so it is said of God that it is in this process of breaking down 'otherness' in the world, that the true nature of God—Love—is achieved, that "God returns to Himself and only in this return is He God," for Love is the 'return' at the top of the dialectical development in which God or Spirit, as he is, is being realized.

This Hegelian view of God, or Spirit, apparent in so many passages, is well captured in the following:

He [God] *is* but is at the same time the Other, the self-differentiating, the Other in the sense that this Other is God Himself and has potentially the divine nature in it, and that the abolishing of this difference, of this otherness, this return, this love, is Spirit. (*LPR*, vol. 3, 99–100)

God as Spirit is the triune God. He is this act of manifestation, this self-objectifying, and it is His nature to be identical with Himself while thus making Himself objective; He is eternal love. (*LPR*, vol. 3, 111)

Here again it can be seen how, for Hegel, *love* is essentially constitutive of the very nature of God, or Spirit, which Hegel took to be the ultimate foundation of reality: God as Spirit is love, and this notion of love is of paramount importance in Hegel, permeating the whole of his philosophy.

To recall Hegel's *ETW* is a reminder that the concept of love was the primary one for him, and especially did this become apparent in the fragment *die Liebe*. But it is also true to recall that *love* was superseded by the concept of *life* and the concept of *spirit;* yet, one must take particular care to notice that this superseding must be understood in the Hegelian sense of *aufgehoben,* for love was never discarded in Hegel's thought. In an important sense it remained quite fundamental, since the three concepts are virtually synonymous: *love* is the principle of union, vividly epitomized by the love relationship between two people; *life* is characterized by wholeness, not separation or division; and *spirit* is the dynamic concept, the living unity of all things. Thus, each of the three concepts is about unity, in which love is a crucial ingredient, for love recognizes the divine life (which is love) that permeates all things.

But it is clear that Hegel became aware of a difficulty with the concept of love as his fundamental concept; and this difficulty became apparent to him because of the use of the term love in describing relations between individuals where it has the connotation of great intensity of feeling, and Hegel was firm in his conviction that feeling can have no place at the level of speculative thought. Thus, he turned to an alternative terminology, even though the concept of love is retained and taken up in those other concepts: love is essential to the concept of Spirit.[83] It is possible to illustrate the point by taking as another analogy the concept of the 'classless society', which is the concept of a society marked by equality and by the spirit of cooperation and love—in other words, it is characterized by the same qualities that mark a genuine relationship between two people, but without the intensity of feeling that is present in the individual personal relationship. Similarly, Hegel said that love is the very concept of Spirit itself, yet 'Spirit' does not have the connotation of that intensity of feeling that characterizes personal love between two individuals—hence the advantage that Hegel perceived in using the term Spirit.

For somewhat similar reasons, Hegel saw the term Spirit to have advantages over the term God, namely, 'God' had become synonymous with certain traditional views about the nature of reality that Hegel found to be unsatisfactory. However, in Hegel's usage the terms 'God', 'Love', 'Life', and 'Spirit' can be regarded as largely synonymous. Further, the foregoing discussion of his use of 'Subject' and 'Person' has shown that his primary model for the elaboration of his meaning of *Geist* is 'Subject', and that he also, though rarely, described *Geist* as 'absolute Person'. There is, of course, a very great danger in using 'Person' as a model for the description of the Absolute, for it has the very definite connotation of individuality; and while this is quite consistent with Hegel insofar as he used 'Individuality' as another descriptive term for *Geist* as the summit of dialectical development, it has to be realized that his usage is not the ordinary one, according to which 'Person' or 'Individuality' refers to the finite individual.

The difficulty in using terms like 'person' and 'personal' in reference to God had been pointed out in Hegel's own time by Fichte, who in 1798 had produced a paper "On the Basis of Our Belief in a Divine Providence," which had sparked off the atheistic controversy (Atheismusstreit), for in it he had asserted that the moral order is God and no other God is needed. In his own defense in the ensuing controversy, he wrote "Appeal to the Public Concerning the Accusation of the Expression of Atheistic Opinion" (January 1799), in the course of which he argued that God cannot be thought of as a being, and that terms such as 'personal' cannot be used to describe God because we think of such concepts only as implying limitation and finitude. The force of this point has really never diminished, and indeed Pannenberg goes so far as to claim that "the crisis of the idea of God since the 18th century is connected chiefly with the problem of how the power that determines all reality can be thought of as a person." [84] Hegel's use of 'Person' in reference to the Absolute is rare—perhaps, in part, as a consequence of an awareness of this point that had been forcefully made by Fichte; and also, in part, because of his distinction (in the Philosophy of Right) between 'subject' and 'person', in which the 'person' is the human with a variety of motives, including selfish ones, and so is not a true 'subject'.

However, the terms 'Subject' and 'Individuality' also have the difficulty of implying finite individuals, and yet these are terms that Hegel frequently employed (especially 'Subject') in reference to the Absolute. Therefore, extreme caution in interpretation is required. The terms 'subject' and 'individual', as well as 'person', all imply, in ordinary usage, finite being; but in Hegel's use of these terms they serve as models for his description of the Absolute, which is thus to be understood as characterized—but only fully at the summit of dialectical development—by Subjectivity, Individuality, and Personalness.[85] However, the usage of these terms here can be justified only if understood in the special Hegelian sense of aufgehoben, so that they are being used at the Hegelian level of speculative thought where they apply to God or absolute Spirit as that which is manifest in the cosmos, underlying and permeating all life, and giving continuity and unity to all.

The relevance of these matters here in this discussion is that they seem to be consistent with, and suggestive of, the notion of the transcendence of the Absolute. But in what sense of transcendence? Certainly not in the sense of a self-contained 'infinite' Being existing alongside other beings—a notion of the Absolute to which Hegel was vigorously opposed! Whittemore wants to say that through

Hegel's use of 'person' in describing the Absolute, he did retain a sense of transcendence, "since 'person', however defined, connotes some sort of transcendent unity." [86] But a sweeping statement of this nature simply cannot be accepted, for it seems quite obvious that 'person' could be defined in such a way as to exclude the notion of transcendent unity. Therefore, is there any way in which 'person', 'subject', or 'individual' can be regarded that suggests a notion of transcendence? If one takes the model of the finite person, one can speak of the nature of that individual, of that nature being expressed through the diverse activities in which the individual engages, and of the growth and development of that nature—that is, the process of, at least the partial, realization of what that individual potentially is.

What is of importance, however, is that there is present here a concept of transcendence, namely, the kind of transcendence that can be identified by the fact that no matter how one may endeavor to speak of the various aspects of the individual, whenever one refers to him as an individual, one is giving to all his various features an embracing unity of nature—indicating a uniqueness of expression in what it is to be human that cannot be totally grasped, and a uniqueness of purpose that cannot possibly be anticipated.[87] It is true to say about an individual that what he potentially is is never exhaustively expressed by his diverse and multitudinous features and activities, nor exhausted in his realized achievements, for it is of the nature of personalness to hope for, strive for, and achieve radical novelty, revealing unanticipated aspects of his potential nature.

However, while one can take these points from an understanding of finite individuality, subjectivity, and personalness, in Hegel's view, true Individuality, Subjectivity, and Personalness do not belong to the finite individual as a separate, distinct, and particular being, but to life in its wholeness—absolute Spirit, or God. Hegel's Absolute can therefore be described as possessing transcendence in an analogous sense to the way in which a finite individual transcends (encompasses, but is not exhausted by) the various expressions and manifestations of his nature: so the Absolute, the true Individual encompasses, but is not exhausted by, the world, the manifestation of its Nature; absolute *Geist* is permeative and formative within the world in a way that is marked by a creative openness to possibilities that lie beyond what has so far been realized.

Allowing this sense of transcendence, one can argue that panentheism still can be admitted as an interpretation of Hegel. But it is an entirely different matter if transcendence is taken to mean that God is 'other than' and 'apart from' his *Dasein* in the world, for it is clear that Hegel did not admit transcendence in that sense, and

pantheism would have to remain as the description of Hegel's philosophy. However, admitting that which is here being suggested as
an alternative sense of transcendence, it becomes possible to go
beyond pantheism, though still more needs to be said in order to
work through the very complex problem to which attention is here
being devoted, namely, how to give expression to Hegel's understanding of the relation of the infinite and finite, of God and the
world. There can be no doubt that Hegel understood that relation
in terms of unity, but it is equally clear that he did not mean unity
as an undifferentiated identity: he saw the presence of distinction or
otherness in that relationship in much the same way as a person
can be said to be distinct from or other than his activities and
relationships. Just how best one can express the Hegelian position
is of the utmost difficulty, because all our thinking is geared to
conceiving relationships in terms of external subject-object relations,
which, for Hegel, must become *aufgehoben*. But this difficulty does
mean that it is extremely easy to overstress either the unity or the
distinction, and so to distort Hegel's position.

Fackenheim provides a good example of the difficulty, for it seems
that he is not completely able to avoid stress on the distinction when
he speaks of the preservation of the double Trinity in speculative
thought. His view is well summed up in the following quotation:
"The pre-worldly trinitarian play is complete, apart from its worldly
manifestation; yet this latter—no mere repetition of the play—is as
real for philosophic comprehension as it is for Christian faith. The
trinitarian God is wholly real apart from the world and wholly real
in it, and only because of His preworldly reality can His worldly
manifestation be complete. *The two Trinities of Christian faith, then,
do not reduce themselves, in one of two opposite ways, to one: they
remain two, for philosophic thought as much as for Christian faith. And
philosophy accepts what faith has asserted: that their relation is Love.*" [88]
By his use of the expression "preworldly Trinity", he obviously is
wanting to represent that for which he finds evidence in Hegel's
references to "God in His Universality";[89] and by his use of the term
"double Trinity", Fackenheim is endeavoring to represent the distinction between God in his universality and the process of God
'othering' himself in the world and 'returning' to himself.

But while Fackenheim is aware of Hegel's view of this distinction
as a distinction-in-unity,[90] his own terminology tends to distort Hegel's view, twisting it toward a much more traditional theistic interpretation. On the other hand, Fackenheim is absolutely right when
he says that unless the truth of religious faith—namely, that of "a
relation *between* the Divine and the human, in which the Divine is
both *other* than the human and yet *inwardly related* to it"[91]—is

retained in philosophic thought, the whole basis of religion would be lost, and philosophy, rather than demonstrating the content of absolute religion to be true, though inadequate in form, would in fact demonstrate religion to be false in content as well as form. However, Fackenheim does seem to see this retention of the truth of religious faith in terms of traditional theism: his use of terminology such as the "preworldly reality" of the "trinitarian God" does strongly suggest the theistic God who is prior to the world and for whom therefore the created world is not necessary. Hence, there is a distortion of Hegel's position.

Does this mean, however, that any admission of transcendence necessarily implies that the Absolute has some *Sein* prior to and apart from its *Dasein* in the world? If so, then the supposed discovery of a sense of transcendence in Hegel's philosophy must always amount to a distortion of it, for, as Min rightly points out, the question "What would God be like 'outside' this relation to the world? " is one that has no meaning for Hegel.[92] This kind of question would be unintelligible to Hegel from an epistemological viewpoint: the only God that the knowing-subject can know is God as he manifests himself in the world—"God-in-himself-for-the-world," but not "God-in-himself." Again, however, even this terminology sug- gests the idea of God-in-himself as 'prior to' and 'apart from' the world; yet, in no way could such an idea be attributed to Hegel,[93] whose view is that the relation between God and the world, the infinite and finite, "is a thoroughly *internal, spiritual* relation".

But the problem persists, for it is "this without prejudice to their relative, mutual otherness and independence. Each is the Other of the other, but this otherness is no mere brute otherness but an internally sublated one." For Hegel, "the fundamental relation of finite and infinite is not the immediate identity of being with itself but the movement of self-mediation through otherness." [94] Now this self-mediation through otherness is God-in-himself-for-the-world, but this movement does not mean that God's being-in-himself would lose "its sovereign objectivity": "God has his *Dasein* in the world, and the world expresses his being-in-himself. This does not mean, however, that this being-for-the-world 'exhausts' his being-in-himself, his interiority or subjectivity as Spirit." [95] A person's activities are an externalization of the person's nature or spirit, but that spirit cannot be said to be exhausted by those activities. "So the world as God's Other does indeed externalize what he is in himself, and yet the world does not exhaust God's subjectivity . . . for God's being consists in the eternal, trinitarian movement of externalizing himself, interiorizing what has been externalized, and remaining in all these identical with himself." [96]

It therefore remains a fact about Hegel's position that, although strenuous efforts must be made to avoid any exposition that would suggest Hegel lapsed into some kind of dualism between God and the world, it is quite wrong to conclude that *God* and *World* are interchangeable predicates for some sort of unity that is mere identity. In Hegel, absolute Spirit or God is conceived of as the prolific, energizing source of the great multiplicity and variety of the world, but it is also true that Hegel considered the Absolute not to be apart from all that is born out of its own fullness. The tendency therefore to identify absolute Being and the world is due to our thinking in terms of definite horizons—even our universal concepts, and our collective concepts such as of the totality of the world, are really horizons in our thinking that can be transcended at any time. In Hegel, the concept of the Absolute is a concept of that which transcends all horizons, because it permeates all horizons as that source of Being or Life in which all things have their being. But the struggle to express this relationship continues, and it is a struggle precisely because of the tendency to think in terms of limiting horizons. It thus becomes almost overwhelmingly difficult to hold in balance the Hegelian concept of the distinction and unity of the Infinite and finite, God and the world.

To attempt to recapitulate: one can recall that Hegel characterized the *Logic* as "the presentation of the divine essence before creation," and that Hegel found the great merit of the Ontological Argument to reside in the fact that it begins with the concept that Hegel declared to be true reality in which all finite things are ontologically grounded. But this is not to say that Hegel admitted the priority of existence of the concept of absolute Being; on the contrary, "the Notion, the Potentiality, is not a state, an existence"—something that is there from the outset—rather, it is "the inner element, the Potentiality," and the existence of particular states of things is due to the Potentiality entering upon existence.[97] The whole created finite world is ontologically constituted in the Potentiality of absolute Being, of which the world is the self-manifestation, and is 'other than' the Absolute in an analogous sense to the 'otherness' that may be attributed to the self-expressive activities of an individual person as being 'other than' the person; and absolute Being is that which permeates, forms, and creates within the finite world. This creative and formative nature is the dynamism that Hegel clearly attributed to absolute Being: the Absolute was not presented as a mere abstract, for crucial to Hegel's presentation was his use of trinitarian thought in his thinking about the nature of absolute Being. And it is this that was reflected in his stress on the Absolute as Subject, characterized by Individuality and Personalness, which permeates and forms all life, in which all finite things and finite horizons are transcended and fulfilled, and which has its own fulfilment in such transcending. As such, the Absolute is infinite, transcendent Being.

A most satisfactory summing up of Hegel's endeavor is provided by Min: "what Hegel tried to do through his 'speculative' approach, it seems, was to provide the ontological foundation for the very possibility of _both_ transcendence and immanence and thereby also to sublate and transcend the rigid opposition often posited between them. This he did, I believe, not by denying either the finitude of the finite or the infinity of the infinite but, rather, by probing into the very conditions under which alone, in his view, the finite could be truly finite and the infinite truly infinite. This condition is the primordial, internal unity of infinite and finite in the true _(wahrhafte)_ infinity and true transcendence of the Absolute Spirit which is itself and yet posits and 'overreaches' its Other out of love." [98]

It is this Hegelian concept of "overreaching" _(übergreifen)_ that clearly suggests the presence in Hegelian thought of that sense of panentheism that has been suggested here, namely, that the Infinite encompasses or includes the finite, though is not exhausted by it.[99] It is this idea that seems to be apparent in Hegel's statement that "only the true infinite, which posits itself as finite, overlaps itself so to speak as its Other, and remains in it, because it is its own other in unity with itself." [100]

The choice of terminology that will capture Hegel's meaning is a task that is fraught with great difficulties: Fackenheim's choice of terms such as "preworldly Trinity" and "double Trinity" appears to be unsuccessful. But if the pursuit of a more adequate terminology is to be continued, then a more successful attempt can be made by turning to, in order to borrow from, the work of Whitehead and Hartshorne, both of whom developed a dipolar conception of God in terms of a _primordial_ nature and a _consequent_ nature of God. The distinction between these 'two natures' of God is, says Whitehead, "a distinction of reason," which enables one to "consider God in the abstraction of a primordial actuality" and also to consider that God "is also consequent." [101] As primordial, God is the ground of actuality; God's primordial nature is "God in himself," the "abstract essence of God." The consequent nature of God is the concrete, relative aspect of God, God "as having in fact created the particular world." [102]

However, to continue to elaborate the views of Whitehead and Hartshorne would be to make it very apparent that there are marked fundamental differences between them and Hegel;[103] but this does not preclude the 'lifting' of these terms from the work of these two writers and applying them to the purpose of expositing this aspect of Hegel's philosophy. The distinction between the primordial nature and the consequent nature of God must be not just a distinction of reason, but a distinction-in-unity, with the primordial nature referring to the abstract, absolute concept of God-in-himself, God as under-ivative,[104] and the consequent nature referring to the derivative nature of God, God's 'Othering' of himself, God-in-himself-for-the-world. The suitability of this terminology in an exposition of Hegel, as distinct from Fackenheim's "preworldly Trinity" and "double Trinity", is that it avoids the implied stress on the distinction between God and the world and the implication that God is prior to and inde-pendent of the world, both of which are quite contrary to Hegel's position.

The suitability of this terminology is also displayed by two other facts. First, in association with the metaphysical distinction between the primordial and the consequent nature of God there is the concept of God as 'the Becoming One', the implications of which are sig-nificantly paralleled in Hegel's concept of God as *Geist*. Secondly, this terminology accommodates another Hegelian thought—one that is also shared by Whitehead and Hartshorne—namely, that God *necessarily* expresses himself in his creating (othering) activity.

It is, however, in this last concept that Pannenberg and others, such as Karl Barth and Hans Küng, find considerable difficulty: as Pannenberg says, "the idea that God necessarily brings the world into being . . . seems to underlie all other theological objections to Hegel's philosophy." [105]

The Hegelian Meaning of Necessity. Thus, the discussion now leads to the role of necessity and freedom, in Hegel's thought, regarding the God-world relationship. Because of Hegel's insistence on the recognition that God necessarily creates the world, it is argued that pantheism prevails in his philosophy, since it means that both God's freedom and man's freedom are abolished.

Pannenberg presents this argument in the following manner: "Thus, from Hegel's assertion of the logical necessity of the creation of the world and the coming into being of evil as the self-assertion of finiteness, *the consequence is drawn* that in spite of all the distinctions which Hegel makes, the world must belong to the process of the self-realization of God, and that therefore Hegel's system is pantheist. Consequently, it is possible to do justice neither to the divine per-sonality, God's freedom with regard to the world, nor to the per-sonality and freedom of man. For both fall victim to the logical necessity with which the divine Idea passes over into the world process and the latter is taken back into God." [106] However, in pointing to the critical arguments against Hegel presented by Tholuck,

Müller and Lütgert, a warning is sounded by Pannenberg to the effect that before one launches into this kind of criticism of Hegel one should carefully consider the Hegelian meaning of the necessity and freedom of absolute Spirit: for it is not the case that Hegel's usage is the commonly accepted one that takes 'necessity' to indicate "a compulsion imposed from outside," and that thus is exclusive of 'freedom'. What is required, therefore, is a consideration of Hegel's meaning in order that this matter might be explored in further detail.

An informative indication of Hegel's meaning can be ascertained from his sense of the inadequacy of both the Cosmological and Teleological Arguments for God's existence. Both arguments begin by identifying certain features of the world as contingent, namely, the world's existence and the world's purposeful design, and then proceed to assert the existence of an absolutely necessary Being as the cause of this kind of world. But in both cases, the absolutely necessary Being remains external to the world, and its necessity is "merely outward and relative": it is said to be independent of the world and yet its necessity is asserted through the process of arguing from the nature of the world—this absolutely necessary Being is "a mere negative." [107]

Indeed, Hegel argued that closer analysis reveals that the commonly accepted distinction between necessity and contingency is permeated by contradiction, necessity being found within the contingent sphere, and freedom within the necessary. The contingent sphere is ordinarily taken to be comprised of the material objects, which are known through sensation and which are regarded as finite and contingent because their existence is accidental and inevitably limited. However, their existence is, in fact, conditioned and subject to the connections of cause and effect and to the laws of nature, and thus they are raised "above the category of contingency into the region of necessity"—or, as Min says, "in this sense, necessity is the 'truth' of contingency." [108] The 'necessary' is ordinarily taken to mean that an existing thing "should stand in some connection with other things, so that . . . it is seen to be completely determined by other existing things." [109]

This dependence of necessary things is the opposite of what is seen to be the independence of contingent things, but just as contingent things are in fact completely dependent, so "it is in necessity alone that we find the independence of a thing." This is because "what is necessary must be [and] this fact that it *must be*, expresses its independence by suggesting that what is necessary is, *because* it is." [110] In this way the concept of necessity as external necessity is abolished: it is supposedly contingent things that are subject to external necessity, but it is a necessity imposed by things that are themselves particular and limited; whereas the truly necessary is not dependent on something external to itself, but "is its *own* inner necessity." Thus, "for Hegel, freedom is the 'truth' of necessity as necessity is the 'truth' of contingency." [111] The conclusion therefore can be drawn that it is in God or Absolute Spirit that the common distinction between contingency and necessity disappears: "God not being dependent on anything—and hence free of the necessity that accompanies contingency—is the only truly contingent being there is. On the other hand he also is the only necessary being because he alone exists by virtue of what he is in himself." [112]

This viewpoint about contingency, necessity, and freedom, which Hegel espoused, evokes a response from Pannenberg to the effect that divine freedom still has been left without firm foundation. It is not that he thinks Hegel was undermining the traditional theological doctrine of divine freedom, for he intimates that traditional doctrine also is unable to deal adequately with the question of divine freedom. The traditional doctrine grounds divine freedom in the absence of any imposition of external necessity on God, thereby making God's freedom to appear as something additional to his being—God himself is the basis of his own act of freedom, not in the sense that freedom belongs to his nature per se, but in the sense that his nature is such that he is not affected or constrained by anything outside himself, and hence he acts freely. Similarly, in Hegel, God is the basis of his own act of freedom, but in a different sense—not in a way that makes God's freedom appear as something additional to his being, but in the sense that his freedom is an expression of his being per se, "as a manifestation of his self-identity, that is, as a necessity inherent in it." [113]

Pannenberg acknowledges that an "insoluble problem . . . exists here in the traditional doctrine of God," and while he asserts that Hegel "did not succeed in removing" that problem, he correctly recognizes that Hegel's aim was to resist "the abstract dualism implicit in the idea of a God who was simply opposed to everything finite, seeing this as effectively making the Absolute finite." [114] The nature of Hegel's error, however, according to Pannenberg, is that "he does not seem to have noticed that the concept of a being as the faculty and 'power' underlying this freedom itself made the Absolute finite," and the concept of such a being means that "Hegel shares with [traditional theology] the acceptance of an absolute being which already exists before the act of divine freedom." [115] Furthermore, since the nature of this prior absolute being is such that the act of freedom is a manifestation of it, an important aspect of freedom has been overlooked: "In Hegel's concept of the freedom both of God and of man, the element which fails to achieve adequate expression is its contingency, in the sense of something that happens on the basis of the future alone, and the impossibility of deriving it from anything that already exists." [116]

In considering Pannenberg's criticisms, it is helpful to keep in mind what Hegel was endeavoring to do, which also involves recalling what he was endeavoring to avoid. He clearly sought to avoid any suggestion that God acts necessarily, where that necessity is externally imposed, for that would finitize God; similarly, he sought to avoid the idea that God acts freely, where that freedom is due to the absence of external impositions, for that would mean that God's freedom is something merely negative. Hegel therefore asserted that God freely acts, but that his freedom is also an inner necessity, for it is of the very nature of God.

One of course is struck immediately by the apparent dilemma in equating freedom with an inner necessity. But, as Min explains, Hegel's way out "is to say that God is 'love' " and that therefore "God posits the world because he 'loves' it. Love alone could unite and at the same time transcend necessity and freedom. Love externally compelled would not be true love; love is free. . . . Likewise, love indifferent to the loved Other would not be true love; love seeks union with its Other. In love one seeks to find his very subjectivity in his Other. Love, then, is both free and necessary; it at once needs and does not need its Other. Love sublates both the mere externality of necessity and the mere subjectivity of freedom into a mutual union." [117] What Hegel was endeavoring to achieve was the sublation (*Aufhebung*) of the distinction drawn by ordinary consciousness between necessity and freedom that regards necessity and freedom as mutually excluding opposites.

It is quite evident that from his earliest writings Hegel had been preoccupied with the concept of freedom, but he never regarded it in terms of the absence of external constraint: even in his early writings it always appeared as a personal autonomy, something that came from within oneself. For example, one acts necessarily when one obeys an externally imposed law; but if that law becomes part of oneself in the sense that one recognizes the intrinsic value of the action that the law is commanding, and so one no longer acts because the law commands but because the worth of the act is part of oneself, then one can be said to be acting freely.

It is this view of freedom that runs through Hegel's early writings, and when one picks up another major concept from those writings—love—one has the concept in which the distinction between necessity and freedom is transcended, for genuine love is both free and necessary: it is free in the sense that genuine love cannot be constrained or compelled, but also necessary in the sense that it is a response toward the beloved that springs from the being of the lover. However, whereas the sense of 'otherness', which always remains between lover and beloved in the finite realm, means that this genuine love—and hence also the sublation of the distinction between freedom and necessity—is never wholly achieved in the finite, the unity of the divine Infinite is coterminous with the completeness of its genuine love, so that it can be said that the necessity with which it expresses itself in its other is an expression of its freedom.

When Pannenberg says, however, that Hegel's treatment of this question implies a being who exists prior to the expression of its freedom, he is attributing to Hegel not only something Hegel wished to avoid, but also something for which there is no definite justification in Hegel. If Pannenberg is correct, it would mean that Hegel said that there is first an Infinite, which subsequently, yet necessarily, becomes finite; but Hegel explicitly denied this, asserting that, "on the contrary, [the infinite] is on its own account just as much finite as infinite." [118] What it means is that Hegel treated the question of finitude and infinity by seeing them "as moments of a movement in which the one presupposes the other, where infinity functions as the immanent *telos* of finitude, so that finitude is meaningful only as a striving towards and a manifestation of infinity while, by the same token, infinity is meaningful only as so manifested through finitude." [119] In Hegel's view, therefore, it is meaningless to speak of the Infinite—God or absolute Spirit—as a being that exists prior to its free act of expressing itself in its Other: both the Absolute and its other are moments of a dynamic movement, the ultimate foundation of which is love and freedom.

Pannenberg is not unaware of Hegel's use of the concept of love in dealing with the dilemma regarding freedom and necessity— indeed, Pannenberg acknowledges this by indicating a significant passage in *SL*: "The universal is therefore *free* power; it is itself and takes its other within its embrace, but without *doing violence* to it; on the contrary, the universal is, in its other, in peaceful communion with itself. We have called it free power, but it could also be called *free love* and *boundless blessedness*, for it bears itself towards its other as towards *its own self*; in it, it has returned to itself." [120]

This quotation is extremely helpful in dealing with a common explanation of Hegel's concept of God's freedom and necessity that employs a distinction between factual and essential necessity. According to this explanation, God's necessity—in Creation, for example—is a factual, not an essential, necessity: in other words, it relies on a distinction between an action that is in accord with one's nature and the actual choice to do that action. Therefore, "while creating is in accordance with God's necessary essence, and even identical with it, the fact 'that God creates . . . is not necessary'," [121] for it is consequent upon God's free choice to actually create.

However, Hegel's concept of freedom as the freedom of love points to the inappropriateness of this distinction being applied to Hegel's view, and a similarity with Plato, to which Hendry draws attention, is indicative of this unsuitable application. "In his account of creation Plato used an idea which has been gratefully taken up by many theologians—that creation springs from the goodness of God, for the good is ever generous in imparting itself to others (Timaeus, 29E). If a free resolve is interposed between the goodness of God and the act of creation, the resolve can no more be freed from the goodness of God than the act of creation. Where would the goodness of God be, should he resolve in his freedom not to exercise it in the creation of the world? " [122] Similarly, in regard to Hegel, it must be pointed out that love, which is the nature of God, is such that love 'necessarily' expresses itself in its 'other', so that it is quite redundant to distinguish some free resolve as intervening between love and its self-expression.

However, Pannenberg finds that Hegel's move—from calling the universal 'free power' to defining it as 'the freedom of love'—involves an unwarranted "leap in thought" that leaves an unmistakable gap unfilled. The gap is caused by the fact that an expressive activity necessitated by the nature of God, even if it can be called free in Hegel's view, can be conceptually anticipated, and to describe it as the freedom of love is to perform an unwarranted leap, according to Pannenberg, because "the freedom of love cannot conceptually be anticipated." [123] Thus, it becomes clear that Pannenberg's concept of geniune freedom is that of the freedom of love, and it is this viewpoint that earlier led him to assert that Hegel's treatment of the necessity and freedom of God's self-expressive activity is wrongly based. It is based on the concept that the freedom of that self-expressive activity is grounded in the nature of God, thus making it "subject to the necessity of the nature of a prior being." The alternative that Pannenberg advocates "is to understand the nature of God itself on the basis of the absolute future of freedom." [124] Thus, instead of the understanding of God's freedom being based on the nature of God, the understanding of the nature of God is to be based on "the absolute future of freedom", for this is the only way that one can employ the genuine concept of freedom as something which cannot be conceptually anticipated, but is truly contingent, in the sense of not being derivable from anything that already exists, but "that happens on the basis of the future alone." [125]

However, two difficulties regarding Pannenberg's comments can be suggested. First, he assumes that Hegel must be interpreted as implying that freedom and creativity are necessary attributes by which the divine nature is to be qualified; and this means, for example, that it is not until the world is brought into being that the Absolute attains to its own nature.[126] But this seems to entail an incorrect reading of Hegel: for him, there is no distinction between divine life and divine creativity, so that the question whether creation is a necessary or contingent act is a meaningless question—creation is identical with the divine life, and so is God's freedom.[127]

Secondly, Pannenberg assumes that Hegel's view of the freedom of God is based on his concept of the nature of God, whereas genuine freedom is an absolute openness to the future. However, is it possible to speak of an *absolute* openness to the future? Surely it is the case that openness to the future is at the most only relative, for from the past are derived the potentialities for the future; but not in such a way or to such an extent that there is no openness to the future, for one can also speak of the *telos* to which the actualization of the potentialities must be open. The difficulty with Pannenberg's concept of "an absolute openness to the future" is that it suggests that the *telos* is the sole cause, with no account being taken of the limitations imposed by the past. Both an element of openness and that which limits openness have to be acknowledged: without the latter there is no acknowledgement of the potentialities derived from the past, and without the former there could be no creativity.[128]

Pannenberg's reservation about Hegel's position springs from the perception that in Hegel there is a priority attributed to the Notion. This priority was expressed when Hegel asserted that God as Universal "is the starting-point," and that "all determinations are contained in the Notion." But this can be only an ontological priority, for the determinations are "not pre-formed," but are contained in the Notion "in a spiritual form," and the development of the Notion is the development of that which it "implicitly contains," of that which "has not yet come into existence." [129] It is this ontological priority that Pannenberg believes removes the possibility of genuine freedom, for any supposedly 'free' activity is really necessitated by its being implicitly contained in the Notion; and, in contrast, Pannenberg speaks of "the ontological priority of the future", in which is grounded "the absolute future of freedom".

Pannenberg here is presenting a concept that is certainly capable of arousing a sense of fascination and excitement because of its bearing on the age-old, and our present, problem of the God-world relationship. But it must be asked whether one cannot also find the same concept in Hegel. Pannenberg's stress on the futurity of God involves the assertion that in a sense God does not yet exist, but is in the process of coming to be—and this sounds very much like

Hegel, for whom the Absolute or God is what it truly is only at the end or result:

> The True is the whole. But the whole is nothing other than the essence consummating itself through its development. Of the Absolute it must be said that it is essentially a *result*, that only in the *end* is it what it truly is; and that precisely in this consists its nature, viz. to be actual, subject, the spontaneous becoming of itself. (*Phen.*, 11)

Furthermore, although Pannenberg accuses Hegel of leaving no room for an element of genuine contingency in human affairs by his assertion of all things being contained in the Notion, one wonders whether Hegel's position entails the elimination of genuine contingency any more than Pannenberg's does, particularly in the light of his disagreement with the Process Theologians regarding the notion of *development* in God, denying such development with the assertion that "what turns out to be true in the future will then be evident as having been true all along." [130]

Thus, both men perceive the Absolute as being that which it truly is only as 'the end', but Pannenberg's emphasis on the future is seen by him as the means of avoiding all thought of necessity and allowing a complete openness to the future. But to what extent is this achievable? The future is the basis of freedom, for Pannenberg, and "freedom is in general the power that transforms the present";[131] yet here there is a limitation imposed on the future in the sense that there is an *actual* present to be transformed. On the other hand, the openness to the future resides in the divine creative process that is genuine love, infinite and inexhaustible in its capacity to transform the actual present.

However, it is certain that this concept of love is present in Hegel just as it is present in Pannenberg. Genuine love does not impose limitations on the freedom of the 'other';[132] complete love is inexhaustible in its adaptibility to the responses of the 'free' and 'independent' other; and yet, also, complete love is ultimately irresistible, so that a positive response to such love is ultimately 'necessary' in the sense of inevitable. It is this ultimate fulfillment of love that is the *Result* that Hegel spoke about as the Absolute *becoming* what it truly is; but it surely is also the future that Pannenberg speaks of as *coming* to be, and which therefore also 'determines' the present in much the same way as Hegel's Notion, for Pannenberg understands the nature of creation as God bringing our present to us out of the future. But it is not a complete determinism in either Hegel or Pannenberg, for both perceive the nature of the Absolute as Love, and the openness to the future is grounded in the infinite and inexhaustible capacity of love to transform and go beyond the present, since in the present the self-expressive activity of love "is never yet its full concept".

Because that is Hegel's view, one can begin to recognize that he also possessed (just as Pannenberg does) a positive sense of the mysterium of God: the divine nature cannot be grasped totally or gathered up. Mystery belongs to the being of God—the triune God— for it belongs to the being of God to be totally open in the outgoing of himself in the externalization and alienation of himself in his 'other' (the world); and to be totally open, to be the inexhaustibility of love, in the overcoming of the alienation, in the return of God to himself. This 'dialectic of God'—the triune God—is God's 'absolute freedom' as 'the "free" infinite'; and this is the mystery of God:

> God is Spirit—that which we call the triune God, a purely speculative content, i.e., the mystery of God. God is Spirit, absolute activity, *actus purus*, i.e., subjectivity, infinite personality, infinite distinction of himself from himself, divinity standing over against itself and objective to itself. . . . in its differentiation within itself, the entire divine concept, Son and God, this absolute unity-in-distinction, is identical with itself: this is *eternal love*.[133]

This mysterium of God belongs to the being of God: it "is not because the divine nature lies 'beyond' a barrier in unknowable darkness, but because it lies infinitely open."[134]

What seems to be the case, therefore, is that the same exciting concepts regarding these matters are to be found in the thought of both men, but that their primary emphasis is different: for Hegel, it is the ontological priority of the Notion; for Pannenberg, it is the ontological priority of the future; for Hegel, as for the Process Theologians, God as absolute Spirit is "the Becoming One", developing toward its end; and for Pannenberg, God is "the Coming One", the power of the future. However, this similarity between Hegel and Pannenberg on this matter points up the sharp contrast between Hegel and Spinoza,[135] for whom a deterministic system was built upon the claim that everything is as it is as modes of the one Substance. But, for Hegel, Substance must be understood as Spirit, whereby infinite divine life is seen to be a creative developmental process, permeated by a *telos*, which ensures the element of openness to the future.

> This Universal is the starting-point . . . It is, however, no inert, abstract Universal, but the absolute womb, the eternal impetus

and source from which everything proceeds, to which everythings returns, and in which everything is eternally preserved. (*LPR,* vol. 1, 95)

Hegel is thereby to be distinguished from Spinoza, and hence also from pantheism.

Concluding Remarks

Throughout this inquiry attention has been drawn to the problem of determining what is involved in Hegel's claim to transform the representative form of religious faith into the conceptual form of speculative thought. By the use of *Vorstellungen*, religious faith seeks to give expression to the true ultimate that transcends the realm of finite reality and that therefore cannot be expressed directly or properly by any finite reality. But Hegel firmly believed that this use of *Vorstellungen* does not allow religious consciousness to escape the realm of finite reality, for although the employing of sensible images as symbols does open up the possibility of a grasp of ultimate reality in a way that would otherwise be closed for us, it still means that religious consciousness is caught within the finite sensible world, and therefore cannot adequately express the nature of the Absolute. This grasping of the Absolute is adequately achieved, in Hegel's view, only in the purer conceptual formulation of speculative thought, where all sensible images derived from the finite world are put aside.

The question that is inevitably raised is whether this transformation of religious images into speculative concepts also means a transformation of religious 'truths' into new *truths*. Hence, the often posed question of whether Hegel's philosophy of religion can be seen as being in any way compatible with Christianity. Copleston, for example, says that it is easy to make out a plausible case "for representing Hegel's philosophy of religion as a stage in a process in which the concept of God is progressively eliminated";[1] and Findlay puts it more strongly when he says that "the religion recommended by Hegel is one in which it is good for God as a separately conceived being to die." [2]

Yet, there can be no doubt that Hegel asserted that the 'truth' of absolute religion is *the* truth, and it is equally certain that he claimed to have retained this truth. But, as Copleston correctly says, this does not necessarily mean that he did. Thus, there is this dilemma running through Hegel's philosophy of religion, a dilemma that Fackenheim clearly indicates: the truth of religious faith is that of "a relation *between* the Divine and the human, in which the Divine is both *other* than the human and yet *inwardly related* to it," and unless this truth is retained in philosophic thought, then Hegel's claim that absolute religion contains the truth, but in an inadequate form, cannot be correct; and if this truth is retained in philosophic thought, then the form in which it is expressed in absolute religion must be true as well.[3]

Copleston says that Hegel's undertaking to give a new and more adequate expression of religious representation of the truth amounts to a demythologization of Christian doctrine, and Fackenheim speaks of Hegel's transmythologization or transfiguration of religious truth. In seeking finally to offer here an opinion about this Hegelian dilemma, it is suggested that Fackenheim's terminology is preferable, for although, as Copleston recognizes, there is no real difference between what they want to say about Hegel's intentions, Copleston does seem to overlook the fact that the connotations of the two terms are not the same, so that there is a real significance in their choice of different terms: what Copleston says about Hegel's achieved position (as distinct from Hegel's intention) is quite different from Fackenheim's conclusion.

Contemporary demythologizers of religion fall into two categories: first, those who wish to do away with the use of myth and symbol—those who, like Bultmann, insist that mythological language must be exhaustively translated into the terminology of ordinary existence. These are 'demythologizers' in the strict sense of the term. Secondly, there are those who—while certainly wishing to abolish existing myths, because these myths have become fixed or accepted at their face value, and thus have caused misinterpretations of religious truth—nevertheless recognize the necessity of myths and symbols in religious expression. This necessity exists because religion is about that which is ontologically ultimate and about man's relationship with the ultimate, and because finite language can never completely grasp ultimacy but can only allude to it by means of myths and symbols. It is therefore seen to be necessary for old ones to be replaced by more contemporarily effective and meaningful myths and symbols before there can be any hope of a more accurate interpretation being rediscovered. Those who adopt this attitude might be more aptly called 'remythologizers'.

It is certain that the term 'demythologizer' cannot accurately be applied to Hegel, for he did not attempt to do away with myths and symbols in religion—indeed, they are the means of expressing the truth of religion; and it is also fairly certain that he did not see the need even to change the myths. He did, however, believe there to be a need to rise above the level of myth. For Hegel, on the one hand, it was imperative that religious life, with its myths and symbols and its cultic practices, remain as an important, indeed essential, aspect of human life: through its myths and symbols the religious truth—of the divine-human relation—is expressed, and through its cultic practices that truth is given practical expression and realized in people's lives. Religion is therefore essential to—it undergirds—philosophy, for without it, the truth to which philosophy gives complete expression would never be known or experienced. But, on the other hand, Hegel believed it necessary to rise above the level of religious mythological expression because of its inadequacy as a means of clearly and distinctly conveying the truth. It is for this reason that Fackenheim describes Hegel's endeavor as a "transmythologization of religion": not the abolition of myth, but the rising above the religious expression of the truth to the higher level of philosophic language, in which the truth is formulated with clarity and distinctness. It is a "transfiguration" of religion into philosophy (to use another of Fackenheim's terms), where transfiguration is understood not as the changing of a thing into something new and different, but the viewing of the same thing from a new and deeper perspective. Therefore, Hegel was not involved in an effort to change religious dogma into new doctrines, but in an attempt at viewing those doctrines from a new and deeper perspective: so that what, at the level of religion, is seen as a divine-human relation is, at the level of philosophy, perceived to be the oneness of absolute Spirit.

To regard Hegel's philosophy of religion in this manner is to become aware of the need to take his endeavor very seriously, for it is of vital importance for religion. In order, therefore, to give a renewed and clarifying expression of the nature of Hegel's endeavor here, one can follow Copleston's suggestion and turn to the language of Paul Tillich, who speaks of the "God above God". It seems that one can identify very close similarities between what Tillich meant by this phrase and what Hegel meant when he spoke of absolute Spirit. Tillich's talk of the need to accept the "God above God" springs from his recognition that the theistic God is objectified as a being who is bound to the subject-object structure of reality and who is really only part of the whole of reality, and that this is bad theology. In contrast, "the acceptance of the God above the God of theism makes us a part of that which is not also a part but is the ground of the whole,"[4] for this is the perception of God as 'Being-itself'.

The same is true of Hegel: motivated by the recognition of the errors of theism, and the inevitable "rebellious" atheism,[5] he attempted, by his concept of absolute Spirit, to express the truth of the ultimate, namely, that we are a manifestation of that which is not also a part but is the ground of the whole. Like Tillich, Hegel also held that this truth is to be found in Christianity; but, given the fact that religion expresses its truth in myths and symbols, which the religious consciousness can easily take literally,[6] it is almost unavoidable that the truth should be distorted in a way that gives rise to the theistic God. Also, like Tillich, who spoke of the "God above God," whom he described as the "ground of our being", Hegel spoke of absolute Spirit, not for the purpose of abolishing the truth of Christianity, but so that that truth may be set free from the narrow restrictions that had become associated with traditional theological forms.

However, there is considerable opinion that says that Hegel's treatment of religious truths is such that they do become diffferent doctrines. If one is, therefore, to maintain successfully that Hegel did not introduce new doctrines, it is necessary to have established that in his final position, in his reenactment of final religion in terms of final philosophy, Hegel—in Fackenheim's words—"reenacted the Christian divine-human relation in thought": in other words, that the religious truth of the divine-human relation is not abolished but is perceived from a new and deeper perspective—a perspective that really simply recaptures the truth revealed in absolute religion—as a complete oneness with Divinity.

Fackenheim is of the opinion that Hegel did reenact the truth of final religion: "That the Hegelian reenactment *means* to reinstate rather than dissipate the religious relationship is shown by statements such as the following: 'God is God only insofar as He knows Himself. His self-knowledge is, *further, man's self-consciousness and the human knowledge of God*, which moves on *so as to become man's self-knowledge in God'* (*EM*, §564, italics added). Man's self-knowledge *in* God does not dissipate the reality of his knowledge *of* God." [7] In this way Fackenheim asserts that Hegel adopted a middle position that preserves Christianity from two extremes—pantheism and atheistic humanisim—that are equally destructive of it.

The earlier discussion of alternative interpretations has shown that there is nothing like unanimity of opinion regarding the understanding of Hegel's position; but that discussion concluded that such interpretations overlook much evidence in Hegel to the contrary. There are, however, other expositors of Hegel—such as Copleston and Taylor—who, while recognizing that evidence, still do not regard Christianity to have been preserved by Hegel, for he so reformulated Christian faith that his formulation could not be regarded as a theism.

Copleston, while admitting that Hegel neither intended to formulate different doctrines nor thought that he had done so, does have strong suspicions that Hegel's own assessment is wrong:[8] that, although it was not his intention, Hegel developed a position of ambiguity that proved to be a significant step on the way to the elimination of the concept of God, a process that came to fruition in the later movements of naturalism, positivism, and the death-of-God theology.[9] Now Copleston may be right in saying that these developments were inevitble, because once one translates language about God into some other language, such as Hegel's language of absolute idealism, one will soon find that one is no longer talking about God; but surely there is a leap in Copleston's argument when he says that it was Hegel himself who introduced the new doctrines. The fact that Hegel endeavored to rise above the misconceptions associated with the term 'God'—that he rose to the *God* above 'God'—by translating language about God into language about absolute Spirit, and the fact that others subsequently developed completely nontheistic philosophies, does not mean that Hegel himself shared these philosophies. It is not the case that Hegel's attempt to transmythologize or transfigure the truth of absolute religion amounts to an abolition of those truths, but just that his endeavor gave rise to the possibility of others interpreting it as such an abolition. And this is no different from any other formulation of religious doctrine, for all are open to the possibility of misinterpretation: indeed, it was Hegel's conviction of the presence of misinterpretation of the truths of absolute religion, in what had come to be the traditional forms of that religion, that strongly motivated his work in the philosophy of religion.

Like Copleston, Taylor speaks of Hegel's 'demythologizing' Christianity to the extent that it becomes a 'de-theologized' Christianity, the spiritual grandchildren of which are the recent theologies of 'the death-of-God.'[10] Christianity was de-theologized by Hegel in that the very essence of the Christian faith was left out—it did not remain a theism (not that Taylor believes Hegel converted it to an atheist doctrine); and not only was the essence eliminated, for Hegel failed also to save Christian dogmas, such as Creation, Incarnation, Resurrection and Ascension. Indeed, Taylor says that "Hegel only accepted a Christianity which had been systematically interpreted to be a vehicle of his own philosophy."[11]

This kind of assertion about Hegel is, of course, based on the interpretation of him as a demythologizer who, by removing the myths, has also removed the 'truths' conveyed by those myths; and those who adopt this approach appear to be following the common stance of religious people, including many theologians, of closely identifying the truth with a fairly literal understanding of the mythological language in which that truth has been formulated. This, however, is a hazardous approach, for one must realize that all myths are formulated within the context of a particular age and therefore reflect the world view and the notion of reality in general and of human life in particular of that age, and to identify a truth too closely with the myth by which a particular age—usually the form-ative age of that truth—expressed it is really to put that truth at risk. This means that myths can never be static: there must be an ongoing process of seeking to perceive the truths that the inherited myths were designed to convey, and express those truths afresh in contemporarily meaningful language—but language that always will be mythological.

This last point is at variance with Hegel. He obviously recognized these problems about myths, but he failed to recognize any need for the use of myths at the level of religious thought to be dynamic and flexible, while he believed it was possible to avoid the use of myth altogether in the expression of truth at the level of speculative thought.[12] He claimed to have the adequate formulation—philo-sophical conceptualization—that provides absolute knowledge of what God is in himself. Thus, Hegel believed he had turned faith into knowledge. He had discussed faith in *Phen.*: believing consciousness, he claimed grasps its object, God, in an act of trust; but its object is a Being that is beyond the world of reality. Faith is a flight from the real world. This is not the authentic religious consciousness, in Hegel's view—not the self-consciousness of absolute Being as it is *in* and *for* itself. When absolute Being is known as it is *in* and *for* itself, absolute knowledge will be attained.

However, while it is clear what Hegel was wishing to rise above, namely, faith in a 'Beyond', it is clearly a fault in his system—certainly an exercise in self-deception—to claim the result of this rising to be absolute knowledge where there is no room for, or need of, the act of trust (the step of faith), and where the use of the language of representation and myth can be entirely avoided. Reli-gious faith can never be turned into knowledge in that sense, and no endeavor, such as that undertaken by Hegel, can avoid the language of representation. No finite mind can fully grasp, and no finite language can adequately express, the Absolute.

Although Hegel claimed otherwise, this is still the case in his system, with his use of the concept of *Geist*, for whatever is said about absolute Being will have *per se* a mythological or symbolic meaning,[13] even when it is expressed—as in Hegel's case—in the speculative language of philosophy. That language is also limited and has a symbolic meaning that can be grasped only by those within the esoteric circle. To believe that one can escape from this kind of limitation by ascending to the esoteric level of philosophy is to indulge in self-deception; and the end of *LPR* indicates that

Hegel finally realized this fact. As Hegel's *Geist* can be spoken of in Tillichian terms as the "God above God", so his 'absolute knowledge' might best be described as 'Faith above faith'.

In the light of this, two important principles can be taken from Hegel at this point. First, that a mere unthinking faith is not truly a faith at all: to accept the myths and symbols of religion on a superficial and literal level without understanding their content is to possess merely a 'blind' faith that is really dehumanizing, for man has the capacity to think, and it is only through the use of that capacity that man can attain a rational faith that Hegel would identify as knowledge of the infinite *Geist*.[14]

Secondly, that the langauge of religion is always imaginative and in a sense mythological, and that to take it to be literally and prosaically true will be apt to lead us into error. What Hegel did achieve in this regard was to recognize the extremely narrow restrictions that had been imposed on Christian symbolism, even to the point where its truth had been lost: he recognized that Christianity had been turned into what Tillich calls an "unbroken mythological" religion, that is, one in which the myths and symbols are taken to be literal; and having recognized this restrictiveness, Hegel broke free from it and achieved a fresh symbol in the concept of *Geist* (even though he himself regarded it, not as a symbol, but as pure philosophical concept), in which the truth of absolute religion could be rediscovered. Thereby, at the very least, and indeed if nothing else, Christianity must take from Hegel the lesson that its mythological language is "a broken myth,"[15] and is never to be taken literally, but recognized as pointing beyond itself to the ultimate ground of all that is.

Hegel's intention in his treatment of religion has been described by the term 'transmythologization'; yet, it may be the case, as has been suggested above, that he did no more than 're-mythologize'. In either case, however, it has been an important argument of this inquiry—in close proximity to Fackenheim—that Hegel did not necessarily abolish Christian 'truths' or create new doctrines, for he can be seen to have been doing no more than anticipate, in the sphere of philosophy, the many twentieth-century attempts, within the sphere of religion, to remythologize those doctrines in order to discover the truth that the myths were intended to convey: for example, by his intended transmythologization of 'God' into 'absolute Spirit', Hegel was doing no more than 'anticipate' the work of recent theologians, such as Tillich, who spoke of the "Ground of Being".[16]

Therefore, it can be argued that, in his own way, Hegel not only presented, but rediscovered some of the truths of absolute religion— truths that had virtually been lost through the misconceptions of the narrow, restrictive literal formulations of traditional theism, which, in turn, had produced reactions in the form of atheism and pantheism. Thus, one can go further than Fackenheim's suggestion of Hegel's preserving Christianity against the extremes of pantheism and atheism,[17] and assert that Hegel provided a means of preserving the truths of Christianity by rising above the misconceptions and contradictions involved in each position—atheism and pantheism, as well as traditional theism. To find a 'label' of this kind to use in reference to Hegel, it seems that the most appropriate alternative is 'panentheism', which conceives the 'all' of the world 'in' God as his inner modification and appearance,[18] even though God is not exhausted by the 'all'. Such a label certainly places Hegel within the broad embrace of theism, while obviously distancing him from the traditional formulation of theism as well as pantheism; but, on the other hand, it is a label that requires qualification, for its use must not be seen to imply that Hegel can be identified in any detail with the views of recent writers, such as Whitehead and Hartshorne, to whom this label has more generally been applied.

There can be little doubt, however, that Hegel's philosophy of religion is characterized by ambiguity: it is very understandable that a variety of interpretations have been imposed upon it, not least that which sees Hegel as having, either unintentionally or deliberately, moved away from Christianity. But here it has been the endeavor to argue that Hegel's position was one that does admit an interpretation that not only remains within the embrace of Christianity,but 'rediscovers' truths of Christianity that had long been neglected without ever having been fully grasped.[19]

Consistent with this view of Hegel, it has been said his philosophy of religion can be described as speaking of "the God above God", as transcending the concept of God so as to achieve the concept of Spirit *(Geist)* in which the truth of God and the truth of man (and the cosmos) is attained: the truth of God is that absolute Being is Spirit (dialectical, trinitarian), the ground of all being, who manifests himself in the finite—for only thereby can he know himself—and who finds self-fulfillment as Spirit by drawing, within himself, all finite reality; and the truth of man (and the cosmos) is that all finitude is a manifestation of absolute Being, deriving its being from 'Being-itself', and it is only in ultimate Being that we, as finite, discover ourselves, and in discovering ourselves we discover Being, or God as Spirit. It is this vision of the nature of reality that Hegel sought to capture by his concept of Spirit; it is certainly one that amounts to a transformation of traditional theism, but it is one that can be seen to be still consistent with the admission of the truth of religion that is manifested in Christianity, the religion of Incarnation.

Nevertheless, at the end, it must be acknowledged that an ambiguity remains: the very fact that there have been such a variety of interpretations is certainly indicative of that—yet, it is an ambiguity that must be grasped as something more profound than a vacillating uncertainity that admits a diversity of, even contradictory, reactions. It is an ambiguity that signifies an important, indeed necessary, allusiveness: such allusiveness is vital to religion, for without it religious language becomes bound by a rigidity that endangers the truth of religion and violates the freedom of the individual to make that truth his own; and such allusiveness is vital to the Hegelian system, for without it an exclusiveness would arise and there would be the marking out of limiting boundaries that would eliminate the Hegelian desire for an all-inclusiveness. But, of course, the basis of that allusiveness lies in the fact that no linguistic expression or concept devised by finite man can embrace ultimate reality: all our expressions and concepts are nothing more than signs or symbols— 'myths'—that can serve as suggestive models of the truth of that reality. Hegel, by his use of the concept of *Geist*, broke free from the erroneous connotations, such as that of an external Being, which has hindered and restricted the use of the term 'God': thereby he formulated an expressive symbol that had all the hallmarks of alusiveness that must characterize religious myths, and thereby he challenged all who would follow in the philosophy of religion to think the relation between absolute and finite being both more exactly and more deeply.

Bibliography

Works by Hegel

Aesthetics: Lectures on Fine Art. Translated by T. M. Knox. Oxford: Clarendon Press, 1975.

The Difference Between Fichte's and Schelling's System of Philosophy. Translated by H. S. Harris and Walter Cerf. Albany: State University of New York Press, 1977.

Dokumente zu Hegels Entwicklung. Edited by Johannes Hoffmeister. Stuttgart: Frommánn-Holzboog, 1974.

Early Theological Writings. Translated by T. M. Knox. Chicago: University of Chicago Press, 1948.

Enzyklopädie der Philosophischen Wissenschaften im Grundrisse. Hamburg: Verlag von Felix Meiner, 1969.

Faith and Knowledge. Translated by H. S. Harris and Walter Cerf. Albany: State University of New York Press, 1977.

"Fragments of Historical Studies." Translated by Clark Butler. *Clio: An Interdisciplinary Journal of Literature, History and the Philosophy of History* 7, no. 1 (1977): 113–34.

Hegels Theologische Jugendschriften. Edited by Herman Nohl. Tübingen: J. C. B. Mohr, 1907.

Jenaer Realphilosophie. Edited by Johannes Hoffmeister. Hamburg: Verlag von Felix Meiner, 1969.

Lectures on the History of Philosophy. 3 vols. Translated by E. S. Haldane and Frances H. Simpson in 1894. London: Routledge and Kegan Paul, 1955.

Lectures on the Philosophy of Religion: Together with a Work on the Proofs of the Existence of God. 3 vols. Translated by E. B. Speirs and J. Burdon Sanderson in 1892. New York: Humanities Press, 1962.

Lectures on the Philosophy of Religion. Part 3. Edited and translated by Peter C. Hodgson, under the title *The Christian Religion.* Montana: Scholars Press, 1979.

Logic. Part 1 of *The Encyclopaedia.* Translated by William Wallace in 1873. Oxford: Clarendon Press, 1975.

Phänomenologie des Geistes. Edited by Johannes Hoffmeister. Hamburg: Verlag Felix Meiner, 1952.

Phenomenology of Spirit. Translated by A. V. Miller. Oxford: Clarendon Press, 1977.

Philosophy of Mind. Part 3 of *The Encyclopaedia.* Translated by William Wallace in 1894. Oxford: Clarendon Press, 1971.

Philosophy of Nature. Part 2 of *The Encyclopaedia.* Translated by A. V. Miller. Oxford: Clarendon Press, 1970.

Science of Logic. Translated by A. V. Miller. London: Allen & Unwin, 1969.

"Two Fragments of 1797 on Love." Translated by H. S. Harris and C. Hamlin. *Clio: An Interdisciplinary Journal of Literature, History and the Philosophy of History* 8, no. 2 (1979): 257–65.

Werke. Neu edierte Ausgabe Redaktion Eva Moldenhauer und Karl Markus Michel. Frankfurt am Main: Suhrkamp Verlag, 1970.

Other Works

Barth, Karl. *From Rousseau to Ritschl,* being the translation of eleven chapters of *Die Protestantische Theologie im 19, Jahrhundert.* Translated by Brian Cozens. London: SCM Press, 1959.

Black, Edward. "Religion and Philosophy in Hegel's Philosophy of Religion." *The Monist* 60, no. 2 (April 1977): 198–212.

Boehme, Jacob. *The Epistles of Jacob Behem.* Translated out of the German language. London: M. Simmons, 1649.

———. *On the Election of Grace.* Translated by J. R. Earle. London: Constable, 1930.

Borchert, Donald M. "The Influence of Hegel in Contemporary God-Is-Dead Theology." *Praxis,* 1971: 203–14.

Cameron, Bruce J. R. "The Hegelian Christology of Paul Tillich." *Scottish Journal of Theology* 29, no. 1 (1976): 27–48.

Chapelle, Albert. *Hegel et la Religion.* Paris: Universitaires, 1966.

Christensen, Darrel E., ed. *Hegel and the Philosophy of Religion.* The Wofford Symposium. The Hague: Martinus Nijhoff, 1970.

Colletti, Lucio. *Marxism and Hegel.* Translated by Lawrence Garner, London: NLB, 1973.

Copleston, Frederick. *A History of Philosophy.* Vol. 7, part 1. New York: Image Books, 1965.

Eckhart, Meister. *Meister Eckhart.* A selection translated by R. B. Blakney. New York and London: Harper Torchbooks, 1941.

Fackenheim, Emil L. *The Religious Dimension in Hegel's Thought.* Boston: Beacon Press, 1970.

Feuerbach, Ludwig. *Lectures on the Essence of Religion.* Translated by Ralph Manheim. New York: Harper & Row, 1967.

Fichte, Johann Gottlieb. *Science of Knowledge, with the First and Second Introduction.* Translated by P. Heath and J. Lachs. New York: Appleton-Century-Crofts, 1970.

Findlay, J. N. *Hegel: A Re-examination.* London: Allen & Unwin, 1958.

Fitzer, Joseph. "Hegel and the Incarnation: A Response to Hans Küng." *The Journal of Religion* 52 (1972): 240–67.

Hallett, H. F. *Aeternitas.* Oxford: Clarendon Press, 1930.

———. *Benedict de Spinoza.* London: Athlone Press, 1957.

Harris, H. S. *Hegel's Development: Toward the Sunlight, 1770–1801.* Oxford: Clarendon Press, 1972.

———. Review of *Das älteste Systemprogramm: Studien zur Frühgeschichte des deutschen Idealismus,* by Hrsg. v. Rüdiger Bubner. *Hegel-Studien* 10 (1975): 299–305.

Hartshorne, Charles. *Man's Vision of God.* Hamden, Conn.: Archon Books, 1964.

Hendry, George S. "Theological Evaluation of Hegel." *Scottish Journal of Theology* 34, no. 4 (1981): 339–56.

Henrich, Dieter. "Hegel and Hoelderlin." *Idealistic Studies* 2, no. 2 (May 1972): 151–73.

Hyppolite, Jean. *Genesis and Structure of Hegel's Phenomenology of Spirit.* Translated by Samuel Cherniak and John Heckman. Evanston: Northwestern University Press, 1974.

———. *Studies on Marx and Hegel.* Translated by John O'Neill. London: Heinemann, 1969.

Kant, Immanuel. *Critique of Pure Reason.* Translated by Norman Kemp Smith. London: Macmillan, 1963.

Kaufmann, Walter. *Hegel.* New York: Doubleday, 1965.

———. "Hegel's Early Antitheological Phase." *Philosophical Review* 63 (1954): 3–18.

Kojève, Alexandre. *Introduction à la Lecture de Hegel.* Paris: Gallimand, 1947.

———. *Introduction to the Reading of Hegel.* Edited by Allan Bloom, translated by James H. Nichols. New York: Basic Books, 1969.

Lakeland, Paul F. "Hegel's Atheism." *The Heythrop Journal* 21, no. 3 (July 1980): 245–59.

Lauer, Quentin. *Essays on Hegelian Dialectic.* New York: Fordham University Press, 1977.

———. "Hegel on Proofs for God's Existence." *Kant-Studien* 55 (1964): 443–65.

———. "Hegel's Pantheism." *Thought: A Review of Culture and Idea* 54, no. 212 (March 1979): 5–23.

———. *A Reading of Hegel's Phenomenology of Spirit.* New York: Fordham University Press, 1976.

Lessing, G. E. *Nathan the Wise.* Translated by B. Q. Morgan. New York: Frederick Ungar, 1955.

Löwith, Karl. *From Hegel to Nietzsche.* Translated by David E. Green. New York: Doubleday, Anchor Books, 1967.

Lukács, Georg. *The Young Hegel.* London: Merlin Press, 1975.

MacIntyre, Alasdair, ed. *Hegel: A Collection of Critical Essays.* New York: Doubleday, Anchor Books, 1972.

McMinn, J. B. "A Critique on Hegel's Criticism of Spinoza's God." *Kant-Studien* 51 (1959–60): 294–314.

McTaggart, J. M. E. *Studies in Hegelian Cosmology.* Cambridge: Cambridge University Press, 1901.

Marcuse, Herbert. *Reason and Revolution: Hegel and the Rise of Social Theory.* London: Routledge and Keagan Paul, 1967.

Min, Anselm K. "Hegel on the Foundation of Religion." *International Philosophical Quarterly* 14, no. 1 (1974): 79–99.

————. "Hegel's Absolute: Transcendent or Immanent." *The Journal of Religion* 56 (1976): 61–87.

Möller, Joseph. "The Problem of Universals: Its Scope and Meaning." *International Philosophical Quarterly* 6, no. 4 (1966): 557–73.

Mueller, Gustav E. *Hegel: The Man, His Vision and Work.* New York: Pageant Press, 1968.

Mure, G. R. G. *The Philosophy of Hegel.* London: Oxford University Press, 1965.

Myers, Henry A. *The Spinoza-Hegel Paradox.* New York: Cornell University Press, 1944.

Norman, Richard. *Hegel's Phenomenology: A Philosophical Introduction.* London: Sussex University Press, 1976.

O'Malley, J. J., et. al., eds. *The Legacy of Hegel.* Marquette Symposium. The Hague: Martinus Nijhoff, 1973.

Pannenberg, Wolfhart. "The God of Hope." In *Basic Questions in Theology,* translated by George H. Kehm, vol. 2, pp. 234–49. London: SCM Press, 1971.

————. "The Question of God." In *Basic Questions in Theology,* translated by George H. Kehm, vol. 2, pp. 201–33. London: SCM press, 1971.

————. "The Significance of Christianity in the Philosophy of Hegel." In *Basic Questions in Theology,* translated by R. A. Wilson, vol. 3, pp. 144–77. London: SCM Press, 1973.

————. "Speaking About God in the Face of Atheist Criticism." In *Basic Questions in Theology,* translated by R. A. Wilson, vol. 3, pp. 99–115. London: SCM Press, 1973.

————. *Theology and the Kingdom of God.* Edited by R. J. Neuhaus. Philadelphia: Westminster Press, 1969.

Parkinson, G. H. R. "Hegel, Pantheism and Spinoza." *Journal of the History of Ideas* 38, no. 3 (1977): 449–59.

Perkins, Robert L. "Hegel and the Secularization of Religion." *International Journal for Philosophy of Religion* 1, no. 3 (Fall 1970): 130–46.

Plant, Raymond. *Hegel.* London: Allen & Unwin, 1973.

Pomerleau, Wayne P. "The Accession and Dismissal of an Upstart Handmaid." *The Monist* 60, no. 2 (April 1977): 213-27.

Prior, Andrew. *Revolution and Philosophy: The Significance of the French Revolution for Hegel and Marx.* Cape Town: David Philip, 1972.

Ramsay, Ian T. "A Personal God." In *Prospect for Theology: Essays in Honour of H. H. Farmer,* edited by F. G. Healey, 53-72. Digswell Place: James Nisbet, 1966.

Reardon, Bernard M. G. *Hegel's Philosophy of Religion.* London: Macmillan, 1977.

Schelling, F. W. J. *Schellings Werke.* Edited by Manfred Schröter. München: Becke, 1965.

Schmitz, Kenneth L. "Hegel's Philosophy of Religion: Typology and Strategy." *The Review of Metaphysics* 23, no. 4 (June 1970): 717-36.

Seidel, George J. *Activity and Ground: Fichte, Schelling, and Hegel.* New York: Georg Olmo Verlag Hildesheim, 1976.

Shklar, Judith N. *Freedom and Independence: A Study of the Political Ideas of Hegel's Phenomenology of Mind.* Cambridge: Cambridge University Press, 1976.

Shmueli, Efraim. "Hegel's Interpretation of Spinoza's Concept of Substance." *International Journal for Philosophy of Religion* 1, no. 3 (Fall 1970): 176-91.

————. "Some Similarities Between Spinoza and Hegel on Substance." *Thomist,* October 1972: 645-57.

Soll, Ivan. *An Introduction to Hegel's Metaphysics.* Chicago and London: University of Chicago Press, 1969.

Spinoza, Benedict de. *The Chief Works of Benedict de Spinoza.* Translated by R. H. M. Elwes. New York: Dover Publications, 1955.

Steinkraus, Warren E. *New Studies in Hegel's Philosophy.* New York: Holt, Rinehart & Winston, 1971.

Strauss, D. F. *The Life of Jesus Critically Examined.* Edited with an introduction by Peter C. Hodgson. London: SCM Press, 1973.

Taylor, Charles. *Hegel.* Cambridge: Cambridge University Press, 1975.

————. *Hegel and Modern Society.* Cambridge: Cambridge University Press, 1979.

Tillich, Paul. *The Courage To Be.* Glasgow: Collins, 1962.

————. *Dynamics of Faith.* New York: Harper & Row, 1957.

————. *Perspectives on Nineteenth and Twentieth Century Protestant Theology.* Edited with an introduction by Carl E. Braaten. London: SCM Press, 1967.

————. *The Shaking of the Foundations.* London: Penguin Books, 1962.

————. *Systematic Theology.* Vol. 1. London: James Nisbet, 1953.

Weiss, Frederick G., ed. *Beyond Epistemology: New Studies in the Philosophy of Hegel.* The Hague: Martinus Nijhoff, 1974.

Welch, Claude. *Protestant Thought in the Nineteenth Century.* New Haven and London: Yale University Press, 1972.

Whitehead, A. N. *Process and Reality: An Essay in Cosmology.* New York: Macmillan, 1929.

Whittemore, Robert C. "Hegel as Panentheist." *Tulane Studies in Philosophy* 9 (1960): 134–64.

General Reference Books

Cross, F. L., and E. A. Livingstone, eds. *The Oxford Dictionary of the Christian Church.* 2d ed. London: Oxford University Press, 1974.

Edwards, Paul, ed. in chief. *The Encyclopedia of Philosophy.* New York: Macmillan, Free Press, 1967.

Rahner, Karl, and Herbert Vorgrimler. *Kleines theologisches Wörterbuch.* Freiburg: Herder Verlag, 1961.

Ritter, Joachim, ed. *Historisches Wörterbuch der Philosophie.* Band 3. Darmstadt: Wissenschaftliche Buchgesellschaft, 1974.

Notes

Introduction

1. *LPR*, 3:151.

Introduction to Part I

1. These essays were first published by Nohl (1907), and, in part, translated by Knox *(ETW)*.

2. Kaufmann (1954), 3–18.

3. Ibid., 5.

4. Lukács (1975), 16.

5. Ibid., 8.

6. Lukács openly agrees that "the core of his work here is religious" (ibid., 9); while Kaufmann negatively asserts that these essays are "not antireligious" (Kaufmann [1954], 5).

7. "The theology he was taught at Tübingen aroused his opposition. It is one of the negative poles *against* which he defines his position in the early writings" (Taylor [1975], 51).

8. It is in the light of this distinction that Hegel's apparent opposition to theology in contrast to religion is to be understood: e.g., in the "Tübingen Fragment." Hegel here was using 'theology' as synonymous with what he termed 'objective religion'—"a matter of the understanding and the memory" (Harris [1972], 487)—to be discussed in detail below.

Chapter 1. The Tübingen Period

1. This antireligious strand was particularly characteristic of the French, though not the German, Enlightenment.

2. Harris (1972), 17.

3. Hegel wrote about this contrast in a school essay in August 1788, "On the Characteristics Which Distinguish Ancient Writers (from Modern Ones)," *Dok.*, 48–51.

4. It is in this same school essay that Hegel gave the first indication of the new depth and significance he will give to the distinction between these two rational faculties. The concept of *Verstand* comes directly from an essay by Garve on which the young Hegel depended heavily in the writing of his own essay, "but as Lacorte has pointed out, Hegel had already taken possession of it, and made a more precise and technical term out of it than it was for Garve himself, in the course of making excerpts from Garve's *Examination of the Faculties* a year earlier:

> From these materials [supplied by sensibility and imagination] *Reason* constructs the system of general concepts by which man governs himself and his affairs. Reason abstracts; if this happens repeatedly it is called Reflection *[Nachdenken]*; and since language supplies the soul with these abstract concepts in association with words, before the soul itself is capable of making abstractions, the understanding [here Hegel used *Verstand* where Garve had written *Vernunft*] is in the first place concerned to determine the meaning of words and to seek out the true general idea of which the word should be a . . . sign (Harris [1972], 36–37, quoting, in translation from *Dok.*, 122).

Harris accepts Lacorte's claim that Hegel's substitution of *Verstand* where Garve wrote *Vernunft* was deliberate, and therefore it seems that we find in Hegel, even as a schoolboy, a theory of two kinds of abstraction based on these distinct kinds of mental operations. There is "direct or legitimate abstraction of concepts from one's own experience, and indirect or illegitimate abstraction of meanings for the words that we have learned" (Harris [1972], 37). In consequence, there are two corresponding types of knowledge: respectively, personal knowledge, the work of *Vernunft*; and book learning, the work of *Verstand*.

5. This essay is titled "On the Religion of the Greeks and Romans, *Dok.*, 43–48.

6. This is the first of a number of essays—the "Tübingen Fragment"—that Nohl has published under the title *Volksreligion und Christentum*, Nohl (1907), 3ff., although the other essays were written in Bern. A translation of the "Tübingen Fragment" is given by Harris (1972), 481–507.

7. Harris notes that Hegel was on leave of absence during his last summer at the *Stift*. H. S. Harris, "The Young Hegel and the Postulates of Practical Reason," Christensen (1970), 63.

8. Harris (1972), 481.

9. An illustration of this view is contained in an earlier diary entry, dated 22 March 1786: ". . . I believe this enlightenment of the common man has always been governed by the religion of his time . . ." (*Dok.*, 37; quoted in translation by Harris [1972], 18).

Wolfhart Pannenberg says, "Hegel recognized that the problem of society itself was a religious problem" Pannenberg, ("Significance of Christianity," 1973, 145).

10. Kant's *Critique of Practical Reason* had been published in 1788, and Hegel had obviously read it.

11. Harris (1972), 484.

12. Ibid., 485–86.

13. In *Critique of Pure Reason* (1781), which Hegel would obviously have studied, Kant had denounced the essentiality of external trappings of religion, and had asserted belief in God and in immortality as the two fundamental articles of belief in the pure religion of morality.

14. In *Jerusalem* (1783), Mendelssohn had argued that the truths of the existence and providence of God and of the immortality of the soul are self-evident to reason and are the ultimate verities.

15. In the famous passage in *Nathan the Wise* (1779), to which Hegel specifically referred (see Harris [1972], 487), Lessing presented the view that good men share a common religious attitude even though the outward expression of religion differs, and that it is the common element that counts, overriding all external differences: in the scene to which Hegel referred, the Christian Friar says that Nathan (a Jew), by his good action, is indeed "a Christian soul!/. . . a better Christian never lived"; and to this Nathan replies, "And well for us! For what makes me for you/A Christian, makes yourself, for me a Jew!" Earlier (Act III, Scene 7), Lessing had argued by means of the fable of the three rings that we cannot know which religion is true, for though they differ in all other respects, "their basic grounds" do not differ, and that therefore one can be true only to the religion of one's inheritance, the sole criterion for genuineness being the religion's power to inspire good actions.

16. Another reference to Lessing's *Nathan* (see Harris [1972], 495) is used as an illustration of Hegel's point that book learning is cold and dead, and does not issue in any personal awareness of meaning.

17. Ibid., 489–90.

18. It is possible to recognize here an affinity with Kant, for whom the existence of God could not be an aspect of objective knowledge, but only a matter of personal conviction arising out of existential moral situations.

19. Harris (1972), 492–93.

20. Ibid., 488–89.

21. Ibid., 491.

22. Ibid., 486.

23. Ibid., 130.

24. This involvement is also indicative of the influence of Lessing, particularly his *Education of the Human Race* (1780).

25. Harris (1972), 499–500.

26. "The young Hegel, intent on the problem of popular education finds reason alone insufficient to raise the masses to Kant's moral level. Sheer respect for the moral law will not do" (Kaufmann [1954], 6).

27. Harris (1972), 502–4.

28. Ibid., 149.

29. Lukács (1975), 29.

30. See above, pp. 1–2.

31. Here one can note Hegel's disagreement with Kant: it is "the aspiration of expressive unity . . . which makes him unable to accept fully Kant's separation of reason and sensibility and cleave rather to Rousseau; it is this which will ultimately turn him against Kant" (Taylor [1975], 54). Kant's position involved a division in human nature, holding that "the Idea *(Idee)* of holiness"—i.e., in Kantian terms, the state in which the moral imperative and human inclinations coincide—is really unattainable because human life is a constant battleground between the moral imperative and human inclinations since there is a radical evil in human nature; and actions are moral only when the moral imperative is the deciding factor, and that requires following reason rather than inclinations.

But, for Hegel, "the ultimate apex of ethical conduct" *[Sittlichkeit]* is a concrete ideal for humanity that can be realized; and in the realization of it 'non-moral motives' cannot be dispensed with (Harris [1972], 495–96), for it is Hegel's view that it is only when human beings are an integrated whole—when all aspects of human nature are brought into harmony and are no longer divided—that humanity, individually and socially, can be renewed.

32. "The regeneration Hegel seeks is thus also and necessarily a political one: the recovery of a society in which men are free and undivided, as the Greeks were, in which the public life is an expression, and a common expression, of the citizens" (Taylor [1975], 54).

Chapter 2. The Bern Period

1. Ibid., 56.

2. Nohl (1907), 30–35.

3. Ibid., 33f.

4. Harris (1972), 165.

5. Nohl (1907), 36–47.

6. "He (Luther) took from the clergy the power to rule by force and [the power] over men's purses, but he still wanted it (power) over opinions" (ibid., 42).

7. "Whoever acts with a pure heart, will at first be misunderstood by the people with the moral and religious yardstick" (ibid., 45).

8. This is Harris's title for the fragment in Nohl (1907), 48–50; a translation of which is found in Harris (1972), 508–10.

9. Hegel's abiding conviction, that religion is indispensible, is apparent: "the supreme purpose of man is to be moral, and among the tendencies that contribute to this end, his tendency towards religion is one of the most important" (Harris [1972], 508).

10. Ibid., 509.

11. Nohl (1907), 50–60.

12. Ibid., 60–69.

13. Harris (1972), 178.

14. Nohl (1907), 52.

15. Ibid., 52–53 n.

16. Harris (1972), 180. This is Harris's paraphrase of Hegel in Nohl (1907), 65–66.

17. Nohl (1907), 75–136.

18. This stage in the development of Hegel's thought is marked by a dominating attraction toward Kant's philosophy. This attraction did not come about quickly, though it could not be said to be unexpected given the vigor of the debate about Kant's philosophy at Tübingen. During Hegel's Tübingen period philosophical issues had been dominated by Kant's *Critique of Pure Reason* (1781), and thus, Kantian philosophy would have been brought to Hegel's attention: it would have been necessary for him to read the *Critique* and to come to terms with Kantian thought. This attention to Kant would have been heightened by the printing of the *Critique of Practical Reason* in 1790, and yet again in 1793 by the appearance of *Religion within the Bounds of Mere Reason*, which sparked off a considerable debate at Tübingen. While there is little evidence of Hegel's active involvement in the debate as a student, there can be no doubt that he rejected the position adopted by his teachers, and it seems that he was already beginning to interpret the Gospels in Kantian terms. This last point is indicated by Harris (1972), 495n.–496n., when he says that the context of Hegel's reference, in the "Tübingen Fragment," to Jesus' discussion with the rich young man shows that Hegel was assimilating "Jesus' instructions to the Kantian distinction between *Legalität* and *Moralität*." But it seems that one cannot go as far as Henrich (1972), 161, who says that "Hegel was a dedicated Kantian even at Tübingen," for it has been indicated already that there were aspects of important disagreement with Kant—disagreements which were so fundamental that they were the source of Hegel's eventual break with Kant. But, for the moment, in 1795, Hegel found Kantian terms to be most adequate for an interpretation of Jesus that would serve as a rational foundation for a *Volksreligion*.

19. In the seminary Kant was taken as providing evidence for the accepted view that human reason requires the supernatural guarantees that the Scriptures offer: the argument was that since Kant had shown human reason to be incapable of attaining knowledge about the supernatural, revelation is necessary for such knowledge to be possible; and this revelation is chiefly

provided in the biblical account of the life of Jesus, and the guarantee of its truth is in the miraculous deeds that are reported.

20. An indication of Hegel's attitude toward the Tübingen theology is found in a letter he wrote to Schelling on 24 December 1794, commending Schelling for his first published essay, "Über Mythen," in which Hegel found that Schelling was "enlightening important theological concepts and gradually helping to clear away the old sourdough" (quoted in translation by Henrich [Christensen (1970), 33]). If this attack on the Tübingen theologians is meant to be a general condemnation of all their work, then it seems Steinkraus is right in saying there is an unfairness and lack of understanding in the attack. Storr, he says, "was something of a pioneer in NT studies, showing an awareness of the synoptic problem by suggesting the priority of the Markan Account" (ibid., 82); but Hegel would not have given praise for this work, since he "had no real interest in scientific biblical scholarship" (ibid.). But Hegel's attack was primarily directed at a general theological stance, and here it is much more difficult to agree with Steinkraus's criticism of Hegel when he says that "Hegel campaigned against a belief [Steinkraus is referring to the idea of the after-life as a heaven managed by a benevolent despot] that no systematic Christian theologian at the time seriously defended though it might have been an implication Hegel thought he detected" (ibid.). Hegel would have been completely justified in thinking he detected such a belief because much of Christian theology has encouraged it as a significant part of popular religious thought: and that is why Hegel condemned it.

21. This is an English title given the essay of 1795: *Die reine aller Schranken,* Nohl (1907), 75–136.

22. For this reason, Kaufmann's statement that here Hegel was attempting "to write the scripture of his folk-religion" (Kaufmann [1954], 11) is too prone to a misinterpretation of Hegel's intentions.

23. Harris (1972), 196. Also, Reardon says that Hegel's purpose "was to comment and interpret. To that extent he felt himself justified in putting words into Jesus' mouth which are not to be found in the gospels themselves. His concern, that is, is not so much with what Jesus might actually have said than with what he *did,* what he accomplished. It is this, he seems to be saying, which will lead us to a proper grasp of what Jesus *meant"* (Reardon [1977], 5).

24. For example, Mueller says that "Hegel's Christ is the name for that life which he understands at that time to be truly and really religious," and Mueller describes "Life of Jesus" as "a desperate effort. It is desperate because even the minimum of texts does not quite yield the philosophy which he would like to see in it; it is desperate because Hegel wants to speak as Christian, *even when the texts say the opposite of what he wants them to say.* He therefore transcribes them until they fit" (Mueller [1968], 49).

25. Nohl (1907), 75.

26. Ibid., 136.

27. It certainly reflects Hegel's attraction, at this stage, to the reinterpretation of Christian doctrine and practice found in Kant's *Religion Within the Bounds of Mere Reason* (1793).

28. Nohl (1907), 87. One can detect here also the influence of Lessing.

29. *ETW*, 67–148: "The Positivity of Christian Religion."

30. Nohl (1907), 233–39.

31. *ETW*, 145–67.

32. Again, one can easily detect Hegel's aspiration for the Kantian notion of autonomy, which is necessary for true morality; for what Hegel means by 'positivity' is the condition created by the suspension of that autonomy in the appeal to authority.

33. *ETW*, 69.

34. Ibid., 71.

35. Ibid., 68.

36. Ibid., 75–76.

37. Ibid., 76.

38. Ibid., 83.

39. Harris (Christensen [1970], 72).

40. Nohl (1907), 233–39. The writing of this essay is generally dated between December 1795 and March 1796.

41. "The thoughts of God are not comprehensible by human reason, they cannot be conceived" (ibid., 235).

42. Lukács mistakenly interprets Hegel's use of the term "that intruder" as a reference to 'the Kantian God'.

43. Lukács (1975), 74.

44. Nohl (1907), 214–33. The writing of this essay is generally dated between May and June 1796.

45. Lukács (1975), 76.

46. *ETW*, 158.

47. Ibid.

48. Ibid., 160.

49. Ibid., 75.

50. Both the authorship and date of this fragment is the subject of much debate, and to place a discussion of it here in this context indicates a following of Harris's view that Hegel wrote it shortly before leaving Bern.

However, the authorship has been ascribed to Schelling and Hölderlin as well as Hegel. The manuscript was discovered in 1917 by Rosenzweig, and his view became the commonly accepted one, namely that, while it had been preserved in Hegel's handwriting, its original author was Schelling. But Harris is firmly of another opinion, for he argues that until convincing evidence to the contrary may be discovered, "it can be shown that all hypotheses about Hegel's copying that fragment that we actually have from another author are gratuitous" (Harris [1972], 249ff.).

Previously, in 1965, Otto Pöggeler became the first to question the opinion for Schelling's authorship and to argue that Hegel was the author, and in 1969 he arranged a conference at Villigst to discuss the matter. The papers presented at Villigst were published in 1973 (*Hegel Studien Beihefte* 9, "Das älteste Systemprogramm. Studien zur Frühgeschichte des deutschen idealismus." Hrsg. v. Rüdiger Bubner. Bonn: Bouvier), and this volume has been reviewed by Harris (1975), 299–305.

Harris acknowledges that at that conference the consensus regarding authorship was shattered, for opinions ranged from uncertainty to Hölderlin, to Schelling, to Hegel. Nevertheless, Harris says "with some confidence that the cumulative case made here for Hegel is a strong one, and that the relation of the fragment to his earlier and later work is canvassed almost as carefully and as completely as one could possibly hope or desire" (ibid., 300).

Among those who argue for Hegel's authorship, it is widely agreed that the fragment belongs to the period shortly after his arrival in Frankfurt. Harris, on the other hand, diverges from this view, for he places it at the very end of his Bern period: "it seems altogether more likely that the author of the "Systemprogramm" was the lonely figure in Bern who had just added a conclusion to his "Positivity" essay in which the 'scientific' claims of Kant were rated very highly (Nohl [1907], 211–13), and had gone on to write a new essay on the downfall of 'natural religion' (*Jedes Volk hat ihm eigene Gegenstände;* ibid., 214–31). He was hearing by correspondence about Hölderlin's plans for a set of 'New Aesthetic Letters'—and quite apart from his own concerns, this would cause him to study Schiller's *Aesthetic Letters* with concentrated attention. He was looking forward eagerly to the day when he would join (or rejoin) the 'Bund der Geister' " (ibid., 305). But, in *Hegel's Development*, Harris had admitted that "since the fragment is a fairly short one we cannot absolutely insist that those scholars who wish to account for the supposed influence of Hölderlin upon it by transferring it from 1796 to 1797 are wrong" (Harris [1972], 249).

The question, therefore, is a very open one, without any means of being conclusive, though here a preference has been shown for Harris's position.

51. Published by J. Hoffmeister (*Dok.*), 219–21, and trans. by H. S. Harris (1972), 510–12.

52. Harris (1972), 510.

53. Ibid., 511.

54. Ibid., 510.

55. Ibid.

56. In one important respect this marks a radical change from Hegel's view as expressed in the "Tübingen Fragment" of 1793, for "the 'subjective' religion that makes reason palpable to the senses in *Religion ist eine* is only a handmaid of *Vernunft*, a childhood governess who remains as an old friend

in the house of the grown man who is governed by his own reason; whereas this 'mythological philosophy' does away with all 'governors', even—by implication—with the authority of Reason. Religion now is neither a governess nor an old friend, but a 'new spirit' of equality and freedom" (Harris [1972], 255).

Chapter 3. The Frankfurt Period

1. Harris (1972), 294 n.
2. Lukács (1975), 91ff.
3. Henrich (1972), 161–62.
4. Ibid., 161.
5. Ibid., 155.
6. In an earlier paper (Christensen [1970], 25–44), Henrich had virtually acknowledged this when he referred to "'various anticipations" of the shift in Hegel's thought at Frankfurt, but he still spoke of the shift as occurring "quite suddenly . . . almost like an incomprehensible break" (ibid., 39). On the other hand, in commenting on this, E. T. Long makes an important point: "There is, of course, no question about there being a change or development here. It would seem improbable that there is a change in the sense of an incomprehensible break almost as if to suggest a change of mind. . . . If, on the other hand, we keep in mind the experimental and fragmentary nature of these essays as well as Hegel's tendency to adopt a point of view disclosing its limits and seeing it point beyond itself, we might see the change or turn in Hegel's thought not as an incomprehensible break but as the disclosure and development of ideas, some of which were already implicit in the early fragments on 'Volksreligion', and which may supply the basis from which Hegel moves beyond Kant" (Christensen [1970], 52). In the other paper, Henrich makes a suggestion similar to this last point when he declares that it was Hölderlin who showed Hegel "that his conceptual framework based on Kant was incapable of maintaining the experience and convictions which they shared from their earlier years" (Henrich [1972], 161).
7. Ibid., 153.
8. Ibid., 160.
9. Harris (1972), 189.
10. Henrich (1972), 160. That such a question occurred to Hegel very quickly is apparent from Henrich's formulation: "how do we advance from that source (of original unity) to that point of development where original truth gets lost in appearance *(Schein)*, so that only a return to what was lost seems open to us?" (ibid., 163).
11. Translated and published under this title in "TFL," 257–64.
12. Nohl (1907), 374–77; trans. by C. Hamlin in "TFL," 258–61.
13. Nohl (1907), 377–78; trans. by Harris in "TFL," 261–63.

14. Henrich (Christensen [1970]) argues that this fragment must be divided into two parts, for he discovers a marked difference in the fragment, viz., that the first part still employs Kantian terms, and that it is only in the second part that the sudden appearance of the doctrine of love occurs. It is at this point, therefore, that Henrich locates the revolution in Hegel's thought.

15. "TFL," 258–59.

16. Ibid., 259.

17. Ibid.

18. Ibid. These two points, viz., that Kant's position can be positive, and that positivity can be overcome, both tell against Henrich's view that there is a marked difference between the two parts of this fragment.

19. Ibid., 260.

20. Ibid., 261.

21. Ibid.

22. Ibid., 262.

23. Nohl (1907), 378–82; ETW, 302–8.

24. ETW, 304.

25. Hegel illustrated his concept of genuine love by the example of the love relationship between two people in which there is a reciprocal giving of oneself completely to the other. Such love strives to annul all distinctions, and the lovers "are a living whole"; but love remains incomplete "if the separable element persists in either of the lovers as something peculiarly his own." To be secretive with each other, for example, is to fail to open one's whole self to the other and thus to place a restriction on the total maturing of love (ETW, 305–6).

26. Ibid.

27. Ibid.

28. One can recognize here an early anticipation of Hegel's concept of the dialectic.

29. Nohl (1907), 382–85; trans. by Harris (1972), 512–15.

30. Harris (1972), 513.

31. Ibid., 514.

32. Nohl (1907), 383; trans. by Harris (1972), 513.

33. This was a controversy, Pantheismusstreit, that had flared during the previous decade as a result of a disagreement between Jacobi and Mendelssohn regarding Lessing's supposed Spinozism.

34. According to Jacobi's report, this phrase had been used in a conversation by Lessing as a summation of his own concept of Divinity; and Hölderlin, in particular, seems to have acquired this phrase as a 'symbol' (Harris [1972], 99).

35. Indeed, it has already been noted that such a surrender, expressed in letters from Schelling, in early 1795, caused considerable puzzlement for Hegel.

36. Henrich (1972), 164.

37. The fragment *die Liebe* has a suggestion of this concept: The unity of love was illustrated by the love relationship between two people, and as a result of such a union a living child comes into existence and is a symbol of that union. But the child himself is only a seed, a new potentiality, as yet undeveloped, who has his own specific existence and who must develop his own consciousness. The child has his specific existence and his own specific personality because he has broken free from the original unity from which he was produced, and he now "turns ever more and more to opposition and begins to develop. Each stage of its development is a separation, and its aim in each is to regain for itself the full riches of life [enjoyed by the parents]. Thus, the process is: unity, separated opposites, reunion" (*ETW*, 307–8). One might add that here, too, was an indication of the concept of the dialectic that was to mature in Hegel's later thought.

38. Henrich (1972), 165.

39. In the light of that early dissatisfaction it is difficult to agree with Kaufmann (1954), 14, when he says that "Kant's distinction between reason and inclination is thus no longer accepted as adequate," for Hegel's conviction about the inadequacy of that distinction was the source of his earlier dissatisfaction with Kant.

40. The manuscripts published by Nohl ([1907], 243–342; *ETW*, 182–301) really represent five essays that were written over a number of months from the end of 1798. These essays evolved through a series of drafts, the original shape of which cannot be identified. It was probably not until 1800 that they were finished in the form in which we have them.

41. Thus is introduced what is, in many ways, a novel feature of these manuscripts, namely, the concept of 'fate', which is the related concept to that of 'spirit'. It is not that Hegel was speaking of these concepts here for the first time, but it is the manner in which they were being treated that provides the novelty. They were present in the "Tübingen Fragment," where the concept of spirit was quite central, but it was the Greek spirit with which Hegel had been concerned, and he treated it as "the operative form in which a community is conscious of its unity." Fate was seen as natural necessity and impersonal power (*Ananke*), against which nothing, not even the gods, could stand; and in this sense fate was seen as contrasted with or in opposition to rational freedom (Harris [1972], 273–75).

But in the Frankfurt MSS there is a new sense of fate. No longer is it used in the sense of the universal might of *Ananke*, and it is now regarded as the correlate of spirit rather than of rational freedom. In Hegel, spirit is a dynamic concept: it is the unity of both creativity and vitality, so that in man it is that which is the motivating or enlivening power within him. In contrast, fate is the consequence of man's reaction to either (a) external situations, such as *Trennung* between a man and his fellows, where the reaction is seen to be necessary because his fellows are regarded as an alien power standing against him and wishing to master him; or (b) an internal consciousness of one's alienation from life and an inadequacy to cope with it.

42. This essay was commenced before the fragments *die Liebe* and *Glauben ist die Art*, but it is agreed that Nohl was correct to place the final draft at the beginning of this collection of essays.

43. "his spirit is the unity, the soul, regulating the entire fate of his posterity" (*ETW*, 182).

44. Ibid., 185.

45. Ibid., 186.

46. Ibid.

47. Harris (1972), 283. Cf. Taylor (1975), 59: "Man's only choice was between two servitudes, to dead things or to the living God. Hence what God promised the children of Israel was not the expressive unity with nature the Greeks achieved, but rather that it would be at their disposal, would serve their needs, the land 'flowing with milk and honey.' "

48. *ETW*, 189.

49. Ibid., 190.

50. Evidence of a similar attitude toward Judaism is to be found in the first of the "Fragments of Historical Studies" (["FHS," 113–34]. While the dating of these fragments is uncertain, it is possible that they belong to Hegel's Frankfurt period). There Hegel spoke critically of the Jewish view of things: to them everything is "something merely real, unpenetrated by the spirit of love" (ibid., 118). However, Hegel's opinion as to what was lacking in Judaism generally seems to have prevented him from noticing exceptions, and this point would seem to justify Warren Steinkraus's criticism of Hegel's treatment of Judaism. Steinkraus complains that Hegel showed "no grasp whatever of the dynamism of the eighth century prophets" (Christensen [1970], 82). On the other hand, and partly in defense of Hegel, one ought to make the observation that Hegel's apparent one-sided criticism of Judaism is possibly a display of his prejudice, not so much against Judaism, as against the Protestantism of his day, which he perceived to be mistakenly enslaved to the spirit of Judaism, and which, therefore, needed to be renewed in the truth of Christianity. Hegel consequently was concerned here only with the spirit of Judaism that he found embodied in Abraham and the Mosaic Law, and so he saw no purpose in discussing other facets of Jewish history, such as the prophets (cf. Harris's response to Steinkraus, ibid., 89).

51. It is in this point that one finds Hegel's account of the failure of Christianity—namely, this 'flight from the world'—which is very different from his earlier account. "From Hegel's point of view it was this weakness that rendered Christianity incapable of becoming in its original form a true folk-religion, since the public life of men as citizens was *ipso facto* excluded from its purview, and thus the third canon of a folk-religion was flouted" (Harris [1972], 345).

52. "For the particular . . . the universal is necessarily and always something alien and objective" (*ETW*, 211).

53. "In the Kantian conception of virtue this opposition remains, and the universal becomes the master and the particular the mastered" (ibid., 214). Thus, as Taylor ([1975], 59), rightly says, the conflict with Kant, that was implicit from the beginning, viz. Hegel's refusal to accept Kant's central thesis of the separation of reason and inclination, is now out in the open.

54. *ETW*, 212. Cf. the fragment *die Liebe*, where Hegel had written that love "is a mutual giving and taking. . . . This wealth of life love acquires in the exchange of every thought, every variety of inner experience, for it seeks out differences and devises unifications ad infinitum; it turns to the whole manifold of nature in order to drink love out of every life" (ibid., 307).

55. Ibid., 215.

56. Ibid., 224.

57. Ibid., 227.

58. Ibid.

59. Ibid.

60. Ibid., 233.

61. Ibid., 231: "This lack is not a not-being but is life known and felt as not-being."

62. Ibid., 238, 232.

63. "For the sinner is more than a sin existent, a trespass possessed of personality; he is a man, trespass and fate are in him. He can return to himself again, and, if he does so then trespass and fate are under him" (ibid., 238).

64. Ibid., 239.

65. Harris (1972), 354.

66. That is why Jesus could declare another person to be 'forgiven'; that is why Peter recognized it in Jesus, thereby indicating his ability to recognize it in others as well, and so Jesus declared that Peter also could pronounce others 'forgiven'.

67. One such example is the incident where Mary Magdalene anointed Jesus' feet, and the reaction of Simon, the Pharisee, indicated that he was unable to recognise *Lebensfülle* displayed in an action of love, for he simply declared her to be a sinner—in Hegel's terminology, he displayed the attitude of the 'positive' Jew—while the reaction of the disciples indicated the more noble attitude of concern for the poor, but they did not recognize the love that motivated Mary; their attitude was akin to that of Kant's rational man.

68. *ETW*, 247.

69. Hegel described the core of Judaism as possessing products of the reflective understanding: "the principle of subjection" and the idea of "the Infinite Sovereign Lord" (ibid., 253).

70. Ibid.

71. Ibid., 255.

72. Harris expresses Hegel's view in this way: God is "the wholeness of life, the one fount from which all separate lives, all spontaneous impulses, and all free actions spring. Jesus expressed this relation of *origin* by speaking of the 'Father', though he did not mean to refer to anything other than life as he himself knew and experienced it" (Harris [1972], 357).

73. *ETW*, 266.

74. Cf. Harris (1972), 365.

75. *ETW*, 258.

76. Ibid.

77. Ibid., 261.

78. Ibid., 262.

79. Ibid.

80. Ibid., 266.

81. Ibid., 265.

82. Ibid., 282.

83. Ibid., 283.

84. Ibid., 285, Hegel also said: "The struggle of the pure against the impure is a sublime sight, but it soon changes into a horrible one when holiness itself is impaired by unholiness, and when an amalgamation of the two, with the pretension of being pure, rages against fate, because in these circumstances holiness itself is caught in the fate and subject to it" (ibid., 286).

85. Ibid., 291.

86. Ibid., 293–94.

87. "Thus Christianity does not really escape fate. Or rather there is a particular fate which awaits those who try to be above fate, try to withdraw from the divisions of the world. And this seems in some ways worse than what it replaces" (Taylor [1975], 64).

88. "This sliding back into positivity" can be seen to be an "important feature of ongoing Christianity" (ibid.).

89. Nohl (1907), 345–51; *ETW*, 309–19. These are the only extant pages of the MS, and from the numbering of those pages, 34 and 47, and the nature of the contents, it has been concluded that these are only two sheets of a 47-page MS on which Hegel had produced a metaphysical treatise as a systematic presentation of his philosophy.

90. Nohl (1907), 139–51; *ETW*, 167–81. According to Hegel himself, he commenced work on this on 24 September 1800, which was only ten days after the completion of the "Fragment."

91. *ETW*, 309.

92. Ibid., 310.

93. Harris (1972), 386.

94. The reflective intellect is caught in the inevitable contradiction involved in a concept of "an infinitely finite, an unrestricted restrictiveness" (*ETW*, 310–11).

95. Ibid., 311.

96. But it is important to note the nature of this process: "The elevation of the finite to the infinite is only characterized as the elevation of finite life to infinite life, as religion, in virtue of the fact that it does not posit the reality of the infinite as a reality created by reflection, be it objective or subjective, i.e., it has not simply added to the restricted that which restricts. If it had done so, the latter would be recognized again as something posited by reflection and thereby itself restricted and would now again seek what restricts it and would postulate a continuation in such a way ad infinitum. Even this activity of reason is an elevation to the infinite, but this infinite is a [false one]" (ibid., 313).

97. "But life cannot be regarded as union or relation alone but must be regarded as opposition as well. If I say that life is the union of opposition and relation, this union may be isolated again, and it may be argued that union is opposed to non-union. Consequently, I would have to say: Life is the union of union and non-union" (ibid., 312).

98. Hegel himself had said as much as early as *die Liebe*: "In love the separate does still remain, but as something united and no longer as something separate" (ibid., 305).

99. "Finite life rises to infinite life. It is only because the finite is itself life that it carries in itself the possibility of raising itself to infinite life" (ibid., 313).

100. Merold Westphal describes this break in terms of Hegel's adoption, in 1800, of what he (Westphal) anachronistically refers to as the Durkheim principle, viz., that "there are no religions which are false," since all, in some fashion, meet " 'some human need, some aspect of life, either individual or social.' " Merold Westphal, "Hegel's Theory of Religious Knowledge," Weiss (1974), 44.

101. *ETW*, 167–68.

102. Ibid., 169.

103. Ibid., 170.

104. Lukács (1975), 232.

105. *ETW*, 172.

106. Ibid., 173.

107. Ibid., 175–76.

Chapter 4. The Jena Period

1. It must be acknowledged, however, that his views were not in advance of Schelling's regarding the notion of 'development'.

2. *Diff*.

3. *FK.*

4. Fichte (1970), 99.

5. Ibid., 104.

6. This is Fichte's third basic principle: "In the self I oppose a divisible not-self to the divisible self" (ibid., 110).

7. Fichte showed some uneasiness about Schelling's work in 1800, and, although he did not want to lose "his greatest and most gifted ally" against Kant, "right from the start he demurred at the autonomy conferred on nature by Schelling's system. In a letter dated 15 November, 1800 . . . he described Schelling's 'self-construction of nature' (i.e., his objective-idealist view of the objectivity of the categories of nature) as self-deception" (Lukács (1975), 250).

8. Ibid., 246.

9. Schelling (1965) 2:326: Schelling speaks of a higher synthesis in nature, "which must be looked for, without doubt, only in nature, insofar as nature is considered to be absolutely organic."

". . . even the distinction between organic and inorganic nature is an object only in nature, and that nature floats (comprehends) both in its [capacity] of being primordially productive."

10. Ibid., 374.

11. Ibid., 388: "The self-consciousness, from which we depart, is one absolute act, and with this one act, not only the I itself, but all being is determined." Further, "the I is nothing other than a producing which becomes its own object" (ibid., 270).

12. Seidel (1976), 99: Schelling "had moved from a pure self which would bring forth nature, in Fichte, to a nature which would bring forth the self in and through the Absolute which brought the two together, or better, which began the two together."

13. Schelling (1965), 324: "a unity which is self-maintaining, and which, contained within itself, requires no ground outside of itself for its movement and interconnectedness."

14. Lukács (1975), 257.

15. *Diff.*, 79. Also, 81: "The principle of Fichte's system is the pure thinking that thinks itself, the identity of subject and object, in the form of Ego = Ego."

16. Ibid., 82: "Ego = Ego is transformed into the principle 'Ego *ought* to be equal to Ego.' "

17. Ibid.

18. Lukács (1975), 258.

19. *Diff.*, 83.

20. Ibid., 156.

21. *ETW*, 172.

22. *Diff.*, 89.

23. Ibid., 82.

24. Lukács (1975), 262.

25. *FK*, 62.

26. Hyppolite (1969), 19 n. 16.

27. Ibid., 6, 19 n. 16.

28. *FK*, 190.

29. *Diff.*, 89, 91, 93–94.

30. This statement made in *Diff.*, 156, was not a new assertion, for it was one that Hegel had foreshadowed in Frankfurt: e.g., "Life is the union of union and non-union" (*ETW*, 312). What Hegel was striving to achieve during these early Jena years was a more systematic formulation of ideas conceived at an earlier stage; and once that is acknowledged, then it has to be said that to refer to Hegel's "transformed perspective" in Jena (as does Taylor [1975], 67), is to overstate the case. This is not to deny that in Jena, Hegel did develop a transformed perspective regarding some questions (as will be indicated); but, regarding the question of the nature of unity, it is more correct to speak of a more systematic formulation, and not of a "transformed perspective." This is so because there is clear evidence, even in earlier Frankfurt writings, that Hegel had perceived the nature of this unity: e.g., in *die Liebe*, he said: "In love the separate does still remain, but as something united and no longer as something separate" (*ETW*, 305). The problem at that stage was that Hegel was still obviously struggling with the concept and was guilty of inconsistencies: e.g., only a few lines earlier he had said, "genuine love excludes all oppositions" (ibid., 304). But by the end of the Frankfurt period this inconsistency had gone: e.g., "Life . . . must be regarded as opposition as well" (ibid., 312); and in Jena his formulation became much more systematic.

31. It is true that it was the influence of Schelling's work that enabled Hegel to come to his mature philosophy in which these concepts figured so prominently. However, this enabling did not take the form of providing Hegel with novel ideas, but rather the form of furnishing insights by means of which Hegel brought to maturity concepts with which he himself had been struggling for some time. This particularly applies to the notion of development that played such a significant role in the maturing of Hegel's philosophy, enabling him to work out systematically the implications of earlier concepts.

Therefore, in speaking about the influence of others, such as Schelling, upon Hegel's development, it must not be overlooked that there were earlier indications of many of these later prominent concepts: e.g., *Ein Gedachtes kann kein Geliebtes sein* (Nohl [1907], 295). Knox's translation ("A thought cannot be loved" [*ETW*, 247]) really obscures Hegel's meaning, which is that "That which is thought cannot be loved." Here 'thought' was being used in the sense of 'reflective thought', which separates and divides, and, thus, destroys the continuity that love sustains. Therefore, Hegel was intending to contrast reflective thought with love, which spontaneously unites.

In *ETW,* love was understood as the clearest, most intense, form in which the primordial unity is retained. It was this earlier, though somewhat latent, idea that formed the basis of Hegel's concept of continuity and infinity.

32. *FK,* 68.

33. *Diff.,* 155.

34. Ibid.

35. *FK,* 55f. Hegel also recognized this view as the consummation of Protestantism in Northern Europe, not only in these three philosophers, but also in the leading contemporary theologian, Schleiermacher: "The great form of the world spirit that has come to cognizance of itself in these philosophies, is the principle of the North, and from the religious point of view, of Protestantism. This principle is subjectivity for which beauty and truth present themselves in feelings and persuasions, in love and intellect. Religion builds its temples and altars in the heart of the individual. In sighs and prayers he seeks for the God whom he denies to himself in intuition, because of the risk that the intellect will cognize what is intuited as a mere thing, reducing the sacred grove to mere timber" (ibid., 57).

36. Ibid., 64, 62.

37. A common fundamental principle of these philosophies is "the absolute antithesis of finitude and infinity" (ibid., 62).

38. Ibid., 63; cf. *Diff.,* 89–90.

39. *FK,* 72.

40. Ibid., 70.

41. *Diff.,* 156.

42. *FK,* 58. Again it is apparent that Hegel linked the theology of Schleiermacher with the three philosophers whom he was discussing in this essay; and the allusion to Fichte is clear, for it already has been noted how he criticized Fichte on the grounds that in his philosophy the "highest unity" remained an unachievable ideal—a mere *"ought."* Cf. *Diff.,* 117.

43. *Diff.,* 93–94.

44. Hyppolite (1969), 4; also 17.

45. As Hyppolite says, "Hegel resists the notion of a subject that pre-exists its predicates. It is the life of the predicates that creates the subject. An Absolute posited apart from its development cannot be anything but an empty intuition" (ibid., 19 n. 16).

46. Taylor (1975) 72.

47. *WK,* 2:195.

48. These forms of religion, along with Revealed (Absolute) Religion, were to be discussed in detail, at the end of Hegel's Jena period, in *Phen.,* but in a slightly earlier work of that period, he referred to them as being amongst the religions that "are imperfect—either because they recognize only the being, the frightful powers of nature, in which the self is nothing, or else the beautiful religion, the mythical, which is a play, that is not worthy of Being, without thought and depth, where the depth is the unknown fate"

(*JR*, 266–67). (This work is the manuscript of lecture notes Hegel wrote in the autumn of 1805 in preparation for a series of lectures he had announced for the winter semester of 1805–6, but which was probably not delivered until the summer of 1806.)

49. "The thought, the principle, the idea of absolute religion is . . . that God, that absolute Being from outside [*das jenseitige absolute Wesen*] has become man" (ibid., 268).

50. Ibid., 269: "The sacrifice of Divinity, i.e., of the abstract, transcendent Being [*des abstrakten, jenseitigen Wesens*] has already happened in its becoming actual [*Wirklichwerden*]."

51. Ibid.

52. Ibid., 268.

53. Ibid., 267. This, too, Hegel found to be manifest in the actual divine man, of whom he said, "this actuality has sublated itself, has become a past one" (ibid., 268).

54. *ETW*, 313.

55. One product of the reflective intellect, Hegel said, is general ideas such as the concept of human nature, but he felt that such concepts are impoverished of content, for 'pure human nature' has never existed. Yet, this emptiness of the universal concept of human nature did not prevent him from speaking of "an ideal of human nature" that "is quite different from general concepts . . . [for] the ideal does permit of particularization, of determination in detail" (*ETW*, 170). This statement, Lukács observes, "represents the first appearance of Hegel's discovery that . . . true philosophical generalizations . . . become richer and more concrete the higher the level of generalization becomes" (Lukács [1975], 226).

56. Hyppolite (1969), 4.

57. *Diff.*, 106.

58. *Diff.*, 88.

59. "This conscious identity of the finite and infinite, the union of both worlds, the sensuous and the intelligible, the necessary and the free, in consciousness, is *knowledge*" (*Diff.*, 96.) (It is important to note that by 'knowledge' Hegel did not mean any specific knowledge, but *philosophical knowledge*, the knowledge of primordial unity.)

60. Ibid., 114.

61. Ibid., 113.

62. Ibid., 100.

63. Ibid.

64. *FK*, 67.

65. "But religion is the represented [*vorgestellt*, pictured] Spirit, the self, which does not bring together its pure consciousness and its actuality" (*JR*, 268).

66. *Diff.*, 171.

Introduction to Part II

1. *LPR*, 1:47.

2. Barth (1959), 285, 286.

3. As Lauer says, "the entire Hegelian endeavour is essentially religious in character. It is unified around one central theme, knowledge of the absolute, and the absolute, terminologically at least, is identified with God" (Lauer [1977], 89).

4. *LPR*, 1:2.

5. "The object of religion as well as of philosophy is eternal truth in its objectivity, God and nothing but God, and the explication of God. Philosophy . . . is knowledge of that which is eternal, of what God is, and what flows out of His nature. For this His nature must reveal and develop itself. Philosophy, therefore, only unfolds itself when it unfolds religion, and in unfolding itself it unfolds religion. As thus occupied with eternal truth . . . , it is the same kind of activity as religion is" (ibid., 19).

6. *SL*, 824.

7. Barth (1959), 298.

8. Black (1977), 207.

9. *SL*, 824.

10. *LPR*, 1:49–50.

11. Ibid., 29–30.

12. Ibid., 37–41.

13. Cf. W. H. Werkmeister, "Hegel's Phenomenology of Mind as a Development of Kant's Basic Ontology," in Christensen (1970), 100.

14. Lauer (1977), 140.

15. Ibid.

16. Werkmeister, in Christensen (1970), 102.

17. Lauer (1977), 143. As Hegel said, "the infinite shall appear in the finite, and the finite in the infinite, and each no longer form a separate realm" (*LPR*, 1:16.)

18. *Phen.*, 128.

19. Lukács (1975), 468.

20. Taylor (1975), 128.

21. Ibid.

22. *Phen.*, 11: "But the whole is nothing other than the essence consummating itself through its development. Of the Absolute it must be said that it is essentially a *result*, that only in the *end* is it what it truly is; and that precisely in this consists its nature, viz. to be actual, subject, the spontaneous becoming of itself."

23. *LPR*, 3:148.

24. Fackenheim (1970), 10.

25. Lauer (1977), 92.

26. *LPR,* 1:54: Speaking generally, religion "is the ultimate and the highest sphere of human consciousness . . . It is the absolute result—it is the region into which man passes over, as into the domain of absolute truth.

"By reason of this universal character of religion, consciousness must, when in this sphere, have already raised itself above all that is finite."

27. Lauer (1977), 93–94.

28. Commentators differ in their understanding of *Phen.,* but it seems to be generally agreed that initially this work was conceived as an introduction to the system, and that in the writing of it Hegel's intention changed. "What was to have been only an introduction to the system grew on its own and . . . became a self-sufficient whole, an exposition of the entire Hegelian philosophy from a phenomenological point of view" Hyppolite (1974), 53.

29. Lauer (1977), 91.

30. Contrary to D. F. Strauss's complaint that Hegel's *LPR* displayed an "excessive subservience to the religious conception" and his contrasting regard for *Phen.* as Hegel's "fundamental work" (reported by Pannenberg [1969], 3:164), it can be stated that there is no aspect of Hegel's philosophy of religion as enunciated in *LPR* that is not really already contained in *Phen.*

31. *LPR,* 1:19.

32. Ibid., 2:63.

Chapter 5. Phenomenology of Spirit

1. Taylor (1975), 123.

2. Here one can note that Hegel was strongly at variance with Schelling, who stressed the immediacy of 'intellectual intuition'. Hegel's profound divergence from Schelling clearly emerged in *Phen.,* and not least on this matter: to Hegel, the Schellingian method of intellectual intuition was in complete opposition to ordinary modes of cognition, and it also suggested an intellectual elitism since knowledge would be possible only for those who can achieve intellectual intuition. When Hegel said that the process toward knowledge will be something other than "the raptuous enthusiasm which, like a shot from a pistol, begins straight away with absolute knowledge, and makes short work of other standpoints by declaring that it takes no notice of them" (*Phen.,* 16), his disenchantment with Schelling was clearly in the open.

3. Shklar (1976), 1. For the sake of accuracy, the qualifying words 'type of' ought to be added to these words of Shklar.

4. That it was not Hegel's original intention to proceed to such extensive historical explorations seems to be indicated by an absence of any reference to them in the introduction, which, unlike the preface, was written prior to the main body of the work.

5. Lukács (1975), 466, 468.

6. Ibid., 470.

7. Hyppolite (1974), 10.

8. Shklar (1976), 7.

9. *Phen.*, 49.

10. Shklar (1976), 7.

11. Ibid., 8, 1.

12. "The analysis of sense-certainty thus demonstrates the reality of the universal and develops at the same time the philosophic notion of universality. The reality of the universal is proved by the very content of the observable facts; it exists in their process and can be grasped only in and through the particulars" (Marcuse [1967], 104).

13. Ibid., 105.

14. *Phen.*, 70.

15. Norman (1976), 39.

16. Shklar (1976), 17. It has been a step forward, in Hegel's view, because there has been the recognition of "a *supersensible* world which henceforth is the *true* world; above the vanishing *present* world there opens up a permanent *beyond*" (*Phen.*, 87).

17. *Phen.*, 88.

18. Shklar (1976), 23.

19. Marcuse (1967), 113.

20. *Phen.*, 104.

21. Taylor (1975), 148: "The dialectic of self-consciousness is thus a dialectic of human longing and aspiration, and their vicissitudes. . . .

"What is aimed at is integral expression, a consummation where the external reality which embodies us and on which we depend is fully expressive of us and contains nothing alien. This goal, which can be called a state of total integrity, is . . . a condition in which the subject is not limited by anything outside. It is this longing for total integrity which for Hegel underlies the striving of self-consciousness."

22. Ibid., 149.

23. *Phen.*, 110: "*Self-consciousness achieves its satisfaction only in another self-consciousness.*"

24. Norman (1976), 47.

25. Prior (1972), 54.

26. Norman (1976), 48.

27. Such points are very reminiscent of Hegel's earlier writings where 'love' appeared as the integration of opposites and the breaking down of objectivity.

28. Shklar (1976), 27.

29. Prior (1972), 55: "Hegel understands man to be a societal being at the deepest level of his individuality."

30. Taylor (1975), 159.

31. *Phen.*, 139.

32. Taylor (1975), 161.

33. Findlay (1958), 103.

34. Norman (1976), 66.

35. *Phen.*, 142.

36. Ibid., 145.

37. Ibid., 210.

38. Ibid., 211.

39. Ibid., 237.

40. Lauer (1977), 176.

41. Lukács (1975), 486.

42. In this fourth section of *Phen.*—"Spirit"—Hegel was immersed in history, and therefore it does not appear necessary to give any further detail regarding the content of these three stages of 'Spirit'. However, as religion is my chief concern, some aspects of Hegel's analysis of history will be considered subsequently in appropriate contexts within the exposition of Hegel's discussion of religious consciousness.

43. *Phen.*, 265.

44. Ibid., 276.

45. Fackenheim (1970), 45–46.

46. Lauer (1977), 235: "Unlike the phenomenology of human consciousness in general, the phenomenology of religious consciousness does not begin with an individual experience which only gradually becomes aware of its social implications. As Hegel sees it, religious experience is from the beginning a corporate experience, whether of human society as a whole at a given stage or of a segment of that society which is taken as paradigmatic of a stage in the overall development."

47. No mention will be made at this point of any content of the dialectic of religious consciousness because, as this is the material that is the object of my concern, a detailed exposition will be commenced in the next chapter. It is necessary to mention it here, however, in order to place religious consciousness in its context within the whole of the Hegelian dialectic.

48. Hyppolite (1974), 10.

49. Shklar (1976), 8–9.

50. In spite of Hegel's confidence about the *naturalness* of this movement of consciousness, the structure of *Phen.* is the result of Hegel's own creative vision of that movement.

51. Hyppolite (1974), 13. Also, Shklar (1976), 6: Hegel "believed that the dynamics of intellectual change always involved intense conflict, and he meant to show that clearly."

52. In Hyppolite's words, "negation is always *determinate* negation . . . this negation of the immediateness of its knowledge is a new knowledge. . . . To be cognizant of one's error is to be cognizant of another truth; the perceived error implies a new truth" (Hyppolite [1974], 14).

53. Literally, and in its most common usage, *aufheben* means "to pick up" as when something has fallen to the floor; but two other, less common,

meanings have been derived from this, namely, "to cancel" and "to preserve or keep." Kaufmann (1954), 159, explains these derivations and Hegel's use of the term in the following way: "Something may be picked up in order that it will no longer be there; on the other hand, I may also pick it up to keep it. When Hegel uses the term in its double (or triple) meaning . . . he may be said to visualize how something is picked up in order that it may no longer be *there* just the way it was, although, of course, it is not cancelled altogether but lifted up to be kept on a different level."

54. It is this process that Hegel referred to as "the negation of the negation". In describing the dialectic, Christensen (1970), 218, says: "By the term 'Notion', Hegel refers to the whole which is the Truth. At every stage of development of life and consciousness, this is to say, there is a wholeness of apprehension which, as the necessary context of what is apprehended, is Truth in the sense which that perspective admits. Hegel's dialectic is a development of successively more adequate apprehensions of the Notion, each including the essential meaning of what has preceded and been transcended, and each implying the Notion in its completeness. It is the Notion as the actuality being apprehended, moreover, which also does the apprehending. Being inclusive, this is to say, it is inclusive of subject and object as of every other discrimination within reality."

Chapter 6. The Role of Religion

1. Fackenheim (1970), 36. Also, Christensen (1970), 241, says: Hegel "suffered a disadvantage in beginning every major exposition of dialectic following the *Phenomenology* with the Notion full-blown as his already justified starting point."

2. Fackenheim (1970), 37.

3. Ibid., 39.

4. Ibid., 46–47.

5. Ibid., 48.

6. Ibid., 49.

7. *Phen.*, 413.

8. Lauer (1977), 91.

9. *Phen.*, 415.

10. Ibid., 413.

11. *LPR*, 1:61–62.

12. Ibid., 76, 61; *Phen.*, 410. Reardon (1977), 38–39, rightly observes that any description of the growth and development of religions will almost inevitably be done on the basis of some assumptions, which in Hegel's case are those of a metaphysician who "holds that the true origin of religion is not to be sought merely in the empirical antecedents or conditions of its historical appearance and progress, but in the *concept* of religion itself as it exists logically (or in *idea*) in the Absolute Mind itself. In other words, he

thinks that philosophy alone can furnish us with an adequate account of religious origins by placing them within that *ideal* framework of thought by reference to which they can be judged for what they really are—'moments' in an unfolding scheme that is at once logical and historical, temporal and eternal."

13. *LPR*, 1:79. Or, as Robert Perkins says, "The religions of nature, of spiritual individuality, and finally of Christianity are not parts of 'religion as a whole' but rather are progressively more adequate understandings of the whole meaning of religion" (Perkins [1970], 139).

14. *LPR*, 1:77.

15. Ibid., 79. Also, *Phen.*, 414: "From the 'shapes' belonging to each of its moments, the *specific* 'shape' of religion picks out the one appropriate to it for its actual Spirit. The one distinctive feature which characterizes the religion penetrates every aspect of its actual existence and stamps them with this common character."

16. *LPR*, 1:83.

17. *Phen.*, 416.

18. Ibid.: "For the shape raises itself to the form of the self through the creative activity of consciousness, whereby this beholds in its object its act or the self."

19. Lauer (1976), 234.

20. *Phen.*, 416.

Chapter 7. Religion of Nature

1. Ibid., 417: "It is in accordance with the specific character of this 'shape' in which Spirit knows itself that one religion is distinguished from another."

2. Ibid.

3. Ibid.

4. Ibid.

5. *LPR*, 1:265. The lectures obviously contain the much more detailed articulation of Hegel's analysis of the dialectic of religion, and while there are some noticable differences of detail, the general pattern is the same as in *Phen.* The *Phen.* was written at the end of Hegel's Jena period and embodies the framework—namely, the pattern of dialectical development— of his comprehensive system as it was in 1807. While the framework remained unchanged, his more mature years saw it elaborated by the addition of a great deal of empirical data that Hegel gathered in the preparation of his lectures on the history of philosophy and the philosophy of religion. There- fore, in looking at this section of *LPR* it is readily apparent that a great deal of additional material has been included, and that, while the basic dialectical pattern is retained, there are some instances where detail has been fitted into that pattern in a different manner. However, as *Phen.* presented Hegel's view of the whole dialectic of human consciousness, it is *Phen.* that will be

generally followed here, where an attempt is being made to relate the dialectic
of religion to the total dialectic of human consciousness. Nevertheless, *LPR*
will be used for the purpose of elaboration, and differences of detail will
be noted.

6. Ibid., 270.

7. Ibid., 271.

8. Ibid., 273.

9. Ibid., 274–75. The Hegelian distinction between the absolute Being, as
it is *an sich*—its Notion—and its manifestations in the dialectical process is
an important distinction to grasp at the beginning of Hegel's examination
of the specific dialectic of the religious consciousness, and the following
quotation is a useful statement of it:

> Spirit as the essence that is *self-consciousness*—or the self-conscious Being
> that is all truth and knows all reality as its own self—is, to begin with,
> only its *Notion* in contrast to the actuality which it gives itself in the
> movement of its consciousness."
>
> *(Phen.,* 418)

10. *LPR,* 1:286.

11. Ibid., 287.

12. Ibid.

13. Ibid.

14. Ibid., 288, 289.

15. Ibid., 79.

16. Taylor (1975), 145. One can here take note of the fact that early in
Phen. some basic Hegelian themes have emerged. Hegel said, "this pure
being is not an immediacy, but something to which negation and mediation
are essential" *(Phen.,* 61). It is negation and mediation that are among the
central themes in Hegelian thought. Sense-certainty is grounded upon the
claim that the object with which the individual consciousness is confronted
is immediately known, but Hegel has argued that the object is unreachable
in its own particularity and can be grasped only through aspects that it has
in common with other objects. In other words, as soon as we try to grasp
particular objects, "they disappear, so to speak; we can hold onto them only
by subsuming them under a concept. In Hegelian language, our attempt to
grasp things in knowledge first negates them as particulars; then, negating
this negation, we recover them by grasping them through mediated conceptual
consciousness. The immediate is negated, but it is retained in mediated form"
(ibid., 145). There is no immediate knowledge of the particular, only mediated
knowledge.

Furthermore, the unreachable nature of the particular was important to
Hegel, and it is advisable to note it in discussing his philosophy of religion,
because it highlights a truth that is crucial to Hegelian thought. It "is not

just an epistemological truth; it reflects the ontological one that the particular is doomed by its very nature to disappear, . . . What is permanent is the concept. So the unsayability of the particular is simply the expression of its ontological status, as that which cannot remain, . . . And, reciprocally, external particular existence is impermanent because it cannot be expressed in concepts" (ibid., 144).

17. *Phen.*, 60, 61.

18. Ibid., 70.

19. "Things are therefore in and for themselves determinates; they have properties by which they distinguish themselves from others" (ibid., 73).

20. Ibid., 74. One is reminded of the significant statement in Hegel's early writings: "Life is the union of union and nonunion" (*ETW*, 312). Indeed, this chapter on "Perception" in *Phen.* really repeats what he had said about 'life' in the "Fragment of a System".

21. Marcuse (1967), 109.

22. Norman (1976), 41.

23. Ibid., 42.

24. Ibid.

25. *Phen.*, 410.

26. While in *Phen.* the Persian religion of Zoroastrianism is not specifically named, the content of this section makes it apparent that it is this religion that Hegel was using here as an example of this elementary stage of religious consciousness. Any possible doubt about this is removed when this content is compared with the content of that section of *LPR* where Hegel did specifically name the religion of Zoroaster. In *LPR* Hegel examined the details of that religion, but in doing so, he no longer placed it as a most rudimentary kind of religious consciousness—instead, that position was attributed to magic.

27. *Phen.*, 419.

28. Ibid.

29. Ibid. Elsewhere, Hegel said that the religion of nature "contains more truth than that found in immediate knowledge" because it "already contains this consciousness of the Divine as being the substantial element, which is at the same time determined, and thus has the form of a natural mode of existence" (*LPR*, 1:328).

30. In contrast to *Phen.*, in *LPR* it is magic that Hegel described as "the absolutely primary form of religion," in which it is felt that "the Spiritual is the ruling power over nature" (*LPR*, 1:290–91). Also, it seems that, at least at this point, Hegel had not rigorously adhered to the features of the dialectic of consciousness, as he did in *Phen.*; yet, even so, that adherence is fairly solid. As in *Phen.*, in *LPR* this type of religion is built on an awareness of spiritual existence that is quite formless and indeterminate; and as in the rudimentary form of consciousness, it is about the individual consciousness who is nothing more than a part of nature, which is nothing more than

particulars that stand 'out there', over against the individual consciousness—there is no awareness of the Universal. But, whereas in *Phen.* the passivity of human consciousness is a feature of its primary stage of development, in *LPR*, regarding magic, "human consciousness . . . is recognized as the ruling power over nature in virtue of his own will" (ibid., 293). Yet, again, the lack of concern for the Universal is displayed by the fact that this attempt to rule over nature is motivated by purely particular, individualistic, selfish and immediate purposes. Further, whereas in *Phen.*, in the "religion of light", Spirit was perceived as manifested in the light of the rising Sun, in *LPR* the Spiritual is "the ruling power *over* nature."

31. *Phen.*, 419.

32. Taylor (1975), 200.

33. *Phen.*, 420.

34. Ibid.

35. *LPR*, 1:317.

36. Ibid., 324.

37. Ibid.

38. Ibid.

39. Ibid., 320.

40. Ibid., 325.

41. *Phen.*, 420.

42. Lauer (1976), 237. It is clear, however, that in *Phen.* Hegel's treatment of this stage of religious consciousness displays a less developed knowledge of religions than in *LPR*, and that his comments are confined to very primitive forms of religion; whereas in *LPR* his discussion includes a comparatively lengthy treatment of Chinese religion, Hinduism, and Buddhism. While Hegel's breadth of knowledge of these and other religions was definitely remarkable, he was quite harsh in his judgments of them, as is immediately indicated by his placing them at this very primitive stage of the development of religious consciousness. Also, a general point of Hegel's attack on this type of religion is one that comes out more fully—and will be dealt with below—in relation to Spinoza, namely, that "substance is not conceived of as the active agent within itself, as subject and as activity in accordance with ends; . . . It is something devoid of content; . . . It is essentially purposeless empty power, which merely staggers about, so to speak" (*LPR*, 1:333).

43. *Phen.*, 421.

44. *LPR*, 2:66–67.

45. *Phen.*, 421: "a form produced by the self, or rather is the produced self, the self-consuming self, i.e., the self that becomes a Thing."

46. Ibid.: "an instinctive operation, like the building of a honeycomb by bees."

47. Taylor (1975), 200.

48. *Phen.*, 421.

49. Ibid., 422.

50. Ibid., 423.

51. Again, the material in *LPR* is much more extensive and is heavily philosophical in contrast to the brief and more historical survey in *Phen.*, and the result is that the kind of material that has been presented here in *Phen.* is really paralleled to any degree only in the section on the "Worship and Cultus" of the "Religion of Mystery". It was Egyptian religion that Hegel was discussing as "Religion of Mystery", but he did not speak only about "Worship and Cultus", for that was preceded by an analysis of "the determination of the Notion of this stage" and of "the concrete idea belonging to this stage". And not only did he speak of "Religion of Mystery" or Egyptian religion, but he also dealt, according to the same pattern, with "the religion of the Good or of Light", or Zoroastrianism, and "the Syrian religion or the religion of Pain".

The inclusion of Zoroastrianism at this point in *LPR* perhaps can be explained only by the fact that here Hegel was presenting a more mature philosophical analysis as opposed to one that was predominantly historical. The "determination of God" in this religion is Light or the Good, which are identical directly and not merely in the sense that one is the outward symbol of the other (*LPR*, 2:77–78). What is achieved in this religion, in Hegel's view, is, first, the idea that "the Good contains determinateness within itself, and in determinateness is the root of the natural existence" (ibid., 75); and secondly, that determination or manifestation can be made real only through the opposite—Light "must strike upon something that is dark" (ibid., 76), and Zoroastrianism supports this in its double principle of Light (Good) and Darkness (Evil). However, the kind of determinateness that is present here is merely "abstract determinateness"—of "nature generally, of Light" (ibid., 75)—it is not concrete; and moreover, the distinction between Light and Dark is absolute and results in an external dualism, and so, in this form of religion, Spirit is not yet Spirit.

The advance that Hegel found—"the essential determinations of the Idea of Spirit which now make their appearance" (ibid., 83)—in Syrian religion or the "religion of Pain" is the disappearance of absolute dualism through the concept of "the annulling of the opposition" by "absorption into infinite unity" (ibid.). The concept of opposition now becomes that of something that is internal, and this is an important new stage in the unfolding nature of Spirit, expressed in this kind of religion in the death-and-resurrection myths; but here it remains at the level of myth, and its true meaning—"the absolute mediation which essentially belongs to the notion or conception of Spirit" (ibid., 85)—is not grasped.

In the "Religion of Mystery", Hegel said, we "approach more nearly to the realm of real actual subjectivity" (ibid., 88), although "we are as yet only in the transition to subjectivity," for "there is still an intermixture here of substantial unity and subjectivity" (ibid., 93). Since there is still the concept of the Other being outside, God is still 'the inner nature' but takes some external form, and that form is an arbitrary and accidental one—"this or the other human or animal form" (ibid., 94. Hegel seems closest here to the material of *Phen.*). But again Hegel's maturer and more penetrating analysis led him to specify another important aspect of this religion, namely, that negation is part of the subject: "Here we have God as subjectivity generally, and the most important moment in it is that negation is not found outside, but is already within the subject itself, and the subject is essentially a return into itself, is self-contained existence" (ibid., 96). Hegel found this in the presence of death and the stress on resurrection in the Egyptian cult of Osiris. However, it is still "subjectivity generally"; and the higher conception, namely, "that negation is that which is posited by Spirit" (ibid., 97), is not yet attained.

52. *Phen.*, 423. In order "to understand the peculiar position of Art at this stage, we have to recollect that subjectivity does, as a matter of fact, begin to appear here, but as yet only so far as its basis is concerned, and that its concept or idea still passes over into that of substantiality" (*LPR*, 2:111). And anticipating what he obviously regarded as a superior form, he said, "the Spirit of the Egyptian notion is, in fact, an enigma. In Greek works of art everything is clear, everything is evident; in Egyptian art a problem is everywhere presented; it is an external sign, by means of which something which has not been yet openly expressed is indicated" (ibid., 114).

53. Reardon (1977), 50. "Subjectivity is not yet grasped in its absolute universality and spiritual nature. Thus it is superficial, external universality" (*LPR*, 2:106).

54. Lauer (1976), 237.

55. *Phen.*, 424.

Chapter 8. Religion in the Form of Art

1. Lauer (1976), 238.

2. *LPR*, 2:124.

3. Ibid., 127.

4. Ibid., 125.

5. *Phen.*, 424, 425.

6. Hyppolite (1974), 548. And correspondingly, in *LPR* there occurs "the Religion of Spiritual Individuality", though there Hegel included more than Greek religion.

7. Norman (1976), 43.

8. Ibid. This is precisely what Hegel had said earlier in the "Fragment of a System."

9. *Phen.*, 425: "Since the ethical nation lives in immediate unity with its substance and lacks the principle of the pure individuality of self-conscious-

ness, the complete form of its religion first appears as *divorced* from *[im Scheiden]* its existential shape *[Bestehen]*."

10. Ibid., 426.

11. Ibid., 425.

12. Ibid., 426.

13. *LPR*, 2:122ff.

14. Ibid., 124.

15. Ibid., 132.

16. Ibid., 127.

17. Ibid., 175.

18. *Phen.*, 426: "This form is the night in which substance was betrayed and made itself into Subject. It is out of this night of pure certainty of self that the ethical Spirit is resurrected as a shape freed from Nature and its own immediate existence."

19. In the Jewish religion, God, as the absolute One, is primarily conceived of as Power. He is creator of the world, which he produced out of nothing and which is totally dependent on him for its existence and preservation, for "natural things have no substantiality or independence in themselves, and the Divine is only in the One" (*LPR*, 2:184–85). The world, as a mere collection of such natural things, is really nothingness—not in the sense of mere illusion, but in comparison with the Divine—and so is totally inadequate to express or manifest the Divine.

That Hegel perceived this to be the basic tenet of this religion is indicated by the fact that he called it "Religion of Sublimity", and this sublimity is found in the concept of God that so directly distinguishes him, as absolute Power, totally above the wholly dependent natural order.

This concept of God, therefore, does present God as Subject who is active in creation, but also as a Subject who comes to stand in an external relation to the material world over which he has complete manipulative control and in which he can manifest himself in a miraculous manner—miracles thus being perceived as the occasional intervention of God through the setting aside of the natural function of things. Thus it is no surprise that it was here that Hegel identified the first inadequacy of this religion. God may be Subject, but he is not really conceived as Spirit (ibid., 178), for Spirit "is simply what mediates self within self" (ibid., 175), revealing nature to be not an external other that is inadequate as a manifestation of God, but as the self-manifestation of Spirit.

However, according to Jewish religion, not only does God let his power be known in his creation, he also declares his wisdom; and this wisdom is revealed by the fact that Creation is arranged in accordance with an end. What may be called the theoretic end here is religion as such, viz., that God, who stands in an objective affirmative relation to self-consciousness, "should be recognized, known, honoured by consciousness" (ibid., 190–91). This produced the moral end, the fundamental requirement to do what is right in accordance with the divine moral law, which, in turn, gave rise to the conviction that all would—and indeed ought—to go well with those who so lived. Hegel perceived this confident faith to be "a fundamental and praiseworthy trait of the Jewish people," for this confidence in the one God, which contained "the consciousness of this harmony of the power, and at the same time of the wisdom and righteousness of God, is based on the thought that God is determined within Himself as end, and has an end" (ibid., 193–94). But, Hegel said, the Jewish people failed to grasp the potential of this thought: although God was perceived as absolute wisdom, it was only in the sense of an abstract wisdom; the notion of end or purpose in the divine, in itself, was devoid of content, with the result that in actual existence this indeterminate end in the notion itself becomes thoroughly limited and particular. Thus, another insufficiency of the Jewish religion is that it possesses "the most rigid possible contrast. God is, on the one hand, the God of heaven and of earth, absolute wisdom, universal power, and the end aimed at by this God is at the same time so limited that it concerns only one family, only this one people" (ibid., 196).

This exclusiveness is not surprising, for as Hegel observed, the close connection between religion and nationality was a feature of Oriental countries. But the extent of the exclusiveness is most striking here because of the contrast with the Jewish idea of God: although God is the creator of all things and the Lord of history, he is the God of this particular people, and there is little evidence (and that only in later writers) of the thought that he may have acted amongst other peoples (ibid., 210). The exclusive relationship between God and this particular people was thought to have been inaugurated by God himself adopting them as his people by means of a covenant and contract. But the basis of this contract, according to Hegel, was "the conditions of fear and service" (ibid., 211): the people's part of the contract was service in the form of conformity to the divinely given law, and their motivation was the fear produced by the idea of a superior power above them; and it was this that gave rise to exclusiveness "because the servile consciousness rests obstinately on its particularity" (ibid., 208). Furthermore, the idea of a contractual relationship between God and man does not admit "an original and immediate unity in union with the Essence, as is the case in the Religion of Nature," for the relation is certainly not seen to be essential and original, and is established only in an external way (ibid., 211–12). This is naturally reflected in the worship or cultus of the Jewish people, in which the act of sacrifice is a testimony of divine power, that God is to be feared, and that the individual, in "his standing before God, has no worth." Clearly, then, for Hegel, Jewish religion is deficient also because in it "man does not yet possess the feeling of his concrete freedom" (ibid., 219); yet, of course, from the dialectic of the master and slave, Hegel regarded the attitude of servitude as the means by which the servant may find that freedom. Indeed, that dialectic, which demonstrates

Hegel's discussion of the 'dependence and independence of self-consciousness', provides a key here. In this "Religion of Sublimity", God is 'holy other', and the relationship of the people to God is based on fear and service, and is one of total dependence. God is other and independent, and the people are dependent on God for their life and for their own recognition of who they are—God's chosen People.

20. Ibid., 224.

21. Ibid.

22. Ibid., 229.

23. Here we find the initial evidence of what Hegel identified as appearing more and more clearly throughout the dialectic of Greek religion, viz., "the unity of the spiritual and the natural" (ibid., 232), which marks this kind of religious consciousness as the means of achieving the transition to true Spirit, for it brings the realization that "what is posited is itself the positing factor" (ibid., 231). Accordingly, the Greeks did not "people Nature with gods" as in the Religion of Nature, for their principle of subjective freedom meant that the natural itself is not "worthy to constitute the content of the divine." But the Greeks still did not attain the Idea, the absolutely free subjectivity, so that, though spiritual, "the content of free subjectivity is still particular; . . . [and] since Spirit has not itself for its object, the particularity is still natural, and is even still presented as the one essential characteristic in the spiritual gods" (ibid., 234). As concrete subjective spirituality, these gods "unite in themselves several characteristics" (ibid., 246), and requiring "the sensuous for its essential representation," the divine "appears as a multiplicity of gods," which indicated to Hegel that still it is "not Spirit as Spirit that is here represented" (ibid., 256).

24. Lauer (1976), 239. In *LPR* Hegel said that in contrast to the limited and inadequate content of the externalization of infinitude through animal life, Greek religion marks thinking man's realization that "the spiritual is expressed in his particular conditions also." Two important concepts follow from this: firstly, "that man even in any one limited condition is at the same time above it, transcends it, is free, and does not go outside of himself, continues to be at home with himself; and secondly, "man has not only this element of mere life, but has likewise an infinite range of higher ways of expressing himself, of higher deeds and ends, the constituent element of which is just the Infinite, the Universal" (*LPR*, 2:252).

25. *Phen.*, 428.

26. Ibid., 429: "to himself as a particular individuality he gave in his work no actual existence."

27. Ibid.

28. Ibid., 429–30.

29. Ibid., 430. The word translated "inspired" is *Geseelte*—meaning "besouled" because it can *talk to us*.

30. Ibid.: The hymn "retains within itself the individuality of self-consciousness, and this individuality is at the same time heard as a universal individuality that is immediately present."

31. Taylor (1975), 204.

32. *Phen.*, 430.

33. Ibid.

34. The kind of perceived manifestation of the divine, of which oracles are an example, is one in which there are said to be two sides, one pertaining to the god and one to the finite spirit. The former is seen as the god revealing himself, but the latter as the merely passive reception by self-consciousness. In anticipation of the perception of 'the Notion', however, Hegel observed that "this double activity is to be conceived of as one" (*LPR*, 2:246, 247).

35. *Phen.*, 431.

36. *LPR*, 2:278.

37. *Phen.*, 432.

38. Taylor (1975), 204.

39. Hyppolite (1974), 551.

40. *Phen.*, 434.

41. Ibid., 433.

42. Taylor (1975), 204. In *LPR* Hegel stated that "the service of God is a reciprocal giving and receiving. Each side gives up something of the particularity which separates it from the other" (*LPR*, 2:267). The Greek sacrifices symbolized this, particularly because they expressed the right concept of the nature of overcoming particularity: they were not "a renunciation, not the offering up of a possession," but rather "an enjoyment" (ibid., 269)—an enjoyment of natural gifts and the affirmation of the concrete fullness of Spirit (ibid., 268); and such an affirmation of the whole of life contained the concept of the overcoming of separating particularity.

43. *Phen.*, 435.

44. Ibid.

45. Ibid., 435–36. Regarding Greek religion in *LPR*, Hegel said that "the gods are duly recognized and revered; they are the substantial powers, the essential, real content of the natural and spiritual universe, the Universal. . . . Thus the world no longer exists for [man] in an external and contingent fashion, but in the true mode. We thus hold in respect duty, justice, knowledge, political life, life in the State, family relationships. . . . The Greek people are hence the most human people. . . . This religion is essentially a religion of humanity" (*LPR*, 2:257).

46. *Phen.*, 437.

47. Ibid., 438.

48. See above, pp. 145–46. Cf. *LPR*, 2:269: It is "not a question of calling a power back to oneself from its place beyond what is here and now, nor of renouncing what, on the subjective side of self-consciousness, constitutes the separation, in order that man may be receptive of the power. It is thus

not a question of deprivation or renunciation, or of the laying aside of something subjective belonging to the individual, nor does the idea of anguish, of self-tormenting, or self-torture come in here. The worship of Bacchus or of Ceres is the possession, the enjoyment of bread and wine, the consumption of these, and is therefore itself the immediate granting of these things."

49. *Phen.*, 438.

50. Ibid.

51. In *LPR* Hegel said that in the representation of the divine in such activities as the Greek festivals, "the divine is revered and acknowledged," for so long as they were freshly and actively produced, they were a means whereby "the subject makes the god present through himself, and makes the god manifest in his own self," and so the divine is seen to be in "the sphere of actual reality" (*LPR*, 2:272, 273).

52. *Phen.*, 439.

53. Lauer (1976), 241.

54. *Phen.*, 439.

55. Ibid., 440.

56. Ibid.

57. Ibid., 441.

58. Ibid., 441–42.

59. Hyppolite (1974), 555. In *LPR* Hegel observed that the Greek who had within him the feeling of this kind of necessity knew only "the pressure of its iron power, in the face of which he could have only obedience and no inner freedom. Yet such a Greek calmed his soul simply by resigning to the fact that *it is so*"; and those who occupied this standpoint could have no aim or interest other than actually existing circumstances and so "retreated into this pure rest, into this pure Being, into this *is*" (*LPR*, 2:240–41).

60. *Phen.*, 443.

61. Hyppolite (1974), 555.

62. The Hegelian concept of 'fate' is essential to the understanding of his analysis of Greek society, but it, in turn, can be understood only in the light of the extremely crucial Hegelian conviction that the universal must be embodied in some particular, which, *qua* particular, is transient. The particular therefore is both posited by and negated by the universal, and can be reconciled with the particular only if the particular understands and identifies with this process. Failure to understand this process will cause the particular to regard its transience as an inscrutable fate; and any identifying of a universal with some particular will cause the universal to be seen also as passing away with that particular, and thus as being just as subject to blind fate as are particulars. Although they were an attempt to understand this process, Hegel found such a position to be reflected in Greek Tragedies just as much as the blind fate of particulars was reflected in the Epic.

63. *Phen.*, 444.

64. Lauer (1976), 243.

65. *Phen.*, 447.

66. These matters were similarly expressed in Hegel's discussion of Greek religion in *LPR*. Showing some development from the mere acceptance of fate—"what is devoid of thought"—which involved the simple "identity of the subjective will with that which *is*," the Tragedy demonstrated that "destiny moves within a certain sphere of moral justice." In the Tragedy the heroes "bring about an alteration in the course of simple necessity," asserting their duty to act in accordance with moral laws. But that assertion gives rise to a division in moral law—that of the family and that of the State—and hence, an inevitable collision. Nowhere is this more nobly expressed than in *Antigone*. Both laws "are recognized as having a value of their own," but they are nevertheless marked by a one-sidedness that results in injustice, and it is this "one-sidedness in their claims which justice comes forward to oppose." Thus, there is a discarding of the one-sidedness—a 'going-under' of the parochial universal—which "reveals itself outwardly in the fact that the individuals, who have aimed at the realization in themselves of a single separate moral power, perish" (*LPR*, 2:263–65). The Tragedy therefore did not escape the notion of an inscrutable fate; and so, regarding Greek religion, Hegel said that "there yet remains for consciousness a 'Beyond'." Man "still feels the need of having above his particular acts and particular lot, an objective determining principle. He does not possess this in the thought of divine wisdom and Providence so as to be able to trust it in general, . . ." (ibid., 274, 275).

67. Taylor (1975), 206.

68. *Phen.*, 452–53.

69. *LPR*, 2:284: ". . . the pictorial representations of comedy, and the giving up by Spirit of its dignity, of its value, of its opinion of itself, and even of its fundamental powers, this entire surrender of all that belongs to self, is just this worship in which the spirit, through this surrender of all that is finite, enjoys and retains the indestructible certainty of itself."

70. Taylor (1975), 206.

71. Hyppolite (1974), 557.

72. The community is "absolute Spirit realized in the plurality of existent consciousness; . . . It is Spirit which is *for itself* in that it preserves itself in its reflection in individuals; and it is *implicitly* Spirit, or substance, in that it preserves them within itself" (*Phen.*, 267).

73. Ibid., 268.

74. Ibid., 290.

75. Ibid., 289.

76. Ibid., 290.

77. Ibid., 293.

78. Ibid.: "consciousness was driven *back* into itself from this actuality."

79. Ibid., 290–91: "What was for Stoicism only the *abstraction* of an *intrinsic* reality is now an *actual* world. Stoicism is nothing else but the consciousness

which reduces to its abstract form the principle of legal status, an independence that lacks the life of Spirit."

80. Ibid., 291.

81. *LPR*, 2:298–305. "The gods are degraded to the rank of means" (ibid., 290).

82. Ibid., 301.

83. Ibid., 294–96.

84. Ibid., 317.

85. Ibid., 290.

86. Ibid., 317.

87. Ibid.

88. Ibid., 319.

89. Ibid., 322: It was "the opposition of Spirit to Spirit in its most complete form."

90. Ibid., 320–22.

91. Ibid., 297: "when, as in the Christian religion, it is said that God wills that *all* men should come to a consciousness of the truth, the nature of the end is spiritual. Each individual is thought of as a thinking being, as spiritual, free, and actually present in the end, it possesses in him a central point, it is not any kind of external end, and the subject embraces within himself the entire extent of the end."

92. Ibid., 323.

93. Fackenheim (1970), 138. Fackenheim expresses (157) his dissatisfaction with the standard accounts of Hegel's treatment of these religions that simply summarize the dialectical sequence—indeed, as has been done here—because he feels that such accounts are in danger of easily implying that "the dialectically later is *ipso facto* spiritually superior." However, it seems that the Jewish base from which Fackenheim works has led him to make too much of this point: he certainly is correct in pointing out that the dialectically later is not necessarily spiritually superior, but it seems that the real point to be made is that Hegel was not particularly concerned to make a judgment about the spiritual superiority of these religions. Hegel presented all of them as deficient in some manner, while also identifying the positive contribution of each in the dialectic of religious consciousness that comes to fulfillment in primitive Christianity, which he clearly presented as *the* spiritually superior religion, manifesting the spirit of love, the true *Begriff*.

Chapter 9. Absolute Manifest Religion

1. *Phen.*, 453.

2. *Phen.*, 455.

3. Taylor (1975), 207.

4. The God described in *LPR* as "self-consciousness, [who] knows Himself in a consciousness which is distinct from Him . . . He distinguishes Himself

from Himself, and is an object for Himself, but . . . in this distinction He is purely identical with Himself, is in fact Spirit" (*LPR,* 2:327).

5. *Phen.,* 457.

6. Ibid., 459.

7. Hyppolite (1974), 68.

8. *Phen.,* 140.

9. Ibid., 140–41.

10. "The immediate existence of *Reason,* . . . and its peculiar shapes, have no religion, because the self-consciousness of them knows or seeks *itself* in the *immediate* present" (ibid., 410).

11. Ibid., 459.

12. *LPR,* 2:327, 330.

13. Ibid., 329, 330.

14. *Phen.,* 459.

15. Ibid., 459–60.

16. Ibid., 459. *LPR,* 2:328: "Here it is revealed what God is; He is no longer a Being above and beyond this world, an Unknown, for He has told men what He is. . . . We have here, accordingly, the religion of the manifestation of God, since God knows Himself in the finite spirit. This simply means that God is revealed."

17. *Phen.,* 460.

18. Ibid.

19. *LPR,* 2:334.

20. Ibid.

21. Ibid., 335.

22. *Phen.,* 460.

23. Ibid.

24. Hyppolite (1974), 559.

25. *LPR,* 2:335.

26. Ibid., 346–47.

27. Ibid., 3:4.

28. Ibid., 7: "Thus, regarded in the element of thought, God is, so to speak, outside of or before the creation of the world. In so far as He is thus in Himself, He represents the eternal Idea which is not yet posited in its reality, but is itself as yet merely the abstract Idea."

29. Ibid. The notion of absolute Spirit *an sich* corresponds to the Idea, in abstraction from its embodiment, with which Hegel dealt in his *Logic,* which he spoke of as "the exposition of God as he is in his eternal essence before the creation of nature and a finite mind" (*SL,* 50).

30. Merold Westphal, in Weiss (1974), 53. Cf. *LPR,* 1:61: "the notion occupies the first place . . . the notion is the content itself, the absolute subject-matter, the substance, as in the case of the germ, out of which the whole tree develops itself. All specifications or determinations are contained in this, the whole nature of the tree, the kind of sap it has, the way in

which the branches grow; but in a spiritual manner, and not pre-formed so that a microscope could reveal its boughs, its leaves, in miniature. It is thus that the notion contains the whole nature of the object, and knowledge itself is nothing else than the development of the notion."

31. *Phen.*, 465.

32. This is, for Hegel, an important aspect of difference between absolute religion and the religion of Israel. Cf. *LPR*, 2:176, 178.

33. *Phen.*, 464.

34. Hyppolite (1974), 564.

35. *Phen.*, 466–67. One is aware of how reminiscent this is of concepts Hegel employed in *ETW*, such as in the fragment "On Love." Also cf. *LPR*, 3:10: ". . . differences are done away with in so far as this differentiation just means that the difference is actually shown to be no difference, and thus the One is at home with itself in the Other.

"The fact that this is so is just what is meant by Spirit, or, expressed in terms of feeling, by eternal love."

36. *LPR*, 3:11: "This eternal Idea, accordingly, finds expression in the Christian religion under the name of the Holy Trinity, and this is God Himself, the eternal Triune God."

37. Lauer (1976), 250.

38. McTaggart (1901), 201–5. "According to Hegel's exposition, the Father and the Son are the Thesis and Antithesis of a triad of which the Holy Ghost is the Synthesis. It will follow from this that the Holy Ghost is the sole reality of the Trinity" (ibid., 204).

39. *Phen.*, 465. Also, *LPR*, 3:11: Men "believe in it . . . although they apprehend it only in the form of a popular or figurative idea, without being conscious of the necessary nature, of this truth, and without grasping it in its entirety or comprehending it."

40. *Phen.*, 466.

41. *LPR*, 3:10, 12.

42. For example, ibid., 12: "God is the beginning; He does this definite thing; but He is equally the end only, the totality, and it is as totality that God is Spirit. God thought of simply as Father is not yet the True."

43. Ibid.: "What [God] thus distinguishes from Himself does not take on the form of something which is other than Himself; but, on the contrary, what is thus distinguished is nothing more nor less than that from which it has been distinguished." Cf. ibid., 1:91–93.

44. Ibid. 3:12.

45. Ibid., 22.

46. Whittemore (1960), 151.

47. *LPR* 3:33.

48. Hyppolite (1974), 565.

49. *Phen.*, 467; cf. *EL*, §244.

50. *Phen.*, 467.

51. Hyppolite (1974), 565.

52. *LPR*, 3:35: "This act of differentiation is merely a movement, a playing of love with itself, in which it does not get to be otherness or Other-being in any serious sense, nor actually reach a condition of separation and division."

53. Ibid., 40–41. These matters have a great deal of bearing on the fundamental question to be examined in Part 3 of this book, and therefore further discussion will be postponed till then.

54. Ibid., 42–43.

55. Ibid., 45.

56. *Phen.*, 467–68.

57. Ibid., 468: "Evil appears as the primary existence of the inwardly-turned consciousness."

58. As Hegel asserted, when discussing these narratives in the context of Judaism, the fundamental note of that account is "that man ought not to have passed beyond that first condition" (*LPR*, 2:202).

59. Taylor (1975), 212: "it is necessary for finite spirit, since spirit is necessarily consciousness of self, and since it is embodied in particularity, its self-consciousness will inevitably be a raising to separate consciousness of particularity. The only way of avoiding this would be for man to remain sunk in nature, unconscious of self like an animal, and hence below both good and evil."

60. *LPR*, 3:54: The serpent "says that Man by the act of eating would become equal to God, . . . God says to Himself, Adam is become as one of us. The serpent had thus not lied, for God confirms what it said."

61. Taylor (1975), 491: Without the Fall, Taylor says (regarding Hegel's view), "God could not be truly God, he could not come to self-realization for he would lack an adequate vehicle. God must have a finite spirit, a will, to come to self-knowledge in; but the birth of the finite will is the Fall. The Fall is thus necessary, an essential step to union with God. Or speculatively speaking, Geist is only *Geist* by returning to itself out of alienation from itself."

62. *LPR*, 3:63.

63. Ibid., 66–67.

64. Ibid., 75–76.

65. Taylor (1975), 208; Findlay (1958), 139.

66. Findlay (1958), 139.

67. *Phen.*, 458. "*sich seiner entäußert, und Ich für das Bewußtsein wird*" (*Phän.*, 527). *Aes.*, 541: "Christ is *divine* love; . . . what is manifest is on the one hand God himself in his invisible essence, and, on the other, mankind which is to be redeemed; and thus what then comes into appearance in Christ is less the absorption of one person in another limited person than the Idea of love in its universality, the Absolute, . . . With this universality of love's object, love's expression is also universalized."

Regarding the use of the term 'God-Man', Hegel said, "This is the extraordinary combination which directly contradicts the Understanding; but the unity of the divine and human natures has here been brought into human consciousness and has become a certainty for it, implying that the otherness, or, as it is also expressed, the finitude, the weakness, the frailty of human nature is not imcompatible with this unity, just as in this eternal Idea, otherness in no way detracts from the unity which God is.

"This is the extraordinary combination the necessity of which we have seen. It involves the truth that the divine and human natures are not implicitly different" (LPR, 3:76–77).

68. LPR, 3:77.

69. Ibid., 78–82.

70. Ibid., 86–89.

71. Ibid., 91, 98.

72. Phen., 461.

73. Lauer (1976), 248.

74. Phen., 462.

75. LPR, 3:99.

76. Lauer (1976), 248. Aes., 543: "the immediate existence of Christ, as this one individual man who is God, is posited as superseded, i.e. what comes to light in the very appearance of God as man is the fact that the true reality of God is not immediate existence but spirit. The . . . absolute existence of God as pure universality . . . is . . . not restricted to this individual [Jesus] who in his history has made visible the reconciliation of human and divine personality, but is broadened into the human consciousness which is reconciled with God, in short into mankind which exists as a plurality of individuals." See also Phen., 471.

77. Taylor (1975), 210. Taylor again correctly observes, though elsewhere and in a more critical context (492), that the Resurrection and Ascension "are never really treated separately by Hegel." However, one might add that neither does the author of the Fourth Gospel, and therefore ask whether this is another indication of the influence of that Gospel upon Hegel.

78. Findlay (1958), 143.

79. Hyppolite (1974), 567.

80. Phen., 463.

81. LPR, 3:6.

82. Ibid., 101.

83. Ibid., 104. In EM §554, Hegel said that in the contemporary emphasis on the subjective side of religion—on "God's indwelling in us"—there was at least that which he regarded as "the correct principle that God must be apprehended as spirit in his community."

84. LPR, 3:107.

85. John E. Smith, "Hegel's Reinterpretation of the Doctrine of Spirit and Religious Community," Christensen (1970), 162: "The third form, or Spirit

proper, is that of individuality and represents God as returning to himself in the spiritual community, having already been manifest as the eternal Idea in itself in the Kingdom of the Father, and in the element of consciousness and ordinary thought which coincides with the Kingdom of the Son. In the first stage, God is, as it were, beyond time in the eternal idea; in the second stage, time differentiates into past and future so that God becomes manifest in time. In the third stage, which Hegel repeatedly describes as *present*, Spirit establishes that present as Truth which cannot be wholly contained by either the past or the future but transcends both. The consciousness of the presence of God immediately in the community is at the same time the proper apprehension of the present."

86. *LPR*, 3:120.

87. Ibid., 121.

88. Ibid., 114–15, 121; John E. Smith, in Christensen (1970), 167–68.

89. *LPR*, 3:125.

90. Ibid., 129.

91. Ibid., 132, 129.

92. Ibid., 134. This distinction between Spiritual Community as an inward reality and the partial reflection of it in worldly existence was presented by Hegel in *Phen.* by means of two terms: *Die Gemeinde,* which is the more usual term for community; and *die Gemeine,* which is much more unusual. The former was, however, used by Hegel to refer to the ideal, inward Spiritual Community *(Aber seine Wahrheit ist . . . die Bewegung, welche [der absolute Geist] in seiner Gemeinde vollbringt),* while the latter was used to refer to the partial, imperfect historical expression of that Community *(die Vorstellungen der ersten unvollkomnen Gemeine). Phän.,* 532.

This usage of *Gemeine* can be traced back to Luther: "The conceptual elucidation [of *Gemeinde*] was first undertaken by M. Luther who pointedly translates *ekklesia* not as *Kirche* [Church] but as *ein christliche Gemeine oder Sammlung* [a Christian *Gemeine* or assembly]" (Ritter [1974], 238).

93. *Phen.,* 462.

94. Ibid., 463: "This *form of picture-thinking* constitutes the specific mode in which Spirit in this community *(Gemeine)* became aware of itself. This form is not yet Spirit's self-consciousness that has advanced to its Notion *qua* Notion."

95. Taylor (1975), 211: "Hegel's reading of Christian religion and theology can therefore only be understood in the light of this final stage of the community which is the self-conscious vehicle of *Geist,* the community which is the true man-God. But Christianity has not yet fully realized this. Rather it lives this community implicitly, . . . in a muddled and obscure way, in a mode of consciousness which Hegel calls 'representation', that is, a mode of awareness which operates with images and symbols and not in the full clarity of conceptual thought."

96. Hyppolite (1974), 567.

97. Ibid., 569.

98. *LPR*, 2:327–30.

99. It is important to include and take note of the German terms, since the English translation is quite inadequate for the purpose of bringing out this important distinction. See *VPR* 17:194.

100. *LPR*, 2:336–38.

101. *Phen.*, 126.

102. Ibid., 127.

103. Lauer (1976), 119.

104. *Phen.*, 128.

105. Ibid.

106. Ibid.: The particular finds "the Unchangeable is a form of individuality like itself."

107. Ibid.

108. Ibid., 129.

109. Ibid.

110. Ibid., 130.

111. Ibid., 131.

112. Ibid.

113. Indeed, Hegel was not opposed to ceremonies as such, for in his earlier writings (Nohl [1907], 20) he had stressed the importance of ceremonies in religious practice that should not neglect the senses and emotions, provided they did not become abstracted into something that is essential in itself.

114. *Phen.*, 133.

115. For the Christian consciousness, external reality has been significantly altered by the Incarnation—all actuality, in a general way, has the significance of "the form of the Unchangeable" (ibid., 133), but only through a divine intervention that is thought of as involving a surrendering of its divine form.

116. That is, "a gift from an alien source, which the Unchangeable makes over to consciousness to make use of" (ibid.). Hegel's language has obvious allusions to sacramental theology, in which religious consciousness sees reality being sublimated, not by its own activity as such, but because that activity sets in motion the power of the beyond; and its own ability to perform this activity is seen to be a gift of God, to whom thanks is given: "the particular individual consciousness *gives thanks* [for the gift], i.e., *denies* itself the satisfaction of being conscious of its *independence*, and assigns the essence of its action not to itself, but to the beyond" (ibid., 134).

117. Ibid., 136.

118. Ibid.

119. Ibid., 137.

120. Hyppolite (1974), 381.

121. That Hegel cited it as being indicative of unhappy consciousness demonstrates his view that this religion is personal, arising from the self,

since unhappy consciousness is a condition of the individual self-consciousness.

122. Hyppolite (1974), 438: "Believing consciousness grasps its object, God, in an act of trust *(Vertrauen)*; that trust is an expression of its own self-certainty. . . . God, here, is not an object which in its transcendence would negate self-consciousness; he is rather the inner certainty that consciousness has of itself. Nevertheless, in faith, that inner certainty appears to me as beyond me."

123. *Phen.*, 297.

124. Historically, Hegel found the attitude of 'faith' typified in the inadequate expression of Christianity that enters into conflict with reason. This was the form of Christianity and its encounter with reason that Hegel experienced most intimately in his own life, but it was a struggle that, in its contemporary form, had its historical origin in the Renaissance and Reformation. It would be easy to assume that it was the Renaissance that gave expression to reason, while the Reformation exemplified faith, and that the clash between reason and faith was represented by the distinction between the Renaissance and the Reformation, especially as lived out in the lives of such personalities as Erasmus and Luther. However, while this is quite true, Hegel displayed a depth of perception in identifying an aspect of the Reformation as part of the struggle of reason. The struggle of reason was for the freedom of the human spirit that began to appear in Luther. In *LHP* Hegel said that "it was in the Lutheran Reformation that the great revolution appeared" (3:146–47), for it was Luther who demonstrated the misconception of seeking to earn union with God through self-denial of the things of this world or to attain that union through priestly mediation; it was Luther who thus taught that it is the human heart "which relates itself directly to God," and that "it is only in communion and faith that I stand in relation to God" (ibid., 149, 150); and it was Luther who insisted on the important principle of human liberty, namely, the "right to speak and think in one's own language. . . . This is of infinite importance, and without this form of being-at-home-with-self subjective freedom could not have existed" (ibid., 150). Thus, Hegel said that "it was with Luther first of all that freedom of spirit began to exist in embryo"; but he immediately added that "its form indicated that it would remain in embryo" (ibid., 148). The great hope of freedom for the human spirit that the Lutheran Reformation offered was not realized, because Luther did not extend the principle of freedom, particularly to the dogmatic content of religion. That content remained very solidly something that was given and could not be open to any development of a speculative kind. The great heritage of the philosophic and speculative theology of the ancient Alexandrian school was definitely lost in the dogmatism of Protestant theology that claimed to admit only external content. Thus, the Lutheran Reformation was only a moment in the struggle of reason, for reason denounced any such externally given content, and this denouncement cul-

minated in the Enlightenment, the climax of the struggle between reason and faith.

125. Hyppolite (1974), 435.

126. Ibid., 431.

127. *Phen.*, 334: Enlightenment "says that what is for faith the absolute Being, is a Being of its own consciousness, is its own thought, something that is a creation of consciousness itself."

This, of course, anticipates the criticisms that were directed at religious faith by Feuerbach, and which will be given some consideration in Part 3.

128. Ibid., 335: "from the other side, it also declares the essence of faith to be something *alien* to consciousness, to be not *its* essence, but a changeling foisted on it." Cf. *LPR*, 1:102.

129. Ibid., 337.

130. Lauer (1976), 205.

131. Indeed, Hegel said, the contrary is the case, for "it does not occur to faith to fasten its certainty to such evidences and such fortuitous circumstances." Faith bases its certainty on a simple trust in God, "an unsophisticated relationship to its absolute object" (*Phen.*, 338).

132. Ibid., 339: "it also affirms as a pure intention the necessity of rising above natural existence . . . ; only it finds it foolish and wrong that this elevation should be demonstrated *by deeds.*"

133. Ibid., 336.

134. Ibid., 333.

135. Ibid., 338.

136. Taylor (1975), 183.

137. Hegel regarded Kant's position as being of this kind: Kant's 'rational faith' resulted in "the sort of God that ought to exist in order to serve a necessary function in the Kantian system," and Hegel thought such a God to be quite inadequate "to satisfy man's spiritual needs." The Kantian position was the result of his emphasizing, from the standpoint of the understanding, the limits of human reason; and in contrast, it was Hegel's endeavor to show, from the standpoint of reason, the artificiality of those limits (Pomerleau [1977], 214). Further, as Merold Westphal notes (Weiss [1974], 31), Hegel's "Lectures on the Proofs of the Existence of God" were devoted to the question 'Can we know God?' for Hegel was extremely critical of both the Enlightenment's severe limitation on "what reason could affirm" and "the Humean-Kantian critique of the traditional proofs." Indeed, "Hegel regularly complains that both philosophy and religion have made it a dogma that man cannot know God."

138. Hyppolite (1974), 443, 436. Cf *ETW*, 171, for an early Hegelian criticism of the Enlightenment.

139. *Phen.*, 349.

140. Pomerleau (1977), 217.

141. *LPR,* 1:51. Hegel's attitude to the position represented by Schleiermacher will again be raised in Part 3.

142. John E. Smith, in Christensen (1970), 172: "Both fail to advance to the truth of the concept, and both fail to appreciate the truth of Spirit as present in the community. The principal error shared by both forms is that of atomic individualism which not only makes community impossible, but works against the acceptance of the religious content at the foundation of the community. Pietism *refuses* to develop the content rationally, and Enlightenment *cannot* develop the content rationally. For the former, religion is enclosed in individual feeling, and for the latter, religion comes to be identified with morality which, at this point, Hegel identifies with abstract subjectivity or individual arbitrariness."

143. *LPR,* 1:51. Hegel's discussion of the contemporary religion (as "Unhappy Consciousness", "Believing Consciousness", the Religion of Feeling) and his reaction to it, is indicative of an important observation that can be made.

His "Speculative Notion of Religion" is a transcending *(Aufhebung)* of his earlier distinction between objective and subjective religion. Religion is not a relation to something purely objective, that comes to us from outside of us, or that arises merely from our own inner experience. Religion is "a relation of the spirit to Absolute Spirit: thus only is Spirit as that which knows, also that which is known. This is not merely an attitude of the spirit towards absolute Spirit, but absolute Spirit itself is that which is the self-relating element, . . . Thus when we rise higher, religion is the Idea of the Spirit which relates itself to its own self—it is the self-consciousness of absolute Spirit. . . . Religion, too, is consciousness, and consequently has finite consciousness as an element in it, but a consciousness which is cancelled as finite; for the Other, which absolute Spirit knows, it itself is, and it is only absolute Spirit in knowing itself. . . . Thus religion is the Divine Spirit's knowledge of itself through the mediation of finite spirit. Accordingly, in the Idea of its highest form, religion is not a transaction of man, but is essentially the highest determination of the absolute Idea itself" *(LPR,* 1:205–6).

144. John E. Smith, in Christensen (1970), 172. It should be noted, however, that though Hegel stressed the speculative form of philosophy as the highest expression of the truth of absolute Spirit, philosophy was not seen as doing away with the need for religion: not everyone will attain the truth in a philosophical way *(LPR,* 2:340), and there will also be an important place for religious cult.

145. Lukács (1975), 518. Lukács keenly wanted to enlarge the gap between Hegel and Marx.

146. *Phen.,* 335.

147. Taylor (1975), 493.

Introduction to Part III

1. For example, it has already been noted, and there will be occasion to recall again, that in the introduction Hegel characterized the *Logic* as "the presentation of the divine essence before creation". It is for this reason that one can be justified for making the systematic discussion of Hegel's philosophy, which is now to be undertaken, solely concerned with his concept of God or absolute Spirit.

2. *LPR*, 1:2.

3. Ibid., 205.

4. Ibid., 92; also, 2:348: "The determination or definition of God here is that He is the Absolute Idea, i.e., that He is Spirit."

5. Ibid., 1:26, 46, 59–60, 66, 74–76, 84.

6. Ibid., 30–31.

7. Ibid., 91. This Hegelian conviction of the Trinitarian nature, or threefold movement, of divine Being has, of course, already been surveyed in the previous chapter under the subsections titled "the Kingdom of the Father," "the Kingdom of the Son," and "the Kingdom of the Spirit."

8. *EM*, §573.

9. *LPR*, 3:317.

10. Ibid., 1:66–67.

11. Ibid., 2:329: "When religion comes to have a true comprehension of itself, it is seen that content and object of religion are made up of this very Whole." At this point Hegel went on to contrast what he took to be the usual pursuit of theology—namely, "to know God as the merely objective [separated] God"—with the Notion of absolute religion, which is "the unity of . . . God with the conscious subject."

12. *EM*, §573: For the 'reflective' understanding there arises the conviction "that the appearance has a relation to the essence, the finite to the infinite, and so on: and thus arises the question of reflection as to the nature of this relation."

13. This is in fact the language of Paul Tillich, which Frederick Copleston ("Hegel and the Rationalization of Mysticism," Steinkraus [1971], 190) suggests can be profitably applied to Hegel.

14. *LPR*, 2:349.

15. Taylor (1975), 494.

16. Hyppolite (1974), 543–44.

17. Westphal, in Weiss (1974), 53 n. 63.

18. Fackenheim (1970), 165.

19. Ibid., 161.

20. Ibid., 162.

21. Ibid., 163.

22. Joseph Fitzer, (1972), 243, goes so far as to say that Hegel may even remind the 'orthodox' of certain elements in their tradition that have been forgotten.

Chapter 10. Two Contradictory Interpretations

1. *EM*, §566–69; *LPR*, 3:1–33; cf. *Phen.*, 465ff. (discussed in Part 2).
2. *EM*, §567.
3. *Phen.*, 465; *LPR*, 1:92.
4. See final chapter of Part 2, pp. 159–78.
5. *Enz.* §564: *"so enthält derselbe das Offenbaren seiner"*, i.e., "it implies the revealing of itself", where *seiner* refers to *Geist*, so that it means *Geist* is revealing itself.
6. *EM*, §567; *Phen.*, 467.
7. *LPR*, 3:1.
8. *EL*, §162.
9. Ibid., §163. The parallel between Hegel's language here and in the context of his discussion of absolute religion is most striking, and thus makes it very apparent that Hegel was discussing the same matter—namely, his understanding of the Absolute—but doing so in two different contexts. In reference to the pure Notion of absolute Spirit, in *Phen.*, Hegel spoke of "Essence", "Otherness of Essence", and "Knowledge of itself *in the 'other'*"; in other words, he was referring to what, in other places, he called the moments of Universality, Particularity, and Individuality—or to what he spoke of in *EL* as "Subjective Notion", "Objectivity", and "the Idea". And in each context it is the third moment—Individuality, or Self-Knowledge, or the Idea—in which the truth of the pure Notion is realized. The correspondence between this and trinitarian theology is also very striking; and the fact that Hegel saw the Idea corresponding to the religious conception of God is made apparent in *EL:* "The purpose of philosophy has always been the intellectual ascertainment of the Idea" (§213, Zus.); and "The objects of philosophy, it is true, are upon the whole the same as those of religion. In both the object is Truth, in that supreme sense in which God and God only is the Truth" (§1; cf. *LPR*, 1:19).
10. *SL*, 50.
11. *EL*, §20.
12. Ibid., §213, Zus.
13. Ibid., §244.
14. Findlay (1958), 19.
15. Fackenheim (1970), 77. However, it seems to me that Fackenheim, although he uses Findlay's term 'transcendent metaphysician', has not really grasped Findlay's meaning, for the latter's definition has a much wider extension than does Fackenheim's, yet he uses Findlay's term thereby implying that his own definition is coterminous with Findlay's.

16. *EL,* §112, Zus: "Another not uncommon assertion is that God, as the supreme Being, cannot be known. Such is the view taken by modern 'enlightenment' and abstract understanding, which is content to say *Il y a un être suprême:* and there lets the matter rest."

17. *Phen.,* 340.

18. *LPR,* 2:335.

19. Paul Tillich, *The Courage To Be* (1962), 178, bears witness to this: "The God of theological theism is a being beside others and as such a part of the whole of reality. He certainly is considered its most important part, but as a part and therefore subjected to the structure of the whole. He is supposed to be beyond the ontological elements and categories which constitute reality. But every statement subjects him to them. He is seen as self which has a world, as an ego which is related to a thou, as a cause which is separated from its effect, as having a definite space and an endless time. He is a being, not being-itself. As such he is bound to the subject-object structure of reality, he is an object for us as subjects. At the same time we are objects for him as a subject."

20. *EL,* §112, Zus, and §213, Zus.

21. *LPR,* 1:172.

22. Ibid., 180–81.

23. The concept of 'Positivity', which also developed early in Hegel's thinking, is relevant here. Positivity occurs at the level of *Verstand,* and, when applied to religion, Hegel believed the question of positivity basically comes down to the metaphysical question of the relation between the finite and the infinite. Therefore, a theism that asserts the ultimacy of divine 'otherness' is, in Hegel's view, fundamentally a theology that is marked by positivity (see above, p. 65).

24. *LPR,* 1:197.

25. Westphal, in Weiss (1974), 48.

26. *LPR,* 3:281.

27. Ibid., 289.

28. Ibid., 290.

29. Ibid., 285.

30. Ibid., 290.

31. Ibid., 286–87.

32. Ibid., 294.

33. Ibid., 1:189: the finite "has become what is fixed, absolute, perennial."

34. Ibid., 197: "In Reflection, the finite stands opposed to the infinite in such a way that the finite is doubled."

35. Ibid., 3:293.

36. *Phen.,* 321ff.

37. *LPR,* 3:296.

38. Ibid., 293.

39. Ibid., 2:331–32.

40. Ibid., 332.

41. Ibid., 1:197–98.

42. Ibid., 3:285.

43. Lauer (1964), 463. This is supported by the following quotation from *LHP*, 2:385: "This relation to the world is then a relation to an 'other', which thereby at first appears to be outside of God; but because this relation is *His* activity, the fact of having this relation in Himself is a moment of Himself. Because the connection of God with the world is a determination in Himself, so the being another from the one, the duality, the negative, the distinction, the self-determination in general, is essentially to be thought of as a moment in Him, or God reveals Himself in Himself, and therefore establishes distinct determinations in Himself."

44. *LPR*, 3:297.

45. Taylor (1975), 100: "Although Hegel takes up the notion of creation, . . . he reinterprets it, and speaks of the creation as necessary. . . . What it cannot mean is what it means for orthodox theism."

46. Westphal, in Weiss (1974), 48.

47. *LPR*, 1:200.

48. Ibid., 2:334–35.

49. Westphal, in Weiss (1974), 48 n.

50. *The Concise Oxford Dictionary.*

51. Edwards (1967), vol. 1.

52. Tillich, *The Courage To Be* (1962), 179.

53. Tillich, *The Shaking of the Foundations* (1962), 64.

54. *LHP*, 3:280.

55. Feuerbach (1967), 23.

56. Ibid., 282.

57. Welch (1972), 1:172.

58. Ibid., 173.

59. Ibid., 172.

60. Feuerbach (1967), 17.

61. Ibid., 23.

62. Welch (1972), 176.

63. Kojève (1969), 71.

64. Ibid.

65. Kojève (1947), 198.

66. Ibid.

67. Kaufmann (1965), 276, 277.

68. Ibid., 275.

69. Ibid., 277.

70. W. Winslow Shea, "Comment on George L. Kline 'Hegel and the Marxist-Leninist Critique of Religion,'" Christensen (1970), 205.

71. Min (1976), 62.

72. Kaufmann (1965), 275, quoting from Findlay (1958), 354: Kaufmann questions the use of the adjective 'liberal', but clearly endorses the term 'humanism' as a description of Hegel's position. It should be noted that the term 'humanism' is being used here in such a way as to include the implication of atheism.

73. Findlay (1958), 348.

74. Ibid., 20.

75. Ibid., 348.

76. Ibid., 350.

77. Ibid., 20. While it is true that Hegel's use of this kind of language is much more abundant in *LPR* than in the works that he prepared for publication, that language is significantly present also in *Phen.* and *EM*.

78. Ibid., 348.

79. Ibid., 20.

80. J. N. Findlay, "The Contemporary Relevance of Hegel," in MacIntyre (1972), 16.

81. Findlay (1958), 20, 152.

82. Ibid., 342: Findlay sees this expressed chiefly in *EM*, §564.

83. Ibid., 348, 354.

84. Ibid., 348.

85. Ibid., 351.

86. Ibid., 348, 354.

87. Ibid., 20.

88. Min (1976), 62.

89. Welch (1972), 177. This, of course, is terminology that Welch uses in the context of his discussion of Feuerbach.

90. Ibid.

91. Fachenheim's definition of 'immanentism' (1970), 81—that "which would confine the scope of Hegel's thought to the experienced world, or, more precisely, to the world as it is *humanly* experienced"—would similarly exclude these interpretations, for it implies the *whole* experienced world. Yet, unlike Min's definition, this one does not obviously accommodate the idea of 'totality' as opposed to a mere 'aggregate'.

92. Löwith (1967), 74.

93. Ludwig Feuerbach, "Grundsätze der Philosophie der Zukunft," quoted by Karl Löwith, ibid., 77.

94. Min (1976), 66–67.

95. Ibid., 67. Other words of Hegel give further force to this question posed by Min: "Because the Truth *is*, it must manifest itself, and its manifestation must be an accomplished fact. Truth's self-manifestation is an inseparable part of its own eternal nature, so much so that if it did not manifest itself it would cease to be, that is to say, its content would be reduced to an empty abstraction." "Reason and Religious Truth": Hegel's

"Foreward" to H. Fr. W. Hinrich's *Die Religion im inneren Verhältnisse zur Wissenschaft* (1822), trans. by A. V. Miller, and printed in Weiss (1974), 230.

96. Min (1976), 66.

97. J. N. Findlay, in MacIntyre (1972), 4–6.

98. Ibid., 6.

99. One is reminded that at Jena, Hegel declared the primary interest of philosophy to be "once again to place God absolutely to the front, at the apex of philosophy as the sole ground of all, as the single principle of being and knowing" (WK, 2:195).

100. Hegel's "Foreward," Weiss (1974), 233.

101. Ibid., 235. Similarly, *LPR*, 1:35–36: "There was a time when all knowledge was knowledge of God. Our own time, on the contrary, has the distinction of knowing about all and everything, about an infinite number of subjects, but nothing at all of God."

102. Hegel's "Foreward," Weiss (1974), 236.

103. Ibid., 239: In this "Foreward," Hegel clearly was indulging in an attack on the theology of feeling developed by Schleiermacher, whose major work, *The Christian Faith*, had just appeared.

104. *LPR*, 1:68.

105. Ibid., 51.

106. Hegel's "Foreward," Weiss (1974), 240.

107. Ibid., 241, 243.

108. Ibid., 243; also *EM*, §564: "if self-revelation is refused Him, then the only thing left to constitute His nature would be to ascribe envy to Him. But clearly if the word 'Mind' *(Geist)* is to have a meaning, it implies the revelation of Him."

This bears out the assertion that in Hegel's view it is from God that knowledge of the divine begins. Hegel can be said to be dealing here with the relationship between the order of Knowledge and the order of Being; and even though Hegel said that Knowledge is necessary for the realization of Being, there could be no Knowledge without the self-revelation of Being or God.

Westphal's point is relevant here: Hegel's "new logic implies a new ontology . . . Knowledge of God cannot be a merely human activity. God himself must be actively involved and present in the knowing process" (Westphal, in Weiss [1974], 41–42).

Cf. Quentin Lauer, "Hegel on the Identity of Content in Religion and Philosophy," Christensen (1970), 269.

109. *LPR*, 1:214.

110. Ibid., 215. Though false, Hegel took this to be the meaning of pantheism that theologians constantly gave. He probably had in mind the theologians of the Tübingen *Stift* whom he remembered asserting pantheism to be the equation of God with individual beings.

111. Ibid., 217.

112. Ibid., 217–18.
113. Lakeland (1980), 256.

Chapter 11. A Contrary View ✸

1. Hartshorne (1964), 10.
2. *LPR*, 3:319. See above, p. 228.
3. *LPR*, 1:96–97, 215–16; 2:318–19; *EM*, §573.
4. *LPR*, 3:320.
5. Ibid., 325.
6. Ibid., 320, 325.
7. *Enz.*, 13–14 n., 15 n.
8. Edwards (1967), 8:25. Similarly, Hodgson says that the philosophical perspective of this work of Strauss "is that of a monistic pantheism." Indeed, "upon near completion of the first volume in February 1840, Strauss wrote Ernst Rapp that the sections on the doctrines of God, creation, and the original state of man 'seem to me especially important because all the principles of our criticism of Christianity lie here; hitherto they have not been adequately expressed. I have surrounded and assaulted theism from all sides and have come forth openly with the language of pantheism. The only consideration that causes me to express myself here and there more mildly than I would like is that my book not be censored'. The monistic, anti-eschatological character of the pantheism becomes especially apparent in the final sections of the second volume on 'The Doctrine of Immortality in Modern Reflection'. Strauss contends that immortality must be understood as immanent and pancosmic (absorption in the World-All) rather than futuristic and personal-individual" (Strauss [1973], xlv–xlvi). In the earlier of his two major works, *The Life of Jesus Critically Examined*, Strauss, in discussing the dilemma of Christology, had expressed himself in the following way: "is not the idea of the unity of the divine and human natures a real one in a far higher sense, when I regard the whole race of mankind as its realization, than when I single out one man as such a realization? is not an incarnation of God from eternity a truer one than an incarnation limited to a particular point of time? " "Humanity is the union of the two natures— God become man, the infinite manifesting itself in the finite, and the finite spirit remembering its infinitude" (ibid., 180). While it is not justifiable to see this view as explicitly pantheistic, it is obvious that such a view is easily so interpreted.
9. Pannenberg (1969), 161. Pannenberg also provided my initial source of the above references to Strauss and Tholuck.
10. Charles D. Barrett, "Comment on Quentin Lauer: Hegel on the Identity of Content in Religion and Philosophy," Christensen (1970), 287–88. Lauer himself notes that "a number of authors—chiefly Roman Catholic—are equally insistent that the God Hegel claims to know rationally cannot escape

the reproach of being a pantheistic God—no matter what Hegel in fact intended. The basic reason for this insistence seems to be the conviction that a total rational system, such as Hegel's, which claims to embrace the absolute cannot escape identifying the absolute with a unified totality of reality" (Lauer [1979], 10).

11. Pannenberg (1969), 170.

12. F. La T. Godfrey, "Hegel's Absolute and Theism," Steinkraus (1971), 168.

13. *LHP*, 3:257. Hegel's regard for Spinoza was an enduring one. In his early Jena period, when he was studying Spinoza's texts, Hegel defended him against Jacobi, Cf. *FK*, 104–10.

14. *LHP*, 3:252.

15. Ibid., 257.

16. Ibid., 280.

17. Ibid., 258.

18. Ibid., 320–21.

19. Ibid., 322.

20. Ibid., 258.

21. *EM*, §573.

22. *LHP*, 3:325. "The 'everything' in what has been called 'Pantheism' is therefore not this or that individual thing, but rather is 'everything' in the sense of the *All*, i.e., of the one substance which indeed is immanent in individuals, but is abstracted from individuality and its empirical reality, so that what is emphasized and meant is not the individual as such but the universal soul, or, in more popular terms, truth and excellence which also have their presence in this individual being" (*Aes.*, 1:365).

23. For the meaning of 'atheism' that Hegel had in mind here, see above, p. 216.

24. *LHP*, 3:280. "In the first place Spinoza does not define God as the unity of God with the world, but as the union of thought with extension, that is, with the material world. And secondly, even if we accept this awkward popular statement as to this unity, it would still be true that the system of Spinoza was not Atheism but Acosmism, defining the world to be an appearance lacking in true reality. A philosophy which affirms that God and God alone is should not be stigmatized as atheistic" (*EL*, §50).

25. Parkinson (1977), 450.

26. Spinoza (1955), part 1, def. 5.

27. *LHP*, 3:260.

28. Ibid., 264.

29. McMinn (1959–60), 307–8: "in short, therefore, Hegel concludes that Spinoza's systematic inadequacy reflects an intrinsic metaphysical deficiency, viz., an unreflective, spiritless universal whose triadic moments of deter-minateness are merely formal, i.e., *in intellectu*, not real or concrete."

30. *EM*, §573.

31. *LHP*, 3:282.

32. Spinoza (1955), part 1, prop. 35: "Whatsoever we conceive to be in the power of God, necessarily exists."

33. Ibid., prop. 25: "God is the efficient cause not only of the existence of things, but also of their essence."

34. Ibid., prop. 1.

35. Parkinson (1977), 455.

36. Hallett (1957), 45.

37. Hallett (1930), 209, 204, 206; also, 37–39. Hallett's illustration of the Whole-Part relationship as a means of grasping Spinoza's meaning is a reminder that Spinoza's distinction between *natura naturans* and *natura naturata* is very much like Hegel's own analysis of the Whole-Part relationship in his *Logic*. This, in turn, indicates Hegel's unfairness toward Spinoza in some of his criticisms of Spinoza.

38. *LHP*, 3:287.

39. Parkinson (1977), 458.

40. Shmueli (1970), 187.

41. Parkinson (1977), 456.

42. *LHP*, 3:288: "distinctions are externally present, it is true, but they remain external."

43. *Phen.*, 9–10: "In my view . . . everything turns on grasping and expressing the True, not only as *Substance*, but equally as *Subject*."

44. *LHP*, 3:288. Hegel's concept of the immanent dialectic is prominent in his criticism of Spinoza.

45. Ibid., 281.

46. Spinoza (1955), part 1, prop. 29, Note; and part 2, prop. 3, Note.

47. McMinn (1959–60), 309, 312.

48. Shmueli (1972), 648.

49. Hallett (1930), 207, 209.

50. Although, as will be pointed out, even this dynamic aspect was not sufficient for Hegel.

51. McMinn (1959–60), 310.

52. Spinoza (1955), part 2, def. 4 and prop. 34 proof.

53. McMinn (1959–60), 310–11.

54. Ibid., 311.

55. Ibid.

56. One is reminded that in criticism of Schelling, Hegel observed that the mere name 'dynamist' is not enough. The dynamic nature of reality is part of the common understanding of things—part of everyday thought; but Hegel, in his philosophical work, may be said to have anticipated what Darwin, through his scientific work, discovered about natural development.

57. *Phen.*, 10.

58. Shmueli (1972), 657.

59. Ibid., 656, 657.
60. Ibid., 657.

Chapter 12. A Medial View

1. Ibid., 656. Shmueli here has in mind Novalis's pronouncement of Spinoza as 'a man inebriated with God'—*ein Gottbetrunkener Mensch.* Cf. *LHP,* 3:282.
2. Pannenberg (1969), 161.
3. Westphal, in Weiss (1974), 48 n.
4. Fackenheim (1970), 106–7, 81. In speaking of "the world of *human* experience," Fackenheim has not really provided an accurate general description of the "left-wing" position; but the point is that such a position does declare *finite* reality to be exhaustive of total reality.
5. Cross and Livingstone (1974). It is this understanding of panentheism that will be taken as the basis of the present discussion.

Historically, the term was used first by Karl Christian Friedrich Krause (1781–1832) as a description of his own philosophical standpoint. Krause was a mystical thinker, influenced by Indian thought, but nevertheless "claimed to be developing the true Kantian position." As his own descriptive term—'panentheism'—suggests, he, too, regarded his system as mediating between theism and pantheism, asserting "the idea that God or Absolute Being is one with the world, though not exhausted by it." In Krause's view, "God is primordial being *(Urwesen),* the being without contrariety; he is the unity of all that exists. Though he contains the world, he is nevertheless other than and superior to it" (Edwards [1967], 4:363, 364).

In more recent times the term 'panentheism' has been used to describe the viewpoints, on the relationship between God and the world, held by Whitehead and, especially, Hartshorne, and those who follow in the tradition known as 'Process Theology'. In this regard the term 'panentheism' tends to serve as a general term, embracing standpoints that, while agreeing on the fundamental direction of their views, do contain differences in specific detail. Hence the difficulty in giving a precise definition of panentheism that will serve for all usages. All one can do is to present the broad terms of the definition that one intends to follow.

6. The distinction between pantheism and panentheism is seen when it is said that the latter "does not intend simply to identify the world and God monistically (God = the 'all'), but intends, instead, to conceive the 'all' of the world 'in' God as his inner modification and appearance, even if God is not exhausted by the 'all'." Rahner and Vorgrimler (1961), 275.
7. *EM,* §573 provides an instance in which theism, pantheism, and atheism are castigated by Hegel.
8. Whittemore (1960), 140–41: "What [Hegel] has to show if he is to lay for once and all the onus of pantheism is that Subject actually does evince

a transcendent aspect. . . . In short, semantic victory is not enough. It is not enough to show that the System *is not*—by definition—pantheism. It must be shown that it *is*—panentheism."

9. *LPR,* 1:95.

10. Ibid., 100.

11. Ibid., 92; 2:335. It needs to be noted that the English translation of *seiner,* as either 'his' or 'its', unavoidably removes an ambiguity that is in the German, and this is quite unfortunate because that ambiguity would seem to be a convenient, but important, thing for Hegel's purposes.

12. Ibid., 1:197.

13. *EL,* §45, Zus.

14. *LPR,* 1:190 (my emphasis). Also, 198: "The finite is therefore an essential moment of the infinite in the nature of God, and thus it may be said it is God Himself who renders Himself finite, who produces determinations *within* Himself" (my emphasis).

15. "Within," rather than "in," seems to be the better translation of the German "*in,*" as it is here used with the accusative, not the dative, case and thus implies movement, not rest.

16. Reardon (1977), 102—though Reardon does not actually use the term panentheism as a description of Hegel's position. Cf. Lauer (1979), 22, who also does not use the term panentheism, but who nevertheless expounds Hegel in the following way: "All being is in God, because the being of all reality is to be in God, the way the being of reality is to be in spirit—in divine Spirit as *creative,* in finite spirit as 're-creative'."

17. This is a passage of considerable importance, and it will be necessary to return to it below.

18. *LPR,* 1:199.

19. Ibid., 200.

20. Colletti (1973), 14, 16.

21. *LPR,* 2:335: quoted above, p. 255.

22. Kenneth L. Schmitz, "The Conceptualization of Religious Mystery: An Essay in Hegel's Philosophy of Religion," in O'Malley, et al. (1973), 127.

23. Chapelle (1966).

24. Schmitz, in O'Malley et al. (1973), 134–35.

25. *LPR,* 1:214.

26. Ibid.

27. Jacob Boehme, Second Epistle, A Letter to Casper Lindern, §8, in Boehme (1649).

28. Jacob Boehme, "Questione Theosophicae" 1:1, in Boehme (1930) [my emphasis].

29. Ibid., 1:3.

30. Meister Eckhart, "The Defence," in Eckhart (1941), 279.

31. Ibid., 278.

32. "Sermons," ibid., 219: "God acts at large above being, animating himself. He acts in uncreated essence. Before there was being God was; and he is where there is no being. Great authorities say that God is pure being but he is as high above being as the highest angel is above a fly and I say that it would be as incorrect for me to call God a being as it would be to call the sun light or dark."

33. Ibid., 218.

34. *LHP*, 3:192, 195, 196.

35. Ibid., 196, 197; also, 191, 193: "what marks [Boehme] out and makes him noteworthy is the Protestant principle already mentioned of placing the intellectual world within one's own mind and heart, and of experiencing and knowing and feeling in one's own self-consciousness all that formerly was conceived as Beyond. . . . This solid, deep, German mind which has intercourse with what is most inward . . ." Elsewhere (ibid, 3:32), Hegel praised Boehme for—though his thinking was of "a rather wild and fantastic sort"—his struggles to reach the truth brought him to "the recognition of the presence of Trinity everywhere and in everything, as, e.g. when he says, 'It must be born in the heart of Man.' "

36. Eckhart (1941), xiii. There is, however, some conflict between von Baader's statement that Eckhart was only a name to Hegel, and Karl Rosenkranz's report that as a young man Hegel copied from various literary periodicals extracts from Eckhart and Tauler. The latter report is to be preferred. But what is quite certain is that Hegel regarded Eckhart's work very highly.

37. *LPR*, 1:217–18.

38. Mure (1965), 103.

39. Copleston, in Steinkraus (1971), 196.

40. Ibid.

41. Ibid., 194.

42. Ibid.

43. Ibid.

44. Ibid., 194, 195. Continuing on from Copleston's analogy of the State, one can insert the analogy of democracy to illustrate this third point of a dynamic process of self-actualization: democracy comes into actuality in the actions of individuals and groups, and comes to 'consciousness of itself' in the ideas or thoughts of the people as they think about the nature of democracy and as they articulate what it is in such a way that it can be recognized. But democracy is not reducible to the behavior of any individual or group, and the 'self-consciousness' of democracy is not reducible to the thought of any individual.

45. Whittemore (1960), 142–43. *EL* §45, Zus.: "The real infinite, far from being a mere transcendence of the finite, always involves the absorption of the finite into its own fuller nature."

46. Whittemore (1960), 142.

47. Ibid., 143–44.

48. Ibid., 146.

49. Ibid., 153, 154.

50. Ibid., 158.

51. Fackenheim (1970), 190–91.

52. *LPR*, 2:335–36. This, of course, is essential to Hegel's concepts of 'love' and 'Spirit'.

53. Copleston (1965), 193. Similarly, Lakeland says, "Religion and philosophy are declared to be identical in content, though different in form. Religion is the truth for all human beings, but in the form of representation. Philosophy, for those few who can attain it, is the recognition of the necessity of the content of religion" (Lakeland [1980], 251).

54. Pomerleau (1977), 219.

55. *Phen.*, 471; also 460: "The divine nature is the same as the human, and it is this unity that is beheld."

56. *SL*, 129, 135. ·

57. Perkins (1970), 141.

58. *LPR*, 3:99.

59. Ibid., 2:347.

60. Pannenberg (1969), 162.

61. *EM*, §573: "All that those who employ this invention of their own to accuse philosophy gather from the study of God's *relation* to the world is that the one, but only the one factor of this category of relation—and that the factor of indeterminateness—is identity. Thereupon they stick fast in this half-perception, and assert—falsely as a fact—that philosophy teaches the identity of God and the world."

62. Ibid. Also, *SL*, 138.

63. Min (1974), 95.

64. Lauer (1964), 451.

65. *Phen.*, 472.

66. Westphal, in Weiss (1974), 51–53; Lauer (1964), 451.

67. Hegel's answer to the charge of pantheism "was that those who made the charge failed to understand, or took no pains, to find out what he meant by unity: they thought of it as 'abstract unity, mere identity', of a kind which entailed a categorical equation of all things with God. What he had in mind is a 'concrete unity', a unity of concrescence which is achieved by the self-unfolding of the concept of God as subject" (Hendry [1981], 348).

68. This is Erik Schmidt's designation of Hegel—quoted by Kenneth L. Schmitz, in O'Malley et al. (1973), 110 n. This is a designation that obviously places Hegel within the pantheistic position, but, at the same time, recognizes the vital distinction between Hegel and Spinoza, namely, Hegel's grasp of the dialectic.

69. *EL*, §50.

70. Godfrey, in Steinkraus (1971), 168, 179. Godfrey's is a typical expression of this kind of interpretation of Hegel's theory, although he himself does not find it a very adequate or satisfying theory, for he says it is one that "is incomplete without recognition of God as distinct from the world, but author of it" (ibid., 169).

It will be suggested here that whereas the kind of interpretation of Hegel represented by Godfrey is not the most adequate one, it is also the case that what Godfrey seeks is not provided by Hegel in precisely those terms, for they are very theistic terms.

71. Whittemore (1960), 141f.

72. Ibid., 142. See above, pp. 255–62. "Evidence for Hegel as a Panentheist".

73. Lauer (1979), 11 n. cites a definition of 'Pantheism' that speaks of it involving "a denial of God's personality."

74. *Phen.*, 10. *EL*, §51, Zus.: "It is true that God is necessary, or, as we may also put it, that He is the absolute Thing: He is, however, no less the absolute Person. That He is the absolute Person however is a point which the philosophy of Spinoza never reached: and on that side it falls short of the true notion of God which forms the content of religious consciousness in Christianity."

75. *LPR*, 3:13f.

76. Taylor (1975), 81.

77. Ibid.

78. In formulating his concept of 'subject', Hegel was influenced by his understanding of Greek and Roman societies. He regarded Greek society as having been governed by customs and characterized by a harmony in which the individuality of each member did not emerge, for each belonged to the whole. Roman society, on the other hand, saw the growth of individuality, as it was strongly asserted in Roman Law, which regarded each member as the locus of rights. This development of individuality, in Hegel's view, was both positive and negative. The negative aspect was the accompanying selfishness, while the positive aspect was the growth of individual awareness. Consequently, Hegel's concept of subject was one in which this positive aspect was retained, and also in which the motives of the individual have lost the sharp edge of selfishness. Further, it is only in such a 'true' subject that authentic freedom exists, for a subject is one who has put aside the awareness of itself as a separate individual and has come to a consciousness of interrelatedness and continuity with others.

79. *LPR*, 1:275.

80. For example, McTaggart (1901), whom Whittemore (1960), 158–62, discusses critically.

81. Pannenberg (1969), 165. Pannenberg also cites *SL*, 583, in which, he suggests, Hegel "explicitly distinguished personality as the logical impulse

of the being of the subject, that is, insofar as the concrete concept of the self is essentially something individual."

82. *LPR*, 1:200.

83. Min (1976), 80 n.: "one is not used to thinking of Hegel as a philosopher of 'love'. . . . Yet it seems clear to me that 'love'—in the sense of the union of subject and object in which other-ness is *aufgehoben*, i.e., both preserved and transcended, in communion—is not only not foreign to but essentially constitutive of the very nature of spirit which Hegel takes to be the ultimate foundation of reality."

84. Pannenberg, "Question of God" (1971), 2:227.

85. This is not a Hegelian term, but one found in Pannenberg, "The God of Hope" (1971), 234: *Personhaftigkeit*—which is not a common word in either German or English, but which will be used here as a means by which the perceived meaning of Hegel can be conveyed. There is, of course, a weight of opinion that regards the use of such terms as indicative of an incorrect grasping of Hegel. Evidence can be found, e.g. as early as *ETW*, where Hegel spoke of the goal of unity as finding "peace in a nonpersonal *(unpersönlichen)* living beauty" (ibid., 301), which suggests a rejection of the concept of personalness. But in the context, the term 'nonpersonal' seems to be used for the negative purpose of denying that it is personal in the sense of "something objective and exclusively personal" (ibid., 300). Furthermore, when one considers that for Hegel the finite, and especially human existence, is the manifestation of absolute Spirit, it is hard to exclude personalness from the Absolute, since all human existence is personal. Therefore, the use of the term 'personalness' is justified, while at the same time avoiding the difficulties of the term 'person' as Hegel used it in other contexts and as it is commonly used to refer to a finite individual.

86. Whittemore (1960), 146.

87. Tillich (1953), 1:270, 283, speaks of an individual person as "a dynamic self-transcending agent," for "in the individual, notably the individual man, there is an inner *telos* which transcends the various moments of the process of his life."

Pannenberg, "Speaking About God" (1973), 3:112, argues: "Human beings are persons by the very fact that they are not wholly and completely existent for us in their reality, but are characterized by freedom, and as a result remain concealed and beyond control in the totality of their existence."

88. Fackenheim (1970), 205.

89. For example, *LPR*, 1:92, 93, and esp. 95.

90. The following quotation illustrates Fackenheim's awareness of this: "The *Enzyklopädie* grasps Nature as other than the Idea in its logical purity, and also as the self-externalization of the Idea, it . . . grasps Spirit as presupposing Nature (hence actual in its finitude) and also as presupposed by Nature (hence infinite) " (Fackenheim [1970], 219).

91. Ibid., 186.

92. Min (1976), 85.

93. The idea of priority is explicitly eliminated by such Hegelian statements as: "*there is not* an infinite which is first of all infinite and only subsequently has need to become finite, to go forth into finitude; on the contrary, it is on its own account just as much finite as infinite" (*SL*, 153).

94. Min (1976), 75–76. Cf. Lauer (1979), 12: "What is basic here is the principle that, concretely, divine being and divine activity are identical."

95. Min (1976), 86.

96. Ibid.

97. *LPR*, 1:275.

98. Min (1976), 87.

99. *Greifen* means to grasp or comprehend; *übergreifen* means to overlap.

100. *LPR*, 1:185. Also, 197: "as universal it overlaps or includes me in itself"; and 208: "At one time Spirit represents the one side, and at another is that which overlaps, which reaches over to grasp the other side, and is thus the unity of both."

101. Whitehead (1929), 521–23.

102. Hartshorne (1964), 231, 234.

103. And for this reason, any attempt to apply the term 'panentheism' to Hegel's position must be carefully defined so that it is not taken to mean the whole system of a Whitehead or Hartshorne, to whom the term has been applied in more recent times.

104. Here another appropriate term is provided by Tillich's phrase "the ground-of-being".

105. Pannenberg, "Significance of Christianity" (1973), 168.

Barth (1959), 304, speaks of necessity in Hegel's philosophy—his "making the dialectical method of logic the essential nature of God"—as being "probably the weightiest and most significant of the doubts about him which might be raised against him from the theological point of view."

Also, Fitzer (1972), 243, says that "what troubles Küng, along with other critics of Hegel, is that Hegel's God seems to be a creator and revealer by a necessity of nature, or essence: even if Hegel's God freely—in the sense of *spontaneously*—decided to create and to reveal, the fact remains that he could not have decided otherwise."

106. Pannenberg, "Significance of Christianity" (1973), 170.

107. *LPR*, 3:266–69.

108. Ibid., 267; Min (1974), 77. Hegel sums up the point thus: "Their isolation gives them a semblance of independence; but the connection in which they stand with other things—with each other, that is—directly expresses the fact that these single things are not independent, shows that they are conditioned and are affected by other things, and are, in fact, necessarily conditioned by other things, and not by themselves. These necessary elements, these laws, would themselves consequently constitute the independent element. Anything which exists essentially in connection with

something else has its essential character and stability not in itself, but in this connection" (*LPR*, 3:268).

109. *LPR*, 3:271–72.

110. Ibid., 270.

111. Min (1974), 78.

112. Reardon (1977), 92. Cf. Taylor (1975), 94. Hegel himself said: It is Spirit that "raises itself above this crowd of things contingent, above the merely outward and relative necessity involved in them, above the Infinite, which is a mere negative, and reaches a necessity which does not any longer go beyond itself, but is in-and-for-itself, included within itself, and is determined as complete in itself, while all other determinations are posited by it and are dependent upon it" (*LPR*, 3:269). The concept of rational freedom— autonomy and self-determination—is the determinant of everything Hegel said about 'God'.

113. Pannenberg, "Significance of Christianity" (1973), 173.

114. Ibid.

115. Ibid., 173–74.

116. Ibid., 174. Taylor (1975), 493, also argues that the freedom of God is eliminated by Hegel's philosophy.

117. Min (1974), 80. Cf. Lauer (1979), 18: if "the essence of freedom lies in self-determination, then it seems abundantly clear that divine activity is preeminently free, precisely because it is preeminently self-determining activity. The identity of being and activity in God precludes the possibility that the determination of the action be other than the very being of God, and that is the only being which can in the fullest sense of the term be called 'necessary'."

This sense of 'necessity' must be carefully distinguished from 'need' (cf. Min's statement that "it at once needs and does not need its Other"). Lauer says, "if God indeed 'needs' the world and man in order to be truly God, then God is a dependent being, and a dependent being cannot be infinite being. But, Hegel is very explicit in denying that God 'needs' the world or man. God is absolute Spirit, infinite being, and, therefore, infinitely self-sufficient. To say then that God 'necessarily' creates is not to say that God 'needs' creation" (ibid., 17). God does not 'need' creation, but God 'necessarily' creates because it is of the being of God to do so: in God there is identity of being and activity.

118. *SL*, 153.

119. Min (1974), 91.

120. *SL*, 603—quoted by Pannenberg, "Significance of Christianity" (1973), 175.

121. Hendry (1981), 350.

122. Ibid.

123. Pannenberg, "Significance of Christianity" (1973), 175.

124. Ibid., 174.

125. Ibid.

126. Ibid., 168.

127. I am indebted here to Paul Tillich's own expression of these ideas (1953), 1:289, for his apparent kinship with Hegel on these matters seems to make Tillich's terminology useful in an exposition of Hegel's meaning.

128. Again an indebtedness to Tillich (ibid., 306), as the prompter of these points, must be acknowledged.

129. *LPR*, 1:95, 61.

130. Pannenberg (1969), 63.

131. Pannenberg, "The God of Hope" (1971), 245.

132. Hegel admitted this element of contingency when he said that each finite determination of itself is such that what is determined "exists as something which is free, as something independent" (*LPR*, 3:36).

133. *CR*, 67–68.

134. Schmitz, in O'Malley et al. (1973), 135.

135. "Thoroughgoing teleology is Hegel's manner of thinking. . . . It set him infinitely far apart from Spinoza" (J. N. Findlay, "Hegel's Use of Teleology," Steinkraus [1971], 92–93).

Concluding Remarks

1. Copleston, in Steinkraus (1971), 198.

2. Findlay, in Steinkraus (1971), 106.

3. Fackenheim (1970), 186.

4. Tillich, *The Courage To Be* (1962), 180, 181.

5. Again, Tillich made the point that atheism is the inevitable and natural rebellion against traditional theological theism, for as Nietzsche said, the God of theism—the imperial ruler, the personification of moral force and the impersonal first principle of philosophy—must die "because nobody can tolerate being made into a mere object of absolute knowledge and absolute control" (ibid., 178).

6. As Tillich (1957), 51, indicates, the desire for security in belief is a strong motivation for such literalism.

7. Fackenheim (1970), 218.

8. It is for this reason that Copleston has said that, while 'panentheism' is the most apt description of Hegel's purpose, he is only a "panentheist in intention", for the position he achieved, in fact, cannot be described as a theism of any kind.

9. Copleston, in Steinkraus (1971), 198–99.

10. Taylor (1975), 495.

11. Ibid., 102; also 492ff.

12. Westphal, in Weiss (1974), 57 n., observes that "one of Hegel's most important claims is to have provided a mode of thinking free of dependence

on the imagination. It is also one of the most difficult of his claims to understand and evaluate."

13. Tillich (1953), 44–45; Copleston, in Steinkraus (1971), 199–200.

14. Lauer (1964), 459.

15. Here I am making use of a phrase employed by Paul Tillich (1953), 54. However, it is not the case that Christianity had to learn this lesson from Hegel; rather, it was a matter of needing to relearn it. There had been many times in its history when the 'truths' of Christianity had been formulated afresh by means of new terminology that was gained from contemporary usage, especially philosophical usage. The New Testament term 'Logos' is a prime example, and other terms—such as 'substance', 'nature', and 'person'—are examples from the classical period of the formation of Christian dogma. Hegel's achievement can be seen to stand in this tradition—even though he himself saw it differently as a rising above the level of representational language—and that achievement can serve as a reminder that this is a living process, for one can never be confident that the 'final' terminology has been attained.

16. Of course, strictly speaking, it was Tillich who followed Hegel's—and especially Schelling's—concept of *Grund*. Nevertheless, all such expressions are subject to the observation just made, namely, that they are never to be taken literally, but must be recognized as pointing beyond themselves to the ultimate ground of all that is. In perceiving this fact about religious language, Hegel, of course, was not anticipating anybody, for it had been recognized long before, the classical example being Aquinas's theory of analogy. Hegel's experience of religion was within the Protestant tradition in which Aquinas had little or no importance, and so Hegel's comments about religious language may be seen as providing the same realization as the doctrine of analogy—for his own tradition, which he found to be so ensnared in the narrow confines of literalism (although one might make the same comment about the Catholic tradition in spite of its Thomism). This imprisonment within literalism was not absolute, of course, for there was always the realization among some theologians that the literal sense of some of their metaphorical language is not intelligible. But Hegel was applying that realization unreservedly to the language of faith, and in doing that he was doing something rather startling, especially in the eyes of contemporary theologians, yet also something of fundamental importance. However, it has been discussed above that the difficulty with Hegel is that he regarded the form of analogies or *Vorstellungen* as completely inadequate, and that he believed the speculative language of philosophy overcame those shortcomings. On the other hand, as already noted, the end of *LPR* shows that Hegel himself again realized—for he had done so early in his career (*ETW*, 312)—that all language is subject to the same condition of finitude.

17. Indeed, Fackenheim does seem to wed Hegel too closely to traditional theism. See above, pp. 281–82.

18. For an illuminating comment about the meaning that can be given to 'in' in such a context, one can again turn to Tillich: "The question is what does this mean in non-spatial terms? Certainly, God is neither in another nor in the same space as the world. He is the creative ground of the spatial structure of the world, but he is not bound to the structure, positively or negatively. The spatial symbol points to a qualitative relation" (Tillich [1953], 1:292).

19. For example, Fitzer reports that Küng, in spite of his critical approach to Hegel, "remains attracted by Hegel precisely because Hegel overcame, even if ambiguously, what he takes to be the fatal insufficiency of patristic and medieval dogmatics, namely its reliance on the concept of the unchangeableness of God" (Fitzer [1972], 244). This observation further indicates Hegel's kinship with recent panentheists.

Index of Names

Analytic Index

Absolute, the (*see also* Infinite, Spirit), 70, 71, 73, 76–85 (passim), 95, 98, 112, 117, 138, 146, 150, 152, 157, 164, 167, 168, 198, 205, 214, 221–25 (passim), 232, 234, 243, 244, 245, 263, 264, 268, 271, 273, 279, 280, 283, 289, 292, 295, 300, 326, 328, 330, 358, 364

Absolute Religion (*see* Christianity, Manifest Religion)

Acosism, 199, 236, 237, 243, 368–72, 364

— Acosmic Pantheism (*see also* Pantheism), 199, 272

Alienation (Division, Estrangement, Separation), 1, 12, 30, 31, 39, 40, 43, 44, 45, 46, 48–55 (passim), 58, 60, 61, 62, 74, 79, 82, 83, 85, 106, 107, 126, 130, 140, 142, 146, 153, 154, 170, 177, 185, 195, 198, 209, 212f., 217, 276f., 321f., 344, 350

— dialectic of alienation, 76f.

— self-alienation of Spirit, 163, 166, 167

Analogy, 375

Appearance, 79f., 103, 129, 134f., 144, 146, 197, 226, 239, 319

Atheism, 3, 69, 199, 200, 203, 215, 216–29, 231, 133, 236, 237, 239, 252, 253, 254, 255, 265, 268, 297, 302, 362, 364, 366, 374

Atheismusstreit, 279

Aufheben, Aufhebung (Supersede, Supersession), 105, 106, 114, 122, 126, 129, 145, 208, 264, 269, 276, 278, 279, 288f., 333f., 371

Authority (*see also* Religion), 12, 24–31 (passim), 43, 56, 153f., 176, 267, 317

Autonomy, 12, 25, 34, 39, 40, 41, 43, 51, 118, 267, 317, 326

— Moral Autonomy, 30

— Rational Autonomy, 31, 91, 117, 118

Becoming (*see* Development)

Being *(Sein)*, 41, 47, 130f.

Being, Essence *(Wesen)*, 45, 146, 147, 179, 197, 198, 224, 232, 330, 342, 345

— Absolute Being, 117, 159–70 (passim), 174, 178, 179, 185, 187, 188, 190, 196, 198, 204, 208, 211, 219, 222, 226, 228, 229, 235, 236, 251, 283f., 300, 302, 329, 336, 355, 357

Catholic, Catholic Church, Catholicism, 36, 60, 183

Christian Religion, Christianity (*see also* Manifest Religion), 1, 3, 9, 13, 17, 19, 20, 22, 23, 26, 30, 33–36 (passim), 40, 59, 81, 85, 118, 139, 151, 155f., 166, 175, 176, 180–83 (passim), 185, 190, 200, 203, 219, 233, 276, 281, 295, 298, 301, 322, 323, 335, 349, 352, 354, 363, 370

— as Absolute Religion, 81f., 146, 165, 170f., 197, 267, 347

— as Folkreligion, 19, 21, 25, 322

— as a 'positive' religion, 9, 26, 28, 29, 59f., 65, 73, 178f.

— 'de-theologized' Christianity, 299

Community, 110, 112, 144, 147, 148, 152, 153, 174, 176–79 (passim), 351, 352

— *Gemeinde, Gemeine*, meaning of, 352

Concept (*see* Notion)

Consciousness, 70, 85f., 89–95 (passim), 99, 100–10, 113–30 (passim), 132, 134, 135, 137, 139, 140, 141, 152, 158, 159, 160, 177, 179–87 (passim), 209, 331, 334, 335, 336, 338, 341, 346

— Believing Consciousness, 179, 184f., 186, 187, 188, 190, 212, 300, 354

— Religious Consciousness, 95, 112f., 117, 119, 122, 123, 124, 126, 127, 139–39 (passim), 141, 144, 148, 149, 150, 153, 159, 160, 162, 169, 177,